Martini Man

THE LIFE OF DEAN MARTIN

by

William Schoell

TAYLOR PUBLISHING
Dallas, Texas

Designed by Carol Trammel

Published by Taylor Publishing Company
1550 West Mockingbird Lane
Dallas, Texas 75235
www.taylorpub.com

Library of Congress Cataloging-in-Publication Data:
Schoell, William.
      Martini man : the life of Dean Martin / by William Schoell
             p.   cm.
      Discography : p.
      Filmography : p.
      Includes bibliographical references.
      ISBN 0-87833-231-6
      1. Martin, Dean, 1917-1995.   2. Entertainers--United States
Biography.   I. Title.
PN2287.M52S36   1999
791' .092--dc21
[B]

10 9 8 7 6 5 4 3
Printed in the United States of America

For my Aunt Helen

CONTENTS

ACKNOWLEDGMENTS

The author wishes to thank people who spoke to or corresponded with him (or with researcher Brian Saunders) about Dean Martin, including those who did not wish to be named in the text. (The dates that follow are either the date of the interviews or of correspondence received.) Jacqueline Bisset (1/21/99), who worked with Dean on *Airport*; Mary Braxton (11/19/98), who knew Dean in childhood; Linda Chesley (11/12/98), who had an intimate relationship with Dean; Fielder Cook (2/1/99), who directed Dean in *How to Save a Marriage (and Ruin Your Life)*; Sunny Daye (11/25/98), who knew Dean in his early days in New York; Terrance Glynn (1/10/98), who met Dean while working on *Cannonball Run*; Marybeth Jaymes (2/8/99), who worked with Dean on *The Silencers* and *The Ambushers*; Janet Leigh (12/4/98), who worked with Dean on *Living It Up* and *Who Was That Lady?* and was a longtime friend of his and his wife Jeanne; Andrew V. McLaglen (2/1/99), who directed Dean in *Bandolero!* and *something big*; Karl Malden (1/22/99), who appeared with Dean in *The Wrecking Crew*; Jeanne (Mrs. Dean) Martin (1/18/99), his second wife and the person he was closest to through much of his life; Joseph Pirone (9/27/98), whose father briefly boxed with Dean in the early days; Eli Wallach and Anne Jackson (2/1/99), who appeared with Dean in *How to Save a Marriage (and Ruin Your Life)*; Christine (Dodd) Werner (10/17/98), who appeared with Dean in *Rough Night in Jericho*; Virginia Wyscott (11/2/98), who partied with Dean in Hollywood; Bud Yorkin (1/28/99) who directed Dean in *Come Blow Your Horn* and once worked on the Martin and Lewis TV program.

The author also tenders his sincere appreciation to film historian Lawrence J. Quirk, who opened his files and his memories and gave access to many contemporary interviews—published and unpublished—with many of the players in the Dean Martin drama, not to mention with Dean Martin himself. Also thanks to research assistant Brian Saunders, who conducted some interviews and corresponded with some of Dean Martin's co-workers.

The author is also beholden to the staff of the Museum of Modern Art Film Studies Center and the staff of the Billy Rose Theatre and Film collection of the New York Library of the Performing Arts, who provided access to literally thousands of articles and documents pertaining to Dean Martin and his life and work; the staff of the Mid-Manhattan Library and O'Donnell Library Media Center, who allowed usage of many video- and audiocassettes as well as showbiz chronicles from which further information or tips for further research were gleaned; and the staff of the Museum of Radio and Television, New York, who provided access to tapes of Dean's—and Martin and Lewis's—television work.

The author also offers his thanks to the folks at Taylor Publishing, especially Mike Emmerich, Fred Francis, Anita Edson, Lynn Brooks, and Dale Gelfand.

Thanks also to: Hal Wallis Productions, Joseph H. Hazen, Howard Hawks Productions, Warner Brothers, Wallis-Hazen Inc., Claude Productions, York Productions Corp., Paramount Pictures Corp., Dorchester Productions, Meadway Productions, Columbia Pictures Corp., Universal Pictures, United Artists, Douglas Netter Productions, 20th Century-Fox, Albert S. Ruddy Productions, NBC Television.

The photographs in this book come from the author's private collection.

"Show business is a ball!"—Dean Martin

Who was the real Dean Martin? A skirt-chasing, heavy drinking, wholly insensitive, minimally talented philanderer and mob pal who dropped friends and wives as casually as he'd discard a candy bar wrapper? Or an underrated, highly amiable, top-flight singer and actor who was loyal to his pals and remained friends with his wives even after he divorced them and who much preferred an evening at home watching a western than a night out drinking with the boys?

Frequently depicted only as a hard-playing, hard-boozing Rat Packer with a dark side, the truth about Dean Martin is much more complex than that portrait, however accurate for the period of the Rat Pack's heyday, might suggest. As more and more of his recordings hit number one on the charts—*Volare, You're Nobody Till Somebody Loves You, That's Amore*—Dean Martin achieved his greatest fame as a motion picture star, rising to become a top-ten box office attraction several years in a row. This book doesn't ignore the wild parties, the multitude of shapely lovers, the three marriages (the third to a twenty-four-year-old when he was fifty-five) that ended in divorce or any of the racier private side of Dean Martin, but it is also a balanced portrait of a gifted man who gave some fine performances in memorable films such as *Toys in the Attic, Career* (as a shoestring theatrical director accused of being a Communist!), *Bells are Ringing*, Howard Hawks's *Rio Bravo*, and many others.

It is oddly commonplace today for celebrity biographers to write only about the personal lives of their subjects while almost completely ignoring the very work that made their subjects famous in the first place. One often gets the impression that some biographers don't even bother to actually *watch* the movies that their subjects have appeared in! In *Martini*

Man I have attempted to put Dean Martin's *work*—as well as his life—into perspective, scrutinizing his film roles and how he approached them and subjecting to in-depth analysis the major films in which he appeared—as well as looking into his most famous recordings—all for the purpose of achieving a better appreciation of what kept him on top for so many decades.

Therefore, this book can be seen not only as a study of the personal life of a complex individual but as a contemplation of his professional and long-lasting artistry.

—William Schoell, February 1999

Introduction

OK, it was a day late, but what did that matter?

It was June 8, 1989. Seventy-two years and one day after he'd first come kicking and screaming into the delivery room, Dean Martin was still performing for enthusiastic crowds in Vegas. Bally's had become his home away from home, and as long as they wanted him there, he'd go into his dance. The career didn't mean much to him at that point—he was, frankly, almost as rich as Croesus—and he'd rather be watching television, but he liked to keep his hand in now and then, hear the applause, remind everyone he was still alive and singing. Some people seemed to think that he'd become a recluse, particularly since the death of his son Dino Jr. It was hell to outlive one of your children. And there were the three marriages and three divorces and other children who sometimes didn't do what he thought was best for them and all that stuff—but otherwise he couldn't complain about his life, which had basically been very good to him.

And now they were giving him a birthday party. Although he had never been an actual alcoholic and rarely if ever got seriously blitzed so that you'd know it, he had been drinking and smoking steadily every day for decades, and it had taken its inevitable toll on him. Plus he was, as incredible as it may have seemed to him, a senior citizen. An old man of seventy-two. Unbelievable.

Bob Macy, a Las Vegas correspondent for the Associated Press, was in the audience and noted that Dean "looked gaunt and barely capable of making it to the center stage. At one point he dropped a glass on stage and it shattered. Some people thought it was part of the act."

Dean somehow made it through his set; then it was time for the audience to celebrate his seventy-two years of life. Dean heard a squeaky noise to his right and turned to see a huge cake being wheeled onto the stage. Behind the cake . . . Jerry Lewis!

Dean could always deal with Jerry more easily when he'd had a couple of drinks, as tonight (it was his birthday party, after all). Smiling as the audience erupted with huge applause and whoops of glee and astonishment, Dean listened as Jerry said: "Here's to the seventy-two years of joy you've given the world." Then he added: "Why we ever broke up I'll never know."

Dean told Jerry, with boozy sincerity, that he loved him. He seemed touched by Jerry's gesture. But both of them knew why they had broken up—what was the point of kidding anyone?

It all seemed so long ago. The breakup. Not to mention even earlier than that, the first day they met. Their rapid, dizzying ride to megastardom, as if they'd been shot out of a cannon together into an unsuspected, inexplicable world of fame and untold riches. Then those uncertain years when Dean tried to make it on his own and found himself shot out of another cannon—the monster of all cannons, with nuclear energy instead of dynamite—that took him all the way to the top of the entertainment world: clubs, casinos, television, movies, recordings—he had it all. It was like that silly song in *The Bells are Ringing*, "The Midas Touch"; everything Dean Martin touched turned to gold.

Dean still had a few years to go. A few years of illness and finding out who his friends were, true friends like his ex-wife Jeanne, for one. A few years of memories, a few more martinis and westerns on TV. It was a quieter existence but not a terrible one.

But he knew his glory days were behind him.

And he of all people knew what days they'd been!

PART ONE

The Barber Of Steubenville

ONE

Steubenville

The Italian barber, Gaetano Crocetti, a nice-looking mustachioed man of average height and build, had come to America with his bride, Angela, on the advice of his two brothers, who had each made the trip some years before. The world was on the verge of the first Great War, and it was said that America offered opportunities that could not be found back home. Gaetano, who later Americanized his name to Guy, opened up his shop in the town of Steubenville, Ohio (population 20,000), where his brothers also lived. Immigrants were attracted to the place because of all the steel mills on the nearby Ohio River. The mills needed workers, and the workers needed all the amenities: grocery stores, bars, churches, prostitutes, even barbers. Thus Guy Crocetti found a place for himself in this new world.

Angela was a plump, pretty brunette with a large nose. Guy and Angela's first child was a boy named Guglielmo (William), who was born in 1914. The second child, also a boy, was named Dino Paul Crocetti, and this dark-haired baby with the big smile and bright if wary eyes would eventually metamorphose into the big-time entertainer known as Dean Martin. It was nearly midnight on June 7, 1917, when he popped into the world, unaware, as were his parents, that one day he'd put sleepy Steubenville on the map.

Gaetano and Angela Crocetti's life was fairly quiet, but the town of Steubenville, while it never exactly transformed into Manhattan, did not stay sleepy forever. As Bill and Dino grew into youths, the town began to supply in ever greater numbers what the hardworking steelworkers and their families were demanding. More gin mills. More pool halls. More houses of ill repute. Many more gambling dens. And when Prohibition kicked in, the cry went out for illegal speakeasies with their bootleg liquor.

"I had a great time growing up in Steubenville," Dean said years later. "There was everything there a boy could want. Women. Music. Nightclubs. Liquor." Then he joked: "And to think I had all that when I was only thirteen."

Actually, at thirteen Dino looked several years older, as he was nearly six feet tall and well-built. Girls were already giving him the eye, this in spite of his extra-large and rather crooked proboscis inherited from his mother. (It wouldn't be until years later, however, that he would become especially self-conscious about his honker.) He lived a rather stereotypical and uncomplicated middle-class childhood with few privations. His father made enough at his barbershop to provide the family with their own house and car, and good, regular meals were cooked with love and care, if no great culinary skill, by his mother.

As his teen years proceeded, Dino proved that he was as good at sports as he was terrible at academics. (In contrast, his brother William was always a good student.) He paid so little attention in school that it was years before he could speak proper English. (In the Crocetti household he had spoken only Italian until he was five.) He felt at home with the fellows, playing football or basketball, trading curse words and dirty jokes, but in these early years he was rather ill at ease with women. Never really shy in the truest sense of the word, Dean knew he lacked poise and sophistication, that confidence so necessary in the pursuit of the opposite sex. He also backed out of conversations with girls because he felt that he had little to say to them. Throughout his life he would seem quiet and even bashful to some people, even though he could be boisterous at parties, because he simply didn't have much to say. In his early years, in particular, he was embarrassed by his bad grammar and the common way he sounded. In any case, Dean never had an interest in talking about the world situation or other weighty matters.

He did have an interest in music, however, and apparently loved to sing even at an early age. "Even when he was a small baby, his mother— my aunt Angela—was sure he was going to be a singer," said his cousin Mary Crocetti. "He sort of crooned all the time. Then, when he was older, you could hear him around the house, always singing. And he always wore a hat, an old soft, slouchy one. First thing in the morning, he put on this hat. He wore it indoors and outdoors and took it off only when he was going to bed." She added, "Dino somehow acquired a record player, an old one, the kind that you had to wind up after each record. His favorites were Bing Crosby and Russ Columbo. He'd play [their] records over and over and sing along with them."

Mary's brother Archie Crocetti remembered, "Dino and I were in the Steubenville Boy Scouts, troop ten, together; Dino was troop drummer. He took lessons; said they'd come in handy when he played in a dance band."

Dino managed to graduate from Grant Junior High and enter Wells High School in the early 1930s, although he didn't stay for long. Like many youngsters who grow up to become entertainers, Dino was the class clown. Private conversations with girls may have been difficult, but he had no trouble showing off: dancing, singing, making a fool of himself for the amusement of the class and occasionally his teachers.

Mary Braxton (née Morelli) knew Dino in high school and confirms that he had the odd mixture of brashness and bashfulness. "He had no trouble getting up in front of a lot of students and acting out a scene or cutting up, singing, that sort of thing, and he would come over to a bunch of us girls and tell us the latest stories in this kind of rat-a-tat-tat delivery. But he would stumble all over himself and look kind of trapped whenever he was in a one-on-one conversation with a girl that he liked. The more he liked 'em, the shyer he got. I guess big audiences didn't bother him but little ones did. I'm not surprised he got out of Steubenville—I certainly did at the earliest opportunity—and even less surprised that he became a big movie star. They always have that certain something, even at that age, don't they? And least surprising of all is that he became such a ladies' man. He may have stammered a bit when we were around, but so many of us had a crush on him—including me."

Girls—and a ready-made audience for his hijinks—were not enough to keep Dino in school, however. He accepted the fact that he would never get good grades; what came easy for brother Bill and his cousins was terribly difficult for Dino, who could not read well and therefore didn't get any pleasure out of books. Whether his father and mother were really as open to his suggestion that he quit school and find a job, as he later intimated, or whether they hoped a dose of good hard work would bring him to his senses is not known. Perhaps they accepted the fact that Dino was not cut out for the discipline of school and didn't have the right kind of head on his shoulders. In any case, he left high school for good during his sophomore year and never graduated. He must have had some good memories of the place, though, because for many years, after he became famous, he sent "a one hundred dollar check every year for an ad in our yearbook," remembered John Maltese, the director of publishing and a teacher of journalism at what was eventually known as Steubenville High. "Just a full page with one word, 'Dino,' in the center," Maltese recalled. (In 1951, when Steubenville's population had swelled to over 30,000, Dino returned to the school with his then-partner Jerry Lewis for "Dean Martin Day," but he was never seen there again.)

Dino was lucky enough to find a number of Depression-era jobs, but like most people destined for show business, he was pretty lousy at all of them. He clowned around too much at the filling station as far as the owner was concerned and was fired within a matter of days. He then begged his uncle Joe, who worked for a milk company, to make him a milkman, but this, too, proved disastrous when Dino's irresponsible tom-foolery, juggling milk bottles and the like, splashed a little too much milk—and glass—on customers lawns and stoops. Lying about his age, he then managed to get a job at one of the steel mills, but he found this too dangerous when a bundle of hot coiled steel nearly flattened him when it fell from a forklift. At least, this was the episode he used as an excuse to quit—he had already decided that working in the noisy, hot, stifling, steamy, and highly uncomfortable confines of a steel mill was not for him.

So the basic pattern for many years to come was established: Dino would not work at or do anything that would in any way numb or deaden his natural exuberance for life, that would suppress or dampen in any fash-ion the sheer pleasure he took in being alive. If that made him irresponsi-ble in some ways, he didn't care. It was his life, and he was free to do with it as he pleased.

Some of the things he was pleased to do did not please his father, who by this time was promising to put in another barber's chair so that his son could join him and his employees in the shop, which had been expanded over the years. There were worse ways, Guy reasoned, to make a living, and Dino didn't seem to be making good at anything else. However, the thought of it was enough to make Dino break out in a cold sweat. He wasn't certain what he wanted to do—except sing, which was a pipe dream at that point—but becoming a carbon copy of his father, no matter how much they might have loved each other, was not an option. Dino didn't want to be just anybody, someone ordinary; he wanted to be special and do something exciting. Becoming "the Barber of Steubenville" was not in the cards—although everyone who knew him at this time pretty much fig-ured that that was to be his ultimate fate. He might as well accept it and be grateful that he had his father's business—and career—to fall back on.

His mother, Angela, had her own fears. Her brother, Dean's Uncle Leonard, had been a restless dreamer who'd gone into show business; now he was a vaudevillian named "Bananas" who did a zany specialty dance act and eked out a living in third-rate theaters. He'd later get a female partner and become a bit more successful (many years later Dino would have him on his TV show), but for now his was an uncertain life of disappointment and privation. Angela didn't want that for her son.

Walking by the local gym one day, Dino wandered in and watched the fighters for a while, sizing them up and coming to the conclusion that he was as well built and athletic as any of them. Now, this was more like it. This was exciting, something that not just any joe could do. He talked to a manager named Tony Romano, who urged him to take some boxing lessons before he would sign him up. It wasn't long before Dino was fighting a few amateur matches as a 146-pound welterweight of sixteen.

Although there have been reports that Dino became known as "Kid Crochet," during this period, if the moniker isn't unlikely enough, it's certainly unlikely that his career lasted long enough for him to have become known under any kind of nickname. According to Joseph Pirone, whose father was one of the men Dino fought against, "My father talked about winning a fight with Dino every time someone mentioned his name, but he never said anything about him being called Kid Crochet. Maybe Martin or somebody made that up years later. [My father] said Dino's heart was never in it. He used to flinch when he got hit in the face. He just had a few fights, lost most of them, and that was it. He had bigger fish to fry."

Guy and Angela weren't crazy about the boxing, but at least it was more or less honest work. The Crocetti family took their religion seriously, and there were some things a good Catholic boy did not do. But while Dino may have believed in God, as he did all his life, that didn't mean he had any interest in being a literal or figurative choir boy. So in his quest for vocational excitement, he next went to work for first bootleggers, then gamblers.

But first there was an automobile trip to California with a friend. A stopover in Chicago widened Dean's eyes as to the possibilities of living in a big city. When they finally got out to Los Angeles, Dean drove out to the Paramount Studios in Hollywood, parked across the street, and stared wonderingly at the gates and beyond, little knowing that one day he'd be making pictures on the lot. When he returned to little Steubenville, there was no way he would ever be satisfied cutting hair as his father did. There was no limit to his imagination or his ambition.

Still, he was very young and would have to bide his time until he had the money and wherewithal to follow through on his nascent dreams. In the meantime, he worked. Dean recalled shuttling bootleg whiskey from Ohio to Pennsylvania with two of his buddies on more than one occasion. "We could have run the car on that shit instead of using gasoline!" he said. It was lucky that hauling hootch was only a part-time, extra-few-dollars sort of thing because the end of Prohibition shortly afterward meant such overnight, after-dark excursions would no longer be necessary. And though by that time the Crocettis had moved to a bigger house in a better neighborhood, for Dean there would definitely be no handouts. Either he worked, his father told him, or he went back to school. He chose work.

This time he settled on the infamous Rex's Cigar Store as his place of employment, which was home to a notorious gambling den. His parents had no idea that the cigar store was just a front for one of Steubenville's most successful illegal businesses. Years later he would say that he got his parents to consent to his remaining at Rex's because he assured them that while he worked there in virtually every capacity—running the roulette wheel, dealing blackjack—he himself did not indulge in the evil vice of gambling. The story is assuredly apocryphal: Not only did Dean gamble, but his parents would never have approved of him working in an establishment that could have been raided at any time—this in spite of Dino's generous salary, which, including tips, was up to twenty dollars a day. It is more likely that they simply couldn't force him to quit, or he told them he was a clerk in the front room, the legitimate tobacco business that served as a front for the gambling operation and where Dino couldn't, therefore, get in any trouble. Whatever he said, it worked—for a time.

Dino really took to working in a gambling parlor. The rush of the roulette wheel, the thrill of the crap game, the snap of cards being dealt, then the swish of them being just as quickly swept away along with the players' wistful hopes of winning—it all seemed so exciting and magical to him that he was in seventh heaven. There was the heady combination of the smoke and the boozy conversation, the tension in the air, the electric charge that permeated everything, the constant sense of anticipation and apprehension, the intimation of fear and a certain danger. The fact that it was all illegal, illicit, only made it more compelling to Dino. This was not an ordinary job, this was not dull and complacent—the very things he couldn't stomach—this was the *real world*. He added to his income by occasionally sneaking a silver dollar or two into his loafers, until the boss caught on and told him to cut it out or else.

Dino's associates in these early days were not the kind to warm the heart of any teenage boy's worrying mother. Dino would later remark that many of them wound up in jail or went to an early grave. His early years at Rex's were responsible for making him feel more comfortable in the presence of "shady" characters years later than the average person might have been. Dino was still too young to be served in a bar, but his friends would get him liquor when he wanted it, and he made an early acquaintance with many of the ladies working in brothels in the red-light district. He had also developed a glib, smooth way with the women that was in sharp contrast to his stumbling, puppylike maneuverings of just a year or two earlier.

He also broke the hearts of many a nonprofessional lady. Dino had developed a new sophistication working in a place like Rex's. He had "important" friends and was being whispered about by all the right people. Young women saw him as dangerous, interesting, someone they wanted to know without their parents ever finding out. Dino was not heartless, but he had no interest in going steady with anyone, and whenever a girl got too proprietary, Dino would disappear, leaving some of them embittered and heartsick for years to come.

Gambling—and the opposite sex—stayed in Dino's blood for the rest of his life.

But this was only the beginning.

TWO

The Sound of Music

Although it would be a couple of years before he could drink legally in the clubs, Dino was no stranger to Steubenville's nightspots during the years he worked at Rex's Cigar Store. A number of gin joints and roadhouses were in the area—many of them owned by mobsters—and Dino made his presence known in all of them. From his teen years on he enjoyed the smoky, convivial atmosphere of bars and lounges, although he was to tire of them by the time he was middle-aged.

Dino had grown up listening to Russ Columbo and Bing Crosby records, and it was the latter who most influenced his own style. He had no singing or musical lessons of any kind and never could read a note of sheet music. He learned by imitating "Der Bingle." It wasn't long before he was doing his Bing impressions in front of the open mike at some of the joints, urged on by his pals and doe-eyed young women. On a dare he had already gotten up to sing with a band at Craig Beach, a resort near Youngstown where he had come with some friends on a day trip, and he was already getting cocky about his performing skills. Still, he would at least wait until his buddies started nagging him to get up and sing. He also took to the microphone at all the social clubs and community centers in Steubenville and its environs, singing with the two-bit orchestras who were at least gratified that the guy could actually carry a tune, even if no one foresaw great things in his future. Before long he was a familiar figure on the circuit, hitting spots like Walker's and Reed's Mill and the Half Moon Club—and dozens of others that catered to a less tony crowd—as well as the more respectable places like the Catholic Community Center, the Polish Hall, and the Capital Ball Room. It wasn't long before he was spotted in clubs and social centers in nearby Columbus and Youngstown. He was an attractive, likable youth who easily made friends among both sexes, winning over both young and old. By this time he was of age and could handle a few beers, and imbibing them only added to his natural insouciance.

A bandleader named Ernie McKay, who was hot stuff for Ohio in those days, caught the now twenty-two-year-old Dino doing his thing on more than one occasion and decided his band could do worse than have a young, good-looking male vocalist who, despite his amateur standing, already seemed to be garnering quite a following. One night he went up to Dino and asked him if he'd like full-time employment as a singer with his band. Dino was excited by the offer, even though the salary McKay dangled was nothing to write home about. He was making more than that at Rex's.

Legend has it that when the mob owners of Rex's heard about Dino's predicament, they offered to pay him the difference in salary on a weekly basis. Others have suggested that the gang in the back room took up a collection to send him on his way. While provocative, neither is very likely. The first anecdote suggests, of course, that Dino was somehow subsidized by the mob in his early days and forever after indebted to them, but there's no real factual substantiation for this. As for the collection, it's more likely that the other croupiers in the back room saw Dino's singing engagement as a step up and were hardly likely to give up any of their hard-earned incomes to bolster his own. As Dino became more and more famous, many people who had once known him only slightly came forward to talk about how they'd once "helped him out" and so on, perhaps hoping he'd read about it and send them a generous, sadly belated thank-you check.

Ernie McKay took it upon himself to change Dino's name to Dino Martini, figuring it would summon up comparisons with a popular romantic singer of the time known as *Nino* Martini. McKay was forever trying to figure out ways to get his group out of the small-time and make it a real winning proposition, so he experimented with different names and vocalists and on occasion hired novelty acts to perform with the band. By the time Dino made his professional debut at the State Chinese Restaurant in Columbus, he was singing with "The McKaymen" and a "Singing Strings Trio." Ambitious to a fault, the three Yee brothers who owned the State hired other acts of all types and varieties so that they could present full-blown vaudeville shows as if they were Chinese Ziegfelds. In the meantime Ernie kept tinkering around with his own act to blow the ballroom dancers and trained dogs they were in competition with out of the water. At one point Dino's billing was as big as Ernie's; a few weeks later he had been demoted to being part of the "Three Well-Wishers Trio," which consisted of him and two other now forgotten male vocalists.

One night singer Lee Ann Lee, the pretty wife of a bandleader named Sammy Watkins, caught Dino at the State and liked what she saw. She sent Dino a note backstage and asked to speak to him. She suggested that he make a record—which could be done relatively cheaply in those days—and forward it to her husband. "I didn't know if she was serious or this was some sort of come on," Dean said years later, "but I figured it was worth a try. I was tired of tripping over those damn dogs [in the canine novelty act] every time I left my dressing room."

Sammy Watkins heard the record and thought his wife, a singer herself, was onto something. Sammy wasn't the first to note that Dino had an absolutely marvelous, easygoing, totally unforced way of singing, a breeziness and spontaneity that other trained singers could strive for but could never quite attain. He was still very much in the Bing Crosby mode, but that was hardly a problem considering the latter singer's popularity at the time. Watkins had little trouble convincing Dino to jump ship from the "McKaymen" with their trios and changeable billing and the State Chinese Restaurant with its dog acts and move to Cleveland and one step closer to the Big Time.

Watkins was tops in Cleveland, where he held court at the ritzy Vogue Room in the Hollenden Hotel. Since Dino had failed to move Ernie McKay into the limelight as the bandleader had half hoped, McKay let him go with reasonably good grace. Dino's salary with Watkins would be thirty-five dollars a week; by the time he was twenty-four, he'd received special billing with the Watkins band and was making nearly twice as much. He decided the name "Martini" was too silly—besides, he was not an operatic tenor like *Nino*—so he shortened it to Martin, keeping a connection to the name he had started out with as a professional. Dino was Americanized to Dean.

"I don't really remember why I changed the name," he said years later. "I guess there were enough Italian singers around, and most of them sang opera. I wanted to do my own thing. 'Dino' was fine for a boy in a small town, but I wanted to sort of cut my ties—not with my family but with those early days when I couldn't stick to nothin' and wasn't gettin' anywhere. I guess 'Dean Martin' was the new me." It sounded classier, more grown up, less ethnic. He made the name change at least a year before the United States and Italy were on different sides of a world war, but there was still a lot of prejudice against Italian-Americans at this time, and almost everyone felt that the U.S. entry into the conflict was inevitable; Dean didn't need a vowel at the end of his name, not during this uncertain period. Lastly, the new moniker helped establish him as an *individual*, someone with his own fresh style and attitude.

Along with the new name, Dean wanted a new contract and more money. Watkins seemed happy to oblige—Dean was popular with audiences—but there was a price to be paid for the increase in salary. Watkins's contract stipulated that Dean would have to turn over 10 percent of any money he made through outside venues, meaning any singing he did without the band. Dean couldn't foresee such a likelihood on the horizon—he was Watkins's lead vocalist and liked it that way—so he had no second thoughts when signing the contract, his mind concentrating on the extra dollars he'd make per week.

Meanwhile a young lady named Elizabeth McDonald had more on her mind than a name change—although that, too, was to happen sooner than she expected. Elizabeth—known to all as Betty—was a shapely, attractive brunette with dark Irish good looks who appeared little like the expert athlete that she was. Due to her athletic achievements she had gotten a scholarship to Swarthmore in Ohio, but she had neglected the academic side of her education and was promptly expelled.

Betty was disconsolate, certain she'd let the family down and afraid of what her father might say, but his reaction was milder than expected. To take her mind off things and to cheer her up, Mr. McDonald decided to take her with him on a business trip to Cleveland. Besides, he had just learned from the liquor firm he worked for that he was to be permanently transferred to Cleveland, so he and Betty could check out the housing situation while Mrs. McDonald held down the fort. Betty looked forward to seeing the sights, staying in a big hotel, enjoying her father's company.

Betty and her father stayed at the Hollenden Hotel, and on that fateful first night in Cleveland, they had supper in the Vogue Room, where Sammy Watkins and his orchestra were entertaining. Out came their male vocalist, a good-looking slender chap, six feet tall, with dark curly hair, bedroom eyes, and an infatuating grin that worked its instant magic on Betty. For his part, Dean could not fail to notice the intoxicating charms of Betty McDonald. During the following days, as Betty's father went to meetings and looked at houses, Betty and Dean began their courtship. Both later claimed that it was the proverbial love at first sight. Dean squired her to some of Cleveland's more interesting attractions by day, and in the evenings Betty would sit at a table in the Vogue Room and listen, enraptured, as her handsome troubadour sang love songs only, it seemed, to her.

Things moved very quickly. Dean was about to go on a tour with the Watkins band, which would keep him out of Cleveland for several months. Thinking it would be a shame to let things cool down just as the two of them were heating up, Dean took Betty to Steubenville for a visit with his folks and friends, who liked her as much as she did them, then popped the question when they were back in Cleveland. Betty gave him an enthusiastic, unhesitant yes. Getting special permission from the church to have an immediate wedding, they got hitched on October 2, 1941, with both families and members of the band in attendance. After a blissful night in which Dean and Betty gave full expression to the passion that the two had ignited in each other from first glance and which had been simmering for weeks, they both got on the bus with the other musicians and, devoid of much privacy, headed for the first stop on the long, uncomfortable tour. It was a hell of a way for them to begin married life.

As madly in love as Dean was, it was Betty who had to learn to put up with the privations and cramped conditions on the bus, the endless series of cheap motels, her mind still agog at the sudden 180-degree turn her life had taken. She had gone from college athlete to married lady in virtually one quick step. She felt with certainty that her being expelled was the best thing that could have happened to her. Dean was proud of his pretty young wife, whose company and wedding ring, cheap as it was, made him feel even more grown up, if not exactly special or unconventional. During the early days they were still awash in their special romantic glow that miraculously airbrushed all the imperfections and nagging doubts out of the picture.

Despite their obvious fondness for and physical attraction to each other, it's likely that Dean and Betty got married for the wrong reasons— or at least at the wrong time. Betty was still reeling from the unexpected blow of being expelled; suddenly there was a gap in her life that needed to be filled, and Dean was there to fill it. Brought up in a warm, nurturing, Catholic family environment, Dean knew—or thought he knew—that there were some girls you tossed aside and some girls you married. There had never been any doubt in his mind that, like his father before him, he would one day find the right girl, the marrying kind, whom he assumed was Betty. But he was still very young and, unlike his father, had appetites that had not yet been, might never be, satiated. The idea of marriage appealed to him; it was part of the growing up process, it was *what one did.*

But he wasn't really ready for it. In some ways, he never would be. For Betty, however, the idea of marriage was never enough; there were certain standards and disciplines that had to be maintained, and it was with standards and disciplines that Dean had always had his trouble. He loved Betty, he wanted to be married, but he wasn't ready to give up being a bachelor. This was essentially how Dean felt throughout his life. Stifling, suffocating things—be they wives, partners, or jobs—should not interfere with his pleasure in life. If life couldn't be fun, what good was it?

Although she was defeated right from the start and didn't realize it, Betty persevered as the bus jolted and bumped from one dreary town to the next. She would watch the band perform most of the time, but when the show was over, Dean would leave her alone in the motel while he had a few more drinks or played poker with the boys. Then he'd come in early in the morning and expect her to have instantaneous sex with him, even though she was half asleep. Dean preferred talking and playing with the guys in the band to quiet conversations with Betty, and the boys would play practical jokes on her that she put up with like a good sport but only served to demoralize her. She told herself that once they were back in Cleveland, things would be different.

But things weren't very different in Cleveland. And Betty was getting tired of waiting around for Dean's show to finish only to have him disappear to a crap game or another woman. There was a temporary reprieve for the marriage when Betty found out that she was pregnant. She used this as an excuse not to go with Dean on any more of the band's tours and stayed home to knit booties as Dean brought home the bacon. During this period the Japanese bombed Pearl Harbor, and all anyone could talk about was the war.

Dean got the first real fright of his life when he got his draft notice in early 1942. His career was going great, he was making good money and enjoying himself—understandably, he didn't especially like the idea of dropping everything and going off to Europe. Unlike most other American men, Dean wasn't exactly gung ho about going off to fight. Practical when he needed to be about certain matters, Dean had no starry-eyed, unrealistic, sentimental notions about the glories of combat. This didn't necessarily make him a coward, though it didn't exactly qualify him as a hero, either. In any case, he figured that his being married with a kid on the way would keep him out of the draft, even if it wouldn't have for long. Betty not only had affluent parents but relatively well off in-laws, so Dean could not be considered her sole means of support. It all became academic when the army doctors discovered a double hernia when they examined him, and Dean was classified 4-F. He could have had the hernia operated on, but he didn't do so until long after the war was over. The steel mill had been bad enough; the miserable conditions endured by soldiers overseas would have been intolerable—definitely not part of the Dean Martin Pleasure Principle. (Years later, he would use his ambivalent feelings about the war and combat to bolster his performance in *The Young Lions*.) In 1944 Dean heard from the draft board again and was briefly stationed at Akron, Ohio, but he was again invalidated by the hernias.

Betty and Dean's first child, Stephen Craig Martin, known as Craig throughout his life, was born on June 29, 1942, with proud papa Dean in attendance. Betty hoped that the birth of their child might make her husband more of a family man, and for a while it worked—but just for a while. Dean was present only for the birth of that first child—his nightclub jobs, and the tours every few months, kept him hopping and away from home more often than not. Betty nursed little Craig and coped as best she could.

Meanwhile things were heating up for Dean in the career department. First he got the thrill of singing for the first time on coast-to-coast radio at the studios of WTAM Cleveland; Sammy Watkins's band had been chosen as the city's favorite in a poll carried out by the popular program the *Fitch* (Shampoo) *Bandwagon*. Dean sang two standards, including a Bing Crosby hit, "Sweet Leilani," as well as two brand new works Sammy had received from New York publishers anxious to get their songs a public airing.

Then he got into a conversation with Merle Jacobs, Sammy Watkins's agent with the powerful Music Corporation of America (MCA). Dean knew of the great success of Frank Sinatra and other Italian-American nightclub singers and wondered if he could ever do a solo the way they did. Sinatra had broken away from the Tommy Dorsey band to go on to even greater fame and riches as a single. Dean casually threw the thought out—he had no idea how Jacobs, who was loyal to Watkins, might react to this possible intimation that he was looking to jump ship—but to his relief Jacobs seemed to go for the idea. "He told me that if ever there was a time for an Italian singer to try to make it in New York, this was the time," Dean remembered. "He said that he could handle Sammy for me, and I believed him."

The way Jacobs handled Sammy was for him to get Dean to agree to a hastily revised contract with Watkins. Watkins would no longer have exclusive rights to Dean's services, but the clause that allowed him 10 percent of all of Dean's outside earnings still remained and would remain in effect for the next several years; the old agreement was then considered null and void, and Dean was free to sign with whomever he wished. But as part of his concession Dean had to agree to stay with Watkins until the end of the year in the event that no major opportunities presented themselves via MCA; even then Dean would need Sammy's approval before he could take off and was required to give him several weeks' notice until January 1, 1944, when Dean would be completely free to do what he wished. Dean then signed a contract with MCA, who also wanted a 10-percent cut of his future earnings. At the time Dean didn't care that he was kissing 20 percent of his income good-bye; he focused on the major success he was sure was just around the corner.

He didn't have to wait long to make his jump. Frank Sinatra canceled an engagement at the Riobamba, a small club in Manhattan owned by Mafia hit man Louis Lepke, and Merle Jacobs wasted no time filling the breach with Dean. The management was not so crazy about hiring a complete unknown—in New York terms—like Dean, but they reasoned that if the crooner had only a portion of Sinatra's appeal, it might work out all right for them.

They told Jacobs it was a go, and the agent called Dean excitedly and told him to start packing for Manhattan; he opened in two days. "What about Sammy?" Dean wanted to know. Again Jacobs told him that he would handle Sammy.

But Sammy was not to be handled so easily. He expected Dean to honor the terms of his agreement and give him plenty of notice before he left the band. Dean knew this was a once-in-a-lifetime opportunity for him, and there was no way the Riobamba, which needed an act *now*, would wait for him for two or more weeks. Jacobs appealed to Watkins on Dean's behalf, but the bandleader would not be appeased. He told Dean he had better forget about the Riobamba deal; there was no way he was walking out on him at a minute's notice. Jacobs told Dean that perhaps he could persuade the managers of the club to hold an opening for him at some future point, but Dean knew the agent couldn't promise that and called the club himself and told them that *he'd be there*. He told Jacobs that *he* would handle Sammy when the time came. He packed his bags, kissed his flabbergasted wife and child good-bye, and fled Cleveland for Manhattan in the night.

Sammy knew that Dean was not easily controllable, and he went to his apartment the following morning to speak to him. Sammy kept jabbing the bell insistently, waking the baby. Betty, still half asleep, answered the door with trepidation. No, Dean wasn't there. No, she didn't know where he was. She *never* knew where he was, didn't Sammy know that?

Finally she broke down and told the bandleader that Dean had gone off to New York. "Don't blame me! I had nothing to do with it!" she said, slamming the door in his face. Sammy kept banging on the door, demanding to know which hotel Dean had checked into. Dean had instructed Betty not to say anything to anyone, but he had run out of there without warning, leaving her behind to deal with all the crap, and there was only so much abuse she could stand. Sammy was yelling at *her*, not Dean. So she told him: "The Astor Hotel!"

Dean was astonished when Sammy himself showed up at the Astor that very night. He got the same treatment as Betty: repeated wallops on the door of his hotel room. When Sammy threatened to do everything he could to queer the Riobamba opening, Dean admitted him to his room, and the two sat down to talk things over—although not very calmly. Dean tried to quell his anger and explained to Sammy that it wasn't just himself; he now had a wife and child to think about. Couldn't Sammy understand that he had a right to think of his future and his family's? A bit mollified by Dean's earnest plea, Sammy told him that he would allow him to stay in New York on certain conditions. Dean had to agree to pay him a small bulk "penalty" fee out of his earnings at the Riobamba plus turn over an additional 2 percent of his future earnings. Anxious to have the man out of his face and out of his life, Dean agreed.

Dean's fleeing Cleveland and deserting Sammy Watkins on the spot has often been cited as evidence of Dean's early ruthlessness as it pertained to his career, his "to hell with everybody but himself" attitude. But this was hardly the case. True, Dean's needs and wishes were always paramount—he was never the hypocritical, self-sacrificing type—but what entertainer in his or her right mind would have turned down such an opportunity? Cleveland was *nothing* next to New York City. Dean also knew that Watkins would have no real trouble finding a replacement vocalist in Cleveland, that he was just being ornery and difficult, angry that someone he seemed to feel he'd plucked out of nowhere was flexing his muscles. Dean helped draw the crowds, sure, but the Sammy Watkins band had always been popular with the audience no matter who was singing. And the bandleader already had other vocalists in his employ.

In any case, Dean's days with the Sammy Watkins band were over—permanently.

He would never look back.

THREE

Manhattan

Whether or not Dean Martin's debut at the Riobamba is viewed as auspicious depends on whether one sees the glass as half empty or half full. On the one hand, his initial two-week run at the nightclub was extended, and eventually there were several New York columnists who sang his praises in print. On the other hand, a lot of critics wrote him off as either a Crosby or Sinatra wannabe with limited prospects, and Dean found himself unemployed before three months were up. *Variety* rightly noted that he had a "small" voice that required a microphone, but the same could be said for Crosby, Sinatra, and all the other crooners—"mike singers" all. It was as if the paper were comparing him to Nino Martini, the operatic tenor. Dean's voice was not an operatic voice nor even a Broadway belt-'em-out voice, the kind that needed no artificial amplification. He was simply a crooner who knew that light and easy was the way to go. If he—and all the other crooners—tried to get too loud or dramatic, it just wouldn't work.

Dean made his New York debut on the evening of September 24, 1943. He was given a grand total of eight minutes to put himself over, as he had to share the spotlight with a number of other acts. The applause he received was polite but not terribly enthusiastic. "I got by," he remembered. "Nobody threw tomatoes at me." Powerful *New York Post* columnist Earl Wilson was one of his earliest boosters, calling him "a hell of a good crooner" in his column of September 25.

Dean wasn't complaining—this was New York, after all, and even if the Riobamba wasn't exactly the even more upscale Copacabana, at least it was a major venue for any entertainer. Still, the irony must have hit him that in Cleveland he'd been the headliner, and now he was just one of a bunch. Then there was the factor that he was working with a brand-new band with hardly any rehearsal time, which must have scared him. But he managed; they were all professionals, and it was easy for the musicians to adjust themselves to his tempo and vice versa. Dean's style was so loose, it was easily adaptable.

Still, Dean was coasting along by singing old standards and the hits of other crooners. There was nothing distinctive enough about either him or his material. Although critics seemed to find nicer things to say about him as he proved a success at the Riobamba, many of them still found him lacking in personality. His natural charisma didn't seem to extend into an audience of blasé New Yorkers who had seen it all. Yet those same audiences were slowly warming up to him as he gradually learned how to work a crowd and command attention.

As soon as he learned that his engagement was being extended, Dean sent for Betty and Craig, and the three moved into a West Side apartment complex known as the London Terrace. Dean was making nearly one hundred and fifty dollars a week at the Riobamba, but he always seemed strapped for cash. MCA assumed that he was taking the 10 percent commission he owed them out of each check that the Riobamba gave him—they cut him some slack as he settled down in New York and paid off some bills—but Dean was doing nothing of the sort. Neither was he setting aside the percentage he was supposed to pay to Sammy Watkins. And tax money never even entered his head; he would worry about the IRS (or not) when the time came. Worse, when the rent was due on the London Terrace apartment, Dean didn't have enough to pay it.

Where was the money going? Like many small-town boys of comparatively limited means who find themselves in the big, exciting city, Dean wanted to live it up, live like the star he knew he was destined to be. He ignored the bad reviews and let the good ones go to his head. Although he was far from the toast of the town, he wanted to pretend that the city was *his*. There was nothing especially monstrous about his attitude, but it has been portrayed as such; in fact, it was all too human.

So after his shows, as Betty minded the kid, he would go out, hit the night spots, look at the ladies, find places to gamble, spend money on women, liquor, and crap games, do whatever the hell he felt like. He ate at the most expensive restaurants, ordered the most expensive brandies and cigars, swallowed martini after martini, and gave away cash and presents to any beautiful showgirl who caught his fancy. When Betty got demanding, he would throw some money at her, let her buy herself a new dress or some perfume or food and clothing for the kid. After a while there wasn't much money for Betty or for the kid. Dean was running through his paycheck practically before the ink was dry, and most of his good times were financed by loans from friends.

Yes, Dean was young and irresponsible, brash and selfish—to put it mildly—but he wasn't really out to hurt anyone. There he was, working in New York, singing at a big nightclub, his name in lights and in all the newspaper columns; he had to keep up appearances. He couldn't accept that he was fundamentally too broke to carry on like a movie star who made thousands of dollars a week. And the women. These were not small-town Steubenville girls with crushes and fancy ideas, but high-toned ladies smelling of seductive perfume and wearing provocative expressions. And they made no secret of the fact that they could be had. It took money—lots of money—to wine and dine these broads, but for Dean, even getting into debt was worth it. Besides, he resented the idea of paying MCA 10 percent—it was him up there singing, not Merle Jacobs. And he sure as hell was not about to send that bastard Sammy Watkins with his black-mailing contracts any money if he could help it!

So Dean made the circuit while Betty watched the kid and stewed. Sometimes he'd take her out, sometimes he'd stay home with her, but he wanted to catch every drop of excitement when he could. Staying home with Betty and the baby just didn't cut it. Meanwhile, Betty would treat herself to a few drinks out of the bottle just to make the evening seem shorter. Wandering around Manhattan unescorted did not especially appeal to her.

There were dozens of women, some of whom he was more success-ful with than others: Gregg Sherwood, a Miss America contestant from Wisconsin who'd changed her name to something more exotic and kicked up her heels on the Riobamba conga line; Janie Ford, a singer from Texas who at one point shared a manager with Dean; and a Brooklyn-born cho-rus cutie who called herself Sunny Daye in the 1940s and fifty years later wound up the widow of a wealthy lawyer.

"Dean knew how to give a lady a good time," Sunny says. "He was very persistent, but in a charming, teddy bear sort of way. Yes, he would give the girls gifts—nothing too expensive but nothing cheap, either. Nobody knew of his money troubles, at least not at first. He spent money like water! Later on I heard he was borrowing from everyone and his brother, and his wife had left him and he'd got thrown out of his apart-ment for back rent. It seemed so odd because he was doing so well for a while—really poised, situated, for the top."

Sunny remembers the first night Dean convinced her to go out on a date with him. "It was kind of off the cuff. He just asked me if I wanted a bite, and I agreed because it didn't seem like an honest to goodness date. I knew he was married, and while some girls didn't care one way or the other, I tried to avoid the married ones if I could. But Dean was so cute. It was like something out of a movie: I was starving, thought he was rich—compared to me, at least—and ordered everything I could get my hands on. He ordered the classic chicken sandwich and coffee. I felt like a heel, but he insisted he wasn't that hungry.

"He spent most of his money on drinks. He could really pack 'em in in those days. As he got older I think he drank less, but in his twenties when I knew him he loved to bar hop and imbibe.

"He made a pass at me—that night, and many others—but he was too drunk by the time he got me home to do anything about it. I had to borrow money from my sister to make sure he got back to Manhattan in a cab. But all the while, even when he was drunk, he was the soul of charm. Dean never grabbed you or tore your clothes. He just sort of offered himself—and you either took him or not."

According to Sunny, there were plenty of girls who took Dean—and with no strings attached. "They knew he was married, so they didn't expect anything other than a nice time. He was good-looking and smooth, so I knew lots of girls who went to bed with him. They didn't have to tell me; I'd just look at them and I'd know. One girl—she worked at a lot of clubs with me—said he was 'quite a man,' if you know what I mean. Some girls saw him as someone who could maybe help their careers, but most just fell under the spell of his charm. He was very attractive.

"One night after his wife walked out on him—which she was always doing for one reason or another—I saw him in a club, just a small bar in the theater district, and he looked a little down, not so much because Betty had left but because he felt a little out of control. He was always happy-go-lucky on the surface, but I think he was bothered by the financial situation. He carried on like it didn't bother him—easy come and easy go and all that—but nobody likes to be in debt, always borrowing from your friends, always having to put yourself in that humiliating position. Particularly when you've thought you've got it made. I will tell you this: Dean could be very generous when he had it. And to everyone, not just the showgirls. He could be very kind when he wanted to be."

Betty might not have agreed, given her situation. She had no solid proof of infidelities—any man who worked in a nightclub with dozens of showgirls was bound to smell somewhat of perfume as well as smoke when he came home—but she wasn't an idiot. She was tired of his late nights, tired of phone calls from friends asking for their money, tired of letters from MCA asking for their commissions. "We're sure it's just an oversight," they'd write, "but please remit." When the engagement at the Riobamba came to an end in December of '43, Betty—as well as Dean—wondered if anything new would turn up and if MCA would continue shopping Dean around when they were already owed so much money. Work came in dribs and drabs for the next few months, but Dean needed a solid, long-term club date to get out of the hole, if it was even possible for him to do so. Adding to Betty's worry was the fact that she was pregnant again. Dean didn't stay out *every* night of the week.

MCA came through in mid-January 1944—sort of. But it wasn't a prestigious club date, just a tour on the Statler Hotel circuit that would take Dean to several northeastern cities, including Boston. Betty had no intention of going with Dean—not that he would have wanted her to—so she decided to stay with her parents, who had moved from Cleveland to Philadelphia since her wedding, while he was out of town. The split lasted somewhat longer than that. Betty had to get away to consider her options, nurse her wounds, make solid decisions about her future. She had learned that when it came to husbands, charm could cover a multitude of inadequacies. On March 16, while with her parents, she gave birth to their first daughter, Claudia. Dean was still on the road, up in Canada and miles away in every sense of the word.

Back in Manhattan Dean ran into an acquaintance from Steubenville named Dick Richards who was looking for a way into show business and swore he had plenty of contacts in New York. Together they came up with the idea of Richards becoming Dean's manager. Dean put one stipulation on the idea first. In return for a 10-percent piece of Dean's action, Richards would have to advance him some money. Richards, happy to finally be part of showbiz, readily agreed.

Desperate for cash, beset by creditors from every direction, and months behind in his rent at the London Terrace, Dean had hit upon a scheme to enrich his coffers. He was constantly running into small-time operators who wanted to become his agent, little Davids who thought they could do better than the Goliath MCA as well as people like Richards who thought because they hung out in clubs and knew a few people, they would make a good manager. All these people wanted to do was use him, Dean reasoned, so why not make them pay for it? In the next few months he would sign virtually worthless contracts with a number of "agents" and "managers," always in return for several hundred dollars of advance money. Eventually he would sign over more than 100 percent of his income to these people, none of which he had any intention of paying.

Dean probably never thought of his actions as being in any way criminal—he needed the money, and when his ship came in he'd be able to do right by everybody, maybe pay them back the advance and then tell them to take a walk. He never imagined that any of these people would ever actually do anything for him, anyway. If they did, then he would buy them off and renegotiate. In those days Dean was only thinking of getting his hands on some money. In the back of his mind he knew it would all implode one day, but that was tomorrow, and in the meantime he tried not to think about it. One more martini might help.

To Dean's surprise it wasn't long before Dick Richards actually managed to book him into the fashionable La Martinique on West Fifty-seventh Street. Only a week or two into the engagement, however, the club shut down, its patronage having slowed considerably due to a surcharge added to the already hefty bill because of a new entertainment tax. Luckily he soon got a new gig at a place called the Harlequin. Dean had so many creditors after him looking to garnish his two hundred dollar a week salary that he asked the management to pay him in cash. Cash that he would promptly spend on lavish meals, lots of martinis, and gifts for the ladies—anything to keep up the lifestyle he had become accustomed to. The management of the London Terrace threw up their hands and evicted him. MCA also let it be known that if he didn't pay something toward all the money he owed them for commissions, he might have to look elsewhere for representation.

Meanwhile, in the Philadelphia suburb of Ridley Park, Betty and her parents wondered if Dean would ever send for his wife, son, and baby daughter. "The girls I grew up with," Betty remembered, "who were all married with their own homes, would make remarks about Dean being out of work again. The leader of the snide remarks was my mother." Betty not only had to wonder if she and her husband would ever have any kind of life together, if they'd ever be a real family, but she knew that her mother and father—especially the former—were losing patience with her and her ne'er-do-well hubby. It wasn't until she went back to New York City that she realized they no longer had a home.

Meanwhile, Dean had other things to worry about besides cash for drinks and babes. He spent a few nights with friends and girls he met in bars, but he needed a permanent address. And what with all the squawking from MCA, perhaps another agent. He knew Dick Richards was weak tea when he needed a cup of strong java. He remembered an agent he had met a few months before when he was working at the Riobamba, a short, thin man with slicked-back hair and an impeccable wardrobe, pushing forty. Like Dick Richards and Dean himself, this man—one Lou Perry—was also an Italian with an Americanized name, and Dean felt sure they would be simpatico. Besides, it was unlikely any other large agency would be interested in him once MCA put the word out on how unreliable he was when it came to commissions.

Going to Lou Perry was just another example of how Dean handled his creditors: by running away from them. If MCA no longer represented him, he figured he wouldn't have to get a reminder from them as to how much he owed every time they called with news of an assignment. Of course, at this point he had no phone that MCA could call him on.

Dean got even more than he hoped for from Lou Perry. Perry not only agreed to sign him and put up some advance money, he offered Dean—who had told him in honest terms of his predicament—a place to stay. It would be an understatement to say that from there on out Dean's living arrangements became utterly absurd and more than a little eyebrow raising. He moved into Perry's digs—room 616 of the Bryant Hotel—even though Perry already had another impoverished client staying with him and only one double bed for the three of them! An arrangement that might have been fun for somebody fresh out of college could not have been a picnic for a twenty-seven-year-old like Dean, but it was better than living on the streets, and he was not about to go back to Cleveland with his tail between his legs. In return for all Perry's help and in lieu of rent, Dean promised him an extra large percentage of his earnings.

Dean's other roomie was another Italian-American singer, named Sonny King. Dean and Sonny would take turns sharing the double bed with Lou Perry while the loser slept on the floor. At one point a fourth "guest" was deposited in the bathtub for several nights. Like college kids instead of grown men, they would drink beer or wine, talk about broads, commit practical jokes on one another like frat boys, and occasionally go out for a drink or a date with a girl when the opportunity presented itself. Dean made the best of it, although years later the whole experience would give him the shivers and permanently sour him on New York. The city would forever become associated in his mind with those horrible days of destitution and struggle, the disappointment of feeling like a failure even though his name was in the columns and his picture on the poster in the lobby of the Harlequin and other nightspots—things that seemed to say, mockingly, that he was a big success. Separated by miles in distance, experience, and aspirations, both Dean and Betty would drink heavily to deal with the fear they felt.

When Betty found out that she and the children had no real home to return to, she felt desperate, nearly disconsolate. Her mother nagged at her to get a divorce, but she could no more admit failure than her husband could. She made frequent trips to Manhattan sans children, moving in with Lou Perry and his troupe at the Bryant, where the sleeping arrangements became even more riotous, but she could hardly have afforded a room of her own. Luckily Sonny and the other part-time roommates had friends they could visit for a night, or they'd stay out till all hours at 24-hour coffee shops to give Dean and Betty a few hours' privacy. Lou Perry was the most patient and tolerant man in the world, but he must have either found it all rather fun and exciting in a it-makes-me-feel-young-again way or else he was the biggest masochist in the world.

Dino legend has it that Dean and Sonny King, who'd also had a brief career as a pugilist, would try to earn extra money by holding boxing matches in room 616, charging five bucks for the dubious privilege of watching them spar in their shorts. According to King, during one fight Dean knocked Sonny straight out the window. "Luckily there were these old-fashioned blinds made out of iron," King told one interviewer. "I just hung on to the blinds and pulled myself up. Dean was laughing; kind-hearted Dean, laughing like hell—I tell you, I beat the hell out of him." King said that Dean was too injured to open at the Hippodrome, so Sonny went on for him as "Dean Martin," but since Sonny was a tenor, not a baritone, the deception was noticed, and he got fired.

Great story, but its veracity is doubtful. It's unlikely that the management wouldn't have known right off the bat that King wasn't Dean Martin, who'd had several engagements in New York, his picture in the papers, and was already fairly well-known. It's doubly unlikely that Dean, whose amateur boxing career had been pretty much a dismal failure, could have knocked anyone out a window. King and other people who knew Dean in the early days have passed on any number of colorful anecdotes to interviewers, but all of these stories—such as the bit with Dean laughing after knocking King out a sixth-story window—should be taken with a large grain of salt. As Dean Martin's legend grew, so, too, did the apocrypha surrounding him, often generated by people who were bitter that Dean ultimately made out so much better than they did.

Besides his financial situation, Dean had two main worries those days: his 4-F status and his nose. To everyone who saw him, Dean looked like the perfect picture of manly health—no one knew about the hernias—and there was hardly a soul who didn't wonder why this able-bodied man wasn't fighting for his country while so many other American boys were losing life and limb in the conflict. Dean was touchy about the subject—and he should have been; challenged by acquaintances or hecklers, he'd figuratively trot out the wife and children, unspecified health problems, anything to get himself off the hook. There are those who feel that, good as he was, Dean's ascent to the top of the profession was greatly aided by the fact that most of the competition was overseas.

Frank Sinatra was also getting flack because he wasn't in the service. His excuse was a punctured eardrum. Later he was exempted because his work was considered "in the national interest." Columnists wondered how singing songs to bobby-soxers could possibly be in the national interest, which was supposed to encompass such professions as engineering, teaching, weapons manufacturing—doing things that could actually be helpful in a *war*. Somehow Dean avoided most of this public criticism; the press by and large spared him, probably because in no way was he as big as Sinatra at this time. He was too small to be a target.

Dean was almost as touchy about his nose as he was his 4-F status, maybe touchier. The funny thing was that his nose, while a bit large and bent, fit his face and looked basically normal. Certainly it had never prevented him from appealing to the ladies or made him seem disfigured. But other performers he knew, jealous of his apparent "success," not to mention the way he scored with the women, tried to undermine his confidence any way they could, and the nose seemed the easiest target. Dean wasn't short or fat or ugly, so it was a case of exaggerating a minimal flaw. Before long Dean had practically developed a complex.

He went to Lou Perry, who was always kindhearted and honest, and asked him what he thought. Was his nose OK? Lou was frank. "Your nose is OK for an ordinary person, but if you really want to hit it big, make movies like Sinatra does and all the rest, maybe you should think about getting it fixed someday." The big screen magnified flaws, Dean knew, and the camera was merciless. Everyone was comparing him to Sinatra, saying he could make it just as big—even the critics who'd formerly scorned him. Maybe Lou was right, and something should be done. If he wanted to go all the way. And he did.

Then another man named Lou entered the picture: Lou Costello of the hit comedy duo Abbott and Costello. Lou saw Dean perform at the Harlequin and tried to interest his own manager, Eddie Sherman, in taking him on. But Sherman had heard too many stories about Dean Martin and how he gave away percentages of himself. Making acquaintance with the singer, Lou found that he and Dean had real rapport, and after a night of cocktails—Lou buying—Dean had himself yet another manager and another cash advance.

He also asked Costello what he thought of his honker. Costello wasted no time telling his new "client" that if he was planning to go into movies someday—maybe he could get him a bit in an Abbott and Costello feature— he had better get a nose job. Otherwise, he should leave it as it was; didn't the women love him already? Dean had to have been struck by the irony of a fat, homely, dumpy guy like Lou Costello—who was already a movie star—telling good-looking Dean he wasn't quite ready for the silver screen. Of course, Costello was *supposed* to look funny, and by now Dean was convinced that his nose made him very funny looking indeed, although such was not really the case.

But Dean didn't have the money to pay for a nose job, and he still wasn't certain he should fool with Mother Nature. It seemed such a feminine thing to do, making yourself over, fussing so much over your appearance. All the ladies' attentions over the years had turned his head, but there had to be a limit to his vanity. Still, the thought of rhinoplasty itched at the corners of his mind night after night. Finally he made up his mind to go ahead with the operation, but each time he managed to get the five hundred or so bucks he would need to pay the plastic surgeon, he would suddenly discover even more attractive uses for the cash—more booze and broads—and a few unattractive ones, such as sending milk money for the kids to Betty in Pennsylvania. By this time a third child had emerged from Betty's belly—apparently she and Dean were as physically attracted to each other as ever and made good use of their hours alone in the Bryant— and she gave Dean another daughter, Gail, on April 11, 1945. She did tell him that she was no longer coming to New York; if he wanted to see her or the children, he would just have to travel to the wilds of Pennsylvania and bear the glares and ire of her parents. He told her he had too many club engagements and couldn't get time off. As for the nose? "It looks fine!" Betty told him.

Dean borrowed money for his rhinoplasty from more than a dozen people, including Dick Richards, Lou Perry, and Lou Costello, none of whom knew that Dean owed percentages to all of them. Eventually Richards and some others got together and agreed to pay the doctor directly, so there was no way Dean could squander the money on other things. They obviously all felt that Dean was a good investment and were sure the new nose would make his prospects even brighter.

Thus Dean faced his first screen test with his brand new, slimmed down, nicely sculptured nose. A Columbia Pictures talent scout had seen the new face when Dean was performing and thought he might be good in pictures. Dean went to the studios on Tenth Avenue, which were used by all the major Hollywood companies for screen tests of New York's show people, and performed with two actresses who were also hoping for a Hollywood break. Unfortunately, new nose or not, Dean's chances were quickly shot down. Harry Cohn, who ran Columbia, wasn't too impressed with Dean. "He cannot talk at all" he wired the talent scout. Dean still had a way to go before he could be convincing and natural in front of a movie camera.

However, another movie notable, producer Joe Pasternak, who'd seen Dean at a club called Leon and Eddie's, thought much more of the test he had Dino do for director George Sidney for *Till the Clouds Roll By*. Pasternak wanted to use Dean in the picture, but this time Dean was nixed by MGM head Joe Schenck, who figured "what do we need with a *Dean* Martin when we've already got a Tony Martin?" At the time Dean felt this was one of the worst, most disappointing blows he could have received—a primary reason for the rhinoplasty was his hope for major movie stardom and an end to all his financial woes, a chance to get out of the awful room at the Bryant Hotel—but after a couple of nights of getting totally blitzed, he took it with his usual the-hell-with-it humor and hoped for another opportunity. Hadn't Pasternak, a movie bigwig, liked his performance in the test? He told himself it was only a matter of time before it happened. All the while he was mortally afraid that it never would.

Nonetheless, this was not exactly a time of despair for Dino. He was still performing in clubs, attracting the ladies, having good times—he always made sure he set aside enough money for his evenings out—and life could have been worse. Which is the only reason he managed to make it through three years in the tiny room at the Bryant Hotel without going utterly out of his mind. And he was still young, which never hurt.

He had no idea that the bottom was about to drop out of everything.

But that love and salvation would appear in the form of a weird, skinny dork who would turn Dean into his reluctant hero.

PART TWO

Jerry's Kid

FOUR

The Unexpected

Although he was working fairly steadily, Dean owed money to practically everyone he knew in New York. "He once hit me up for five dollars," says Sunny Daye. "I was a chorus girl who was making peanuts next to what he was making. But I lent it to him anyway. I never got it back." Dean would always give the people he borrowed cash from the equivalent of "the check is in the mail," telling them he'd settle accounts on payday. Of course, they never saw him until the entire paycheck was gone. Eventually people knew that if they lent Dean money, they'd never get it back. "They really just *gave* him money because they liked him," says Sunny.

Meanwhile his various "agents" and "managers" were becoming all too aware of one another. Dick Richards was furious when he learned that Dean had signed with Lou Perry even though he was still out there trying to find him work. Richards had gotten him a return gig at La Martinique, but that fell apart when Dean's "manager" decided to sue him for fifteen thousand dollars. Dean laughed when he heard about it. He didn't have two nickels to rub together, so where the hell was he going to come up with that kind of money even if Richards won his suit? Jerry Sears, busy doing new arrangements for the old standards and Bing Crosby songs that Dean interpreted, also threatened a lawsuit when he learned it was unlikely he'd ever get any of the 10 percent Dean had promised him in return for his work. Dean convinced him that he couldn't get blood from a rock and later paid him off with several hundred bucks. Lou Costello finally dumped him when Dean bought thousands of dollars' worth of clothing and charged all of it to the portly comedian's account. Costello liked Dean but figured he was just too costly and irresponsible to give a damn about.

Dean was having trouble getting cash from friends, and nobody was left who wanted to buy a piece of his action—too many people were now clued in to the little scam he'd perfected. And now that his nose was fixed he couldn't use the "God help me, I gotta get a nose job or I'm sunk" excuse any more. Restaurants had been only too happy to open an account for him as a "celebrity," but when the charges for meals hit the three figure mark, they wanted cash or it was no deal. Everyone from bartenders to barbers refused to serve him until he paid his often staggering tabs. He'd bought ads in the trade papers that he never paid for, and they were after him, as were the management of the London Terrace apartments and, of course, MCA, which he still owed thousands. "Everyone I ran into I owed money to," he said years later when he had his own TV show and was worth millions. "I think there are *still* people in New York I owe money to. That's why I hate that place. Too many bad memories."

But his luck was about to change. It wouldn't be long before he'd never really have to worry about money again.

In the summer of 1945 Lou Perry, by now his only agent, got Dean booked into the Glass Hat supper club in the swanky Belmont Plaza Hotel. Although Dean was the headliner, several other entertainers were on the bill, including a young guy with a weird novelty act who also served as emcee. His name was Jerry Lewis. He had entered the world as Jerome Levitch, though all his life everyone had called him "Joey" until he decided to take back his real given name, or at least its diminutive, as part of his theatrical non de plume. Lewis was an Americanization of Levitch, the name under which his father, Danny, performed as an Al Jolson imitator.

By all accounts—especially his own—Jerry had a fairly lonely if not exactly miserable childhood, being shunted from place to place as his parents traveled the third-rate vaudeville circuit and "Borscht Belt." Often he was left with his grandmother or other relatives. Like Dean, he'd had a natural inclination to clown around in front of his classmates. He also had a tendency to occasionally overdramatize the hardships of his youth, but it's safe to say that he did feel genuinely shunted aside by his parents, who hardly made him feel as if he were the most important thing in their lives. Father Danny was ambitious to break out of the bottom tier and rarely had the time or attention to waste on his small, needy son. Jerry didn't make friends easily, but when he did, he was a friend for life, whether they wanted him to be or not.

During his spare time, and craving the applause that seemed so important to a lot of insecure youths who felt ignored, Jerry came up with his own act, which he referred to as "practicing." Essentially, he would put on a record and lip-sync the words while making funny faces, wearing comically inappropriate outfits (say, a grown man's tuxedo several sizes too big), and cavorting crazily. Exuberant and undeniably talented, he managed to parlay this lip-syncing stunt into a genuine stage act and got himself booked into various clubs at the lowest end of the bill. He did double duty as the guy who introduced the other acts for no extra pay, or else he might have had trouble finding regular employment. He also landed a sharp agent named Abner (Abby) Greshler.

At this point in their careers, Dean Martin was much more successful (even if the scarcity of loose change in his pockets might have belied it) than Jerry. He had appeared in most of the top spots on the East Coast and Chicago, and had he managed money better and not owed so much to so many, he probably would have been sitting pretty. Of course, Jerry was only eighteen and hadn't had as much time to make good.

Despite other accounts of their first meeting, Jerry Lewis says they first set eyes on each other at the Belmont Plaza. When Dean came up to him one night after the show and told him he was a funny kid, "I was in love with him immediately," Jerry remembered. It was a platonic love, but it was real, as Dean not only became a father substitute but the big brother and best friend that Joey Levitch had always longed for. "Dean was my big brother, the father figure, the handsome figure, the hero figure," Jerry said in 1992. "He was schlepping me through life. He was the schlepper, and I was his luggage."

Dean, who was nearly ten years older, saw Jerry primarily as that "funny kid," a teen, a youth, a boy whom he liked and had fun with, but he had no special idea of working with him or making him part of his social circle; he was a *kid* and a bit nerdy. Yet, according to Lewis, Dean was not as sophisticated as he liked to think he was, despite the women and his minor celebrity status. Unlike Dean, Lewis had been born in a busy urban area—Newark, New Jersey (on March 16, 1926)—and was raised on the Lower East Side of Manhattan, a far cry from Ohio.

Of Dean, he said, "He was very macho, very down to earth, [a] very plain, simple guy. He was not a bon vivant; he was still from Steubenville and pretty naive about a lot of stuff." Dean learned the score soon enough, however. "He grew into a sharp, know-what-it's-all-about kind of guy very, very quickly," Jerry recalled. "And his instinct about people was tremendous." Jerry remembered that Dean would study someone for a while, mull it over, then give Jerry either a thumbs up or thumbs down. "That would tell me that whoever I was dealing with I should watch."

It wasn't long before the two both found themselves booked into the Havana-Madrid Nightclub on East 51st Street, and this was where the magic began to blossom. It started when, on an impulse, Jerry began to do some comic shtick, a little humorous heckling, as Dean was finishing up his act. Dean, who'd always had a good sense of humor and a spirit of fun, "retaliated" by heckling Jerry when the latter was doing his lip-syncing act. Recognizing the on-stage rapport they had and anxious to skewer the monotony of doing the same act several times a day, several nights a week, they got together for the midnight show—Jerry mimicking Dean's singing and Dean coming up with the wisecracks as quickly as his impromptu partner did. Jerry was always amazed at the way Dean was able to play it back to him when he, Jerry, trotted out one of the old vaudeville routines he'd seen his father perform—what Danny called the "pastrami list" after a popular menu item at the hotels he played in the Catskills—even though Dean had no prior knowledge of the material. According to Lewis, "Dean was the greatest straight man who ever lived because he had such a great sense of humor, and a sense of timing that was incredible. The other key is he had that sensational delight in making an audience laugh."

The verbal comedy quickly metamorphosed into physical hijinks, as well. Jerry would pretend to be a clumsy busboy and knock glasses and plates over while Dean was trying to sing. They'd run out into the audience and knock over customers' drinks, getting everyone into the show— and not a few people wet. Jerry would pull off tablecloths and sit in women's laps, and Dean would rush around playing it all back to him, frequently getting as many laughs as the younger man did. They'd also get physical with each other, slapping, punching, grabbing one another or just tapping each other to make a point. "Touching was very important to us," remembered Jerry, "although we weren't aware of it, and it, too, wasn't part of the strategy; it became part and parcel of everything we did because we enjoyed being close." *Billboard* and other trade papers took note of their kibbitzing for the midnight show and gave them shining notices.

As this was going on, they grew close, becoming good friends despite their many differences. Jerry liked to call Dean "Paul," his middle name, just to be perverse. Dean would call Jerry, as the latter put it, "pallie, Jew [in an affectionate way], or pardner." Dean would occasionally invite Jerry up to Lou Perry's hotel room, where he was still sleeping, and the two would sit up until the wee hours, shooting the breeze. Dean would always finagle someone—Lou or another friend—into supplying the late-night booze. Jerry could not be counted on for spirits since he was not much of a drinker. He'd seen one too many sloppy, disgusting drunks while accompanying his parents to the Borscht Belt and had almost an aversion to alcohol—at least compared to Dean.

Dean thought of young Jerry as a "kid," but he was a married man with a wife and child. In 1944 he'd gotten hitched to a former singer who'd called herself Patti Palmer; she had retired to take care of their baby son, Gary. In the meantime, Dean's neglected wife, Betty, decided to take her and Dean's brood from her parents home in Philadelphia and knocked on Dean's parents' door in Steubenville. They had moved into a bigger house, and with the two boys grown and out on their own, they would now have room for her and the kids.

The situation had become untenable in Pennsylvania. Betty's mother would rail against Dean and insist that her daughter demand Dean become more of a father. *"Do these children even know what their father looks like?"* she'd scream. Betty would argue that Dean *had* to stay in New York because that was where the work was. "He'll send for me when he's settled." "Settled?" her mother would say. "In what century will that happen? A married man who can't even provide a home for his wife and children!" Betty's parents would have suggested that Dean give up the show business foolishness and get a real job, only they were hoping Betty would come to her senses and dump the guy, period. The loneliness Betty felt, her dismay over Dean, the difficulty of raising three children without a father, and the fact that her parents were feeling exploited and were therefore not as welcoming as before combined to make her utterly frantic and miserable. Then her mother would nag her that she was drinking too much. *"What other pleasure do I have?"* Betty would scream back. If her parents didn't want her and their grandchildren around, she'd go to her in-laws. Once she and the kids had settled in, Dean visited them and his folks now and then, but club engagements, and his distaste for Steubenville, kept him hopping and mostly away.

Jerry Lewis was booked into the outsized 500 Club in Atlantic City in July 1946. There was already a male vocalist on the bill, a fellow named Jack Randall, but when he fell ill, a quick replacement needed to be found. Everyone and his brother has since taken credit for getting Dean the plum assignment—at that time the 500 Club was the best, biggest, and most prestigious nightspot in the New Jersey resort town—but odds are it was, as he claims, Jerry Lewis: Jerry and Dean were already friends; Jerry knew that he and Dean worked well together and might have further opportunities to clown around as they had at the Havana-Madrid. Furthermore, Jerry looked up to Dean, enjoyed his company, and would not only have wanted to do the singer a favor but have him around for company. Given that, it's only some writers' hostility toward Jerry Lewis that make them dubious that Lewis was instrumental in getting Martin hired at the 500 Club. In the entertainment world people do tend to take more credit than is justified in getting somebody, however inadvertently, a big break, but in this case Lewis's claims seem justified.

"Skinny" D'Amato and Irvin Wolf, who ran the place—and who had an illegal gambling operation in the back that attracted FBI attention—did not need too much persuasion to sign Dean. Lou Perry told them that his client was not only a top nightclub act but a "recording star," as well. This was a slight bending of the facts but not just an agent's hyperbole. Dean had just recorded a record on the Diamond label, and he and Perry were hoping it would take off. The four songs included a smooth rendition of "All of Me," which Sinatra had already recorded, and a bouncy variation—just right for Dean—of Irving Berlin's almost jazzy number from *Annie Get Your Gun*, "I Got the Sun in the Morning (and the Moon at Night)." Dean may not have been a bona fide recording star, but he had enough experience and a big enough, if modest, following to suit D'Amato and Wolf. He was hired.

The engagement at the 500 Club was just the beginning of Dean and Jerry's meteoric rise. Although they were booked as solo acts, they did so much shtick together that they were practically a combo. Right from the very first, as Jerry acknowledges, Dean pulled his weight, even when it came to the comic interplay between the two, although Jerry's on-stage behavior was often so attention grabbing and maniacal (which was simply his style, not necessarily an attempt to steal the limelight away from Dean) that it took quite some time for certain critics to perceive this. In any case, something in the duo clicked, and audiences were spellbound.

They had their naysayers, those who found them crude, their antics too "hysterical" in the wrong sense of the word, those who didn't care to have drinks spilled on their laps, those who thought all the audience-interaction stuff was lifted from Olsen and Johnson's *Hellzapoppin'*, those who recognized routines that were as old as the hills even if interpreted somewhat differently, but by and large they won over the box-office record-breaking crowds in Atlantic City.

It was at this time that Dean switched agents from Lou Perry to Jerry's agent, Abby Greshler, a slick thirtyish operator who has often been described as albino pale, cadaverous, and skeletal, a barely warmed-over Bela Lugosi in an expensive, carefully tailored silk suit. Dean's making the switch after Lou had done so much for him has been trotted out more than once as proof positive of his ruthless "screw everyone" nature, but the truth is a little more complex. Again, to get at what really happened one must examine the actual circumstances and ignore all the spurious stories circulated by embittered, so-called friends of Dean's from the old days.

Dean had never attracted the kind of crowds as a solo artist as he did at the 500 Club when he worked with Jerry. As soon as news of their antics hit the papers, people were lined up outside the club for blocks. Lou Perry had been handling—more than handling, virtually supporting—Dean for almost three years and was getting a little tired of it. (A story has made the rounds that he tried to sell off Dean's contract to a hoodlum just to get rid of him, but its veracity and source are suspect.) Perry had always been more than interested in Dean's career, but the same did not hold true for Jerry Lewis, who already had his own representative in any case. And Perry had never really done enough for Dean in a professional sense—Dean still couldn't afford to move out of the man's hotel room and needed to declare bankruptcy to get rid of most of his debts—and Perry wondered if Dean's chances as a solo were limited. In any case, once Dean and Jerry decided to make it a twosome, there could only be one agent. Perry had always been a small-timer, and Greshler was one of the biggest agents in the business. Should Jerry have *dropped* superagent Greshler and joined up with Dean and Perry, which would have made no sense at all? If Dean wanted to work with Jerry, which he did, he really had no choice but to sign with Greshler.

That Perry sued Greshler (but not Dean, interestingly enough) only means that he was, understandably, attempting to get *something* back from all that he'd spent on Dean over the years. (He eventually got several thousand dollars from Greshler.) It didn't mean he saw Dean as a stinker. During the years after the breakup when Jerry and Dean weren't speaking to one another, Jerry would imply that Dean had simply dumped Perry unceremoniously and unconscionably via some practically Machiavellian maneuverings, but at that point Jerry could hardly be considered an objective source. The same goes for Betty Martin, who told the same story as Jerry but only after her divorce from Dean.

In any case, Abby Greshler was now in charge of the careers of both Martin and Lewis. And that's who they had become: Martin and Lewis, team extraordinaire. How did this come about? Each of them had their reasons. Dean may have publicly discounted the negative and even positive reviews that mentioned his comparative lack of personality and his "sameness," all those who said he was OK, perfectly acceptable, just not very special or distinctive, but the notices stayed in his subconscious. Hollywood didn't seem interested, and he was afraid that he had gone as high as he could go as a solo act. Jerry Lewis had never even gone as high as Dean; he knew his lip-syncing act had its limits, so as far as he was concerned, anything would be an improvement. Both men got along well and liked the idea of working together. Teaming up didn't mean they couldn't do what each did best—Dean's singing, Jerry's clowning—it didn't mean each wouldn't get his moment in the spotlight. And then there was ol' Skullface, Abby Greshler, who knew he could make a lot more money out of Martin and Lewis than he could out of Lewis alone and who told both of them that as a *duo* they might very well grab that proverbial brass ring. Entertainers before and since Dean Martin have been swept off their feet by the smooth manipulations of canny, high-powered talent representatives, some of whom, like Greshler, could actually make good on their promises.

In January 1947 Greshler got them booked into the Loew's State Theater in midtown Manhattan for fifteen hundred dollars a week. This was their first official engagement as a "couple." He hired the famous George B. Evans, the same man who created a sensational furor over Sinatra, as their publicist. Jerry put away the records and the phonograph and pretty much dropped his lip-syncing routine for good (although he'd revive it now and then over the years). Instead, after Dean sang a number or two, he would heckle Dean in the guise of assorted zany characters, finally joining Dean onstage for some banter and sketches. The formula was simple, but it worked. And Dean was an equal partner in the fun; sometimes he started the heckling by saying something rude to Jerry. He yelled at the audience and interacted with them, verbally and physically, as much as Jerry did. The equality of their partnership explains why he was so angry later when people would dismiss him as the "untalented" or minor half of the team.

"He's what made me as good as I was in that period," Jerry would admit years later. "I believed then as I believe now, and I know I'm right: I would never have been as funny without him." Although Jerry was decidedly the clown half of the team, and the one who garnered most of the chuckles, Dean could also be funny—in perhaps a less ostentatious manner. For a man with his sense of humor, it was effortless. The two working in tandem were a well-oiled machine, each line and limb functioning perfectly with Swiss-watch precision. Part of the fun was simply watching the two of them keep it up for an hour, running around like loons, with Jerry the untrammeled, maniac adolescent and Dean the at first forbearing and then exasperated authority figure who would finally lose control and give as good as he got.

Notices were almost universally favorable, and the sold-out engagement at the State was carried over to the Capitol and the Paramount. The boys were employed for months—instead of days or weeks—on end, and they were rolling in dough. The first thing Dean did with his newfound fortune was rent an apartment—ten rooms, no less—on Riverside Drive. Now that he had cash to burn and the creditors off his back, he also went on a buying spree. "What I remember most," recalled Jerry, "was that first look at Dean's bedroom closet, every square foot filled with handmade suits and tuxedos, racks and racks of shoes, ceiling-to-floor shelves containing imported silk shirts and cashmere sweaters—we'd come a long way and awfully fast since that day when Dean blanched at the thought of buying a two-hundred-dollar suit." Dean was determined to be the classy dresser that he felt his major new success warranted, to look like the big celebrity he, with Jerry at his side, had become.

Throughout most of his life, until his later years, Dean was always the picture of sartorial splendor, wearing expensive custom-made suits and tuxes, very formal, very dapper, but never overly elegant or even remotely epicene. It was part of his image and his reality, but it was also what he thought was expected of him. Baseball caps and casual clothing were all right for Steubenville but not for New York or Hollywood.

Sales for Dean's debut record on the Diamond label went up due to all his new exposure, although he was still far from being a recording star at this point. Nonetheless, he was making enough money off his club and theater engagements with Jerry to feel financially secure enough to send for Betty and his children. How much Dean really wanted to have Betty and the three children with him in Manhattan is debatable. Certainly Betty had her say in the matter; there was no way she'd stay in Steubenville with his parents now that he was finally on the right fiscal track. Dean had gotten a place with ten rooms for two reasons. First, after being in a cramped hotel room with two, three—and sometimes more—people, he needed as much space and privacy as possible. Second, with ten rooms, he could always find a place to hide from Betty and the brood when they became bothersome. For decades after what seemed like his near incarceration in the Bryant Hotel, Dean would need room to stretch out and get away from everyone. There were times he simply needed to be by *himself.* Anyone who couldn't understand that—Betty, Jerry, the children—would find themselves shut out.

Too much has been made of the fact that throughout his life, many of the clubs and casinos Dean played in were owned and run by mobsters. That was the situation industrywide, and every entertainer had to accept it or get out of the business. One could spend pages, as some have done, listing every mob figure that Dean encountered in his steady climb to the top, both before and after he became friends with Sinatra, who palled around with these grim, colorful figures a lot more than Dean did. They were part and parcel of show business. Because of his early association with such types back in Steubenville, Dean was more comfortable—or at least less uncomfortable—with them than others, but they were hardly close friends; he just didn't take them that seriously. Some accounts of Dean's life overemphasize these types, making them a much larger part of the story than they deserve to be, in an attempt to portray Dean Martin as some kind of "Mafia singer," which is simplistic at best, and simply inaccurate at worst. No entertainer—from Debbie Reynolds to Wayne Newton—could have played these clubs and casinos without now and then running into mobsters.

So Jerry and Dean played clubs that were in some way—at least in people's minds—associated with the mob or that were partially or solely owned by underworld figures. There was no way they could avoid it, and neither of them was exactly inclined to inquire of the management if they were, say, part of the Bergen County mob or some other family. It must also be said that many if not most of the spots they played in were perfectly legitimate. Greshler booked them into any venue that would pay their asking price: the Riviera in Fort Lee, New Jersey; the Chez Paree in Chicago; on up to the Copacabana in New York. He never cared if the profits went into the pockets of honest businessmen or Mafioso, as long as the boys got their fee and he got his commission.

One thing that has not been exaggerated about Dean is his philandering. Now that he had plenty of cash on hand, he was pursuing the chorus girls with a vengeance, making up for the time lost when he had no place to call his own and nowhere to bring the women. Now he could afford hotel rooms and room service, lots of champagne for him and his lady love of the evening. Sunny Daye remembers, "Everyone was happy for Dean, but more than a few were upset. It was like, how could someone as irresponsible as him become so successful while the people who'd lent him money were still struggling? He did pay some people back, people who really needed it. And I never saw him without a woman on his arm. I don't think I ever even met his wife. She just wasn't a *presence* in the clubs he went to. I don't think he wanted her around; he was afraid she'd cramp his style. Dean did not get a swelled head that I remember; he was still as charming as ever to people he liked and that he knew liked him. But to people who'd been snotty to him—the ones who'd made fun of his nose? He'd just cut them dead. They'd try to rub up against him now that he was doing so well, but he'd just turn his back on them."

In the lonely ten-room mausoleum that Dean had constructed for Betty, his wife took care of the kids and herself: one bottle for the baby and a different one for herself. She was back in New York, they had a beautiful home and plenty of money—but she was still alone. She began to wonder if Dean had ever really belonged to her in any concrete fashion. She kept up a brave front with her folks—Dean was doing swell, she was doing swell, the kids were swell, everything was perfect—how could it not be with a ten-room apartment on Riverside Drive? But things weren't swell, they were lousy.

Martin and Lewis broke records at the Copa, supplanting the nominal headliner, songstress Vivian Blaine, who quit when she was demoted to the number two spot. No one could compete with the refreshing lunacy and high-energy exuberance of the boys. That some of their routines were borrowed from ancient comics and practically sported varicose veins did not matter to the crowd, who had never heard them before. And Jerry and Dean put their own fresh spin on all the material. It wasn't the jokes or the skits that mattered, anyway; it was the way they put them over.

In the meantime, Abby Greshler was not ignoring Dean's solo singing career. He got a new deal at Apollo Records for Dean, who recorded two albums on the label. At least one of the numbers, "Oh, Marie," proved that Dean could sing with subtlety and relative power when he wanted to. He later jumped from Apollo to Embassy, but while sales weren't dismal, they were not enough to put him in Sinatra's league. Still, Dean was happy. He had major success—the Copa, no less!—with Jerry and could pursue his solo career on the side.

And a new element would soon enter the equation, one that would make the recording and nightclub deals seem like small potatoes.

FIVE

Hollywood Schemes

Just as their debut at the Copa in New York became legendary, so, too, did Dean and Jerry's premiere engagement at the hottest club in Los Angeles, Slapsy Maxie's on Wilshire Boulevard. All of the big names in Hollywood came to see them. Abby Greshler got on the phone and called his contacts at the movie studios. He knew the big money was in pictures, and if two middle-aged, homely guys like Abbott and Costello could become film stars, there was no reason why the younger, better-looking Martin and Lewis couldn't do the same. Besides, straight man Bud Abbott couldn't sing and Dean Martin could.

As he usually did, Dean began their act at Slapsy Maxie's by singing a solo number or two. Early critics had compared him to Sinatra because he was also Italian and did many of Sinatra's numbers, but now people were hearing in him his true mentor, Bing Crosby. Dean added a certain suggestiveness to Bing's basic style, and the drawl he'd had from birth—odd for a boy from Ohio and not the South—further distinguished his sound from Bing's. Still, more and more people began noticing the similarity. Some dismissed him because of this; others felt there was nothing wrong in a singer being influenced by another singer, as long as he eventually found his own path and his own material, which Dean did in time. For Jerry's part, his shenanigans had the sophisticated crowd in stitches. There were still those who felt Martin and Lewis were a second-rate act who only got away with their lowbrow hijinks because nobody had ever dared do such childish material in a swanky nightclub before, but most people adored them.

Among those in attendance on the highly promoted opening night was Joan Crawford, who felt the boys were amusing if a little on the silly side. "That Dean Martin is rather attractive, though," she told her friend, film journalist Larry Quirk, adding that the weird little Jerry Lewis was probably "the better lover. Those types always are." Joan predicted that, whatever their flaws, Dean and Jerry would go places. "The crowd really loved them. Not every entertainer gets that kind of response, and if they do they'd better act fast."

Greshler *was* acting fast, urging any number of producers and studio heads to catch the act. Those who missed opening night caught the show on a subsequent evening. Legend has it that there were bidding wars among all the studios for the boys' services, but too many of them wondered if the chemistry they had could be transferred intact to the movie screen and therefore made no offers. Columbia and MGM put out feelers but let it be known they wanted exclusivity, which was unacceptable to Greshler. He knew of too many entertainers who signed exclusive contracts with movie studios, only to sit around waiting for work or winding up in inappropriate vehicles or loaned out to another studio to their loss and their own studio's financial gain. Producer Hal Wallis, who was associated with Paramount, only expected the boys to accept no other work while they were filming one of his movies, but otherwise they were free to do as they chose. Greshler figured Wallis was the man.

Hal Wallis was one of the prime movers and shakers in Hollywood, having by that time produced about a hundred movies, many of which were classics: *Casablanca, The Man Who Came to Dinner, Little Caesar, The Adventures of Robin Hood, The Maltese Falcon, King's Row, Sergeant York,* not to mention a handful of top Bette Davis starrers such as *Jezebel, The Old Maid, The Letter,* and *In This Our Life.* Wallis's tastes never really ran to the "women's" pictures he did with Davis and other femme notables, but he continued to make them because they made a lot of money. He preferred comedies and action films, but ultimately he'd work on anything that could turn a profit. Eyebrows were raised in Hollywood as this man who was considered a producer of more or less "classy" fare went after a stake in Martin and Lewis, but obviously Wallis saw the duo as probable moneymakers or he'd never have bothered.

The deal Greshler finally cooked up with Wallis was for ten pictures over the next five years. Dean and Jerry's starting salary would be fifty thousand dollars, but it would eventually go up in ten-, fifteen-, and twenty-five-thousand-dollar increments. Greshler also engineered what would turn out to be a long-term Capitol recording contract for the boys: Dean would do solo albums, and with Jerry he would do special comedy platters of songs and patter, with a guaranteed one hundred thousand disks cut for each release. Then there was a plethora of radio guest spots, and even an NBC radio show of their own that would pay them twenty-five hundred dollars a week for doing basically what they did in a nightclub but without all the physical shtick that needed to be seen to be appreciated. And their weekly nightclub fee had skyrocketed to ten thousand dollars.

Everything was happening so fast on the professional front—and on the personal, as well. Dean remembered being so overwhelmed by it all in one sense that conversely it seemed to make no impression on him, as if it were a natural series of events. "I don't remember pinchin' myself and askin' myself if it was all happening," he said. "I was over thirty and tired. I had been up and down and up and down in the game for years already. So I guess I felt like it was about time my ship had come in. That was it: not so much grateful—though I was—but more like 'it's about time.'"

Still, there were hurdles in the road ahead. Hal Wallis arranged two screen tests for the boys and was dismayed by the results in both cases. They exhibited very little of their patented charisma when they had to perform with a script and as characters they couldn't relate to. He began to wonder if these two would ever have any kind of future in Hollywood. Then he decided to just film them in their usual personas, ad-libbing and carrying on as they did on the stage. The results were just what he'd hoped for.

The first two movie vehicles for Dean and Jerry were based on a popular radio show about a dizzy gal named Irma who was always getting into all sorts of trouble due to her essential imbecility, driving her long-suffering roommate, Jane, to distraction. However, she was sweet and good-natured and hard to stay mad at. Marie Wilson, who played the role of Irma on the show, would star in the movie version. It was suggested that Dean would be perfect as Irma's boyfriend, Al, a con man straight out of Damon Runyon who knew all the angles; clearly stories about Dean and his percentages had followed him to Hollywood. But Dean was a little too handsome and normal to be a good match for the ditzy Irma, so it was decided to turn that part over to Jerry and make Dean the more sensible Jane's beau, Steve—Jerry and oddball Marie Wilson, it was thought, would play well together. There were more problems, however, when the part as written didn't give Jerry ample opportunity to play his usual stage characterization. Since, as noted earlier, at this point neither Dean nor Jerry could be trusted to stray too far from what they did in their night-club act, Wallis decided a new character would have to be invented just to give Jerry something to do. This was Steve's buddy at the orange juice stand where they worked, a zany character named Seymour, who was basically a variation on the same nut Jerry played in their shows.

But Jerry didn't want to play Seymour. There was nothing romantic or heroic or sexy about the guy, and he was, Jerry felt, just a tacked-on supporting character who hadn't even appeared on the radio series. He was sure he was being shunted aside. He insisted on playing Al; when that didn't work, he suggested Dean play Al, as originally proposed, and he would play Steve. But by this time John Lund had been hired to play Al, and he was perfect for the part. Wallis told Jerry that the role of Seymour would give him a chance to shine doing what he did best, but Jerry wasn't convinced. Finally Wallis told him he either played the part or he was off the picture. Jerry complied—and got the last laugh, because he got the lion's share of the praise when the picture was released.

Meanwhile, on Dean's family front, Betty had given birth to a fourth child, Deana, and she stayed in New York to look after the children. Dean found that the starlets of Hollywood were as easy to bed as the chorus girls of Manhattan. Jerry's wife, Patti, thought Dean was a bad influence on her man, foolishly unaware that Jerry was as much of a philanderer, if not more so, than Dean, and he needed little encouragement. Offscreen, particularly as the years went by, Jerry was hardly a geek but rather a sharp, intelligent, crafty, and rather handsome smoothie who could practice the seduction routine as well as anyone. Gradually Patti would catch on to Jerry, but it would be many years before she finally divorced him.

One of Dean's earliest L.A. conquests was actress June Allyson, who was married to Dick Powell at the time. Patti was livid when she found out about it, and she went straight to Betty. Betty had already heard so many of these stories of Dean's women that she figured one more or less didn't make a difference. Whether she believed it or not, she was inclined to just let it go. But she came across a copy of an oft-quoted telegram that Dean had sent June—"I'm still tingling"—and confronted him with it, vowing to tear out Allyson's hair if she ever ran into her. Dean was nearly apoplectic—not because of the discovery of the telegram but because he was at first afraid that Betty had found out about a much more serious threat to their union. Dean had apparently fallen for someone else.

As for that telegram to June? No matter how many different women Dean was sleeping with at the same time, he treated all of them with a kind of perverse respect. He wanted them to know how much he enjoyed them and how desirable he found them, hence his flattering love note to Allyson.

Who Betty didn't know about was the next major lady in Dean's life, the woman who was to become his soul mate. Jeanne Biegger was a pretty blond twenty-one-year-old who was acquainted with Abby Greshler's wife through her parents. A Florida resident, she had first seen Dean Martin when she sat in the audience at the Riviera on a trip north with her parents. For her it was love at first sight, as it had been for Betty, but she didn't get to meet Dean until some time later, when Dean and Jerry were booked into the Beachcomber Club in Miami in 1948. Jeanne had been crowned Orange Bowl queen the year before—she briefly became a model for mail-order catalogs in New York and appeared in advertisements for toothpaste and hair tonic—and would ride in the parade after she crowned the new queen. Later, she looked down from her chair on the float and spotted Dean and Jerry riding alongside in a convertible. Of Dean, she remembered: "He was like a big hick, the way he gaped up in wonderment at all the celebrities and the pretty girls."

Her beauty didn't really rivet Dean's attention until she attended a New Year's Eve celebration at the Beachcomber and the two men took to the stage. This time Dean's eyes locked on hers as hers had locked on his at the Riviera. Dean was smitten. "I knew: This was it," she recalled. From then on, Dean had become the ultimate man of her dreams, and eventually he'd feel the same way about her.

Dean had once loved Betty, but they'd been through too much shit together. He felt about her the way he felt about New York once he'd moved permanently to California: too many bad memories. Although there were tremendous bright spots to his total Manhattan experience—his and Jerry's triumph at the Copa, for instance—they weren't enough to wipe out all the negatives of debt and defeat. (Dean would come to feel that everything didn't really begin to come together for him until he hit Hollywood in the late forties.) Even though he and Betty had had many good times together—not to mention four children—as with New York, Dean couldn't get past the negatives. There was that constant hurt, accusatory look on Betty's face, that look that reminded him of his neglect of both her and the children. The kids were cute, he loved them, but they weren't *fun*, they threatened to tie him down just at the greatest period of his life, when he needed to be untrammeled, free to explore every option in and out of the bedroom. His paternal instincts were never the sharpest.

Then there were the constant fights, bolstered by the fact that both parties were often drinking heavily. Dean would try to do right by Betty, or so he remembered, but she would nag and kvetch, as Jerry would have put it, and drive him out the door. She wanted to know where he was and what he was doing all the time, and that was intolerable. Dean Martin was not accountable to anybody—never had been, never would be. She would screech if he didn't call when he promised, even though it was difficult to get to a phone when you were in a meeting, having a drink with Hal Wallis, talking to Abby Greshler, doing the town, networking, working all the angles, meeting people who could do for you. "Or bedding some broad?" Betty would demand.

Still, Betty didn't take any of the other women seriously, not even Jeanne at first. With four children, a ten-room apartment, and Dean rolling in dough, she thought for sure that whatever their marital difficulties, she and Dino were a permanent item. Meanwhile Jeanne, who at first didn't even know Dean had a wife, moved from Miami to California at Dean's urging—and without her concerned parents' blessing. Jeanne continued seeing Dean even after she learned about Betty. By that time their whirlwind affair was going hot and heavy, and she was too much in love, she was in too deep, to back out. Dean assured her that he and Betty were married in name only, that it was only a matter of time before things fell apart completely; he just had to figure out the easiest, kindest way to sever himself from a woman who was, after all, the mother of his children. While he was saying all this, he might have even meant it. Betty represented negation, restriction; his relationship with her had become claustrophobic. Jeanne represented youth and freedom, a fresh start. A new woman to complete his new life.

Just before the boys began working on *My Friend Irma*, they decided it would make sense to have homes in Los Angeles or its environs since they'd be working in Hollywood for years to come. Dino had a real estate agent show him some properties and settled on a six-hundred-dollar-a-month rental of a comparatively modest (for the Bel Air neighborhood) mock English-style "manor" at 850 Stone Canyon Road. Betty packed up the brood and flew out to their new home; even her in-laws, Guy and Angela, moved in for a time. She thought everything would work out OK; that after years of struggle and disappointment and loneliness, finally she and Dean and their children had nothing but pure happiness to look forward to.

She didn't know that Jeanne Biegger was now a house guest in the home of Dick Stabile, whom Dean and Jerry had hired to be their permanent bandleader. Dean would go out for "appointments" and squire Jeanne around town or stay in for romantic evenings. Occasionally, Jeanne would sit at the side of the stage while Dean and Jerry performed, clearly functioning as his date once the show was over and the boys retreated to a table for some food and libations. Patti Lewis was outraged at the way the two of them were flaunting their affair and tried to make Betty realize that this time she was facing some genuine competition, the most serious threat to her marriage yet. Anxious to marry Dean, Jeanne would send gifts and love letters to his home, which Betty would find, telling herself that this Jeanne person was simply an ardent fan. Despite what Patti—and others—told her, she was convinced her marriage was solid, especially when Dean moved her and the whole clan into an even bigger home in Holmby Hills—this time it was a sale not a rental—where their neighbors included original Rat Packers Humphrey Bogart and Lauren Bacall.

Dean was in for yet another move, however, when Betty finally acknowledged the truth about Dick Stabile's house guest and what was going on behind her back. She ordered Dean out of their Holmby Hills dream pad and forced him to move into a small rented house on Sunset Boulevard. Jeanne, of course, moved in with him. For a time Dean was torn between both women. Jeanne was wonderful, but the two of them barely knew one another; the whole basis of their relationship was an intense sexual attraction. Dean reacted to Jeanne's beauty, and young Jeanne was intoxicated not just by Dean's virility and charm but by all the trappings of success and power that came with it—heady stuff to a young former beauty queen who had her own ambitions in life.

Betty consulted a lawyer. Like most Catholic girls at the time, the idea of a divorce was abhorrent to her. She did, however, demand a legal separation, custody of the children, and three thousand dollars a month. Some columnists gleefully noted that there was no way Dean could marry his honey pie until Betty agreed to a divorce. Dean and Jeanne kept house while Dean mulled over his options, Jeanne whispering sweet nothings—and marriage plans—into his ear.

Now it was time to report to the Paramount lot to make *My Friend Irma*. The boys had fun doing the picture, though for most of their scenes they were off by themselves and didn't always get to interact with all of the cast members. Jerry would indulge in dozens of childish practical jokes, sometimes with Dean's bemused or enthusiastic assistance. When they spotted Paramount studio head Y. Frank Freeman on the lot, they'd go up to him—especially when Freeman was accompanied by important visitors—and ask him if he'd finished washing their cars or some other menial duty. Dean approached the assistant director on the picture one day and introduced a janitor from across the street as his father. The AD spent his lunch hour escorting the old man on a tour of the lot.

My Friend Irma is notable only as the first vehicle for Martin and Lewis, although they are just supporting players. The minimal plot has Al cooking up yet another get-rich-quick scheme by becoming manager to singer Steve (Dean) and comedian Seymour (Jerry), who are hoping he can make good on his promises to hoist them to stardom. Instead Al gets hoisted on his own petard. He spends as much energy ducking Irma's marriage proposals as he does getting bookings for the boys, although at one point they do appear on a television show, and Steve gets a chance to sing while Seymour clowns. Dean was a natural in his very first picture, as smooth and charming as he was on stage, although no one would have taken him for a heavyweight. The picture was hardly a stretch for his or Jerry's talents.

The same was true of the sequel, *My Friend Irma Goes West*, which was hastily rushed out once news of the tremendous grosses of the first *Irma* flick reached the front office. In this one, Dean and Jerry were given more to do, and there were a few more laughs than in the first picture, but they were still supporting players. Steve is still Al's client, his only client, in fact —apparently Seymour has fired him—and the whole bunch take a train to Hollywood because a producer has offered Steve a job in a movie. Unfortunately, the producer turns out to be a mental institution escapee (which Martin and Lewis at various times during their careers would think was true of all producers), and there's no job waiting. This is just as well since they never get any farther than Las Vegas, where they run afoul of a gang of crooked casino owners. The film was careful to include a line, spoken by the sheriff of Vegas, intimating that most casino owners were entirely legitimate, which was anything but the truth. The best scene had Jerry interacting with a chimpanzee that could have rivaled Cheetah for adorableness—and scene-stealing ability—as the ape first imitated Jerry chewing gum and then blowing smoke rings. The chimp also made distressing offscreen advances on Corinne Calvet, a pretty French actress who was hired to play—guess what?—a pretty French actress who herself makes advances on Dean.

This picture also made money, but apparently not enough to continue the franchise—or at least to convince Martin and Lewis to participate. There were plans to film *My Friend Irma Goes to Europe* with the usual suspects, but Dean and Jerry were tired of playing second fiddle to Marie Wilson and John Lund. It was Jerry who was the draw, not Marie, so there was no point in continuing without his presence. Lund later complained, "Dean was mostly a pleasure to deal with, but Jerry just wanted to hog all the action." Marie never publicly criticized Dean or Jerry, but she never worked with them again and did mostly supporting parts thereafter. Stories that Dean was also annoyed with Jerry's allegedly expanded role seem inexplicable on viewing the picture: Dean has as much to do as Jerry, is given a couple of song numbers, and his character provides the impetus for the plot. It would be a few pictures down the line before Dean would start to feel, rightly or wrongly, that he was getting the shaft.

In between the two *Irma* films Dean finally got to settle his marital woes, although it remains unclear who ultimately got Betty to forget the trial separation and head straight for divorce court. Betty had always maintained that she never wanted a divorce, not only on religious grounds but because she was sure Jeanne Biegger was just a fling—she and Dean had known each other for such a short time, for one thing—but she finally lost her temper and decided to file when Jeanne sent out phony gold-embossed wedding invitations for her and Dean to all of their acquaintances. Dean's story was that he importuned Betty to grant him a divorce by appealing to her fair play and by getting her to face reality—as well as promising her a hefty cash bonus in return. In any case, Dean did get her to go to Las Vegas to get a quick divorce—Guy and Angela watched the kids—instead of waiting a full year for the California one to become final. Jeanne was pestering him to get married, and besides, he was in love. Given how little Dean and Jeanne knew about each other, how quickly their romance had flowered, it was probably not an emotionally mature love, at least not at that time, although it would grow over the years into something warm and meaningful.

Dean's Catholic parents were not at all thrilled with his decision to, in essence, throw away his first wife, the mother of his children, for a pretty blond "chippie." Still, they loved Dean and would love whomever he loved, so they gradually warmed to Jeanne and made her feel welcome. In the meantime, Betty, who had fulfilled her six-week Nevada residency, stood alone before Judge Frank McNamee in Clark County Court in Las Vegas on August 24, 1949, and had her marriage dissolved on the grounds of "extreme mental cruelty." She would receive over forty thousand dollars a year.

A week later Jeanne and Dean were married in the home of Herman Hover, who owned Ciro's, the nightclub where Dean had performed and hung out. Jerry Lewis was the best man. As a gag he put on one of Dean's best suits and jumped into the pool. Then the bride and groom—and Jerry—were on their way to Las Vegas, which a numb, angry Betty had just vacated. Martin and Lewis had been booked into the Flamingo hotel and casino. It was there that the newlyweds had their honeymoon.

Guy and Angela may have gotten around to accepting Jeanne, although they felt terrible for Betty, but Jerry and Patti Lewis were another story, especially the latter. While Jerry also felt bad for Betty, he didn't identify with her and didn't really care whom his partner was married to. But Patti saw in Betty her own possible future, and she was enraged at what Dean had done. She saw Dean as having browbeaten Betty into divorce and Jeanne as a miserable home wrecker who had pursued Dean without any thought of the consequences nor of the wife and four children waiting for him at home. Patti and Jeanne would learn to tolerate each other, but they would never become friends. As far as Patti was concerned, Jeanne represented all those fresh young things who were out there hoping to land successful, wealthy husbands without regard for the loyal, older wives who had stood by their men throughout the dark days.

To many people, Dean had gone Hollywood in every sense of the expression. It was typical for movie stars to dump the reliable old roadster of a first wife and trade her in for a snappier new coupé. Betty was the homey Chevrolet to Jeanne's sexy Cadillac.

Judging from how quickly Dean and Jeanne went from first meeting to marriage, it's easy to dismiss their relationship—at least in those early days—as one inspired by out-of-control hormones; Dean had thrown away eight years of marriage for some gal he hardly knew. Yet Dean and Betty had also married very shortly after first acquaintance, and they had seemed to be genuinely in love—at least in the first years of their marriage. Dean's actions directly before the divorce—buying a new house in California, moving in the family, including his parents, lock, stock, and barrel—did not add up to a man who was planning on dumping his wife. Jeanne was simply to be his gal on the side, safely ensconced at Dick Stabile's, somebody ready to be with her adored older man at a moment's notice. Perhaps Dean figured she would eventually get lost in the mire of her own ambition, meet other young men or heavy-breathing producers, or he could send her back home older and wiser when they were through with one another. What altered the equation was that Dean came to truly care for the girl—and to care what happened to her. Yes, she had worked her wiles, but Dean was not the type to be too easily manipulated by any woman unless he wanted to be. And he wanted Jeanne.

Had his relationship with Betty been going more smoothly at that time, he might never have left her—although he would certainly have strayed. But he was no longer in love with her; familiarity had bred contempt. They'd had sex often in the intervening years—the four children were proof of that—but there was too little quality time, too little talking, too little sharing of feelings and needs. Dean had simply not seen enough of Betty to feel that close to her. Ironically, one of the songs he recorded during this period was "Absence Makes the Heart Grow Fonder (For Somebody Else)."

So it was a bit more complicated than a heel of a husband dumping the old wife for the new one. He didn't love Betty anymore, and she couldn't give him what he needed. He needed to be hero worshipped—and not the platonic kind he got from Jerry. Betty knew Dean, knew all of his habits, too well to see him as a hero any longer. Jeanne, on the other hand, was still very young. She may have been callow, immature, incapable of understanding what Betty was going through, but she was not necessarily the villainess that Patti and Betty painted her. Dean, needing her worship as well as her body, encouraged her. And what they felt for each other the day they said their "I do's" *was* a kind of love.

New developments were also in store for Dean professionally. While the two *Irma* pictures were well received by the public if not the critics, Dean and Jerry were having less luck with their NBC radio show. As suspected, their kind of physical comedy did not play well over the non-visual airwaves. Dean's Capitol albums kept coming out with regularity—he did duets not only with Jerry but with such genuine singers as Peggy Lee and Margaret Whiting—and sales were respectful if not spectacular. Meanwhile Abby Greshler had come up with their next film project—or rather he'd come up with a new movie to put them in—with himself as producer. Just as the two *Irma* pictures could not really be considered bona fide Martin and Lewis movies, neither could their third film, *At War with the Army*.

At War with the Army began life as a successful Broadway show of that title by James Allardice, and indeed the film has a certain stage bound, overrehearsed feel to it (many actors from the play were used in the movie). Dean played Sgt. Victor Puccinelli, a nightclub singer—naturally—who's bored to tears stateside in the army and anxiously hoping for action overseas. Puccinelli is also tired of constantly having to cover up for his friend and all-purpose screwup, Private Korwin (Jerry). Throughout the movie Puccinelli refuses to cut Korwin any slack and is always irritable with him, while Korwin keeps reminding him of what good friends they were. "Just remember," he says, "you were the best man at my wedding." To which Puccinelli replies, "I sure was!"

The only person whom Puccinelli finds more exasperating than Korwin is his old girlfriend, Millie (Jean Ruth), whom he finds very stupid, to say the least. She has important news for him, but he's too busy avoiding her to hear what it is. It turns out Millie is pregnant, and we're led to believe that Puccinelli is the father. In a complication reminiscent of *The Big Clock*, Puccinelli is instructed by his superiors to find the man—himself!—who put Millie in the family way. Puccinelli tries all sorts of subterfuges to get out of this predicament, one of which results in Korwin being named as the father. It turns out that the pregnant woman in Korwin's life is actually his wife, and the father of Millie's baby isn't Puccinelli, but her new husband. The film ends with Puccinelli busted to private and Korwin made sergeant.

Anyone viewing the film today can't help but be struck by how prescient the picture seems to be, as eventually Jerry's and Dean's relationship would become just as it is in *At War with the Army*, with Dean quite cold to Jerry and tired of dealing with his crap. In his portrayal, as he sometimes did offscreen, Dean perfectly delineates how embarrassed a "manly" guy can be of a buddy who is *comparatively* girlish.

Their contract with Hal Wallis permitted them to make one outside picture per year, and *At War with the Army* would be it. And with Greshler producing it, he'd make much more money than he did strictly as Dean and Jerry's agent; in effect, as producer, he could hire his own clients! The antitrust laws eventually put this kind of arrangement to rest, but by the time *At War with the Army* came out, it was all academic. Martin and Lewis had found themselves a new representative. They also formed their own production company, York Productions, and entered into an agreement with a new picture-releasing group called Screen Associates, Inc., under whose auspices *At War with the Army* would be released. The powers that be at Screen Associates hoped to have a long and rewarding partnership with York—i.e., Dean and Jerry. That was not to be the case.

At War with the Army was filmed under difficult conditions because Dean and Jerry weren't talking to the producer, and their now ex-agent, Abby Greshler. The trouble all started when Greshler booked them into two popular nightclubs at the same time. When Jerry and Dean got sued by one of the clubs for breach of contract, they argued that Greshler had negotiated the deal without checking with them first and that it was his fault they were in trouble. They also had other bones to pick with

Greshler. They had allowed him to handle their financial affairs, but firm letters from the IRS made it clear that Greshler had not been sending part of their income as he was supposed to, and they now owed tens of thousands of dollars to the government. Plus there were allegations of other misappropriations and financial misconduct. To add to their desire to rid themselves of Greshler, now that they were superstars, Dean's old representatives, MCA, had begun sniffing in their direction.

Abby Greshler had been a power player, yes, but only by their old standards of wannabe entertainers; he was still just an independent agent, if one of the better-known ones. Now that they were stars, Greshler looked as quaint and ineffectual as Lou Perry had once seemed. This was not the case with mega-agent Lew Wasserman, who worked for powerhouse MCA. They had written Dean off years ago not just because he didn't pay his commissions but because he seemed to have a success ceiling; but his partnership with Jerry had changed the whole situation. MCA wanted Dean and Jerry in their roster of stars, and Wasserman was just the man to get them. As filming proceeded on *At War with the Army*, Wasserman wined and dined them.

Considering his feelings toward ex-clients Dean and Jerry, Abby Greshler spent as little money on *At War with the Army* as possible, and the production values are nil. Dean gives a perfectly solid, more or less "serious," performance in the film, and proves he can perform well as part of an ensemble. He has a particularly good, funny scene telling off Jerry in the mess hall, telling him to "SHUT UP!" at the end of each sentence without ever allowing the private to get a word in edgewise. In a soft shoe duet that the two boys have together, Dean wasn't quite nimble enough to actually jump over his cane as Jerry does, but Jerry had more trouble with another bit in the same number, letting his hat roll down his arm and catching it, which Dean did with ease.

Both men were given a couple of songs to sing by Mack David and Jerry Livingston. Dean's number, "Tonda Wanda Hoy (It's Easier to Say 'I Love You')" is rather awful—Dean recorded it, however, to help publicize the movie— but he sings it in his best Bing Crosby style during a stage show rehearsal at the army camp. He also has a nice duet with Polly Bergen (who was "introduced" in this picture)—"You and Your Beautiful Eyes"—in a small recording booth. Jerry gets to warble "The Navy Gets the Gravy but the Army Gets the Beans," but surely one of the most grotesque, if admittedly amusing, moments in cinema is Jerry in drag singing "Tonda Wanda Hoy" in a bar to a perplexed sergeant played by Mike Kellin.

By this time Dean was being compared to Bing Crosby on such a regular basis that he didn't mind spoofing the whole business in his act and in the movies. One of the film's highlights is when he and Jerry do a great parody of Barry Fitzgerald and Bing Crosby from *Going My Way*. Dean, singing "Tarra Ta-larra Ta-Lar," which he had already recorded, is dead-on as Bing, but at that point it wasn't really much of a stretch for him. In another scene Jerry tells a reluctant, dyspeptic Dean that he wants to make a demo record with him. Dean: "Get Bing Crosby!" Jerry: "I like you better." Dean: "Now I know you're crazy!"

The trouble with the picture is that most of the comedy scenes—such as Jerry dealing with a berserk soda machine—are more loud and busy than funny, and Hal Walker's direction is static and just plain bad. A former actor, Walker had already directed the boys in *My Friend Irma Goes West*, but he completely fails to open up the action in any compelling way in *Army*. He would do two more pictures with the team before switching to television and *I Married Joan* with Joan Davis.

By far the worst thing in Fred F. Finklehoffe's script, which may have been taken from the original play, is when Jerry, bored and put-upon in the army camp, says: "If I ever get overseas, the first thing I'm gonna do is surrender. Concentration camps have gotta be better than this." This is surely one of the most idiotic and tasteless lines to be found in any movie.

Still, *At War with the Army* proved to be a financial success. With three hit movies in a row, Dean should have been sitting pretty. But he was about to enter a world of litigation that would make the debts and lawsuits of his New York City days seem penny ante in comparison.

SIX

Stooge

When you start soaring to the stratosphere, somebody has to try to knock you down.

Dean Martin should have had everything by this time in his life. His
career was going great—the records were coming out (not million sellers,
maybe, but not doing badly), there was one movie after another, he got
terrific (and terrific-paying) club assignments; in short, everything he
could have asked for. He even had a young new wife to replace the eternally frowning, disapproving old one. Sure, he had to pay out a lot in
alimony and child support, but that shouldn't have made that much of a
difference to a man with his income. And maybe it wouldn't have if there
hadn't been complications from all directions.

Because of Abby Greshler's manipulations, or so Dean and Jerry
alleged, they weren't bringing home half as much money as they'd
expected. Lew Wasserman, anxious to bring them into the MCA fold, also
reviewed Greshler's deals and told the boys they had been shortchanged;
MCA could have done—and would do—much better. Greshler's turncoat
assistant, Fred Fields, clued them and Wasserman in about all his boss's
fiscal shenanigans because he was hoping that if he helped bring the boys
to MCA, the agency would offer him a job, which they did. Because
Greshler had not paid the IRS, the duo discovered that much of the
money they had would have to be turned over to the government. And
then there were the lawsuits.

When Dean and Jerry fired Greshler, they filed a suit demanding
that all agreements with him be terminated and certain monies be
returned. He turned around and sued back. Greshler also sued MCA—for

a cool million—when the boys signed with Wasserman. Even Sammy Watkins, the bandleader from Cleveland who'd had Dean sign a contract promising 12 percent of his earnings for seven years, was back in the picture. The seven years were nearly up, and Sammy wanted a piece of Dean's unexpectedly major action. And Lou Costello was miffed because Dean hadn't come over to pay homage to him one night when both men were at Ciro's, so he decided to file a suit over their old management contract.

Yet another suit was eventually filed by Screen Associates, Inc., the firm that had agreed to release *At War with the Army* with Dean and Jerry's York Productions. Although the picture grossed over three million, the boys saw little of it, due to creative accounting at Paramount. What's worse, since Abby Greshler had been the producer, there was no chance they'd ever see a dime of profit—assuming anything trickled down to Greshler. They wanted nothing more to do with Screen Associates, even though they were supposed to do several more pictures with the group. Screen Associates sued York Productions, Hal Wallis, MCA, and Dean and Jerry themselves, the latter for two million. They also tried to keep Martin and Lewis's fourth film—their third with Wallis as producer—from starting production. To top it all, Capitol Records was now claiming that they'd accidentally overpaid Dean in royalties, and he owed them five thousand dollars!

With all this litigation going on, Dean was understandably disgusted. Sure, the situation was not as bad as it had been back in Manhattan during the Lou Perry days—he didn't need handouts from friends or have to cadge drinks—but he wondered if his financial entanglements would ever be unraveled. With less cash at his command than he expected and a new wife who needed clothes and goodies, Dean tried hard to have his alimony reduced. When that didn't work, he simply stopped sending checks, and Betty made a move to have his salary garnished. It was hard for any judge to take seriously a movie, recording, and nightclub star who claimed he was dead broke, no matter how many lawyers argued his case, so she succeeded. At this point in his career, Dean's many lawyers were probably all getting more take-home pay than he was.

The Sammy Watkins lawsuit dragged on for months, as did the various litigations involving Greshler. The boys got free of their former agent, but he managed to get the courts to give him over ten thousand dollars in lost commissions. Greshler managed to outwit his opponents, and nothing concrete could ever be proved against him. Watkins's whole case should have been jettisoned by the bankruptcy Dean had declared some years earlier—more than once he'd thought about going back to bankruptcy court to get rid of his current problems—but Dean had afterward made the mistake of telling Watkins in front of witnesses that he would do his best to someday settle accounts with him. Watkins's lawyers argued that this statement, which Jerry had to back up since he had been one of those witnesses, meant that Dean still owed Sammy the money, bankruptcy or no bankruptcy. Dean's lawyers argued, and the judge concurred, that even if this were true, Dean should only have to pay what he owed up until the day he said those fateful words to Watkins. Eventually Dean forked over twelve thousand to Sammy, who in spite of everything still thought of Dean as his friend. Dean's assessment of their relationship? "Fuck him."

As for the suit filed by Screen Associates, Dean and Jerry eventually settled it for eight hundred and fifty thousand dollars. Lou Costello dropped his suit, but Hal Wallis made him go away, anyway, with a token check for twenty thousand to hopefully avoid future problems. Dean already felt bitter about the way he was treated or dismissed in Steubenville, Cleveland, and New York, and now he was getting increasingly revolted by all the "parasites" and "jackals" who were out to leech off of him now that he was a success. "People either wanted nothing to do with me, or they wanted half of everything I made," he said years later.

But there were happier things for Dean to involve himself in besides lawsuits, such as the TV deals cooked up by his and Jerry's hotshot new representative, Lew Wasserman. He got them a plum deal hosting Colgate's new television program, the *Comedy Hour*. Whatever its moniker, this essentially became the Martin and Lewis show, which made its debut on September 15, 1950. The critics were favorable, and, even better, the ratings were high. Radio may not have been the best venue for the duo, but television—so visual, so "in your face"—was just their apple. The boys were paid one hundred thousand dollars for the first show and one hundred and fifty thousand for every show thereafter.

Dean was as much a natural on TV as he was in the movies. Looking at kinescopes of those early shows, it's hard to imagine why some critics ever thought he was bland or humorless. By 1950, of course, he'd had time to hone his act, but even after that year there were still reviewers who thought of him only as Jerry's kid, someone Jerry was carrying—and anyone would do. Actually Dean displays a great deal of appeal and humor and frequently cracks up at the proceedings the way Carol Burnett, Harvey Korman, and Tim Conway would years later on the comedienne's CBS series. He's right there with Jerry every step of the way—for instance, in a sketch telecast on November 13, 1950, in which he plays the head of a dance school trying to give instructions to Jerry on how to be suave with the ladies. One can't imagine the bit being as good without Dean in it.

There are those who insist that the scripts were all tailored for Jerry, to make sure he got the laughs—he was the comedian, after all—but in the tapes Dean never seems shunted aside, and he functions as much more than a straight man. They seem like equal partners. Norman Lear, who wrote scripts for the boys before he became a top television producer (of *All in the Family*, among other shows) was to say, "Jerry couldn't stand it if Dean got laughs. He would wind up in the corner someplace with a bellyache." But both Dean and Jerry appear to *revel* in the laughs that they're producing, singly or together, in the studio audience. (Comments about Jerry Lewis have to be taken with a grain of salt because he apparently rubbed so many people the wrong way.)

Television was in its infancy in those days, and everything was done live. Almost from the first Jerry was seen as a control freak, but this may have been due to the fact that in comparison Dean was so laid back and disinterested in everything. Dean did not like to spend a lot of time rehearsing, which was the case his entire career, so he wasn't there as much. He didn't wander around asking questions about all aspects of the production as Jerry did. He didn't write scripts for the show as Jerry did. But since Dean had no writing or directing aspirations, why should he have? And since Jerry *had* ambitions in those areas, why *shouldn't* he have? Jerry hung out with the writers and other *Comedy Hour* staff members, but Dean left when the work was done and did his own thing. He was liked by everyone but seen as distant.

Perhaps if Dean had been as enthusiastic about the behind-the-scenes details as Jerry was, Jerry wouldn't have gotten his reputation as a controller. In any case, once Jerry learned the score, the way to make TV shows and movies, he wanted to get more and more involved, to make them the way *he* wanted to, not always with felicitous results. This also led to friction with his cocreative artists and all the bad blood that may have made their memories years later so selectively negative.

Dean and Jerry seemed funnier on their program than in the movies—or at least the laughs were more consistent—because theirs was the type of act that worked better in short skits than in drawn-out sections. Each movie became a kind of overlong Martin and Lewis sketch. Dean was also allowed to be funnier on TV than he was in the movies. He's half the fun in one sketch where he pretends to be a ventriloquist, and Jerry masquerades as one of his dummies. And his reactions are price-less in a great 1950 sketch when he's a newlywed in the bridal suite, and Jerry is an intrusive bellhop on a motorized golf cart. To say that the two worked well together is a massive understatement; they are hilarious pouring water all over each other on a 1951 *Comedy Hour*. Dean was also given plenty of numbers to sing, ones he had recorded or sung in the movies as well as new tunes. He wasn't afraid to eschew the laid-back singing approach if a song required something different; in one early show he sang "San Fernando Valley" with a great deal of generally uncharac-teristic dynamism.

Although he might have made a lot of writers mad, Jerry was entirely accurate when he said, "Whatever Dean and I brought to each other spontaneously far exceeded whatever the writers came up with." It's not that Martin and Lewis didn't need good material but that good material was worthless if it wasn't well played, and bad material could be saved by expert clowning. Also, ad-libs, accidents, and lost lines sometimes brought in the biggest laughs, such as when a towel dispenser that refused to work added hilarity to a skit that was dying on the vine. Thinking quickly, Jerry went offstage and dragged the prop man onto the set to fix the machine while the audience roared.

In their club act Dean and Jerry often employed what was called "nance," or mock-homosexual, material as many comics of the period did, and they also utilized it on TV, only in a less extreme form. Usually it took the form of Jerry playing a character who seemed to have a crush on Dean—which was to become a mainstay of the dynamics of their screen characterizations—but sometimes it went further. In a 1952 sketch on the *Comedy Hour*, Jerry and Dean are caught, actually crushed between, the clothing on the hangers in a closet; face to face, their lips brush together until they're practically kissing. (This was in the days before the term "coming out of the closet" existed, so it's unlikely any hidden meaning was implied.) Later in the same sketch the two go over to bunk beds, and Dean reminds Jerry to take his clothes off before he gets into bed. A petulant and mildly scandalized Jerry says, "I will sleep in my full attire, so noth-ing will ever be said."

Were things being said about Dean and Jerry? Not of any serious nature, mostly because they were decidedly heterosexual offstage, but remarks were certainly passed. These remarks came from two distinct—and very different—quarters. First there were the more sophisticated fans (although Dean and Jerry hardly appealed to the true sophisticate or intel-lectual), often but not always gay, who noticed the way Dean and Jerry were always carrying on, constantly touching and thrusting their lips into each other's faces as in the sketch described above, and who, while they didn't necessarily believe the team were actually gay lovers, couldn't help but notice the homoerotic dumb show that was going on and be curious about whatever happened when the show was over.

The other quarter consisted of less sophisticated types who never really questioned the "manhood" of the team but saw how Jerry minced around, how his on-stage character seemed so smitten with Dean, and half-seriously suggested that the boys were a couple of "fags"—or at least they portrayed same in their act. Dean was eventually made aware of these factions and, since it was Jerry who did most of the nance stuff, he became a bit uncomfortable with this type of material.

Ginny Wyscott, an actress who appeared in a few of the TV sketches in bit parts and in a couple of their movies, was at a party that Dean attended—sans Jerry—and remembered how angry he got at a fellow guest who'd imbibed too much liquor. "This man kept coming over and poking Dean in the chest, which was bad enough. Then he said to Dean, 'Where's your boyfriend?' People were always asking Dean where his 'boyfriend' was, only usually it was just in fun, totally harmless. There was nothing meant to be insinuating about it. But this guy was really obnoxious and kept saying, 'Is he the wife or are you? Where's your wife? Are you top or bottom?' Stuff like that. Frankly, some of it had to be explained to me later. Dean took as much of this from the guy as he could and then finally blew up at him; the guy dropped his drink and ran off. That hero-worship stuff was just part of their act, but Dean really hated if anyone implied there was more to it than that. When they broke up, I really wondered if that was one of the reasons—Dean's embarrassment over people's misconstruing what he and Jerry were doing, their whole relationship. I saw Dean casually many times over the years, but I never saw him angrier than he was that night."

The nance material was the one aspect of their act that drew the most criticism. It isn't that people found it homophobic, as it could be termed today—this was decades before Gay Lib—but rather unspeakably vulgar. Even intimations of homosexuality were not considered in good taste.

Some things thrilled Dean even less than the nance material, however. For instance, he wasn't especially fired up to learn that the chamber of commerce of Steubenville had decided to christen October 6, 1950, Dean Martin Day. It meant that he would have to put in a personal appearance—with Jerry—or he would look like a heel and an ingrate. It was mostly for his parents that he decided to go back to Ohio for the weekend; left to his own devices he would have forwarded a curt refusal. He and Jerry performed at the Steubenville High auditorium, and there was a parade with marching bands, floats, and banners.

Dean's distaste for the whole business was threefold. First, he felt it was just another example of his being exploited—he knew the chamber of commerce saw it mostly as an opportunity to rake in tourist dollars the way they did during, say, a county fair. Second, he had no reason to go back to Steubenville; even his parents didn't live there anymore, and if he wanted to see his cousins or old friends, they could come out to California for a visit. Third, Dean Martin was not a man who liked to look backward; Steubenville was yesterday's news, plain and simple. But his parents were proud and excited—all of their neighbors would see them and know how far up in the world their son had come—and he didn't want to disappoint them. Jeanne was in her element; it reminded her of when she'd been the Orange Bowl queen, but to Dean the whole day was just excruciating.

Joseph Pirone, whose father had once boxed with Dean, recalled his father telling him about Dean Martin Day. "My father watched the parade, and later on he wanted to see Dean. He went to a tavern, one of Dean's old haunts, where Dean was having drinks with some of his old gang, but there were so many people around that Dad couldn't even get near him. Suddenly everyone who'd once just passed him on the street had become Dean's 'friend.' Dad was disappointed, but he'd never really been close to Dean." Mary Braxton, who'd gone to school with Dean, had long since fled Steubenville for San Francisco, but she remembered reading about Dean Martin Day in the paper. "There was a small item about it in the newspaper. I swear to God I remember thinking, 'I bet Dino hated it.' And then I wondered why I thought that. After all, he'd been a bit of a showoff in school. I think it was that even after clowning around, Dino hated to be fussed over. He wanted to be appreciated, but he didn't want to be fussed over, especially by women. It embarrassed him."

Whether or not Dean wanted all the attention, his fame as half of Martin and Lewis continued to grow. The team's first three films had been so successful that they were named the Number One Stars of Tomorrow in the annual poll tallied by the *Motion Picture Herald*. Hal Wallis was anxious to find them a property that might wash the taste of *At War with the Army* out of his mouth. The film had made money, but only for Abby Greshler and Paramount, and Wallis had been appalled by its low production values. He was determined to come up with something for his boys that would showcase their talents but also be something "different." This time they would be the main characters and the only stars.

Cy Howard, who had created *My Friend Irma* for radio and written the scripts for the two features, came to Wallis with a screenplay that was alleged to be inspired by Wallis's relationship with his own son, which was problematic at best. Wallis couldn't seem to understand that his son wanted to follow his own path. Apparently Wallis never caught on that he was a prime influence for *That's My Boy*, but something must have struck him on a subconscious level. He always maintained that *That's My Boy* was the best of the Martin and Lewis vehicles. "It was perhaps [Jerry's] finest screen characterization," he said.

In the picture Jerry plays "Junior" Jackson, and Dean is Bill Baker. Junior is the son of former football hero "Jarring Jack" Jackson (Eddie Mayehoff), who is appalled that his son seems to be such a sissy. He hires Bill Baker, a more macho college boy, to "butch" Junior up by becoming his friend and teaching him athletics, hoping that through osmosis some of Bill will rub off on his boy. Junior falls in love with a pretty coed named Terry Howard (Marion Marshall), but of course she only swoons for the manlier Bill Baker. A trip to a psychiatrist determines that Junior really *does* want to play football, only he was always unable to because he was "overawed" by his father. After various complications and misunderstandings involving Bill and Terry, Jerry joins the team, and all is well.

That's My Boy emerged, incredibly, as a more or less serious picture, and there are very few laughs in the film. To many people this was seen as Martin and Lewis's—and especially Jerry's—dramatic debut. Both of them are quite good in the movie, but the mawkish and mindless script does them in. Instead of being a story about how people must be true to themselves, that sensitivity can have value over moronic machismo, instead of allowing Jerry's character to find value in himself as *he is*, the movie turns him into a chip off the old block, making him a football star and proving his essential "normalcy" before the supposedly happy fade-out. Some people felt Dean had only a "glorified supporting role" in this, but he was given two classic song numbers to perform, both of them made to order for his talents: the great swing number "Ballin' the Jack" and the quintessential romantic ballad "I'm in the Mood for Love."

The movie was a tremendous hit, but the critics were divided. According to the *Saturday Review* critic, the movie dealt "in a conventional, almost soporific way with what Hollywood assumes is college life. As a freshman football star, Dean Martin is approximately fifteen years older than he ought to be, and the farce, based on the psychosomatic difficulties of Jerry Lewis, who, sensibly I thought, preferred animal husbandry to football, only becomes agreeable when Eddie Mayehoff is participating in it." Mayehoff would go on to star in a television spin-off sans Jerry and Dean.

The female lead, Marion Marshall, had recently canceled her engagement to director-producer Howard Hawks when she felt he wasn't personally doing enough for her career and wouldn't even talk her up to other Hollywood players who might have used her in their movies. It was a fitting revenge for her to accept a contract from Hal Wallis because Wallis and Hawks were mortal enemies. She made a beeline for Jerry Lewis, hoping he would do what he could to advance her career, but aside from appearing in the next Martin and Lewis movie, nothing ever happened. After that she quickly married producer Stanley Donen in 1952, then actor Robert Wagner, before becoming an exclusive dress designer in Beverly Hills.

Cy Howard, the writer and co-producer of *That's My Boy*, was afraid Jerry was doing too much mugging and wanted him to exploit more of the screenplay's soggy pathos. Howard thought he had come up with a real work of art—Eugene O'Neill or something—and wanted Jerry to follow suit. Howard was squiring Paulette Goddard, the ex-Mrs. Charlie Chaplin, around town at that time and even went so far as to have her talk to Jerry. Reportedly, it was Paulette's comments to Jerry—something along the lines that he was talented enough, like Chaplin, not to have to resort to mugging—that gave Jerry his Chaplin complex. Unfortunately this approach meant that the film sacrificed any meager laughs it might have engendered. There was very little pathos, genuine or not, in the remaining Martin and Lewis films, and this was the last "drama" they did together as a team.

The Martin and Lewis movies did such socko business at the box office that they couldn't be pushed into release even when they'd been fully edited and scored and were ready to go. Paramount and Wallis didn't want to foist a new movie onto the public until they'd had their fill of the old one, which might take many months. Many fans, especially children, went to see *At War with the Army* and *That's My Boy* over and over again. That still doesn't explain why the next picture they made, *The Stooge*, was kept out of release until two other movies the boys made afterward were shown in theaters. Some have theorized that the studio felt the picture was too serious, but the more dramatic *That's My Boy* did such good business that that shouldn't have been a concern. It's more likely that Paramount didn't want two serious pictures in a row, and they held on to *The Stooge* for a couple of years as they pondered the best time to release it. In any case, the somewhat biographical *Stooge* was their next cinematic project.

The Stooge took its cue from the real-life adventures of Sid Silvers, who had been a professional stooge for an accordionist for many years. Fred Finklehoffe and Martin Rackin's screenplay incorporated elements of the lives and styles of Martin and Lewis to come up with one of the duo's better movies. Director Norman Taurog, who garnered an Oscar nomination for *Boys Town* and also directed *Girl Crazy* and many others, worked with Dean and Jerry for the first—but certainly not the last—time on this picture. In the 1970s Taurog told Arthur Marx: "Dean was a very peculiar guy. He knew his words every morning when he came in. But he did it a la Crosby. He was a lousy rehearser. He'd just mumble his way through a scene until I turned the cameras on. Then he'd be fine. He wanted to get through the scene as quickly as possible so he could get onto the golf course." (Dean had first played golf on a day outing during his New York days and fallen hard for the game; it would be a lifelong love affair.)

Dean and Jerry, especially the latter, continued all the practical jokes they had played on others with Norman. The director would half jokingly give them lollipops as a reward if they behaved themselves. One afternoon when Dean, who'd been up late the night before with a bottle and a broad, was particularly lethargic and finally went off to his dressing room for a nap, Taurog had the trailer towed three miles away, where Dean woke up to find himself inexplicably alone on a beach.

When it took too long to set up a scene and Dean got bored—which was often—he'd get one of the studio flunkies to go to the nearest candy store and bring him back a stack of comic books—Superman, Batman, Wonder Woman—about all Dean ever read. Ironically, the childlike Lewis (at least on screen) never read the things and often teased Dean about his interest in them. For Dean, they were just a pleasant way to pass the time when he couldn't get off the lot and do anything else. He was not the sort of man who'd have picked up a thick book or a play by William Shakespeare. His late nights often made him tired and therefore unable to concentrate on anything heavier than the adventures of "long-underwear" characters, though all his life he was never much of a reader, regardless of his mental condition.

The Stooge takes place in 1930s New York, although there's so little period atmosphere that it never seems like anything other than 1950s Hollywood. Dean plays Bill Miller, a singer who's always done an act with a comedian partner named Ben Bailey (not Lewis). Bill has just gotten married and is itching to finally break off from Ben but his agent tells him "You're not a single, and you never will be!" No one but his wife, Mary

(Polly Bergen), has any faith in him. Bill gets an old gag writer to come up with an act for him, but all he gets are—old gags! Bill's solo act bombs because of this, and meanwhile Ben Bailey is successful with a new partner. Things look bleak for Bill until he hires an idiot named Theodore Rogers (Lewis) to be his stooge during his act and heckle Bill from the balcony and so on. Ted has no idea of what he's doing or even that he's part of the entertainment, but in spite of this he's an immediate hit. Ted goes far beyond being just a stooge, he becomes half the act, but to Mary's consternation, Bill refuses to give him any billing. "Why is he so thoughtless of everyone?" she asks. "I know it's just ambition. Underneath he's a great, sweet guy. I brought it out of him once, and I will again."

When Bill is too inebriated to go on one night, Ted goes on in his place and gets an even bigger reception. The kindhearted Ted is so grateful to Bill for the opportunity that he still doesn't expect any billing, but his angry partner fires him. His new solo act is an even bigger bomb without Ted, so much so that Bill halts the show and apologizes to the audience. "I can play the accordion and sing a song," he tells them, "but I need that spark, that something, the chemistry that makes two men a successful team." Bill accepts a loving Theodore back into the act, and the two go on as happy equal partners. *Fade out.*

Dean's character was based on an old-time vaudevillian and not himself, but it's hard not to see all the parallels between Bill and Ted and Dean and Jerry. Dean gives an excellent, thoroughly convincing performance, perhaps because he was tapping into his ambivalent feelings about Jerry. His drunk scene late in the picture is effective, as are the scenes when, as in *At War with the Army*, he's being nasty to Jerry. He also isn't bad when he's being humble, like during the climactic speech he gives to the audience at the end; as in real life, he may have been down but never totally defeated.

The character Dean plays has always been considered an out and out stinker only partially redeemed by the love of a good woman, but Bill Miller has his side of it. He has a right, after all those years of hard work and upward struggle, to refuse equal billing to a geek he essentially took out of nowhere and who, unlike the real Lewis, has no real talent of his own. As for Jerry, the more serious tone to the script makes him seem almost pathetic and mentally deficient, although he gets to do some great physical gags in the picture, such as when he deliberately does all sorts of things to break up Bill's act at the Palace. One of his typical nance scenes is also hilarious. On a train, Ted climbs in bed with Bill in the lower berth instead of climbing up to the upper berth where he's supposed to sleep. "You—up there!" Bill snaps. "You—*get up there!*"

Polly Bergen always thought highly of Dean's talents. "Dean is a marvelous actor," she said, "much better than he thinks he is. His only drawback is that he looks down upon himself as an actor. He is insecure because he hasn't been trained as an actor. With a top-notch director, Dean could be superb." Marion Marshall was back on deck as Theodore's girlfriend, Genevieve Tate, also known as "Frecklehead," still pursuing Jerry as ardently offscreen as she did on.

No one could say Dean didn't get enough song numbers in *The Stooge*, all of which he recorded. "A Girl Named Mary and A Boy Named Bill" took its basic melody from "Cheek to Cheek," but it's a pleasant minor tune sung by Dean to Polly as he accompanies himself on the accordion; he and Polly also do it as a duet in a nightclub scene. This is the only song attributed to the song writing team of Mack David and Jerry Livingston; the other numbers were mostly period tunes. "With My Eyes Wide Open" is a song about Polly, but Dean sings it to Jerry as a lullaby in the aforementioned train sequence. Dean and Jerry both do "I Feel a Song Comin' On" separately in a montage of their act, and Dean warbles "Just One More Chance" during Jerry's hijinks at the Palace. The best song, far above the level of typical Martin and Lewis numbers, is "I'm Yours," nicely rendered by Dean in the best Bing tradition but with his own baritone twist—and without too much of Dean's by-then patented vowel wobbling.

It was around this period that Dean also recorded one of his best received numbers, the Italian standard "Come Back to Sorrento." Although not really suited to his voice—in a later era Pavarotti would become the foremost interpreter of this song—Dean manages to give a good account of himself.

Dean and Jerry's professional and personal relationship was spoofed not just in movies like *The Stooge* but also on their TV show; one of their best sketches aired on the night of December 30, 1951. In this Dean comes up to a friend, Danny, on the street in a state of near hysteria. "Danny, you gotta help me," he says. "This little monster I'm workin' with is driving me crazy. We're workin' in nightclubs, I see him seven nights a week; we make a picture, I see him every single day. Between radio and television, pictures and nightclubs, he's got me crazy, I don't know what to do." Danny tries to calm Dean and says, "He's you're partner, you've *got* to see him." To which Dean replies, "But I see him when

I'm *not* working." Danny: "You mean you keep imagining you're seeing Jerry?" Dean: "I'm not imagining. I take a cab, the cab driver's Jerry. I see a cop, the cop's Jerry." The next second Danny literally turns into Jerry as Jerry's face is superimposed over his own. "Don't be upset, bubbie," Jerry says. Dean screams in horror and runs off.

As the sketch continues Dean runs home only to find Jerry in his liquor cabinet, under the bed, in his bathroom, anywhere and everywhere. Everyone who shows up turns into Jerry. Finally Dean determines to kill Jerry in his latest incarnation, a shrink who's come to hear Dean's problem. As exaggerated and absurd as the sketch was, it illustrated a problem that was to become very real to Dean as the years proceeded. He may have loved Jerry in his own way, but there was just too darn much of him. The sketch, like *The Stooge*, might have been cobbled together from a cup of tea leaves.

Doing hit films for Paramount Pictures, it was only natural that Dean and Jerry be booked into the huge Paramount Theater in New York City. Their engagements broke all existing records, and fans—mostly teens and younger but quite a few older people, too—waited in line in the early-morning hours for tickets. Afterward, these same fans would jam Forty-third Street in all directions as Dean and Jerry appeared at their dressing room window in the back of the theater on the second floor and went into an impromptu performance. Dean threw photographs at the crowds and Jerry threw kisses. Adoring teenage girls and many of their boyfriends would nearly swoon as they caught a glimpse of their sacrosanct idols. Dean and Jerry were legitimate superstars now—they'd conquered virtually every medium—and the mere sight of them was enough to thrill the average spectator.

The only people they didn't thrill were each other.

SEVEN

Living It Up

Sailor Beware (1952) had originally been envisioned as a sequel to *At War with the Army* and was to have been titled *At Sea with the Navy*. It eventually emerged as a remake of the William Holden–Dorothy Lamour starrer *The Fleet's In*, made ten years earlier. (*Sailor Beware* was actually the fourth film version of this well-worn story about a sailor who bets that he can get a kiss from a pretty—and pretty standoffish—movie star.) Since Dean and Jerry and their York Productions were being sued by their partners in the releasing of *At War with the Army*, Screen Associates, it was decided that the original idea for a sequel would be scrapped, and an old screenplay would be dusted off and tailored for the boys. Jerry would get the William Holden part, and Dean would, as usual, be his best buddy.

There were two new arrivals in Dean's life at this point. Herman Citron had taken over from Lew Wasserman as his and Jerry's agent at MCA. And Jeanne presented him with their very own baby boy, born on November 17, 1951. They named him Dean-Paul Martin Jr., but they'd always call him Dino. Dean played the proud papa to a fault.

Sailor Beware emerged as fair-to-middling Martin and Lewis. Jerry, of course, made the Bill Holden character, who had merely been shuffling and bashful in *The Fleet's In*, a bit more of a spastic and a ninny. In the original, Holden got the reputation of a ladies' man simply because he's on the scene when a quick-thinking photographer asks him to pose with a gorgeous celebrity and give her a kiss. His buddies see the picture and figure he's hot stuff and the perfect guy to win the aforementioned bet. In the remake, Jerry is picked to select the winner of a contest and is pursued by dozens of lascivious women who want him to make one of them the lucky choice. When he shows up all smeared with lipstick from his cap to his collar, he's mistaken for a stud supreme. Dean put up with Jerry's nonsense in this with his usual aplomb and was given his usual one or two numbers to do. Corinne Calvet was again on hand, as the dispassionate sexpot whom Lewis has to win a kiss from although she of course hungers more for Martin. Perhaps the story was just showing its age, but the team was unable to resuscitate it—especially with Hal Walker at the helm—and *Sailor Beware* fell flat. Even the songs Dean was given were pretty forgettable.

Although Hal Wallis had paid Lou Costello off with twenty thousand dollars, the chubby comedian was feeling litigious again when he got a look at *Sailor Beware*. One of the writers for the film, John Grant, had originally worked for Costello, who was convinced Grant had lifted material from the Abbott and Costello service comedy *Buck Privates* for *Sailor Beware*. Lou steamed and simmered, but nothing ever came of it. One of the reasons was that some jokes in Martin and Lewis films were so old that no one alive could claim ownership of them or knew where they had actually originated.

One of the odder "perks" of Dean and Jerry's showbiz achievements was that they were now popular and successful enough to inspire imitation, primarily from two guys who'd worked with them in a minor capacity. Dean's imitator was a singer named Dominick "Duke" Mitchell, who had a small role in *Sailor Beware* as a corner man during a boxing sequence. Jerry's was a eighteen-year-old named Sammy Petrillo, who had appeared on one of the *Comedy Hour* broadcasts two years earlier in a cameo as Jerry's son. While Duke was really nothing like Dean, Sammy was such a good impressionist that he was almost mistaken for the better-known comic on more than one occasion. Sammy teamed with Duke to form their own duo, and the two of them managed to get booked into clubs and even make a movie.

Bela Lugosi Meets a Brooklyn Gorilla (aka *The Boys from Brooklyn*) came out later the same year that *Sailor Beware* was released, and it was the one and only film made by the knock-off team of Mitchell and Petrillo. At this point in his career, the drug-addicted Bela Lugosi would lend his name and presence to virtually any production, no matter how dismal, that would help him support his habit, which is how the former Dracula not only got into the movie but into the title. Sammy and Duke play entertainers who parachute onto the island of Cola Cola. A three-hundred-pound island girl gets a crush on Sammy, while Duke catches the eye of a prettier island princess. Bela, who is doing experiments with apes on the island, is in love with the princess and decides to get rid of his rival by turning Duke into a gorilla. Sammy wakes up in the nightclub where he's working, only to realize that everything that happened on the "island" was only a dream and that all of the characters have real-life counterparts in the club. (Bela is the disapproving nightclub manager.) He realizes that the three-hundred-pound gal is actually a good kisser, and all ends happily.

The picture was a megabomb and disappeared in a matter of weeks, although today it has become a cult trash classic in certain nondiscriminating circles. The only really funny scene is when a chimp locks Sammy in a cage with him and throws away the key. With its low-grade, almost nonexistent production values and with hack B-movie director William Beaudine at the helm, *Bela Lugosi Meets a Brooklyn Gorilla* more resembles a cheap Bowery Boys flick (many of which Beaudine directed) than a more expensive Martin and Lewis feature.

Sammy does a shameless though rather expert imitation of Jerry Lewis, better than the chimp in *My Friend Irma Goes West*—but that's all he does; there's not a bit of originality or inspiration in his entire repertoire of stolen-from-Lewis bits and movements. As for Duke Mitchell, he comes off a bit more like Tony Curtis, reeking more of the Bronx than of Brooklyn, than he does Dean Martin. He has an OK voice and does a nice job with a pretty ballad he sings to the princess, but when he does a kind of rock number, he sounds like an aging, hokey make-out man, and when he tries to imitate Dean he just comes off like a sleazy lounge singer. His unintentionally comical style, and the stereotypical "Negro" jive that he effects, are awfully campy by today's standards. As an actor he was minimally capable and mostly amateurish, with none of the smooth skill or charm of Dino, who seems like a renaissance intellectual and Laurence Olivier in comparison to the dead-common Duke.

Jerry and Hal Wallis were outraged by Mitchell and Petrillo, who were even turning up on television programs. Dean never seemed all that bothered by them, however. Duke was to tell interviewers on more than one occasion that Dean "don't want no trouble. He used to tell Jerry, 'Leave the kids alone, let 'em make a buck.' I'm sure Dean never, *never* bum rapped us once."

Duke had gotten to know Dean casually on the set of *Sailor Beware* and thought the other singer was a square shooter. Sammy never blamed Dean for their subsequent troubles, either. Of course, Dean knew that in no way could Duke Mitchell ever be compared to him—they didn't even look alike, and Duke was a head shorter—while Jerry felt lookalike

Sammy was an evil twin who was out to supersede him, as unlikely as that development would have been.

Another reason Dean didn't want to lay into the guys was because the press was taking their side. Mitchell and Petrillo were seen as a couple of mugs who only wanted their piece of the pie—which greedy, supersuccessful Martin and Lewis, so the press claimed, wouldn't allow them to nibble. Sammy's people argued that it wasn't his fault if he looked so much like Jerry that he couldn't get a job doing anything other than imitating him. This reasoning didn't take into account the fact that Sammy stole every single tic and gesture, however brilliantly, from Jerry. Sammy would tell a story that he was supposed to be on a *Comedy Hour* guest-hosted by Lou Costello, but Lou told him that Jerry had nixed his guest appearance. Of course, Costello may still have been miffed over the alleged similarity of *Sailor Beware* to *Buck Privates* and could have had his own agenda.

Wallis was afraid someone would tune in Mitchell and Petrillo or see their movie and think they were actually Martin and Lewis on the downslide; he wanted to smash them in the courts. He importuned lawyers at Paramount, MCA, York Productions, and Jerry and Dean's representatives to get behind him on this, but either they didn't see Duke and Sammy as such a terrible threat, or they felt any litigation would only backfire. Afraid public sentiment would go for the "little guys" and against the superstars (plus the fact that Dean was somewhat sympathetic with Duke and Sammy and could well understand their desire to make it big), Dean and Jerry never sued. But they still got in trouble when misinformation leaked that they had filed a lawsuit against their imitators, and they took a licking in the press. In any case, Mitchell and Petrillo lost their meal ticket when Dean and Jerry split in the late fifties, and by that time both their solo and combined careers were over. Mitchell died in 1981, and little has been heard of Petrillo, though with their weird little movie they both earned a spot in outré cinema history. Nowadays there are geeky film buff conventions that would probably love to have Petrillo as an honored guest more than they would Jerry Lewis!

Dean and Jerry's next film, *Jumping Jacks*, was one of their best, even if many of the gags and jokes seemed to be taken from Bob Hope and Bing Crosby movies of a decade earlier. Still, much of the movie is genuinely funny and inventive instead of just silly, and it just misses being really special. The story, some of which was photographed at the Infantry Center of Fort Benning, Georgia, has Jerry and Dean as yet another showbiz duo who are broken up when one of them, Chick Allen (Dean), joins the paratroopers. Chick's partner, Hap (Jerry), falls in love with his new female colleague, Betsy (Mona Freeman), but all she wants is a professional relationship; the sight of Chick, however, sends her motor racing. Chick sends for Hap when he needs help with his "all army" revue, even though the latter is still a civilian and is forced to masquerade as a paratrooper to participate. The show is so successful, Chick's superiors send it from base to base, along with a hapless Hap, who has a big Broadway engagement coming up and keeps trying to escape from Chick and his fellow soldiers. Afraid they'll all get in trouble if it's uncovered that Hap is only imitating a soldier, they bring him back kicking and screaming every time. Totally by accident, and to Chick's increasing exasperation, Hap impresses his sergeant with his alleged "skill" during maneuvers, but Chick gets the consolation prize of the girl.

The team employ their usual psychosexual dynamics in *Jumping Jacks*. Once again Dean is the macho partner embarrassed by the antics of girly-boy Jerry, whose unwilling cooperation he has to rely on. Hap flounces around the camp like a sissy, and when he goes to bed in the barracks, he insists on the men holding up a blanket in front of him so that he can undress in privacy! Not to be outdone, Chick asks Hap, "Wouldn't you like to see your buddy with an extra stripe" with a breezy flirtatiousness that proves he had the ability to do camp humor with that certain insouciance as well as Jerry. When the grouchy sergeant, superbly played by Robert Strauss, tells Chick that Hap is the only man he'd trust "and I know men," Chick's response is classic. "He knows men," he says with disgusted understatement as the grumpy guy goes off with his new best little pal skipping beside him. When Jerry affects an uppercrust British accent, Dean responds in kind, right there with him all the way. Jerry may have gotten the big, funny scenes—trying to fold and pack an open, voluminous parachute; hurtling down from the parachute tower during training—but Dean made an amusing anchor and contrast. And as usual the two worked together beautifully. "We've been flying at a high altitude, but we're going down for the jump," Chick says to Hap as they prepare for their first leap with a parachute. "Good," Hap says. "I'm going to wait until we're three feet from the ground." Jerry was the everyman, reacting as most of the fans would in similar situations, while Dean was the man, at least on-screen, that some of the fans—even Jerry—wanted to emulate.

Even the songs were better in *Jumping Jacks*, genuine highlights instead of stuff to fill the time until the comedy starts. The bouncy and kind of sexy "Parachute Jump," perfect material for Dean, is sung expertly by him as he's backed by a contingent of male dancers in uniform. Dean moves well in front of them as he sings, not *really* dancing but rather moving to the rhythm with relative grace. "The Big Blue Sky is the Place for Me" is also performed by Dean with the soldiers in backup, perfectly performed by him and written to order, a nice song with great orchestration. Another pleasant tune was "I Know a Dream When I See One," the only one from the movie that Dean recorded, well sung to Mona Freeman on the dance floor during a date. The only forgettable number is Dean's duet with Jerry, "Keep That Dream Handy," the sole notable aspect of which is that both men imitate Al Jolson at one point. (Jerry's father, who'd changed his name to Danny Lewis by this time, had made—and was still making—a career for himself imitating Jolson.)

One can only imagine what Lou Costello thought of *Jumping Jacks* when he saw it; the screenplay had originally been written for Abbott and Costello ten years earlier by Robert Lees and Fred Rinaldo, who did a lot of scripts for the older comedy team before being blacklisted in the '50s. Since he and his partner had never made the movie, Lou couldn't really accuse Martin and Lewis of lifting any of his material this time. The genesis of the script may explain why Jerry seems to be borrowing a lot of shtick from Costello throughout the movie, or maybe the veteran comedian was an influence on Lewis. In any case, Dean was a much better straight man than Costello's partner, Bud Abbott, ever was. Abbott was good, solid, professional, but he lacked Dean's charm—and he couldn't sing.

Sailor Beware and *Jumping Jacks* were both big hits for the boys. When *The Stooge* was finally released after the other two, Dean and Jerry were right up there with such major movie stars as Cary Grant and Bette Davis and Gregory Peck; they were household names who seemingly could do no wrong. It didn't matter that many critics turned up their noses at them; their fans were hysterical and clamoring for more, more, more, which they were only too happy to deliver. The *Comedy Hour* was still going strong, with Jerry's catchphrase "I like it, I like it" becoming part of the national language. They had even been given another chance at a radio show. At thirty-five, Dean was happier than he'd ever been before.

Hal Walker, who'd directed them in several movies, was working on *The Road to Bali* that year, 1952, and asked the boys if they'd come over and do a cameo in the picture. As the likes of Jane Russell and even Dean's neighbor Humphrey Bogart had already agreed to do spots, Jerry and Dean were only too happy to comply. (Bing and Bob would return the favor in Martin and Lewis's next feature, *Scared Stiff*).

The addition of Martin and Lewis caused an awkward moment for Dorothy Lamour, who got annoyed one afternoon when her costars were

LIVING IT UP

blowing all their lines and were more preoccupied with the golf game they were looking forward to than with the script. "Better warm up Martin and Lewis," she said, half seriously. "They're not only funnier but younger." Everyone on the set cracked up except for Hope and Crosby. The former looked at Lamour and said, "Be careful how you talk to us. We could always replace you with an actress."

This was also the year that they did their first telethon—March 15, 1952. It lasted sixteen and a half hours and raised over a million dollars for the construction of a New York hospital devoted to cardiac treatment. Some of the proceeds were donated to the Muscular Dystrophy Association, which had already become Jerry's pet charity. Jerry put his father on the show; Dean employed his uncle Leonard "Bananas" Barr, the vaudevillian; Dean and Jerry also worked with Frank Sinatra, whom they'd met fleetingly over the years and who for the first time was on a serious downslide in 1952. The telethon was extremely well received by the public and critics, and the press almost universally gave Martin and Lewis high marks for their class and professionalism as hosts.

Hal Wallis might have begged to differ when his stars refused to report for the first day of shooting of their next film *Scared Stiff* (1953); Dean, for one, had gone to Palm Springs for a much-promised vacation with Jeanne, and he and Jerry, never having any idea of just how success-ful they and their movies would become, had come to feel that they'd been shortchanged by their original agreement with Wallis. Their five-year contract with him was almost over, but they had no desire to wait for addi-tional compensation. Since *Sailor Beware* had been a rewrite of a thrice-filmed script, and the screenplay for *Jumping Jacks* had been a decade old, they used the fact that *Scared Stiff* was simply to be a remake of an old Bob Hope picture—*Ghost Breakers* (1940)—to charge Wallis with saddling them with dusty, dated scripts in an attempt to exploit them and shove them into any piece of refashioned tripe he could make money from. They hadn't objected to the scripts for the earlier pictures, but this time they charged that the "new" screenplay was "degrading, offensive, and insulting" and that Wallis was indifferent to their futures as artists as long as they could bring in a few bucks during their tenure with him. "We do not propose to burn out the candle, so to speak, to make inferior pictures so that you can capitalize on our current popularity without regard to the future," their letter to Wallis stated.

Wallis wasn't fooled for a minute. He knew that the whole issue was money, not artistic integrity. He also knew that Dean and Jerry would pull this holdout every time they started a movie unless he renegotiated with

[79]

their agents at MCA. In the meantime, the boys couldn't fulfill any club dates because they were supposed to be working for Wallis. In spite of that, Wallis threw up his hands and offered them a new contract that would pay them one million per year for seven years in return for one picture annually. In addition, they could do anything else they wanted, including other movies, when they weren't filming a Wallis production. Because he lost the big battle, Wallis decided to win a few small skirmishes by refusing to do them any more favors or grant them any perks. Dean had wanted the Paramount construction division to make some furniture for Jeanne, but Hal called the division head and told him not to bother—or else. And so on.

Wallis's greater revenge was in having the boys do *Scared Stiff*, which was probably worse than *Sailor Beware* and certainly a step down from the amiable lunacy of *Jumping Jacks*. Jerry plays Myron M. Mertz, a hopeless busboy in a club where Larry Todd (Dean) is a singer. The two of them flee a bogus murder rap and jealous gangsters and wind up on a ship heading for Cuba with Mary (Lizabeth Scott), who's inherited a spooky place called Lost Island. On the ship Myron tries to avoid colorful Carmelita (Carmen Miranda) because he once inadvertently got her fired, but she has since found a better job and subsequent stardom and forgiven him. After receiving numerous warnings from unknown parties to stay away, the boys and Mary explore the eerie castle on Lost Island and discover there's a vein of gold in the cellar that runs all through the island. The gold-seeking desperadoes who have been pretending to be ghosts are dealt with, and a couple of real ghosts pop up, too.

One of the problems with *Scared Stiff* is that it takes 80 minutes out of 108 to get to Lost Island. As directed by George Marshall, who had also helmed the original Bob Hope version as well as the boys' first film, *My Friend Irma*, the picture has absolutely none of the atmosphere of the classic Abbott and Costello "horror-comedies" like *Hold That Ghost* (1941) and *Abbott and Costello Meet Frankenstein* (1948). Despite some good moments, it never really comes alive. Even the final gag—in which Dean and Jerry look through a hole in the wall of the castle and see chained skeletons with Bob Hope's and Bing Crosby's heads on them—falls utterly flat.

Dean and Jerry, genuinely superior to the material as they'd charged in their otherwise bogus letter to Wallis, give their usual fine performances. Dean in particular gets some especially good scenes, such as when he survives a shoot-out between mobsters in a hallway and dashes into Liz Scott's apartment for safety. Frightened and quivering from his narrow escape, he plays the scene as if it were written for "cowardly" Lewis but in his own inimitable style. He's just as good as Jerry only different, and he's given a comparatively rare opportunity to show his genuine flair for out-and-out comedy.

The boys resuscitated one of their earliest nightclub bits in this picture when Jerry does the busboy routine, this time spilling heaps of spaghetti all over everyone as he interrupts Dean's singing act. Jerry may have been playing the Bob Hope part—Dean, of course, was Crosby—but he reacts to fright in much the same way Lou Costello did in his horror-comedies. Jerry also brought back his old lip-syncing act for one of the few times in a motion picture, dressing up like Carmen Miranda and mouthing the words to her famous number "Mama Yo Quiero." The record skips, sticks, speeds up, slows down, all the while Jerry tries to keep pace with it. It's the exact same stunt Lucille Ball performed on an episode of *I Love Lucy*, only Lucy was a lot funnier.

Carmen Miranda would have agreed, since she did a better Carmen Miranda than Jerry did if only there were more of her in the movie. Making *Scared Stiff* was a demoralizing proposition for the Cuban singer and comedienne, as she was quite ill and heavily addicted to sleeping pills and uppers. Many of her scenes with the boys were left on the cutting room floor. Hal Wallis had thought she might pep up the picture but it only pulled her and everyone else down. She found Lewis's impersonation of her rather offensive, but she was subdued when she spoke to the press: "Oh, zose boys, they drive you nuts. I have several offer for to go to London and Paris, but I am so tired I tink I will just go to sleep beside my swimming pool."

Wallis had other reasons for casting Lizabeth Scott, who'd already appeared in several of his productions, such as *Desert Fury* (1947), in the film, but it had more to do with his *own* morale. He was married to Louise Fazenda but had an eye for many of his attractive leading ladies, Liz Scott among them, whether they felt the same or not. He instructed director George Marshall not to let Scott and Martin get too heated in their brief kissing scenes, and as a result said scenes are quite tame. Scott gets in the maniacal spirit of the piece very capably. "I found Martin and Lewis amusing and great fun to work with," she said years later.

Dean, however, was more interested in sultry Dorothy Malone than in Lizabeth Scott. Malone, who briefly played a showgirl and gangster's moll very early in the picture, had just lost her brother in a tragic accident and always felt that Dean had gotten Wallis to hire her because he knew the best therapy for grief was work. Malone wasn't alone in sensing the sometimes hidden kindness at Dean's core. "Dean and Jerry were nothing alike," she remembered. "Dean was very felicitous and very helpful to me in our scene together. I thought he was a very nice, *very* attractive man, and like most women I was attracted to him. I didn't really see Jerry that much that first time out." Malone would work on another Martin and Lewis film two years later.

Dean got a kick of another kind out of another supporting player, Frank Fontaine, who essayed his fantastic and funny drunk act in this and other pictures and many TV shows. "Why don't you go home and lie down on a sponge!" his character says to Fontaine's. Occasionally over the years at a bar or party Dean would say, "I have to go home and lie down on a sponge," even though he was never one to drink himself into insensibility.

The songs in *Scared Stiff* were again by Mack David and Jerry Livingston: "When I'm with My Baby" was the right kind of bouncy material for Dean, and he made the most of it, surrounded by lots of pretty chorus girls; while "When Someone Wonderful Thinks You're Wonderful" turned out to be one of Dean's best numbers. Standing on the deck of the ship in the fog with Liz Scott, Dean hears the bleat of the foghorn, says, "That's my key," and begins to sing—and sing very well— a lovely romantic ballad that he does full justice to.

Unfortunately "The Enchilada Man," sung by Dean in a quasigaucho outfit with another bevy of lovelies, is a pretty mediocre ditty, and it isn't saved even when Carmen and then Jerry join in. There wasn't room in the running time for Carmen to have a solo number, so she was also given part of Dean's "San Domingo," a lousy Latin-by-way-of-Hollywood piece in which he had to wear a silly outfit with some sort of ludicrous lace-crepe concoctions on the arms. Dean not only felt ridiculous in the costume, he was not thrilled that he had to share the number—again— with Carmen and especially Jerry. Dean had fun with them in his good-natured way, he liked Carmen and felt sorry for her, but he felt one trio should have been enough—and he was right. He never recorded even his solo numbers from the film.

One number he did record while he was making *Scared Stiff* was Price, King, and Stewart's "You Belong to Me"—the song that begins: "See the pyramids along the Nile, watch the sunrise on a tropic isle . . ."— which over the years would become a standard. Unlike other versions, Dean's only rose to number ten on the charts, but it has a superb arrangement, beginning with a lazy alto sax played by bandleader Dick Stabile, who brings in the strings as Dean's smooth, insinuating, smoky voice intones the lyrics.

Dean brought his brother, William Crocetti, into the fold when he and Jerry decided to do an outside picture under the auspices of their York Productions after finishing *Scared Stiff*. William became business manager for York, while his brother and Jerry mulled over ideas. *The Caddy* grew out of a sketch that they had done on the *Comedy Hour* in April 1951. Writer Danny Arnold gave Jerry a half-page synopsis based on the sketch, and Jerry brought it to Paramount for approval, but the story needed to be fleshed out by another writer before the production chief would OK it. More Dino mythology has sprung up around this film about how Dean's part was just a walk-on, but such is simply not the case. It *is* true that Dean gives a performance of real charm and personality, but he seems in part held back by the foolish Jerry.

Jerry and Dean are—yet again!—a showbiz duo named Harvey Miller and Joe Anthony, and the picture is mostly a flashback showing how the team got together and became stars. It had nothing to do with the bona fide origins of Martin and Lewis. In what the screenwriters concocted with earnest flimsiness, Joe (Dean) is a fisherman who suffers from seasickness, and Harvey (Jerry) is an inept department store worker engaged to Joe's sister and living with his family. Harvey suggests that Joe become a golf pro and he'll be a caddy. While Joe makes a name for himself and attracts the interest of an heiress, Cathy (Donna Reed), Harvey is shunted aside and treated like a servant. But throughout the movie his antics terribly amuse a supporting player who turns out to be a theatrical producer. He thinks Harvey and Joe would make a great showbiz team, and the rest, as they say, is history.

Jerry's affection for Dean comes through in every scene, and his strictly on-screen crush on the fellow is more vivid than ever, a development that would never have worked in a less naive era than the '50s. At one point a character even says to Jerry, "You're quite a tomboy," and in a nightclub Jerry interrupts Dean's singing by whining and begging him to come home, like an abandoned wife.

A pretty bad movie, *The Caddy* hasn't a single highlight except for one or two of the songs by Jack Brooks and Harry Warren. The duet, "What Would You Do without Me?" is enlivened by the fun, spirited performances of the fellows. When Dean sings "You're the Right One" to Donna Reed, he seems to be doing an outright imitation of Crosby and sings in too low a register. "A Wonderful Kind of Whistling Moment" is the number interrupted by Jerry's "abandoned wife." Part of Dino's legend is that he hated the song "That's Amore," which he introduced in this picture and became his first hit record (and perhaps the one he's most identified with), and he had to be pressured into doing it in the film and then recording it. The reason this bit of apocrypha came into being is that many years later, after Dean had sung the song literally thousands of times, he told an interviewer, "Y'know, I hate that fuckin' song"—but actually he liked the number right from the first. Although, frankly, Dean recorded better songs, "That's Amore" was a catchy tune with a nice Neapolitan flavor, and it was right up his alley. It sold over two million copies and received an Academy Award nomination—and Dean would never be quite the same. After all these years he had a hit record; he had finally made it as a singer. This certainly contributed to his slowly growing feeling that he could also make it as a solo.

In any case, Dean could not have been pleased that when he sings "That's Amore" in the movie, Jerry gets to join in. Jerry was even given his own solo number, "The Gay Continental," to sing at some swells' pool party—another irritant to Dean, who was beginning to wish Jerry would stick to the comedy stuff and just let him do the vocalizing. Dean had never really enjoyed the records they had done together, not only because they were, in his opinion, "pretty stupid," but because while Jerry could carry a tune he couldn't actually *sing*. Their voices did not blend well together no matter how you sliced—or dubbed—it.

The Caddy inveigled a couple of actual golf pros—Ben Hogan and Sam Snead—into becoming a minor part of its nonsense. Costar Donna Reed told an interviewer on the set, "Dean and Jerry are marvelous. They play practical jokes all the time and have lots of fun. I'm really enjoying making this movie." But one can't imagine she considered it one of the brighter spots on her resume.

Dean had finished filming *The Caddy* when Jeanne told him abruptly that she wanted to try a trial separation. He had been through this before, with Betty, and for some of the same reasons—and not necessarily the infidelities. Today Jeanne Martin admits that Dean was never a Boy Scout but says, "I never cared about that. I knew he was off at a studio or a club surrounded by beautiful women; it was part of the business." Still, Jeanne couldn't help but feel disillusioned. The long honeymoon, the frantic, dizzying, spellbound early days of their romance were over, and they'd come to know more about each other—or had they?—through months of daily living. The real problem may have been one of communication, or lack of same.

Jeanne's attitude at that time, typical for the prefeminist period, was, "A husband should be the boss, the strong man around the house. He should have the final say." The trouble is, Dean didn't say much of anything. "He's a man of few words," she would state, "but to women, he's a man of no words." (In contrast, columnist Joe Hyams once wrote of Dean:

"Over the years I've found Dean Martin to be a man of many words on many subjects.") She didn't want a "sensitive" man who would help her with the housework (and since that would never be a description of Dean, she had gotten her wish) but she did want the brute to be around sometime, to act as if she existed. What with Dean always being off making movies or doing club gigs and God knew what else, she at least wanted him to be attentive when he was home. Jeanne was very liberal and understanding when it came to Dean and other women—Hadn't she felt that irresistible tug from his attractiveness and charisma herself? Hadn't he been married to somebody else when she met him?—but she wanted to feel that she actually had a viable partner she was going through life with, come what may, something Dean did not make her feel at this time. Instead she felt that she was just there like the TV set or the radio, something to be turned on to provide amusement whenever Dean felt like it. Otherwise, it was as if she weren't even there. Things might have been different if she had also been in showbiz, if there were mutual things they could discuss, but this was not the case. This separation, the first of many, would last a little over a month, until Dean found out Jeanne was pregnant with their second child by reading about it in Louella Parsons's column; Jeanne had not wanted it to influence Dean either way but the news got out and that was that. She gave birth to Ricci James Martin (pronounced "Ricky") on September 20, 1953.

Money from Home, the first of Martin and Lewis's 1954 releases and their one and only in 3D, might have the distinction of being the worst movie ever made from a Damon Runyon story, and there have been plenty. Directed by George Marshall, the story takes place during Prohibition (though again there's virtually no 1920s period atmosphere) and has Dean as New York operator "Honeytalk" Nelson—he can talk the honey out of anyone—and Jerry as his cousin Virgil Yokum, who works for a pet hospital. Fleeing from yet another mobster, the boys disguise themselves as a sultan and one of his wives on the train and wind up in Maryland. Jerry is mistaken for a famous (and alcoholic) jockey, Bertie Searls, by a pretty horse owner, Miss Phyllis Lee, who, naturally enough, falls for Dean. But Jerry finds his own true love in Dr. Autumn Claypool (Patricia Crowley), who's a veterinarian at an animal hospital and ahead of her time: "Women can do anything men can do—and have babies, besides." After steeplechase races and chases from sultans and mobsters, all ends happily for the two couples if not for the audience.

Money from Home illustrates Dean's almost supernatural ability to maintain his dignity no matter how silly Jerry—and the pictures—became. He's just as good as Jerry if not better. Jack Brooks and Joseph

Lilley contributed a couple of new songs to round out such standards as "Moments Like This," which Dean sings very nicely (and which he recorded) while dancing with Phyllis, and "I Only Have Eyes for You," which Dean croons just out of sight of the same lady, who's mad and isn't speaking to him. Jerry stands below her bedroom window and lip-syncs the number as Dean pours forth a notable rendition of it. Dean sings the new song "Love is the Same All Over the World" while dressed as a sultan to a bevy of beautiful harem girls; it's nice and bouncy but forgettable. The other new tune, "The Be Careful Song," was a charming number given to Jerry to sing to his menagerie of injured dogs, cats, and monkeys in the animal hospital.

Aside from the song numbers, the film has few highlights, one of which occurs when Jerry, dressed as a harem girl, is pursued across a boudoir by a fat sultan. A bit of business when his pet ants escape their ant farm, crawl all over party guests, and cause them to break out into a "strange new dance" never erupts into hilarity, although it must have looked good on paper. But how to explain some of the dialogue, which wouldn't have looked good under any circumstances: "I know I sacro'd my illiac," Virgil says after he jumps off a train. When he remarks, "Ain't he quaint" about Honeytalk to a party guest, the gentleman corrects his grammar and says, "One doesn't say 'ain't,' one says 'isn't.'" To which Jerry replies, "Isn't he quisn't?" Virgil taps Honeytalk on the shoulder while he's dancing with Phyllis, then waltzes off with Honeytalk and leaves the lady just standing there. "What's the matter with you?" Honeytalk asks grumpily. When, referring to Phyllis, Honeytalk asks Virgil "What do you think about us getting married?" Virgil replies, "I can't. I'm gonna marry Autumn."

Sheldon Leonard had portrayed so many mobsters by this time that he could play "Jumbo" Schneider in his sleep and probably did. (In his own memoirs, he completely ignored the boys.) Jerry's love interest, Pat Crowley, who had made her movie debut a year earlier in *Forever Female* with Ginger Rogers and William Holden, is so attractive and charming that she lights up every scene she's in. She was to appear in the last Martin and Lewis feature also, this time as Dean's romantic partner.

Their final feature for 1954, *Living it Up*, helmed by Norman Taurog, was a remake of the Fredric March–Carole Lombard starrer of 1937, *Nothing Sacred*, directed by William Wellman. The original film teamed an allegedly dying woman (Lombard) with a reporter (March) whose paper is covering her tragedy and treating her to a final fling in New York. Underneath the farcical humor, Ben Hecht's screenplay had trenchant and intelligent things to say about human nature, and the black comedy was one of the most memorable of the thirties.

The Martin and Lewis sex-switch version took the basic idea—Lewis as Homer Flagg has supposedly been exposed to radiation poisoning (Dean is the hometown "Doc" who made the original misdiagnosis), and Janet Leigh is the reporter "Wally"—and just turned it into an excuse for Jerry to clown and Dean to sing. Wally isn't teamed with the "dying" Homer but with Doc, of course, although at one point out of compassion she asks a smitten Homer if he'll marry her. Homer had supposedly become radioactive by entering a nuclear testing site in Desert Hole, Nevada. Doc realizes his mistake—Homer doesn't have only three weeks to live—but at first agrees to keep the truth from Wally until it all blows up in their faces as Wally's editor, played by Fred Clark, fumes.

Dean first appears in his cabin strumming a guitar and accompanying himself to "Kiss Me Baby" as a wide-eyed Jerry observes. A better number is "How Do You Speak to an Angel?" which Dean croons to Leigh in his inimitable style while dancing with her in a nightclub. Dean wasn't thrilled when Jerry got to reprise the same tune and tried to sing it seriously instead of in his usual goofy fashion. Dean also sings "Money Burns a Hole in My Pocket" to Leigh in a gift shop and teams with Jerry for "I Love New York" (which Dean certainly didn't) on a strictly Hollywood-soundstage Manhattan street.

Living It Up emerged as a rather dull movie far below the level of the original, but it does have its moments. "You're going all the way to New York," Wally tells Homer, "because you have radiation poisoning." Homer asks, "How far can I go on a sinus condition?" A waiter gives some advice to Homer: "Don't eat the food here; it'll kill you." A headline showing a close-up of Jerry's backside as he's carried over Dean's shoulder reads HOMER'S END NEAR. And Dean, smooth and professional as usual, gets a good bit to do as he's desperately hanging from a widow ledge while Jerry, on the same ledge, calmly answers a call on the telephone. On the other hand, a scene with Jerry impersonating three specialists—one each from Paris, Austria, and China—is excruciatingly silly and unfunny. Dean was good-natured but he almost lost his patience when one comedy bit—his accidentally catching a ride on a serving cart and jumping off it just before it crashes into a door—had to be done over and over again until director Norman Taurog thought it was "just so."

By far the most exciting moment in *Living It Up* occurs when Sheree North, in her film debut as a dance contest winner (but referred to in the film as "Sheree North") does an incredibly sexy jitterbug with Jerry.

There is no way Dean could not have noticed this totally hot and energetic performer, who steals the picture without uttering one word. The Paramount publicity flacks billed her bit as "the screen's first rock and roll dance," apparently unaware that the jitterbug was not exactly invented by Elvis. A year later North was appearing—and shaking—in *How to be Very, Very Popular*, which drove nominal star Betty Grable into retirement.

An odd thing about *Living It Up* is that for some reason Jerry Lewis looks better than Dean, which was normally not the case at all. Jerry was certainly not an unattractive fellow, but Dean was always considered the looker, if for no other reason than Jerry always contorted his looks with funny faces. Perhaps he consciously made an effort to do less of that sort of thing in this movie—he plays a "poor soul" more than he does a "spastic"—and it also must be remembered that Jerry was twenty-seven to Dean's thirty-six. Whatever the case, Dean still looked great, but he was no longer a youth.

Janet Leigh had already known Martin and Lewis for some years when she made *Living It Up*. In fact, Jerry and Patti had been best man and matron of honor at her wedding to Tony Curtis, and Janet and Tony enjoyed many evenings at Jerry's home playing word games and charades. At this time she didn't know Dean and Jeanne all that well—although that would change—as the two partners and their wives had never been much for socializing together (they saw enough of each other at work) even before the problems that led to their breakup began. "Dean had his group, and Jerry had his group and all of that," Leigh remembered. And, of course, Patti didn't approve of Jeanne and tried to avoid her out of loyalty to Betty.

Janet and Tony appeared in many of the zany home movies that Lewis was directing with his friends at that period, learning the ropes and honing his craft, experimenting on his own time without spending any of Hal Wallis's money; he was itching to direct his own feature someday. Dean appeared in only one of these gems—he did enough acting and line memorization at the studio without having to do it on his days off—playing a mobster named Joe Lasagna in a parody of Humphrey Bogart's 1951 mob movie *The Enforcer*, which Jerry christened *The Reinforcer*. Janet played his moll, Mary Muck. Jerry probably only got Dean to do it because Dean's favorite movie star was George Raft, whom he socialized with on several occasions, and he'd grown up watching many of Raft's tough gangster melodramas. Dean got to speak in a thick, stereotypical Italian accent as he went around the makeshift set threatening all he encountered with violence.

Leigh was at first uncomfortable with her part in *Living It Up* because it had been modeled on the original Fredric March characterization and was "full of caustic one-liners" more appropriate for an Eve Arden type. She didn't feel she would be believable playing it that way and importuned Norman Taurog to make some minor script changes and allow her to try a warmer approach. She recalled Dean as being "relaxed, easygoing, open and sexy—and it resulted in a seemingly effortless, honest, warm portrayal." She says today that she and Dean were to become "friends besides co-workers—dear friends. He was a joy to work with, fun and easygoing, but," she emphasizes, "he also cared about his acting and was very proud of his movie career—he was a natural. I adored Dean." She recalled Norman Taurog as being a director who really "understood comedy, and he knew his people. He allowed Jerry and Dean to have their heads, when that served the purpose. But he also reined them in when *that* was necessary. He didn't lose sight of the balance."

Perhaps the same could not be said for Martin and Lewis themselves, whose great success had also engendered great paranoia. A wonderful sketch they did on the *Comedy Hour* in May 1953 had each of them fearing the other would kill him when they take out million-dollar life insurance policies on one another. Their feelings were not quite so extreme in real life, but they did have their doubts.

It wouldn't be long before each would be accusing the other of figuratively stabbing him in the back.

EIGHT

Busted

"Dean just felt he would have been better on his own," says Jeanne Martin in 1999 of the breakup of Martin and Lewis over forty years earlier.

Of course there were a lot of factors that led to Dean coming to this conclusion, and a thousand theories as to what went on behind the scenes. Most agree, however, that the trouble started with their twelfth film together, *Three Ring Circus* (1954). The screenplay had been written by a friend of Jerry's and Frank Sinatra's, Don McGuire, who had already penned a script for Frank—with Frank's eager participation—called *Meet Danny Wilson* (1952), a thinly disguised account of the singer's career and his mobster ties. McGuire would also bring the director of that film, Joseph Pevney, along with him at Jerry's urging. (Pevney later directed the fascinating psychosexual thriller *Female on the Beach*, with Joan Crawford and Jeff Chandler.)

Most accounts present McGuire as a struggling writer, a Hollywood wannabe, who'd hitched his wagon to Sinatra's—and then Lewis's—star, but McGuire had already had a successful career as an actor, appearing with Ida Lupino in *The Man I Love*, Joan Crawford in *Humoresque*, and costarring with Red Skelton in *The Fuller Brush Man*. Although he'd had some solid parts in the forties, he'd never broken through into major stardom, and like many actors in that situation wanted to work on the other side of the camera. A big handsome man with personality to spare, he had no problem attracting powerful friends.

Everyone had a different story about who was upset by the screenplay McGuire fashioned, which was known at that time as *The Big Top*.

According to Hal Wallis, Jerry wouldn't approve the script because he didn't show up until ten minutes into the picture. According to Jerry it was Dean who was furious because the screenplay "relegated him to a supporting role. At least Dean thought so, and when I looked at the script, I had to agree."

It is largely due to Hal Wallis that the idea was firmly planted in everyone's minds that Jerry wanted to shove Dean to the side and reduce his role in their movies practically to a bit part. This has never really made a lot of sense. It is true that Jerry took more of a role in the basic film-making process—now that he was writing and directing his own home movies he wanted to try out his ideas on the real thing—but why would he have wanted to completely exclude Dean? It was Jerry who was getting the lion's share of the positive notices whereas Dean was frequently overlooked and dismissed, so Jerry could hardly have felt Dean was getting too much time and attention. Some have argued that it was because of this that Jerry got a swelled head, thought he was the whole show, and didn't really think he needed Dean anymore, which would sound more than reasonable if it didn't completely ignore the real affection that Lewis felt for his partner, especially but not exclusively in the early years. It's more likely that when Dean started complaining, Jerry took it too personally.

When Jerry had his friends—McGuire and Pevney—making their movies, Dean couldn't help but be paranoid. All the years of being the so-called second banana in the eyes of the critics and some of the fans had left him vulnerable and susceptible to any story that was passed along about Jerry and his wiles. Jerry, who'd always been a bit insecure to begin with, wasn't in much better condition. Wallis, annoyed at how they'd bamboozled more money out of him, undoubtedly played both against each other.

Adjustments were made to the screenplay, but Dean was never happy with it, primarily because it only gave him room for two songs, one of which was a duet with Jerry, and because his character was so unpleasant, especially as compared to Jerry's lovable, heart-tugging clown. "For Christ's sake, Duke Mitchell could do this!" he ranted, and he reportedly had to put up with jealous extras on the set taunting him about how little he had to do. "Are you still part of the act?" they'd say in mock commiseration. According to Jerry, Dean was difficult and glowering and kept threatening to quit all through the shoot, "saying he was fed up to the ears with playing a stooge."

A look at the pair's previous movies could have made it clear to any objective observer that Dean was an important part of the proceedings and hardly a stooge, but Dean couldn't see it that way. He kept taking hits to his ego—only one solo number in this new flick—and there were other things, such as the time a still of him, Jerry, and Sheree North from *Living It Up* was supposed to be in *Look* magazine, only the *Look* staff clipped him out of the photo. Another problem was that the hit recording of "That's Amore" had made it clear to him that perhaps he did have a chance to be another Frank Sinatra if he didn't allow himself to be totally enveloped by the Martin and Lewis hilarity engine. Each half of the team had his cheering section telling him that he could do just as well if not better on his own.

There was still another factor, which their famous sketch on the *Comedy Hour* had parodied: Dean and Jerry still saw too much of each other, even if they rarely socialized these days. Jerry had no problem with it; the once-lonely kid liked his friends around him, was fascinated by the film medium, and loved to talk shop with writers and directors. But Dean wasn't into any of that, and besides, he was a *singer*. Dean had grown up in a small house with loving parents and an older brother, he had a wife and children (*two* wives and children, actually), and he didn't need any more pulls on his time and emotions. Jerry was so emotional; Jerry was so oppressive. He loved him, but Jerry could be so damn *suffocating*. Talented and likable he may have been, but a little of Jerry Lewis went a long way.

Jerry may have felt that touching was part and parcel of their act, but there were times he got too carried away. In January 1954, the two did a very funny sketch on *Comedy Hour* in which an angry Lewis orders the cameras to close in and nearly crush Dean while he's singing—we see Dean backing away from multiple camera viewpoints as they start to move in. As the bit ends, Jerry jumps up on Dean's shoulders and keeps repeatedly clapping him on his head and boxing his ears. It's clear that Dean is not only uncomfortable but in genuine pain as Jerry keeps hitting him. "You're overacting, Jerry," Dean says as Jerry continues to pummel him and pull on his hair. Dean seems torn between laughing it off—the cameras were rolling after all—and throwing Jerry off his back and stomping on him. And it's also obvious as he tells Jerry, "It's over! It's over!" (referring to the sketch) that he's so angry, he can barely contain himself. This sort of thing was happening too often—Jerry overdoing everything and getting too rambunctious—and the slapping and hitting were undoubtedly his way of expressing his anger and frustration, that demon paranoia, at Dean.

Somehow they got through the new movie, whose title had been changed to *Three Ring Circus*, a big top run by Joanne Dru. Dean is attracted to a trapeze star played by Zsa Zsa Gabor, and Jerry (playing "Jerry"), who wants to be a lion tamer, is beset by a jealous clown. Instead of a romantic solo to a pretty young gal, Dean gets to sing "It's a Big, Wide, Wonderful World" to a bunch of animals in cages. The other Jerry Livingston–Ray Evans song, "Punchinello," was a duet with Jerry. Most of the critics found Don McGuire's script to be formulaic and unoriginal and felt the film only came alive in the second half when the circus scenes took over, "with the stars as prominent components," as the *New York Times* put it. "The boys, at long last, are beginning to relax," though the critic added, "Mr. Martin blandly wows the two ladies." *Three Ring Circus* has some good moments, but it's not one of their better vehicles.

Nobody had much fun making this movie, with the exception of Zsa Zsa, who spent her free days enjoying hotel assignations with famous playboy Porfirio Rubiroso. Elsa Lanchester was cast as a bearded lady in the movie, but she never had anything good to say about it or Martin and Lewis. Hal Wallis remembered, "Our cast stayed at the Arizona Biltmore in Phoenix. In the evenings when Dean and his wife came into the bar for a drink and Jerry and his wife were there, they ignored each other." During breaks in shooting, Jerry and Dean did not speak but went off in separate directions. Wallis claimed that some sections of the film were so bad, they had to be reshot. "I got an attack of the gout due to *Three Ring Circus*," he told interviewers. He also had his own attack of paranoia, wondering if the boys' feud was for real or just an MCA-inspired stratagem for getting more money or control.

The director, Joseph Pevney, remembered it differently. "Hal Wallis was the major problem behind *Three Ring Circus*. He didn't care about anything but getting things done as quickly and as cheaply as possible. He didn't give a damn about the final result, just as long as he had *something* to release." It may well be that the producer of movies like *Casablanca* and *Jezebel* really couldn't take Martin and Lewis—and their movies—at all seriously on an artistic level and figured their generally unsophisticated fans would sit through anything no matter what its quality. In other words, he might pay them a lot of money because they made a lot of money for him, but that didn't mean he had to spend a lot of money on production costs. A work of cinematic art, maybe, but Martin and Lewis? *No.* Martin and Lewis made the commercial movies whose success would more than pay for a few artistic flops. (The story that Wallis tried to hire such prestigious directors as Billy Wilder, Frank Capra, or William Wyler to helm *Three Ring Circus*—whether originally circulated by Wallis or not—is ludicrous in retrospect!)

When the shooting was over, Jerry told Wallis that the situation was completely intolerable; he couldn't make movies with Dean when his partner refused to talk to him, and he wanted to work on a solo project. Wallis wasn't interested—not at that time. Besides, Dean and Jerry more or less made up, or at least came to terms temporarily. In their next film, *You're Never Too Young* (1955), Dean was given five Sammy Cahn–Arthur Schwartz tunes to warble, and only one was a duet with Jerry. More importantly, Herman Citron, their agent at MCA, sat them down in his office and got them to understand that no petty grumbles should interfere in the multimillion-dollar partnership that they'd spent so much time and energy developing. Why destroy everything they'd worked so hard for? Couldn't they put their differences aside? Citron told them that it was only natural that some pictures would favor one performer, and the next might give the other a chance to shine, but it all balanced out in the end, didn't it? For the time being, Jerry and Dean shook hands and agreed to go on as a duo, although things would never really be the same for them after Martin's "mutiny," as it was perceived by Jerry. The mutiny had begun when, in Jerry's eyes, Dean became comparatively incommunicative, moody, hostile, sullen, and generally uncooperative, and the truce between the two men didn't change him all that much.

Since the press had uncovered the feud and reported on it, Jerry and Dean weren't afraid to refer to it publicly to get a laugh. In a classic spot on their September '55 *Comedy Hour*, Jerry played a contestant on a sixty-four-million-dollar quiz show. Dean, as the emcee, puts him underwater in a six-foot-high tank so that he can't hear anyone shout out the answers. Climbing a ladder to the top of the tank, Dean reads the questions off a scroll that unrolls all the way to the floor. Dean keeps pushing Jerry's head under the water until Jerry finally gasps and says, "Haven't you heard? The feud is over."

They may have been laughing about it, but behind the scenes the same insecurities, tensions, and frustrations were at play. Hal Wallis tended to blame it on the women the boys were married to. "Their wives didn't get along," he said. "Each wife was protective of the relative importance of her husband in scripts, films, and publicity, and this ultimately led to the breakup of the team." That may have been a factor, certainly, but Wallis was being simplistic.

You're Never Too Young was another remake, this time of *The Major and the Minor* (1942), which had starred Ginger Rogers as a young woman who disguises herself as a twelve-year-old and winds up in an all-boys school run by Ray Milland. It had been Billy Wilder's first directorial effort (Wilder would later do a notorious film with Dean), and was just silly enough for someone to think it would make a good vehicle for Jerry Lewis. Sidney Sheldon, later to become famous as best-selling author of several movie-influenced potboilers, reworked Charles Brackett's original script and put Lewis into the Rogers role. This time a grown man pretending to be twelve would, naturally, hide out at an all-girls' school.

Again one of the duo is on the run from the mob, or at least a robber played by Raymond Burr. Jerry is an apprentice barber who witnesses the robbery and tries to hide from the thief-killer in a kiddy sailor suit. Dean is a teacher at the school who falls for one of his colleagues, Diana Lynn. (Lynn was not only a carryover from Martin and Lewis's first two films, the *Irma* pictures, in which she played Marie Wilson's more sensible roommate, but she'd even had a role in *The Major and the Minor.*) Veda Ann Borg, a hard-bitten blond who played a number of villainous roles in movies and on TV during this period, is Burr's accomplice, and Nina Foch is another gal who competes with Lynn for Dean's affections.

Foch found Martin and Lewis pleasant, but she was appalled by their lack of culture and their semiliteracy and had no great desire to know them better off the set. Although both could certainly read, neither of them ever cracked a book, unless, in Dean's case, it was a comic book. Raymond Burr recalled that Dean and Jerry seemed never to speak to each other while making the film, but according to Jerry they *were* speaking; they were just rather cool and "tentative," as he put it, with one another. Filming a climactic chase with Dean in a motorboat and Jerry on water skis, which was considered the highlight of the picture, Jerry was hit by a ski and had to be rescued by Dean. Jerry wasn't really in danger of drowning, but the Paramount press flunkies, anxious to wipe away the bad publicity over the boys' feud, issued releases that made it sound as if Dean had risked life and limb to save his partner, who had nearly died.

Still upset and frustrated and not sure how to handle his frustration or what to do, Dean had taken to drinking between scenes, with two-martini lunches more the rule than the exception. Jerry recalled this as the time he realized that "our luck as a team was running out . . . . Maybe the core of our difference was the insoluble problem every straight man has to face." Jerry felt that Dean was fed up with always having to hear how great and funny Jerry was, particularly when, as Jerry put it, "in his heart he knew *he* was the reason we were successful." When Jerry would suggest one little script change or a new bit of business, Dean would fly into a rage, overreacting to what he perceived—and had been told by others in his camp—as Jerry's need for total control.

Dean also thought it was Jerry's need for control that led to his partner suggesting that they hold the premiere for *You're Never Too Young* at

Brown's Hotel in the Catskills, where Jerry had once been a busboy while his father was doing his Al Jolson routine up on the stage. For Jerry this would sort of be the equivalent of Dean Martin Day in Steubenville, since he'd moved around so much as a child, he didn't really have a hometown as such. At this point every other movie the team was doing was produced by their own outfit, York Productions (with Wallis producing the other films); *You're Never Too Young*, like *The Caddy* and *Living It Up* (and the upcoming *Pardners*), came out under the auspices of York. As a partner in the business Dean deserved to be consulted, and he was livid when he was told by Jerry, *after* it had all been arranged, about the premiere at Brown's. Jerry argued that the owners of the hotel had agreed to foot half the bill, so they'd be saving money, but Dean, who had no sentimental feeling for the Catskills where he'd never worked, argued that the area was out of the way and a lousy place to hold the premiere of a major Hollywood film. Although by some accounts Jerry refused to change his plans, by this point Dean was so disgusted with everything that he told Jerry to do what he wanted—and to go to hell—and he went off with Jeanne to Honolulu for a little R and R. He never did show up at Brown's.

Dean's singing career was really taking off, no doubt in part because of all of his exposure in films and on TV, and he asked Herman Citron at MCA if there was a chance he could have his own television program without Jerry. The emphasis would be on his singing, and he would no longer be a second banana to his partner. He'd recorded some nifty numbers by this time: the clever, amusing "Naughty Lady of Shady Lane" (who turned out to be only nine days old), which had been a hit for the Ames Brothers; "Let Me Go, Lover"; "Long, Long Ago," with Nat King Cole; the prophetically titled "We Never Talk Much, We Just Sit Around," with Helen O'Connell; "Georgia on My Mind"; and he even spoofed himself in "If I Could Sing Like Bing." One of his best and sexiest numbers from this period originated as a Mexican hit called "Quién Será?" that was Americanized into "Sway," an irresistible mambo number with a provocative beat and lyrics that didn't suffer too much from that awful chorus going "Ping! Ping!" at the start of the record. The chorus in "Memories are Made of This"—which whispered "sweet, sweet" instead of shouting "Ping! Ping!"—also didn't add much to the arrangement, but it didn't prevent the song, which had a pleasant if unspectacular, almost country-and-western-type melody, from becoming Dean's second hit record, selling over a million copies and staying in the number one position on the national charts for over six weeks. No wonder Dean was feeling his oats! As for the solo TV show, Herman Citron, who knew how to handle his stars, told Dean that he still had contractual obligations to fulfill with Jerry but that they would "wait and see."

You're Never Too Young was well received by fans and critics, although it had its naysayers. "Too young for what?" asked the *New Yorker*. "I have known six-week-old babies who were too old for *You're Never Too Young.*" Dean's ego and troubled feelings weren't assuaged by *Variety's* report that he did "his best with his usual straight man assignment, but he is hampered by the underdeveloped character provided by the scripter. He gets the girl, but it's Lewis who gets the audience." He did get to sing "Every Day Is a Happy Day," a kind of march-and-drill number, with about a hundred pretty gals, as well as "Simpatico," "Love Is All that Matters," and "I Know Your Mother Loves You," while Jerry only got "I Like to Hike."

Their next film, *Artists and Models* (1955), was another Hal Wallis production and was helmed by forty-two-year-old Frank Tashlin, who'd done stellar work on some Bob Hope comedies such as *Son of Paleface* (1952). The plot of the movie didn't really allow Tashlin too many opportunities to indulge in his trademark cartoon-style sight gags, but that would be rectified when he also directed the last Martin and Lewis film, *Hollywood or Bust*, the following year.

Rick Todd (Dean) and Eugene Fullstack (Jerry) are pals who have come from "Steubendale" to make their fortune in New York (actually, Hollywood's version of a Greenwich Village that never existed). Rick wants to be an artist, and Eugene wants to write children's books. Rick blames all of their problems on Eugene's obsession with comic books—he spends more time reading them than doing his job; his particular favorite is the Bat Lady. Comic book artist Abby Parker (Dorothy Malone), who draws Bat Lady, quits her job when her boss tells her he wants more gore in the stories. Apparently TV presents too stiff a competition, what with several murders a night, and soon, says the editor, the wounds will be gushing in color, no less. Rick takes her place while Eugene, a pawn in the hands of anti-comic-book organizers, goes on TV to denounce Bat Lady and all the rest. Rick and Abby fall in love while Betsy (Shirley MacLaine), the comic book editor's secretary and Abby's model for Bat Lady, pines for Eugene, her numerological match. When a top-secret military formula coincidentally winds up in Rick's comic book *The Vulture*, which Eugene gives him ideas for, a sultry super-spy (Eva Gabor) is sent in to seduce him. After the spies are taken care of, it all ends happily at an artists and models ball, where the boys paint patterns on Anita Ekberg's back. Got it?

The movie was based on a Broadway play by Michael Davidson and Norman Lessing that had been adapted by Don McGuire, although Frank Tashlin, Hal Kanter, and Herbert Baker worked over the screenplay. *Artists and Models* took its cue from the contemporary controversy over the graphic horror comics that were sweeping the industry and the country, but it only used the debate as a backdrop; wisely the picture never really takes sides, since many of Martin and Lewis's fans, not to mention Dean, were comic book fans. Jerry is held up as an example of "what can happen to the human brain on a steady diet of comic books," but *Artists and Models*, while a lot of fun, is even more mindless and silly than a typical comic book of any era! Social critics of the fifties argued that comics, particularly of the gruesome shock variety, contributed to juvenile delinquency, even though studies showed that normal kids who never got into trouble loved the darn things just as much as delinquents did. Having its cake and eating it, too, the movie acknowledges that there was a so-called problem regarding the bad influence of comic books, but it doesn't take the problem very seriously.

The toll that the feud and his conflicted feelings were taking on Dean can be seen in his appearance in this picture: he looks so lean that he's almost gaunt. His bemused, somewhat affectionate, and highly ambivalent, exasperated attitude toward Jerry is reflected in the characters they play in the film. "A divorce is the only way out," Rick says to Eugene. "We've been together too long." Teary eyed when Rick changes his mind and decides to stay in New York, Eugene makes a candlelit supper for them of pork and beans. The mock-homosexual humor continues when Eugene kisses Rick twice—once for the landlady and once for himself. (Tashlin always included this kind of humor in his Bob Hope films, but of course Martin and Lewis had been doing it for years before he worked with them.)

Tashlin did get a chance to work in two zany sight gags of the type he was famous for: The funniest bit has a masseuse bending Jerry's legs around in impossible cartoonish positions as he reacts with hysteria; the second has Shirley MacLaine backing Jerry up against a water cooler that begins to steam and boil over as she kisses him—an old gag but an effective one. Shirley and Jerry are terrific together, and they make a good team against the malevolent youngster George "Foghorn" Winslow, whose neurotic mother has dropped him off at the comic book offices while she goes shopping so that they can see firsthand the effect of his "horror literature on undeveloped minds." Jerry is also very funny talking about the bad effects of comics on the human brain.

That left only the song numbers for Dean to make an impression in, and he delivers, especially in a number called "Innamorata (Sweetheart)," a lovely Spanish-flavored ditty with a nice orchestration that he sings to a sunbathing Dorothy Malone. If his rendition sounds gruff and careless, it's probably because "Innamorata," while clearly a popular tune, is structured a bit like a song from an operetta with a middle section that rises and rises dramatically. As he sang, Dean had to lower his voice a bit so that he could hit the high note, with felicitous results. Malone is unaware that Dean is on the roof deck with her and asks MacLaine who's singing the number on the radio. "That's the guy who had the hit with 'That's Amore,'" Shirley tells her. (Shirley does a comical reprise of "Innamorata" and gives it even more oomph.)

Songwriters Harry Warren and Jack Brooks provided "Innamorata" and several other numbers for the picture. "When You Pretend" is sung—badly—by Jerry to Dean; when Dean takes over in the second verse, he sounds like Caruso compared to Lewis, making the forgettable, derivative number sound better than it is. Dean also sings "You Look So Familiar" to Dottie Malone, but his voice sounds kind of wobbly on the track. A more successful number is "My Lucky Song," which Dean sings after he gets his first paycheck from the comic publisher. The song isn't necessarily that great, but it's well performed by Dean, who is clearly enjoying himself, and well staged by Tashlin, who has Dean march down the street and all over the place, encountering a small black street band and a cute Shirley Temple-type moppet who dances with him. Alas, the title song, which Dean sings over the credits and reprises at the end, is quite dreadful. Dean wisely declined to record this number, but he did go into the studio for the others as well as a jazzy, brassy cover of "Standing on the Corner," the snappy Frank Loesser watching-the-girls-go-by song from his Broadway smash *The Most Happy Fella*.

Artists and Models wears out its welcome after a while, mostly because of the long, tiresome climax with Rick and Betsy rescuing Eugene from the clutches of the bogus Bat Lady (Eva Gabor) as she and her bed of spies try to wrest secrets that Eugene has no knowledge of from his brain. Otherwise, the movie is more entertaining than most Martin and Lewis films, and for once Hal Wallis seems to have spent, relatively speaking, a lot of money on the production (reportedly one and a half million).

Dean and Dorothy Malone were delighted to be working together again, with Malone in a much bigger part than she had in *Scared Stiff*. Supposedly Tashlin didn't think she had much sex appeal and wanted her to play it cute instead of sexy, but this seems inexplicable considering she was one of the most sensual actresses in Hollywood at the time. However, Hal Wallis and Shirley MacLaine had no love lost between them. She would later claim that Wallis had chased her around a desk, and Wallis would call the incident "totally fictitious. She was a cheap chorus girl living in a cold-water flat. She hasn't a grain of gratitude in her." Wallis would also claim that he had "started her career in pictures," but MacLaine had actually made her debut in director-producer Alfred Hitchcock's *The Trouble with Harry* the year before *Artists and Models*. She and Dean would work together often in the future.

Playing the Queen of the Art Student's Ball in the film's final scene, but with no dialogue, is gorgeous Swedish starlet Anita Ekberg, who'd be seen to better advantage in Tashlin's next Martin and Lewis movie. Stunned by her good looks and fantastic figure, Hal Wallis had bought her contract from John Wayne's Batjac productions (Wayne, incredibly, had cast Ekberg as a Chinese mother in *Blood Alley*), and Wayne's contract as well, and decided the former model would be very decorative in *Artists and Models*. *Playboy* magazine applauded the decision, lauding the production as the first to "showcase the Anita Ekberg fuselage in anything approximating the way it should be showcased." Jerry paints tic-tac-toe on her back during the ball sequence.

Artists and Models got mostly negative reviews, but decades later it's one of the most fondly remembered of the team's musical comedies and not just for the performance by Jerry Lewis. "Dino is given more opportunity to shine than in most other Martin and Lewis vehicles," opined David J. Hogan in a retrospective *Filmfax* review of 1997. "He's not just a supporting player, here; to the contrary, the story is propelled by Rick's predicaments and ambitions. Martin was an outstanding straight man but given a chance, he could more than hold his own against Jerry in the comedy arena. The script allows Dean plenty of funny lines . . . . Tashlin, Lewis, and Martin are giants of American entertainment. *Artists and Models* is a delicious, not-to-be-missed showcase for their unique gifts."

Hal Wallis decided, temporarily, that his next production with the boys was going to be called *The Story of Martin and Lewis*, which would not only capitalize on all the publicity they got—their feud, Dean's marital problems—but which would really have them playing themselves instead of some made-up comedy duo as was usually the case. But Dean had other things on his mind besides movies, hit records, Jerry Lewis, and a possible solo career. He was given a whopping tax bill from the IRS, and a temporary lien was put on his bank account. And he and Jeanne were having troubles again—or at least the same old troubles had resurfaced. Some say that Jeanne was annoyed that Dean wouldn't make the permanent break from Jerry, whom she disliked, along with Jerry's wife. Others say Jeanne was tired of staying home all day with the kids and staying home all night with Dean, but Dean was pooped after a long day at the studio, especially after getting up so early, and just wanted to relax and watch TV. He probably would have let her go off to social occasions on her own or with an escort, but like most wives, she understandably wanted her husband beside her.

This time, reportedly, Dean suggested that Jeanne take the kids and go off for a while to cool down. He could see how bothered she was—he'd had lots of experience with dissatisfied wives—and the last thing he wanted was for her to start drinking to deal with her distress the way poor Betty had. Jeanne left for Palm Springs, where she rented a house with the boys while Dean stayed in their new Beverly Hills estate on Mountain Drive. Dean did not want the marriage to end and begged some of his friends to talk to her, to explain how it was—that he loved her, but he worked hard and had to have *his own space*. Both made it clear to the press that the problem was *not* another woman, at least not the *whole* problem. During this separation Dean accompanied Dorothy Malone to the premiere of her film *Sincerely Yours*—most famous as the picture that for all time made it clear that Liberace was no movie star—and shared a passionate kiss for the cameras that had the whole town talking.

But it was not Dorothy Malone who was the threat to Dean's marriage. A starlet named Lori Nelson, who'd appeared in *Revenge of the Creature* (of *Black Lagoon* fame) the year before, had been tapped to appear in *Where Men are Men*, the next Martin and Lewis film (for their York Productions), with a script by Sidney Sheldon and with Norman Taurog again at the helm. This was yet another remake, of the Bing Crosby starrer *Rhythm on the Range*, which Taurog had also directed. By this time Jeanne and the boys were back from Palm Springs, and Dean had moved back into that house on Sunset Boulevard he'd employed when he'd been separated from Betty. Although Lori Nelson didn't make much of an impression in the new movie, retitled *Pardners* (1956), the twenty-two-year-old made quite an impression on thirty-nine-year-old Dean, who wanted her to keep house with him.

It was the whole Jeanne–beauty queen thing all over, Dean now needing the hero-worshiping adoration of a comparatively unspoiled young girl to stave off the fact he was just about to hit the big four-O. Was the responsibility of a wife and family—plus the first cast-off wife and the children from that union that he never saw—too much for him to handle? Was he eternally seeking bachelorhood, wanting to start fresh over and over again, falling in love and getting married until he got it right? Could someone like Dean Martin *ever* get it right? He wanted someone to come home to, someone who could keep him company without complaining—or even talking to him unless he wanted her to—someone who saw him as her hero, while at the same time he wanted the freedom to bed as many women as possible. As Jeanne would say ruefully many times over the years, "Dean Martin was not the ideal husband."

Meanwhile Dean wondered if Lori Nelson might just be that ideal wife who existed only in his dreams and imagination. Their relationship ran hot and cold as Dean debated the relative merits of a fresh young babe with ambitions versus the warm, loyal love of the mother of his youngest children. He didn't want to cause more pain, which a divorce would inevitably engender. But Jeanne was turning into Betty—he could see that same discontent in her eyes—and who wanted to go home to *that* every night? He balanced a reconciliation with Jeanne while keeping Lori in reserve. Lori kept his interest by holding off on the ultimate prize, knowing full well that once Dean had sampled her wares, his interest might wane. But Jeanne played the trump card and got him back: She was pregnant with their third child, Gina. Reluctantly, Dean returned to their home to play husband again, but his heart wasn't really in it. It must be remembered that Dean was exceedingly restless during this period, and despite a couple of number one records, he was not certain he could sustain a career without Jerry. The man had much on his mind.

In the prologue to *Pardners*, which takes place in 1885, Wade (Jerry) and Slim (Dean) are killed by the Hollister gang, and as they expire they express the hope that their sons will avenge them. Twenty-five years later, Wade Jr. goes west to escape an unwelcome marriage along with a petulant Slim Jr., who falls for a pretty ranch owner (Lori Nelson) and tries to protect her from a group of masked raiders led, of course, by the Hollister clan. Wade and Slim defeat the villains, and all ends happily, with the boys addressing the audience at the conclusion. "You keep comin' to see us, 'cause we sure like seein' you," Dean says.

In truth, their working and personal relationship had become a grim affair. In his autobiography Jerry wrote about how he just went through the motions all during filming, and due to the breakdown of communication with Dean he felt isolated even on the crowded set: "'It's a take!' Then walking off across the lot back to the trailer and sitting there, drowsy, indifferent, thinking of nothing and nobody . . ." It wasn't just that Dean was avoiding Jerry but that he was preoccupied with his attractive leading lady.

On the road doing club dates Jerry and Dean mostly got along fine. But once they were back at home or at the studio, their assorted sycophants would start to work on them, passing along gossip, feeding their paranoia, until the old jealousies and insecurities would begin to resurface. Jerry was described as being tense and nervous, while Dean, even with his tax and marital problems, was generally calm and relatively acquiescent. After the contretemps over *Three Ring Circus*, he had come to a certain acceptance: He would make his break when he could. The same went for his marriage. Two people felt especially strong emotional ties to him— Jeanne and Jerry—and he would deal with them when the time came. He would not let either of them *get* to him. Nothing was worth having a stroke over.

Certainly not *Pardners*, in which Dean is in fine fettle, exhibiting his trademark cocky insouciance in every scene. He's particularly good as he dramatically tells Jerry's mother (Agnes Moorehead) about the legendary day her husband and his father died in a gun battle. All the while Jerry mugs, and in contrast he seems sillier than ever. Whatever was going on offscreen, the two still play well together, but they had stiff competition in the acting department from the aforementioned Miss Moorehead, who really perks up the picture as a wealthy harridan, and Jeff (*This Island Earth*) Morrow as a gravel-voiced hoodlum, Rio. An extremely underrated actor, Morrow is terrific and nearly unrecognizable in the part. The long fight scene he has with Jerry and Dean in the saloon and elsewhere is one of the film's highlights. The picture also demonstrates the sad comedown of Lon Chaney Jr., who had given a superb performance as Lenny in 1939's *Of Mice and Men* and was now given not a single line of dialogue— only a few muttered asides—as one of Hollister's gang, but he needed the work. Lee Van Cleef, who went on to greater fortunes in "spaghetti westerns," also had a small role as a gang member.

Jimmy Van Heusen, who composed the songs, was no Richard Rogers, but his numbers were pleasant and tuneful. Dean was handed "Whistlin' Wind" and "Me and You and the Moon," which he sings to Lori Nelson with more vowel-twisting than usual. The number ends, oddly, with a quick fade-out before their lips can meet. Jerry was given "Buckskin Beauty," and he and Dean team on the catchy title tune.

By now Hal Wallis had given up his idea of doing the Martin and Lewis story as a film project—the way things were going, they might not be together too much longer—and looked around for something he could substitute. He had an old script entitled *Route 66*, which he had commissioned years earlier as a vehicle for Shirley Booth with perhaps Humphrey Bogart as her costar. The two would have played strangers who jointly win a car in a sweepstakes and decide to take to the highway for some adventures and romance. When Frank Tashlin reworked it as *Beginner's Luck*,

MARTINI MAN

Dean and Jerry were to win the car and head out for Hollywood and excitement.

The two men were not speaking by the time filming began on the new movie, which had been retitled *Hollywood or Bust*. There had been arguments, hurt feelings, ego clashes—each was afraid the other wanted him *out*—and there just seemed so little to say. After years of being both kissed and clobbered by Jerry onstage and on-screen, Dean had had enough. Jerry reacted by becoming livid at Dean's dispassionate attitude toward him; he couldn't stand the way he just didn't seem to give a damn. Because he was afraid to confront Dean directly, to really tell him how upset he was and how angered he was by his actions, Jerry, as he admitted years later, took it out on everyone around him. He was also angry at himself, as he put it, for not being able to accept that the long ride with Dean was finally over. First he risked the wrath of former light-heavyweight champion Maxie Rosenbloom, who had a small role in the picture, by mocking him mercilessly. Then he made an issue over the presence of a Great Dane in the story, even though the script had been approved months before. (Perhaps he remembered that scene-stealing chimp in *My Friend Irma Goes West*.) Then he zeroed in on the director, whom he called Tish. "I laid it into him, grandstanding, playing the king, reacting intemperately to his directions before each take." Tashlin finally freaked and ordered him off the set. *"You are a discourteous, obnoxious prick!"* Tashlin screamed. *"An embarrassment to me and a disgrace to the profession!"* Jerry apologized to the director over the phone later that evening, and "Tish" agreed to take him back.

How ironic that the last movie Dean and Jerry did together is one of their better ones. After winning the car, they head out for Hollywood, where Malcolm (Jerry) hopes to meet the movie star of his dreams, Anita Ekberg (playing herself), and Steve (Dean) just hopes to find work. Steve schemes to rid himself of Malcolm, but his plans all go awry. On the road they have two lovable companions: Malcolm's pet, Mr. Bascombe (the aforementioned Great Dane who, as Jerry feared, practically steals the picture); and Terry (Patricia Crowley from *Money from Home*), who falls for Steve and vice versa. A little old lady hitchhiker holds up the boys, and at one point Mr. Bascombe drives off in the car by himself. Tashlin kept the sight gags coming and put together an exciting scene when the boys have to push their prize automobile off the train tracks before its gets mulched by an oncoming locomotive. The movie, unfortunately, loses steam when the boys actually get out to Hollywood, although Ekberg's voluptuous presence certainly bolsters the proceedings. Ekberg became the centerpiece of the advertising campaign—for obvious reasons, given the title—which featured a full-length picture of her in between the name of the movie and cast list on one side and head shots of Martin and Lewis on the other.

Dean is fine in the picture, although he seems a little disinterested during the prologue when he's introducing assorted movie fans (all played by Jerry) from around the world. The songs by Sammy Fain and Paul Francis Webster include "Let's Be Friendly," which Dean sings to Pat in an insinuating manner when they're preparing for sleep at the side of the road. This was Dean's only solo number; the rest he had to share with Jerry, Pat, or both: "It Looks Like Love" is a duet by him and Pat at a recording session in Hollywood; "The Wild and Woolly West" is a trio as the group sing about each state of the union they pass. The highlight is "A Day in the Country," a pleasant tune well visualized by Tashlin, which has Dean and Jerry again singing in their car as they drive past bicycling beauties and cuties on tractors, through covered bridges, past bucolic streams, even standing up in the front seat at one point with no hands on the wheel. The two join forces for the title song over the credits, but in the film Jerry makes it a solo with *the dog*. But the ultimate indignity for Dean was the scene when Pat and Jerry chat in the front seat while he lies down in the back seat of the car with Mr. Bascombe, whose head is on his shoulder. Dean had to put up with the animal's flatulence for an entire afternoon of shooting. Enough was enough!

According to Jerry, as the final day of shooting drew near, he approached Dean and tried to revive their friendship. He told him that what had made them really click as a team was "the love that we still have for each other." Dean supposedly replied (and it was this reply that convinced Jerry to call it quits): "You can talk about love all you want. To me you're nothing but a dollar sign." (Subsequent retellings of the story generally make Dean's language a little saltier.) This anecdote is generally used to illustrate Dean's callousness and cynicism, his hardness and unforgiving nature, but given his emotional state as well as his distrust of Jerry at the time, it hardly makes him a monster.

But did he even say it? The only source is Jerry Lewis, who was never objective about his ex-partner. When questioned about it years later, Dean said: "How the hell do I know what I said back then? We weren't speaking to each other; I was fed up with the whole business. If I did say something like that, that he was just a dollar sign, it was probably afterward, after he attacked my wife in print. I was *really* mad afterward."

Whatever the case, Martin and Lewis were *through*.

PART THREE

Solo

NINE

On His Own

Now that Dean and Jerry had decided irrevocably to split, there were still contracts to honor and legal decisions to be made. Their MCA agent, Herman Citron, continued to represent both of them, but he had to renegotiate everything as if they were two distinct and separate parties. Paramount was compliant, but Hal Wallis still expected pictures from the team in addition to one per year in which they would star individually, and he wanted over a million dollars if they wanted to buy out their contract with him. Eventually he settled for four more movies from each of them for a total of eight pictures instead of the four more Martin and Lewis movies he had originally been entitled to. NBC maintained that their deal had only been for Martin and Lewis as a duo and balked at tearing up their contract and starting over, but a suit from Jerry and Dean's York Productions (which Dean retained an interest in for many years and which was *not* dissolved along with the partnership) got the network to change its mind. Their last TV appearance together was on a muscular dystrophy telethon. All opposition and other entanglements were slowly falling by the wayside; Dean would soon have his wish and be a solo.

"I think we'd still be together today if it wasn't for the outside forces that broke the team up," Jerry said in 1992, but he conceded that "it broke at the perfect time; it was time for it to break." He maintained, "I was never concerned with how the public was going to accept me. I was concerned with how they were going to accept Dean. Because if the public didn't accept me, I'd have made adjustments, but if they didn't accept Dean, it was my fault, and I could never have recovered from that."

Before acceding to their demands, Paramount did try to get them to make one more picture for them, a script entitled *Damon and Pythias* that had been written by Don McGuire of *Three Ring Circus* fame. Dean mustered every objection he could to the script because the simple fact was that he no longer wanted to work with Jerry. Don McGuire claimed that his screenplay did not shunt Dean to the side, as Dean charged, but that he had to give the comedy to Jerry because "Dean was a terrible actor. He could barely talk," which was patently untrue. At a meeting with Jerry and Paramount execs, Dean listened patiently, then stormed out of the room after voicing a few salty expressions.

Dean and Jerry made separate announcements about the breakup on the penultimate day of filming of *Hollywood or Bust*. Hearing of the split, Lou Costello, in what many saw as an act of a certain perversity, took out an ad in the trades imploring the boys to reconsider for the sake of their fans. (Ironically, Costello would split from Abbott shortly afterward.) By the time their final film was released in theaters, everyone knew of their animosity, and few of their fans were interested in seeing them playact their friendship and affection on the screen. It was as if they couldn't accept the fact that the two had been actors all along. Whatever the names of the characters they essayed, to their public Dean and Jerry were always Dean and Jerry, and now that they were no longer together and no longer speaking, going to see *Hollywood or Bust* would be like viewing a corpse. The film made the least money of any Martin and Lewis picture.

They were importuned to honor some club engagements and appeared at the 500 Club in Atlantic City, where their act had gotten its start. Then they did the Copacapana in July of '56, the scene of some of their biggest triumphs in New York. One night, during a particularly boisterous bit of business, Dean's shoe came down hard on Jerry's foot, fracturing two toes and making him cry out in such obvious agony that everyone in the audience was alerted that something was wrong. Dean told both Jerry and the reporters that the whole thing had been an accident; they'd gotten carried away and he'd lost his balance, and his foot wound up coming down, much too hard, where Jerry wasn't supposed to be in the first place, and gosh he felt awful. But some observers noticed how much Jerry had pulled on Dean's hair, smacking him a little too hard, and many wouldn't have blamed Dean if he'd just had too much and snapped, getting even for months of rough treatment. Jerry saw a doctor, got his foot bandaged, and wore slippers.

The last night at the Copa was packed full of celebrities who'd come to see the swan song of Martin and Lewis, among them Jackie Gleason,

Milton Berle, Steve Lawrence, Jack Benny, and Sammy Davis Jr., who'd become Jerry's next best friend as well as a member of Sinatra's Rat Pack along with Dean. There were foes as well as friends; some were just as glad the machine had ground to a halt and that the world would soon see the last of Martin and Lewis. By all accounts it was a rousing, electrifying finish. They encored with the "best pals" theme song from *Pardners*.

Jackie Gleason, who'd overimbibed that evening, managed to lift himself up to the stage and told the crowd that this terrible thing must not happen, that these wonderful, talented boys must not go their separate ways; he wouldn't allow it. "We *can't* let them split up, can we, everyone?" Jackie asked the crowd morosely. But it was much too late for reconciliations; deals had been broken, contracts shredded, new deals made. It was just too late.

The consensus of opinion was that Jerry, who'd always been the chief draw of the Martin and Lewis comedies, would have no trouble going it alone but that Dean would have a tough row to hoe as a solo. Still, fellow entertainers were very supportive in the press. Jackie Gleason said of Dean: "He's got a great sense of timing. He never presses. He gives the impression that he's a nice guy, which audiences love. He's coordinated like an athlete, which means he can dance when he sets his mind to it. Wait and see—in a couple of years Dean will be bigger than Jerry."

Bing Crosby, who'd apparently come to be rather flattered by Dean's emulation of him, also felt sorry for him. As Louella Parsons reported in her column of May 12, 1957, "I like Jerry, too, but there's a certain depth of sincerity about Dean Martin, a sweetness that I find very attractive. In our town Bing Crosby and certain of the other singers like Dean immensely. I remember New Year's Eve meeting Bing, who said he was going over to Dean's house to a small party. I sensed that Bing wanted Dean to know that he was very much his friend. I hope I haven't given the idea that Bing isn't Jerry's friend, but I think he felt, as many did, that at that point Dean needed friendship." Bing's name was being linked with Dean's in the columns because he, Dean, and Frank Sinatra had recently done a TV special in which they introduced soon-to-be *South Pacific* star Mitzi Gaynor to everyone in televisionland.

Perhaps Dean and Jerry could have remained friends, been like exspouses who've had an amicable divorce, but they couldn't resist making public comments, and this only intensified the paranoia and resentment. The trouble started when Jerry wrote a story for *Look* magazine in which he attacked not only Dean but Dean's wife, Jeanne. Dean felt he could defend himself, but how dare Jerry make negative public remarks about his wife, who should have been out of bounds. She had nothing to do with their problems—Jerry was just jealous of her, he told the press. The article only served to revive their feud and cement their permanent separation.

After Jerry's piece was published, Dean no longer held back. To *TV Guide* he said: "I'm not sore. I've just severed all connections, that's all. As far as I'm concerned, Jerry Lewis doesn't exist anymore in my life. I like it just fine that way. But I'm tired of being the heavy, that's all." He expressed great irritation at the way Jerry had thrown out all of his pictures of Dean. "I still have pictures of Jerry all over the house," he said. He added: "Jerry acts four. He's pressing. He's trying to go too far too fast." He complained about the way Jerry would be so busy messing in production matters on their movies that he would run off and leave him with a stand-in to rehearse with. Of course, Dean had never been much for rehearsing, anyway, so it's likely that in his anger at Jerry he not only carried on about the major things that stuck in his craw but anything he could think of. Jerry countered by charging that all Dean wanted to do was make one movie in a month and then play golf for the rest of the year. "I couldn't be that lazy if I tried," he said. Dean shot back with: "Jerry's trying hard to be a director. He couldn't even direct traffic."

Asked on *America After Dark* on NBC if it was true that Jerry had a "desire to inject pathos and heart into their act," Dean replied that he "wouldn't have objected if he knew how to do it—or felt it!" His attacks on Jerry on the *Tonight* show so appalled radio personality and columnist Barry Gray that he indicted him in print, essentially asking why he had stayed with Jerry for so long if he had been so awful. Jerry countered with several volleys of his own. And so on and so on.

Despite whatever fears he had about his future, Dean displayed one positive change that friends noted with approval. He had become much more socially and conversationally outgoing now that he'd severed from Jerry. A lot of this simply had to do with the fact that when Jerry wasn't around, Dean didn't have to compete with him or wait for a chance to get a word in edgewise. He was also more relaxed knowing that a decision had been made, he would never have to feel like a Siamese twin again, and his fortunes would rise or fall, however it went, on their own. Just making that basic decision, regardless of the repercussions and the financial losses that he and Jerry would take because of it, had put his mind at ease. He was drinking less and sleeping better. Jeanne was also very supportive, standing by her man in his hour of need as she had done and would do again many, many times over the years.

While Paramount and Hal Wallis were mulling over exactly what to do with Dean, Joe Pasternak, who'd once tested Dean for *Till the Clouds Roll By*, contacted MCA and offered the singer the starring role in a new film he was producing for MGM. Pasternak had been considering working with Dean on this project or others in the past, but he had always seemed inseparable from Jerry. Now that they were officially defunct as a duo, Pasternak made his move. Dean had also been offered the lead in the film version of the Broadway musical *The Pajama Game*, but he passed when MGM offered him a quarter of a million dollars to do Pasternak's *Ten Thousand Bedrooms*. Anna Maria Alberghetti, another typical, transplanted Italian starlet of that era, if even more beautiful than the average, was a much more appealing leading lady to Dean than *Pajama Game*'s Doris Day. In the final analysis, however, it was Dean's agents at MCA who advised him to do the picture, primarily because their commissions would be that much higher. Dean would live to regret ever listening to them.

In *Ten Thousand Bedrooms* Dean plays a hotel tycoon, modeled on Conrad Hilton, who travels to Rome to check out a possible new addition to his hotel chain. There he meets a flighty, flirtatious young lady, played by Alberghetti, who complains that she can't get married until her three older sisters have tied the knot. Dean romances Anna but slowly begins to fall under the more subtle spell of one of her sisters (Eva Bartok), who is more demure and dignified, which is OK because Anna has really fallen for Dean's pilot (Dewey Martin, no relation). But what to do about the two older sisters (Lisa Gay and Lisa Montell)? Dean hatches up a plan to fly in eligible males from New York, but a big mix-up results with all the sisters matched up with the wrong guys and so on. Finally things are straightened out, and everyone is more or less happily wedded.

None of Dean's co-workers noticed any tension or apprehension in him while he was making the film that might make him or break him in show business. That was because he was so happy to be making a picture without being Jerry's sidekick that he failed to notice that *Ten Thousand Bedrooms* was essentially a stinker. He loved filming on location in Rome, and his relationship with his wife, who had accompanied him to Italy and who was pregnant with their daughter (Gina Carolyn was born in December of 1956), had never been better. He got four songs to sing all by himself. His female costars were lovely. And everyone from director Richard Thorpe to dapper film veteran Paul Henreid, who played a count in name only who's also in love with Eva, were more than cordial. "Dean was happy-go-lucky, whistling to work, pleasant to everyone," Thorpe remembered, "as if he'd just lost the weight of the world on his shoulders. One of the easiest actors I've ever worked with."

The picture was decked out in Technicolor and Cinemascope with lots of prettily photographed scenic views of Rome such as the Fontana di Trevi, but nothing could compensate for its empty core, for that forgettable script. Never more than pleasant fluff with a mild chuckle or two, someone had left the humor and whimsy out of *Ten Thousand Bedrooms*. The only thing that might have saved it would have been if something actually went *on* in any of those bedrooms, but the title of the movie was just a tease. Even *Hollywood or Bust* eventually delivered the bust. *Ten Thousand Bedrooms* delivered little. Years later Paul Henreid pronounced it "downright awful." (Nowadays it is often confused with the 1961 Rock Hudson–Gina Lollobrigida starrer *Come September*, which also took place in Italy and had Bobby Darin singing the suggestive "Multiplication.")

The critics agreed, although some were kind to Dean. Jerry Lewis was referred to in virtually every review. The *New York Herald-Tribune* opined that "Dean Martin himself is a personable hero, who really seems to think that these antics are amusing. When things get dull, he bursts into song and then suddenly, everything is just as dull. It would do no harm at all to have Jerry Lewis around." The *New York Times* was less merciful, pronouncing the film "ridiculous and trite; it wears pretty thin in the course of two hours," and adding that "more than a couple of vacancies are clearly apparent in *Ten Thousand Bedrooms*. One is the emptiness alongside Dean Martin, who here plays the lead without his old partner Jerry Lewis and that's an emptiness indeed! He's just another nice-looking crooner without his pal . . . a fellow with little humor and a modicum of charm."

Dean was not thrilled. All the critics who had lambasted Jerry for his dizziness and over-the-top performances now acted as if they couldn't live without him. But he did come to agree with the critics about the picture. "I wanted to be in *serious* pictures. I knew I could do it, I *knew*. So what did they put me in? *Ten Thousand Bedrooms*. That picture stunk up the place so bad, even my best friends wouldn't talk to me." In reality the movie was no worse than a few of the Martin and Lewis features, but *then* Dean could have blamed Jerry's excesses, and now he had no one to blame but himself. He was furious at his advisers but mostly at himself for not having stuck it out and waited for something better, but he knew Jerry was rushing through *Damon and Pythias*—retitled *The Delicate Delinquent*— and he wanted to have his own feature ready. What made matters worse was that *The Delicate Delinquent* was a big hit, establishing Jerry as a major movie star on his own, while *Ten Thousand Bedrooms* failed at the box office. Adding insult to injury, Jerry had done a solo album entitled *Jerry Lewis Just Sings*, and it was a hit. One of the tracks, "Rock-a-bye Your Baby with a Dixie Melody," even went gold!

Adding to Dean's angst was the fact that he was now forty years old, a difficult period for a man or woman who's thirsting for major success. Not old but hardly young, he *felt* old, and he feared becoming a has-been, being seen as washed up. He wondered how he'd pay all his bills, keep the house, keep up his lifestyle, pay for all those children. It seemed as if he'd been in show business most of his life, and he still felt insecure, still felt—incredibly, after all the good that had happened—that he hadn't really made it.

Dean and everyone else thought his movie career was over, but at least he could count on club dates and recordings to take up the slack. He hadn't performed on his own for many years, except for a time when Jerry came down with a high fever and had to stay in bed the night before an important engagement at Ciro's. Dean went on by himself, but the first night there were many celebrities in the audience that he could call on to pinch hit for Jerry, so he didn't have to just talk to himself or sing number after number. He rounded out the week with singer Tony Martin (no relation) as his partner.

But now he had to face the fact that he had to go on alone night after night with no help from anyone. Sure, he'd had a singing act before he met Jerry, but that's *all* it was, and after all those years of clowning and badinage with Jerry, the audience was expecting more. What could he do? He asked some of his creative friends for help, but nothing they came up with seemed right for him. Finally he got together with Ed Simmons, one of the comedy writers from the Colgate show he'd done with Jerry, who wrote some jokes for his solo debut at the Sands hotel and casino in Las Vegas, and also suggested it might be a good idea if he develop a new character to go with the new act. Dean had always been the exasperated parent to Jerry's child, but that would obviously no longer work unless he wanted a new partner—which he most certainly did not. Simmons thought that the mock heavy drinker bit had worked for some nightclub performers in the past, and it might work for Dean, who liked his spirits. All he had to do was exaggerate it a bit for a comic effect; the audience would know he was joking and wasn't really a lush. Dean was at first hesitant, then decided to go with Simmons's ideas. On his own he came up with the idea of occasionally throwing out a screwy, often sexually suggestive, line instead of the real lyric. You could get away with a little more with a pleasantly blitzed nightclub audience, and they seemed to appreci-ate his substitute lyrics. The drunk gags, the new lyrics—it all seemed to work.

Simmons later claimed that he got not a single penny in recompense, but perhaps Dean felt compensation wasn't required when all Simmons had really done was suggest he do a drunk act like Joe E. Lewis and offer a couple of gags. Besides, Dean had been referring to his love of liquor on-stage, if not quite as emphatically or as often, when he was with Jerry and even before. Rightly or wrongly, Dean felt Simmons, who had recently broken up with writing partner Norman Lear and was looking for work, was trying to take too much credit, another one of the "parasites" who Dean felt had plagued him throughout his career.

The crowds loved him at the Copa Room (not to be confused with the real Copacabana in New York) at the Sands and begged for more when he left the stage. Dean endeared himself to owner Jack Entratter by keep-ing the show short so that the audience could get back to the gambling tables quicker and lose a lot more loot. Dean couldn't have cared less about that, although he loved to gamble himself; he felt a forty-minute act was more than enough work. Entratter signed him up for five years at twenty-five thousand per week every time he played the Sands. Dean also wowed 'em at the Coconut Grove in Los Angeles and got respectful reviews from the trades and sometimes even better than that.

But it wasn't enough. He needed more hit records—which weren't coming—and he *needed* to be in the movies, where the really big money was, if he wasn't going to be considered a Hollywood has-been. While Herman Citron at MCA told him he'd see what he could do, he took off on a tour across the country with his new act; Jeanne went with him. As Dean remembered it: "I was in Pittsburgh in 1957 with no prospects, seven kids, and enough alimony and child support to start a foundation. Jeanne and me was [sic] just wondering what bar I could make a deal with when the phone rang." It was Herman Citron. Dean had been offered a role in the film adaptation of *The Young Lions*, which was to costar two of Hollywood's most acclaimed young actors, Marlon Brando and Montgomery Clift.

The Young Lions began life as a novel by Irwin Shaw that was deemed eminently filmable. As writer David Shipman put it, "Shaw had written precisely the sort of second-remove stuff that Hollywood understands best." The three main characters were a feisty Jewish American G.I. (Clift), a Nazi officer (Brando), and a Broadway star who does what he can to avoid the draft. The two Americans encounter the German only at the very end of the picture.

Tony Randall, whose agent at that time was the cast-off Abby Greshler, was set to play the Broadway star, Michael Whittaker. But Herman Citron thought the role would be perfect for Dean—dramatic but not too much of a stretch—and contacted the film's director, Edward Dmytryk, to plead his case. Citron reminded Dmytryk how the supposedly washed-up Frank Sinatra had surprised everyone and won an Oscar for *From Here to Eternity* the year before. "Dean Martin is not Sinatra!" Dmytryk said. By the time of *Eternity*, Sinatra had played several serious roles, but such was not the case with Dean. Nevertheless Dmytryk said he'd think it over and got in touch with Montgomery Clift. Clift only knew of Dean as the "other half" of the silly Jerry Lewis combo and was horrified at the idea of casting him. But then he caught Randall's film debut in a sex farce entitled *Oh Men! Oh Women!* and decided he'd rather go with Dean (Randall was a fine actor in the right part, but his light style might not have been suitable for *Young Lions*). Dmytryk agreed to hire Dean for the role. A furious Greshler circulated the untrue story that Dmytryk had dumped Randall only because MCA had told him, "No Martin—no Brando and Clift!"

When Dean found out about the offer in that hotel room in Pittsburgh, he was overjoyed, squeezing Jeanne and singing and dancing around the bed. He was also a little daunted—*Brando*, for heaven's sake, and Montgomery Clift! Talk about going from one extreme to the other. But he felt sure—almost sure—that he was up to the challenge. There was one disappointment; a big one. Citron was only able to get him about ten percent of the fee he'd been paid for *Ten Thousand Bedrooms*, but he assured Dean, who concurred, that appearing in the film would ultimately increase his coffers many times over, which it did.

Almost everyone working on *The Young Lions* was coming from a bad place. This was the first film Clift had appeared in since a devastating car accident had destroyed his face and necessitated expensive reconstructive surgery (he did finish parts of *Raintree County* after the accident, however). Dmytryk had been one of the Hollywood Ten blacklisted during the McCarthy era and had spent one year in jail before being reinstated in the director's guild. Marlon Brando was making the difficult transition from young stud roles to older, flabbier character parts. And of course Dean, after the foolish debacle of *Ten Thousand Bedrooms*, knew that this might be his only opportunity to redeem himself and prove himself to the many—and they were legion—naysayers. *The Young Lions* was his *From Here to Eternity*.

There were other problems, as well. In the novel Brando's character, Christian, became more committed to Nazism as the story progressed;

Brando wanted his part to be more sympathetic and influenced screen-writer Edward Anhalt to make Christian *less* committed to the cause as the story unfolded. Shaw was enraged when he heard what had happened; *The Young Lions* was always meant to be virulently anti-Nazi, not just the comparatively tepid antiwar film that emerged. Brando and Shaw got into screaming matches on the set—Clift sided with Shaw; he didn't especially like Brando, although the two were not exactly feuding as many people believed—while Dean did his best to stay out of it.

Brando had his clique; Clift and Dean had each other. Clift helped Dean with his lines, as he had done for Sinatra on *From Here to Eternity*, and the two became good drinking buddies and close friends. Monty was attracted to Dean's easygoing, amiable nature, may even have found him sexually appealing, and tended to monopolize his time when they weren't in front of the cameras. Dean enjoyed Clift's sense of humor, such as the time during a party scene when Monty, who was not in the sequence, hunkered down out of sight next to a piano Dean was standing beside and started mischievously tickling the other man's leg. Dmytryk had to stop the action until he could figure out why Dean was laughing; Clift was then told to go to his dressing room and behave. Sometimes it was Dean who cracked up Monty, such as the time they were filming an outdoor sequence in an icy storm when Dmytryk read them a telegram from the Fox production chief, Sid Rogell, who was wondering why a little bad weather should hold up the production. When a clap of thunder suddenly reverberated after Dmytryk was through, Dean looked to the sky solemnly and said, "Massa Sid, we're really trying!"

Martin's nickname for Clift was Spider, not only because he spoke with exaggerated, theatrical flourishes, but because his abuse of drugs and alcohol gave him a whole complement of nervous gestures. He would be standing up one minute, slouching the next, off crouching in the shadows a few seconds later, always working his hands and arms. He was almost as spastic as Jerry Lewis but a lot more fun. Dean never had a lot of fun clubbing with Jerry, who didn't drink. That was certainly not the case with Monty. Still, there were times when Dean wanted to be left alone—as usual, he needed breathing room, no matter how much he may have liked a person—and he would have to hide out in a café, his face hidden by a newspaper, to keep Monty from finding him.

But Dean, perhaps because he needed a new best friend and was grateful for the time Monty took to help him, felt genuine affection for Clift. He had some of the crew members make up a special chair for him with an arachnid insignia on the back for his friend Spider. After Clift's death, Dean described Monty in effusive terms as "another friend very dear to me. Nobody wanted him around, nobody would eat with him. So I took him to dinner, or I would have a drink with him, or I would put him to bed 'cause he was always on pills, you know. He was such a sad, sad man, and he was like a boy, so unhappy and rejected, and so I'd say. 'Come on, Clift, let's go.' And I'd bring him with me everywhere, and I'd say, 'If you don't want him, you don't want me.' And he'd leave the party. But first I'd spit in their faces for him."

Most people on the set of *The Young Lions* knew that Clift was gay, though in those far-away fifties he was seen as tormented, and it was also theorized that he only entertained the notion of homosexual activity when he was drunk. The talk—some of it sympathetic, some of it less so—must have eventually made its way to Dean, who might have become suddenly wary of his drinking companion and a little guilty of his suspicions. This is likely why he claimed he hung out with Clift because "no one else would," so no one would think he had ulterior motives, although it's also true that Clift's drinking and drugging left many people impatient and angry with him. Dean would have felt about homosexuals the way most straight men did in that era: revulsion for the more flamboyant, ridiculous ones, whom he and Jerry had lampooned in their act; and honest pity and sympathy for those who, like Monty, could pass. Dean simply liked Monty too much, was too grateful to him for all he'd done—the friendship in a difficult time, the acting lessons in his first serious picture—to ever turn against him completely, whatever his proclivities.

Monty and Marlon nearly came to blows when it was time to film the final scene. In the novel the Nazi character kills Monty, then the actor kills the Nazi, but in the film only Brando dies. Brando wanted to make the most of his death scene and told Dmytryk he wanted to stagger into some barbed wire and stretch out his arms in the hoary cliché of a Christ figure. Clift thought the idea was ludicrous and said so, and Dmytryk concurred. On more than one occasion Clift noticed Brando watching surreptitiously from the sidelines as he did a scene and told the director, "Tell him he doesn't have to hide his face when he's watching me." Clift also restored some dialogue that Brando wanted cut.

Dmytryk later said, "Clift was clever and seemed not to be; Brando was stupid and pretended not to be." Of Dean he said, "I knew he could rise to the occasion. He had that ethnic, working-class background that gave him a real toughness. And I knew from all the other movies he'd made that he was a real pro. I mean, after Jerry Lewis, why would he be afraid to stand up to Brando or Clift?"

Dean comports himself well in the film, although the part of Michael Whittaker—a boozing, womanizing singer—was made to order for him.

Playing someone who at first does what he can to stay out of the war brought back uncomfortable memories for Dean, who had never served in World War Two and been heckled for it more than once. He certainly understood where Whittaker was coming from. He took the character and adapted it to himself instead of the other way around with effective results, though he plays it too unemotionally in the scenes when they liberate a concentration camp. (Dean would always have trouble expressing strong emotions on camera, as he often did in real life.) Brando gives one of his best performances in the film, and Monty is reminiscent of Maggio, Sinatra's character in *From Here to Eternity*.

Barbara Rush played the woman who embarrasses Dean into enlisting. She got to know him fairly well and had interesting things to say about him a few years later. "I think Dean hasn't much to say to a woman. I think a woman is to him something soft and cuddly and pretty, and he hasn't much time to waste on them. As for the modern aggressive woman, he doesn't even recognize her. I would be very surprised to hear about any adventures of Dean because I've seen many women in love with Dean—you have no idea how many—and he's always behaved with great kindness toward them, great patience, but also a sort of detachment and maybe embarrassment. They simply aren't very attractive to him. He prefers men because he can talk to them, play cards, and say rough words."

The Young Lions is breathtaking to look at, but like the novel it's simply too removed and Hollywoodish to become the important film it could have been—though it was certainly important as far as Dean's career was concerned. For each scene that's vivid and effective, two are phony and contrived. In its study of three men of war and the effect that war has on them and those around them, the picture lacks the certain, sharp, clear ring of truth that distinguishes a truly great motion picture.

Half the film was made on soundstages in Los Angeles, the other half in Paris, which Dean did not care for. "The only things I liked about Paris were the planes leaving it. I went there for seven days and stayed twelve weeks. The French don't like us, and I don't like them." One can imagine how Dean felt about the French once their film critics proclaimed his former partner a cinematic genius!

There was a new partner in Dean's future, however, another superstar who would team with him repeatedly and in some ways prove just as difficult to deal with as Jerry was.

TEN

Enter Sinatra

Jerry Lewis had the Muscular Dystrophy Association; Dean had the City of Hope. It had started out as a sanitarium for tubercular patients but now the City of Hope needed a new division devoted to leukemia research. Dean was tapped in May 1957 to be solo host of the Parade of Stars telethon broadcast from Manhattan from 10 P.M. until 5:30 P.M. the following day. Dean's guests included comedian Eddie Cantor, fellow crooner Perry Como, columnist and TV host Ed Sullivan, Phil Silvers of *Sergeant Bilko* fame, Polly Bergen from *The Stooge*, Milton Berle, George Jessel, and many, many others. By the time it was all over, the telethon had raised $804,000 in pledges, and the City of Hope began building what was christened the Dean Martin Blood Disease Center in Duarte, California. Dean did telethons for the City of Hope each May for the next few years, but it was never seen as a way to keep his name before the public as some believed Jerry Lewis's telethons were.

The telethon wasn't the only TV work Dean was doing. Five months later came the premiere of a series of specials on NBC billed as *The Dean Martin Show*. On his second show he had Frank Sinatra as his guest star. The first show was produced by Cy Howard of *My Friend Irma* fame, but the subsequent shows were produced and directed by Jack Donahue, a former choreographer who later directed Dean and Frank Sinatra in *Marriage on the Rocks*. Mae West of "Is that a gun in your pocket or are you just glad to see me?" fame was a guest on one of the later programs, and she and Dean—sort of the king and queen of leer—made a terrific if somewhat grotesque combo, albeit sexier than Dean and Jerry had ever been. "That Dean is something else!" Mae purred to reporters. "A man's man and a ladies' man, and that's just my type. Working with him was more fun than a barrel of monkeys. *Ooh!*"

The early programs were broadcast live, but by late 1958 the show was done on tape, losing some of its spontaneity. The ratings were good, but not everyone was crazy about Dino. "Dean Martin may be a devil with the ladies, a roisterer with the boys, and a real demon down at the pool room, but on America's home screen he can sometimes be a rather offensive young man," wrote TV critic Harriet Van Horne in the *New York World-Telegram*. "I had the feeling that this pretty laddie with the pretty ringlets and roguish grin would take pleasure in spitting in the eye of the audience. His offhanded air, his apparent lack of rehearsal, and his highly personal ad libs all bespeak a faint contempt for his work."

Van Horne didn't realize that it was those very same qualities—that casual, laid-back, I-don't-take-myself-too-seriously demeanor—that endeared him to his many fans. It wasn't that Dean had contempt for his work or his audience but that he couldn't stand entertainers who believed their own publicity and expected everyone to genuflect, and his at times exaggerated informality was a reaction to that attitude. "Who the fuck am I? Caruso? Sinatra?" he once said. "I do what I do, and if people like it, that's OK." Although he never used four-letter words on television, even at this early stage a certain vulgarity would creep into his asides, which would eventually get him into trouble with NBC censors, as did the preoccupation with the jokes about alcohol consumption. Some critics genuinely believed Dean got plastered—as opposed to pleasantly buzzed—on a regular basis and thought his admitting to and even making light of it was in questionable taste. And here Dean had honestly thought everyone would know he was kidding. In truth, few did, but since most of his fans liked a drink or three now and then, or even got plastered from time to time themselves, they responded with identification and even glee to the grape and barley humor.

It was around this time that Dean ran into Jerry Lewis again and even appeared on a program with him—sort of. Dean was working at the studio when Bing Crosby suggested that they just drop by Eddie Fisher's show, which was taping down the hall. Jerry Lewis was that evening's guest star, and Dean simply poked his head out the curtain behind Jerry to tremendous applause. The two men didn't speak, however. From time to time this sort of thing would happen, or they'd see each other on the golf course, but it never amounted to anything or changed the way they felt about each other.

1958, the year *The Young Lions* was released, Dean came out with several wonderful recordings, some of which had him singing both English and Italian lyrics in the same song; Dean was one of the few Italian-American singers who would do this on a fairly regular basis. Lombardo/Di Minno's "Return to Me/Ritorna a Me," a pretty multilingual American song co-written by bandleader Guy Lombardo's brother, Carmen, had a nice arrangement despite a rather too-wailing chorus in the background. The Milanese "Nel Blu Dipinto di Blu" by Domenico Modugno was transformed into the snappy, suggestively sung "Volare," another tune that became firmly identified with Dean despite many other versions of it. One of his very best recordings was Taccini/Bertini/Fredericks's "On an Evening in Roma," another catchy, transplanted Italian number that Dean sounds just great on. With its snazzy arrangement of guitars and organ, an irresistible beat, a properly muted chorus, and Dean's knowing way with the lyrics, with their intimations of private and even public sex ("You can see 'em disappearin' two by two; do they take 'em for espresso? Yeah, I guess so . . ."), "On an Evening in Roma" emerged as quintessential Dean Martin. All three records were hits, although none rose above number four on the charts.

Dean had millions of fans, but his singing left just as many people cold. Part of the problem was the Italianate nature of his material and his style. Just as some people, for whatever reason, are repelled by, say, a Boston accent, a Scottish burr, a Southern drawl, or a low-class Brooklyn pronunciation, there are those who are turned off by the stereotypical Italian-American way of expressing oneself—"Hey, paisano!" or talking about food with the fingers pinched—which permeated Dean's way of singing. (Sinatra generally evoked New Jersey more than he did Little Italy.) The vowel-twisting he occasionally employed was found sexy by some and vulgar by others. Then there was the fact that he never took any of it that seriously. He himself would have agreed that he was not the musical genius that Sinatra was, but Dean couldn't have cared less. He enjoyed what he did as did his fans, so he was happy. He didn't care if he was an "artiste." For those nonfans who could get past the Italianate trappings of his style, Dean would nevertheless reveal himself as a skilled, talented singer with a strong baritone voice that he, wisely, rarely forced to go beyond its natural range or volume.

Dean hadn't been joking when he'd talked about "making a deal with a bar" back in Pittsburgh, although that particular city was in no way where he wanted the bar, his own place, to be located. L.A., the "happening" city with few skyscrapers and even fewer elevators, was where he wanted to open what would come to be known as Dino's Place. It had originally been called the Alpine Lodge of Sunset Boulevard, but Dean and one Maury Samuels contacted the three owners of the Alpine and made them a deal. Dean and Maury bought 50 percent of the place, and Dean was to be paid one thousand dollars a month in exchange for the right to use his name. Dino would drop into the place now and then, occasionally get up to the piano and sing a song, but he never did his act there. He made his brother, William, the general manager, but this didn't prevent the original owners from eventually buying up Samuels's percentage and taking control, with the result that William was fired in a couple of years, and Dean stopped getting his thousand per week. Weary and disgusted, Dean would find himself—or at least his by now rather well-off lawyers—back in the courtroom suing for money owed him and trying to deny the owners the right to use his name and image. He got the money, but the place was still called Dino's for years after Dean himself had nothing more to do with it. This further cemented his feeling that the world was full of parasites seeking to suck all the blood, money, and energy out of people who'd made good. Whether Dean partially blamed his brother, Bill, or not, the Dino's Place debacle at the very least forever altered their professional relationship; Dean's brother went to work for Rockwell Aircraft as an engineer. He'd apparently had enough of showbiz and, perhaps, of Dean.

Things were now looking up for Dean on the professional front, but there was more personal upheaval to be endured. He got back from the studio on the night he did his first *Dean Martin Show* and found his three daughters from his first marriage—Claudia, fourteen; Gail, thirteen; and Deana, ten—tearfully waiting for him with Jeanne at 601 Mountain Drive. They told him that their brother, Craig, the oldest at fifteen, had been living in the spare room of a friend for some time. Their aunt Ann had brought them to their father's house because their mother could no longer take care of them. Jeanne and Dean exchanged apprehensive glances. What was going on with Betty? Hadn't he been paying enough in alimony and child support?

Betty had become a pathetic figure since her divorce from Dean. She had watched him climb to the stratosphere of the entertainment industry with Jerry Lewis—him and the "young blond"—and she felt bitter and resentful. She hated the way Dean would always make it sound in interviews as if Jeanne were his first wife, as if Betty and their years together had never existed. It would be unfair, however, to claim that the divorce was responsible for all of her problems. With enough money for herself and her children, a beautiful home on Sunset Boulevard, Betty could have rebuilt her life as many other ex-wives had done before and since, but she just couldn't get beyond her pain and self-pity. She began to drink so heavily that she didn't know what she was doing half of the time. A scandal sheet charged that she held wild champagne parties while her kids lived on a box of spaghetti for a week, but whether or not things were ever that bad, it's clear that she was not doing all she could for herself or her children. Police were called to her house frequently to respond to loud yelling or fights, and more than once highly disreputable characters were discovered partying with Betty. She just didn't give a damn anymore. She had taken that unexpected turn so many years before, and nothing had turned out as she'd hoped or had supposed it would. Still, underneath the haggard, swollen-from-alcohol face and prematurely gray hair there were vestiges of the pretty young woman Dean had fallen in love with.

It did not help Betty's situation that her children, understandably, didn't want to be with her. Part of the problem was that their father, the wealthy star Dean Martin, could do so much more for them, so it was only natural for them to gravitate to his nicer house and more fully stocked kitchen. Preoccupied with his career, Dean had concentrated paternally on his children with Jeanne; dealing with the other four children meant he had to deal with Betty, which he did not want to do.

Now the children had no choice but to stay with Dean because their mother no longer had a home and was living with her sister, who had no room for the girls and couldn't afford to take care of them. Betty was loathe to ask Dean for help, to have him and "that woman" know what had become of her, but her sister Ann knew steps had to be taken. Jealous of all the things she perceived Jeanne as possessing because she had "her" husband, Betty had gone on buying—and drinking—sprees and now had as many creditors as Dean had had when he was living in Manhattan. Look at how irresponsible he had been and how wonderfully things had turned out for him, she thought. Betty told herself and friends that perhaps Dean, who'd never listened to her when he was gambling and drinking away the rent money, had had the right idea after all. She would spend and spend like he did. She would make him pay for everything. He could afford it, couldn't he? She had made the mistake, she would say, of taking straight alimony instead of asking for a percentage of his income. Before long the IRS came to her with a whopping tax bill, and there was no way to hold off her numerous creditors and also hold on to the house. Betty moved in with a male friend after her sister put her out and paid numerous visits to Mountain Drive, telling her children that they would all be together if they'd only be patient. But the children would much rather have stayed in Dean's elegant pad.

Dean felt Betty was an unfit mother. He liked the idea of having all seven children under the same roof—there was a governess to take care of them, after all, so what did he care?—but Jeanne had understandable reservations. They talked the whole thing out over a period of days. Jeanne was the kind of woman who saw her husband as boss and probably knew the decision was therefore preordained. But she wanted whatever would make her husband happy, and she felt sorry for the children. She was in more or less complete agreement when Dean filed for custody.

Betty did not contest the suit, stating that she felt Dean could take better care of the children since he had much greater resources than she did. They wanted all the things that Dean's other children had: a beautiful home and pool, horseback riding and piano lessons, private schooling, expensive toys and equipment—things that Betty could not provide them. Reluctantly, she let them go with Dean.

Now she had nothing. Dean was granted custody in Superior Court on December 11, 1958. The children doubled up in the four bedrooms while Dean mulled over the idea of boarding school. Hearing this, a couple of the kids threatened to run away. Dean built an addition on the house eventually, but it was already a large property on spacious grounds. Jeanne did her best with seven children, sometimes losing her temper and wondering why she'd acceded to her husband's request. But she felt—they *all* felt—it was for the best.

It was Dean's acquaintance with Frank Sinatra that led to his next motion picture assignment. Sinatra was going to star in a film adaptation of James Jones's *Some Came Running*—a kind of sequel to *From Here to Eternity* about a serviceman who comes back after the war to the small town he was raised in—and there were still some parts to fill. Frank and Dean had worked together on TV and met in clubs and they knew each other casually and enjoyed each other's company, but they were not close friends. Dean, never a shrinking violet, simply asked Frank if there was a role in *Some Came Running* that he could fill. Frank clapped his hand to his forehead and said, "Why didn't I think of that? Now that you mention it . . ." The two became good buddies while they were making the picture. *Some Came Running* was directed by Vincente Minnelli, who'd previously helmed such films as *Kismet*, *The Band Wagon*, *Brigadoon*, and *Tea and Sympathy* and would work one more time with Dean.

Dean played Bama Dillert, a man Sinatra (as David Hirsch) meets in a local tavern in his hometown and moves in with. Bama is a gambler, which Dean could identify with, one of those restless gadabouts that Dean might have become had he not had any talent. Like the role in *The Young*

Lions, Bama Dillert is not too much of a stretch for Dean, and he makes the most of it. He always admitted the role posed no special problems for him. "Let's see," he told one reporter. "[As Bama] I sit around most of the day playin' cards with Frank. When the director yells 'cut!' what do I do? I sit around playin' cards with Frank. Hard work, I'm tellin' you." He didn't even have to bother affecting a southern drawl as he sort of had one—or at least an Ohio variation of it—already. Since Bama constantly wears a battered old hat, Dean had to wear one practically the entire time he was making the movie. Late in the film Bama's doctor tells him he has diabetes and has got to stop drinking, which brought looks of shocked disbelief from everyone. "Can't even imagine having to go through life without having my lunchtime martini or a glass of wine with spaghetti," Dean said about the scene later, shuddering at the thought. Dean had done some brief crooning in a party scene in *The Young Lions* (it wasn't a "song number," however), but he did no singing whatsoever in *Some Came Running*, which was for him a first. It made him feel like he'd finally "gone legit."

Frank Sinatra, haughty after winning an Oscar for *From Here to Eternity*, underplays so much and seems so negative and blasé in the picture that Dean makes the better impression if only because he's more likable. As Hirsch, Sinatra was supposed to be the sensitive writer full of emotion and feelings of love, but Dean registers much more sensitivity—his actual basic good humor and good-natured sensibility coming through—as Bama, even if he does refer to Hirsch's choice of fiancée (Shirley MacLaine as Ginny) as "a pig." Hirsch is torn between Ginny, a girl he invited home with him while under the influence, and Gwen (Martha Hyer), a local schoolteacher.

MacLaine had worked with Dean before in *Artists and Models*, but this was her first picture with Frank, whom she'd already encountered socially. *Some Came Running* signaled the start of a long friendship with both men, although Sinatra would later cut her out of his circle when she was too frank about him in one of the many volumes of her memoirs. "Until *Some Came Running*," she would say, "I don't think Frank was fully aware of Dean's brilliance. His performance in *Some Came Running* was his best. He was a lot like Bama, a loner with his own code of ethics who would never compromise, so maybe it wasn't really a performance." Shirley sort of fell into the role, but Martha Hyer pursued her part with a vengeance after meeting James Jones socially and having him tell her that she'd be perfect for Miss French. She immediately and unceremoniously dumped her longtime minor-league agent and replaced him with the more top-drawer Burt Allenberg of the William Morris Agency, who sat next to her one night at a dinner party. The director, Vincente Minnelli, ran some of Hyer's previous movies and told her she'd be OK if Sinatra approved her, which he did upon noting exactly how badly she wanted to be in the picture; besides, Allenberg was also *his* agent. Allenberg's clients Eleanor Parker and Jean Simmons had been up for the part, but he in effect betrayed them for Hyer by either telling them they were wrong for the role or quickly getting them the consolation prize of another movie.

Hyer had been Jerry Lewis's leading lady in his first solo film, *The Delicate Delinquent*. There was some apprehension about how Dean would react when he heard she'd been cast—not that he had enough clout at that time to veto Sinatra—but there was nothing to worry about. Dean knew people had a perfect right to work with or even be friends with Jerry regardless of how he might have felt, and he never held it against her or anybody else.

"Dean was wonderful in the picture," Hyer noted. "I've always felt that if he had accepted a billing cut down to a supporting role, he might have gotten nominated for an academy award, had he gone after it." In truth, Dean's role *was* only a supporting part, even though he was billed between Sinatra and MacLaine above the title, as Sinatra wanted it. Sinatra had come through his own long dark night of the soul before *From Here to Eternity* had rescued him from obscurity, and he was so grateful to be back on top again that he wanted to do what he could to help Dean. Hyer and MacLaine did receive supporting Oscar nominations, however.

The women were put up in a hotel in Madison, Indiana, where much of the movie was filmed, while Dean and Frank, like the characters they played in the movie, rented a house together for the duration. Many of Frank's mob friends would drop in for card games and drinks, bringing hookers from Chicago with them, but Sinatra was more bothered by the often obsessive female fans who would camp outside his door and try all manner of strategies to make their way into the house and pounce on him. The poker parties would sometimes go on until dawn, and Dean and Frank would report to the set hung over and bleary-eyed, to director Minnelli's consternation—and they found Minnelli a little too prim and proper for their taste to begin with. Dean had never liked to spend too much time rehearsing before he teamed with Frank, but now he really got influenced by Frank's often lackadaisical approach to making movies, and it would get worse before it got better. At least he never just tore pages out of the script the way Frank did so that they could get done faster and go off and play golf.

Frank's mobster friends felt drawn to Dean—there was that rough, unconventional manner he had—but it didn't work in reverse. He'd been used to types like that since his days in the back room of Rex's Cigar Store, but that didn't mean he craved their company. They were part of the equation, part of what you had to put up with when you were with Frank. Their presence didn't necessarily bother Dean, but he wasn't in awe of them, anxious to consort with them, like Frank was. Like Frank, Dean recognized that these guys were party-hearty fellows who loved gambling, women, and booze, just as he did, but other than that they were not alike. Some of them wondered what sort of vocation Dean would have taken up had he not been a nightclub singer—mobster maybe? He seemed the type—to them at least. What other job gave you the same hours, kept you in the casinos and the bars until dawn, and got you the money and the women? If Dean himself wondered about it, he never said.

Frank and Dean would take off on minivacations, mostly to nearby Cincinnati or infrequently to Las Vegas to gamble or carouse. One time they were in an elevator when Frank, a little high, wondered what that little red button did and began to press it. "Dago! Stop right there!" Dean shouted, but it was too late. "I ended up walkin' down seven floors," Dean remembered. "I was lucky. He stopped it close enough to a floor so I could crawl out. But that's why I ride the freight elevator; it's usually open on top. I have to be able to see out. Otherwise I get this feeling I'm in my own casket." Dean's claustrophobia was another reason why he didn't like New York City. "Too many damn elevators."

Annoyed one day by the artsy-fartsy way Minnelli was taking too long to set up a shot because he wanted a Ferris wheel *just so* in the background, Sinatra fumed and decided to walk. Picture making could be boring enough without having to sit around and sit around just for one lousy shot. Undoubtedly he talked Dean into walking out with him; Dean knew there was no picture without Frank, so what was the point in remaining? They flew all the way to Los Angeles, where the producer, Sol Siegel, followed them in an attempt to try and talk Frank into resuming his work. Frank was probably just tired of hanging around in a one-horse town like Madison and needed a week's vacation. When the week was up, he and Dean returned to Indiana and finished the picture.

Some Came Running was an even higher profile movie than *The Young Lions*, and it made a lot more money, two factors that did Dean's career a world of good. The movie is entertaining but minor, never really striking sparks until the melodramatic conclusion when MacLaine's old boyfriend shows up out of the blue to shoot her in front of Sinatra. Still, it has enough good sequences and performances to hold the attention, which was not the case with every film Dean and Frank appeared in. In the meantime they had become fast friends and would work together on stage in the Copa Room of the Sands shortly after *Some Came Running* was released. Sinatra would also serve as conductor on Dean's *Sleep Warm* album for Capitol Records. By that time Humphrey Bogart had died, and Sinatra had taken over as Leader of the Rat Pack.

Dean's association with Frank, despite the career advances it engendered, was not 100 percent positive. When working with Frank, Dean often absorbed all of his friend's worst habits—a sloppy attitude toward the picture business, an arrogant, unprofessional booze-and-broads-come-before-the-job posturing—that in some ways erased all the good done since his split with Jerry. But Dean couldn't afford to carry on as Frank did. Frank had his Oscar; Dean did not. Frank was called "The Voice," and Dean was not. Frank was taken seriously and respected as a performer, something Dean had coveted during all his years with Jerry; in other words, Sinatra could risk goofing off, but Dean was still trying to prove himself. Sinatra increased Dean's profile, but it was Dean himself who made Hollywood sit up and take notice.

Dean's next picture, a big splashy production from one of Hollywood's most respected producer-directors, would get him plenty of attention, but it was his work in a much quieter, almost forgotten movie immediately afterward that would prove he could really act.

ELEVEN

Bravo

If getting a role in *Some Came Running* was a feather in Dean's cap, being tapped for *Rio Bravo* (1959) was the whole darn cap ablaze with feathers.

Vincente Minnelli and Edward Dmytryk were busy, respected directors, but they weren't considered the auteur that producer-director Howard Hawks was. For many people, being in a Hawks film was the height of prestige. After *Rio Bravo* few people could look down their noses at Dean Martin as an actor. If Hawks would hire him, he had to have something going for him.

In the film, Dean, who was second-billed after John Wayne, plays Dude, an alcoholic deputy to Wayne's Sheriff Chance. Dean's cousin Archie Crocetti remembered that he "got a kick out of seeing Dino in *Rio Bravo*. When we were kids, we were all nuts about cowboys, but Dino took it real serious. Spent hours practicing the draw." Which may or not have come in handy for *Rio Bravo* all those years later. The basic plot has Dean trying to overcome his penchant for liquor, brought about by heartbreak over a woman who deserted him, so he can be of use to Wayne during a coming moment of crisis. Wayne has arrested a murdering gunslinger named Joe Burdett (Claude Akins) and is holding him in jail, but he knows that Joe's brother Nathan (John Russell) will do anything he can to get him out. Nathan has virtually an army of nasties at his disposal, while Chance has only Dude, the old crippled jailer Stumpy (Walter Brennan), and a young gun for hire named Colorado (Ricky Nelson) on his side. Meanwhile a girl on the run named Feathers (Angie Dickinson) is stuck in town because the stagecoach is disabled; she and Chance draw closer as Nathan rallies his forces and prepares to lay siege to Rio Bravo. Dude comes through in the end, and he, Chance, and the others manage to retain Joe Burdett as prisoner while rousting his brother and his army.

Although Wayne was playing the film's main character and chief protagonist, many saw Dean's role as being more central to the film. According to Randy Roberts and James Olsen in *John Wayne, American*, "*Rio Bravo* revolves around Dude even more than around Chance. John T. Chance is as constant as John Wayne; he might get shot or even die, but he would never betray a friend or go back on his word. Dude, on the other hand, battles psychological demons; his great fear is not so much that he will betray a friend as that he might betray himself."

Dean's presence in the film sort of pales next to massive Wayne's— who was six foot four (as was his opposite number in the movie, John Russell) to Dean's six feet and had a much longer history as a dramatic actor—but the two played well together and liked each other enormously. They would play chess and chat when they weren't in front of the cameras, and they became good friends.

Hawks had hated Fred Zinnemann's *High Noon* with Gary Cooper and wanted to make a film that was its ideological opposite. "I didn't think a good sheriff was going to go running around town like a chicken with his head cut off asking for help, and finally his Quaker wife had to save him," he explained. Hawks wanted to take "a real professional viewpoint. As Wayne says when he's offered help in *Rio Bravo*, 'If they're really good, I'll take them. If not, I'll just have to take care of them.' We did everything that way, the exact opposite of what annoyed me in *High Noon*, and it worked." Early titles for the new film were *El Paso Red* and *Bull by the Tail*.

Wayne also hated *High Noon*—he saw it as leftist—and agreed to star in Hawks's new movie despite some lingering resentment regarding Hawks; almost a decade earlier he'd had to haul the director into court to get his full salary for *Red River*. Screenwriters Jules Furthman and Leigh Brackett were in semiretirement when called in to work on the script because Hawks liked and trusted them both. In an outrageous, blatantly sexist development, Furthman was paid twenty-five hundred a week while Brackett got only six hundred.

In the original script, worked on mostly by Brackett, there was no Dude character as eventually played by Dean Martin. A man named Jim Ryan, a hired gun whom the sheriff reluctantly takes on, was eventually divided into the characters Dude and Colorado. The MPAA objected to some of the violence and sexual implications of the revised script, so Hawks instructed the screenwriters to tone things down further—just a bit—before shooting began. The famous opening silent scene was cobbled together just before the first day of filming. Hawks tinkered with the dialogue and other small bits of business as shooting proceeded.

Kirk Douglas was an early choice to play the Wayne role, and he would have brought more passion to the part. Montgomery Clift was first choice for Dude, but given his real-life problems with drink, he wasn't crazy about playing an alcoholic, and he'd had enough of Wayne and Hawks and what he thought of as their tiresome machismo in earlier films. Hawks had nineteen other names on his list for actors to play Dude: His top choice was Sinatra and after him James Cagney, Richard Widmark, and Edmund O'Brien. When none of the nineteen worked out for one reason or another, Hawks drafted a second list of names that included such as Spencer Tracy, Robert Mitchum, William Holden, Van Johnson, Ray Milland, and even Cary Grant! Jack Warner wanted Grant, but Hawks had his reservations. Hearing that none of these names had been hired yet, Dean's MCA agent got in touch with Hawks and practically begged him to consider his client; he knew how important it would be for Dean.

Hawks insisted that Dean meet with him the very next morning, which necessitated Dean chartering a plane to fly him directly from Las Vegas after his act in the wee hours. Although he was bedraggled and red eyed—which actually suited the character—Hawks was impressed with the way he'd just dropped everything to show up at considerable personal inconvenience. Hawks reasoned that if Dean would do that, he probably had the stuff in him to work hard to give a good performance in the picture. He was hired immediately, with Hawks agreeing that Dean could take time off from filming to act as host for the second City of Hope telethon.

Ricky Nelson was hired strictly because of his popularity on TV's *Adventures of Ozzie and Harriet* and his hit records for the younger set; Hawks reasoned that his participation could only help the box office. Nelson turned eighteen while the picture was being filmed, and to celebrate the occasion, Wayne and Dean presented the young man with a 300-pound bag of cow manure. As "Little Ricky," as he was known (after a character on *I Love Lucy*), stood there wondering what to say, they first lifted the bag—pouring the contents out onto the ground—then lifted Nelson and threw him bodily into the manure. A minor contretemps later erupted when not-so-little Nelson (he was an inch taller than Dean) had the gall to object to the tune he was to sing with Dean, "My Rifle, My Pony, and Me"—he wanted to do an inappropriate Johnny Cash number that would have been out of sync with the time period and setting—but he was finally persuaded to do things Hawks's way.

Walter Brennan was hired not only because of his acting ability but because of his very successful TV show, *The Real McCoys*, which had made him a national star in his own right instead of just a well-known character actor. Unfortunately, Brennan first played the part too much like the codger on *McCoys*, and Hawks had to tell him to make old Stumpy much more dyspeptic and unpleasant.

Assistant director Christian Nyby was the one who suggested Angie Dickinson to Hawks because Nyby had directed her on some TV programs. Twenty-six at the time, Dickinson had already appeared in a western, *Gun the Man Down*, with James Arness in 1956, but the picture had made little impact. *Rio Bravo*, on the other hand, was to make her a star. (She tested with, of all people, Frank Gifford playing Sheriff Chance.) Hawks was determined to turn her into an actress the way he'd tried to make Lauren Bacall into an actress decades earlier by casting her opposite her future husband, Humphrey Bogart, in *To Have and Have Not*. With her overt sexuality, Dickinson reminded Hawks of Bacall, but she was more voluptuous and not nearly as shy or inexperienced. Dickinson was to say in later years that she was so much in awe of her then current amour that if Hawks had been sexually obsessed with her—or even made a pass—she wouldn't have noticed. The same was true of Dean, whom she liked very much and whom, unlike Hawks, she found attractive. "Had I not been really crazy about the guy I was involved with at the time," she said, "I definitely would have developed a crush on Dean. He was charming, wonderful, and very masculine. A real doll." On another occasion she added: "Dean is a very, very funny man, naturally amusing, like Charlie Chaplin. He did normal things, and they were hysterical. Whereas Jerry tried to be funny, Dean just *is* funny." She, Dean, and Wayne all had fun and made jokes during a sequence when she gives Dean a suggestive shave while the sheriff warily watches. Signing her to a personal contract and recommending she change her name—which she didn't—Hawks tried to take as much control of her as he did Bacall, but Dickinson was a different kettle of fish, and Hawks never used her again.

Scenes were filmed on Hollywood soundstages with exteriors shot at Old Tucson, a replica of the original city, which had been built for the movie *Arizona* in the forties. Hawks used part of the budget to make enough changes in the town so that it wouldn't look exactly as it did in *Arizona* and numerous other pictures since. Temperatures rose to over one hundred degrees during filming, during which the cast and crew would long to get back to their hotel or resume work back on the air-conditioned Hollywood soundstage. Otherwise the seven-week shoot proceeded with little unpleasant incident; everyone got along and enjoyed making the picture. A true actor's director, Hawks even allowed his stars to make changes in the dialogue so they'd be more comfortable with their lines.

Hawks was gratified when Dean gave him the performance he'd been hoping for. Hawks could see beyond the actor's casual manner and perceive how earnestly he was trying to get it right. This time he was advised by his other *Young Lions* costar, Marlon Brando, on how to get to the bottom of his character—either Dean didn't want to impose on Montgomery Clift, or he wasn't especially anxious for his company—and Hawks gave Dean some critical direction that set him unerringly on track. Initially afraid that he was going to do the comical "nightclub drunk" that he did in his act, Hawks told him about how he once saw a guy with a severe hangover "pound his leg trying to hurt himself to try and get some feeling into it." Dean used this suggestion in a jail scene late in the picture, when he's sitting in a chair, desperate for a drink, beating himself in frustration; it's one of his best moments in the movie. He is also especially good in an early scene talking with Ward Bond as rancher Pat Wheeler, who sits on horseback as he tells Dean that the Indians avoid him because of his taste for alcohol. Dean has virtually no dialogue; most of the time he merely looks at Bond, listening and reacting, but he somehow comes closest in this scene to creating a real and different characterization.

Still, Hawks found that he had to keep on top of Dean or else. "He was a damn good actor," Hawks said, "but he also is a fellow who floats through life . . . . He has to get some kind of a hint . . . otherwise, hell, he won't even rehearse!" Dean was still operating under the Sinatra School of Motion Picture Making, which is why he may have held back too much in certain sequences. Hawks was unable to get him to completely overcome his aversion to depicting strong emotion, such as in the scene when, disgusted by himself, Dean tells Wayne that he's quitting. He's going through the motions, but he isn't *feeling* it, which makes the scene almost a comical catalog of the kind of once-removed, second-rate acting that most Hollywood stars indulged in more often than not. But Dean makes up for it a bit in the following scene in the jailhouse (although he's still a little self-conscious) as Dude sits at a table with Chance and Stumpy, clearly trying to decide whether he should take a drink or not. Despite his own love of drinking, Dean could not really tap any hidden feelings to help him in these scenes; he liked a few drinks, may even have been a heavy drinker during periods of his life, but he was not *addicted* to the stuff and had never gone through the should-I-or-shouldn't-I torment that Dude had. Whatever problems Hawks may have had with Dean, the director liked the actor, and after shooting was over would bring his lover, model Chance de Widstedt, to Dino's Place in the hopes that Dean himself might drop in for a quick one.

Dean appears in the film's very first shot, opening the door into the recreation hall where he has a fateful encounter with Chance and Joe Burdett. The next few minutes are a fascinating, totally silent interplay of the characters played by Akins, Wayne, and Dean: Dude comes in longing for a drink; Burdett taunts him by pouring himself one, then throwing a coin into a nearby spittoon. Chance kicks the spittoon away before Dude can debase himself by digging for the coin, and Dude, maddened by his desperate longing for alcohol, knocks him out with a board. Burdett is beating up Dude when a bystander tries to interfere; Burdett shoots him. There is no dialogue, only Dimitri Tiomkin's music punctuating each movement. The sequence sets up the story and all the hidden conflicts within it.

Another fairly tense scene has Chance and Dude pursuing a hired gun who has run into the saloon and may still be hiding there. Dude decides he can identify the culprit by looking at the boots of everyone inside and seeing whose are muddy. (Which begs the question: Wouldn't everyone's boots be somewhat muddy? There was no pavement in the Old West!) It turns out that the desperado is clinging to the rafters, but Dude takes care of him before he can do any more damage. The scene when the jailed man's brother comes to speak to Chance at the jailhouse, each menacing the other, is also a crisply acted confrontation. Unfortunately, such scenes as when Dude tells Chance, "I could hold your hand if you're nervous" as they go on night patrol or when Chance gives Stumpy's bald head a big smooch when the latter complains that his job is thankless smack a little too much of Martin and Lewis. There's also a little too much comedy relief provided by both Stumpy and Carlos, the owner of the hotel.

Although he has his moments, John Wayne is too lethargic and laid back as Sheriff Chance. Even at the tense moments he looks like he's about to fall asleep, which hardly helps to make the leisurely paced film more riveting to watch; even old Walter Brennan has more energy. Brennan had become a comical old caricature of himself by this time, but his bright, flavorful performance blends well with Wayne's more laconic one. Ricky Nelson is pleasant but amateurish; you keep expecting Wayne to diaper him or put him to bed. Dickinson, one of the first of the new

breed of more intelligent sexy actresses of that period, is saucy and inso-
lent, exuding her full-frontal wave of patented sensuality, but her acting is
sometimes too subdued. She certainly isn't bad, although she makes a
highly unlikely bed partner for a paunchy, middle-aged Wayne, even if the
wind-up with her and the sheriff in her hotel room is quite charming. One
actor who appeared in the credits, Harry Carey Jr., was completely cut
from the film. There were a lot of heavy drinkers in the cast of *Rio Bravo*
—Dean, John Wayne, Ward Bond—but unlike Carey they could handle
their liquor and never reported for duty while inebriated. Carey's role was
greatly reduced and then eliminated altogether.

    Rio Bravo was not taken very seriously by the critics when it was
released—although that would change over time—and received no
Academy Award nominations, but it was one of the ten most successful
films of the year and made nearly five and a half million dollars in profits.
Dean got mostly rave reviews, with *Time* calling *Rio Bravo* "his best film"
and describing his performance in it as "the rare movie portrait of an alcoholic that skirts both sensation and sentiment." Some film critics find
deep meaning in the movie (which Hawks probably never intended) and
see it as a masterpiece of cinema. Critic Robin Wood—one of those types
who turns films topsy turvy, admittedly in an often fascinating way, to dig
down for supposed truths—has said of the film: "If I were asked to choose
a film that would justify the existence of Hollywood, I think it would be
Rio Bravo." And French New Wave director Jean-Luc Godard hailed it as
"a work of extraordinary psychological insight and aesthetic perception,
but Hawks has made his film so that the insight can pass unnoticed." Of
course it must be remembered that sometimes the heaviest of criticism
comes from the shallowest of minds. Hawks would only have been amused
by all the pretentious analysis of his movie, which at its heart was merely
a relatively well-made B western. It's entirely reasonably to suggest that
Chance rolls cigarettes for Dude as a way of expressing his support for his
friend, but when *Rio Bravo* is talked about as if it and Hawks were on the
level of Shakespeare, the enthusiasm gets a little carried away.

    Despite some wonderful moments, a lot of humor and charm, and
some solid performances, *Rio Bravo* is sometimes tedious and overall
second-rate, and certainly nowhere in the league of its counterinfluence
High Noon. Dimitri Tiomkin contributed a haunting opening theme for
the film, Spanish-flavored music that sings of dust and longing, loneliness
and melancholy, but the film that follows has none of its depth or
poignancy. Hawks's apologists claim that the film's slow pacing was
because Hawks wanted to take the time to explore his characters, but if

that was the case, their lack of dimension is as inexplicable as it is ironic. Angie Dickinson's character, Feathers, is never developed beyond the cliché of the mysterious girl with a past; we learn some of her history but little about what makes her tick. All the characters are types more than they are real people—but for stick figures they certainly talk a lot, even during the fight scenes, which pretty much ruins the slack climactic gun battle. The shame of it is that *Rio Bravo* pulls the viewer along from that terrific silent scene for about thirty minutes until it just starts meandering, and it's all too clear that the promise of its opening moments are not going to be fulfilled. Lots of people like the movie, but one suspects *Rio Bravo* is profound only to those film critics who spend their whole time watching movies but never crack a book.

Ironically, considering that this picture assured Dean's future designation as a serious actor, the highlights are the musical numbers (by Tiomkin and Webster), which really shouldn't work at all but do—beautifully. "My Rifle, My Pony, and Me" is not only well-integrated into the story but is sung excellently by Dean as he relaxes in the jailhouse, with Ricky accompanying him on guitar and Brennan on harmonica. Dean whistles the tune as Ricky sings the second verse, and then the two make it a duet. (Dean recorded this both as a solo and with Nelson.) This is followed by a second number, "Get Along Home, Cindy, Cindy," which is sung by Ricky, Dean, and even Brennan, as an amused Wayne looks on. These delightful sequences did much to endear the film to its admirers. The melody played over and over in the saloon was supposed to be "De Guello," reportedly the music played at the actual Alamo, but Tiomkin wrote something new because Hawks didn't find the original piece evocative enough.

Over the years Dean's next film—and performance—hasn't gotten nearly the attention that *Rio Bravo* has, although *Career* (1959) was in many ways a worthier picture. Dean still had a few movies to do for Hal Wallis, who thought he had a role for him in an adaptation of a Broadway show by James Lee, which detailed the heartbreak and struggles of a young man fighting against hope for success as an actor. Dean wanted more money to do the part, but one of the concessions he'd made to dissolve old Martin and Lewis obligations was that he'd do each movie at the same old fee. Wallis refused to up the ante, but as Dean still had to do four more movies for the man and since the colorful part of Morey Novack intrigued him, even though it wasn't the main role, he agreed to do *Career*. It was a wise decision. Dean was not only perfectly cast but delivered one of his greatest performances. Wallis apparently came to loathe Jerry Lewis and vice versa, but of Dean he was to say, "He was never a problem."

Wallis chose forty-seven-year-old Joseph Anthony to direct the picture because he'd had a lot of Broadway experience before helming such film adaptations as *The Rainmaker* and *The Matchmaker*. Anthony Franciosa (in the performance of his career) was picked to star (although he was second billed after Dean) as Sam Lawson, who leaves Lansing, Michigan, and his sweetheart behind to try for success as an actor in New York. One of the first professional contacts he makes is with Morey Novack, an impoverished director at a shoestring theater company who gets Sam to buy him what is probably his only meal of the day: a hot dog. Lawson appears in some of Novack's productions but can't get anyone important to come to see them. He finally importunes a major agent, Shirley Drake (Carolyn Jones) to take him on as a client, unaware that the lonely woman is rather smitten with him. Lawson's girl (Joan Blackman) follows him to New York and they marry, but Sam doesn't make enough money to make their life bearable, so she leaves. After all sorts of trials and tribulations, as well as another marriage to Sharon Kensington (Shirley MacLaine), the neurotic daughter of a theatre bigwig, he gets a job as a waiter at O'Malley's, the cinematic equivalent of Sardi's. He's humiliated when he sees his ex-wife with her successful new husband but more determined than ever to succeed. He finally gets the lead role in a smash Broadway play. What follows is one of the most powerful endings of any Hollywood film, as Sam, now middle-aged, asks his loyal, loving agent: "Why did it have to take so long?" She tells him, "You give a wonderful performance. Perhaps a great deal had to happen to you to make it what it is." Then she adds in a sudden outburst: "Such an awful one-sided bargain. No life, no family, no home. Just existence. And all those precious years for what—a name on a marquee? Tell me, Sam—was it worth it?" With his head held high Sam marches on stage to tumultuous applause after telling his agent, "Yes, *yes*, it was worth it!"

Dean is wonderful and amusing as a lovable freeloader on the fringes of showbiz who runs an actor's rostrum in a low-rent district of Manhattan. His character goes through quite a lot of changes during the course of the story, but Dean keeps up with all of them, becoming first a hot-shot Hollywood director (exactly the sort of person he once despised) who doesn't do a hell of a lot for his old friends and later a down-on-his-luck suspected Communist whose career has been destroyed by the blacklist. Dean effectively limns the three separate stages of this man's life: the cocky, hopeful, poor-but-happy artist with theater in his blood and an eternally upbeat nature; the Hollywood player who makes and breaks deals and gives a show of concern for those less fortunate whom he's left behind but who really, inevitably, feels he's above them now and in a separate universe; and the down and out yet still undefeated older and wiser struggler who goes back to his theatrical roots after being rejected by Hollywood and, against all odds, hands Sam the part that finally makes his career. Wallis was remarkably astute in seeing how this role would work for Dean and vice versa. Dean called upon all his years of struggle, the assorted ups and downs and highs and lows of his own career, to evoke a totally convincing portrait.

Given how some accounts of Dean Martin's life like to depict him as being totally coldhearted and self-centered, it's inexplicable that this portrayal has escaped scrutiny since Dean plays a man who—at least in the middle stage of his career—doesn't seem to give a damn about anybody else, perhaps because for too many years nobody gave a damn about him. One senses Morey Novack has lived by his wits for most of his life and never had anyone to count on. When he's in a position to help, he doesn't want to. He's partially redeemed late in the movie, although by this time he needs Sam as much if not more than Sam needs him.

Anthony Franciosa is superb as Sam Lawson. Some have criticized him as being overwrought, but he's playing a man who is often overly sensitive and self-destructive—in other words, a real, imperfect human being. Sam is too intense, he lacks charm and that ability to schmooze; he doesn't even seem able to have fun, which can't be said for his buddy Morey. Joan Blackman offers a sensitive portrayal of his initially understanding but then utterly disillusioned wife who just can't comprehend how truly driven he is or what he will endure to achieve his dream. Shirley MacLaine offers her usual fine performance as loopy rich Sharon Kensington. She really gets into her kissing scenes with Dean, which isn't surprising since she was slowly falling in love with him at the time. When she puts her head on his knee and looks up at him with a wistful, adoring expression, it isn't acting. Carolyn Jones gives her usual sharp portrayal as the agent so devoted to Sam and so pathetic in her loneliness.

Playwright Lee and director Anthony were successful in opening up the play so that it never has that stage bound quality that has sunk other play-into-film adaptations. The picture is full of crackling dialogue and memorable scenes and details: the sweet little old lady at City Hall who watches the happy couple of Sam and his bride get married as Dean throws rice at them and then (in what was probably an ad lib) at *her*; the kind, understanding speech his ex-wife gives Sam when she sees him, mortified, in O'Malley's; Lawson's comment on the eve of his being sent to Korea ("After Broadway, I'm going to welcome a nice quiet war"). Dean and Tony Franciosa have a very good scene in a restaurant where

Sam practically begs Morey for the lead in his new production. Even better is their subsequent confrontation when Sam begins to strangle Morey, screaming, "I'm going to kill you!" which actually turns out to be his way of auditioning for the role when Morey suggests he may lack the killer instinct.

One dated—or daringly modern, depending on how you look at it—aspect to the film is its oblique exploration of the frequently expressed dictum of the fifties and even later that the theater was "dominated" by homosexuals and that there was even a conspiracy of gays helping out others of the "brotherhood" in Hollywood. Sam's heterosexual pedigree is established in an early scene when Morey doesn't realize he's got a girlfriend and mistakes his disinterest in other women for something else. "You *do* go out with girls?" he asks warily. Later, when Morey is showing Sam around the studio, they meet a handsome movie star and his manager, both of whom shake hands in a distinctly epicene manner. "It's amazing," Sam says. "They're both left-handed." One could also quibble that *Career* never *quite* cuts into the nitty gritty of show business, yet in its successful attempt to portray many different points of view, it's also undeniably wise and trenchant and often penetrating. And one of Dean's all-time best pictures.

In a sense, *Career* is the forgotten Dean Martin movie, even though it is head and shoulders above the stuff he'd do while a member of the Rat Pack.

TWELVE

Who Were Those Ladies?

Years earlier, before he'd even met Jerry Lewis, Dean had done a screen test for Joe Pasternak that had been directed by George Sidney. Dean had finally worked for Pasternak—in the ill-fated *Ten Thousand Bedrooms*—but he'd never actually worked with Sidney in a film until he was cast in *Who Was That Lady?* (1960), an adaptation of Norman Krasna's hit play *Who Was that Lady I Saw You with that Night?* (Dean would also work briefly with Sidney later that same year when he did a cameo in the director's film *Pepe*, starring Mexican comedian Cantinflas and about fifty other special guest stars—all to no avail.) In between that old screen test and *Who Was That Lady?* Sidney had helmed such films as *Show Boat* in 1951 and *Pal Joey* with Frank Sinatra in 1957.

In *Who Was That Lady?* Dean was teamed with old buddies Janet Leigh and Tony Curtis, still a married couple in real life although not for much longer. In the film, however, Ann (Janet) sees her husband David (Tony), a chemistry professor, kissing one of his pretty students and wants to throw him out of the house. A panicky David asks his buddy Mike (Dean), a TV scripter, to help him come up with a scenario that will explain why he was smooching with the girl. Mike tells David to tell his wife that he's a special agent working for the FBI and he *had* to buss the girl, who's secretly a spy, so as not to blow his cover. This not-so-little white lie eventually snowballs to such an extent that a real FBI agent (James Whitmore) as well as real foreign spies are embroiled in the action and hot on Mike and David's trail after information they think they possess. At the end of the film the two nitwits are caught in the basement of the Empire State Building, which is being flooded by a burst pipe, only they believe they're really in a sinking Russian sub. The pedestrian if somehow engrossing script was dotted with racy one-liners.

Dean had great fun making the film with Tony and Janet. As Leigh recalled, "The personal familiarity of the three of us allowed absolute freedom, and the interplay was wild and woolly and inventive." The three would do their best to crack each other up while the cameras were rolling—occasionally in the finished film you can see them struggling valiantly not to laugh and fall out of character—and between scenes they would pursue one another with water pistols (yes, even forty-three-year-old Dean). After the final scene in the basement/submarine had been filmed, Sidney pretended he needed a few more shots and kept Dean and Tony writhing in the gushing water so that Janet, who had presumably left the lot and gone home, could float merrily by them and let them think she had ruined the take.

"I don't know whether Dean was as driven as Frank Sinatra," Leigh says today, "but I know he liked and tried and was good in his film work. I don't know a lot about his skirt chasing—obviously he did so. Jeanne was and is one of my best friends, and I do believe she understood a lot and put up with a lot. I truly don't believe he drank as much as he pretended—it was part of his 'act.' A lot of times there was Coke or 7-Up in his mug. He was professional in his work—that I can say. If he caroused, etcetera, it was on the club circuit, not the movie part."

Who Was That Lady? was good fun with good performances, and most believed, as did *Variety*, that "Curtis and Martin work nicely together. Dean Martin strengthens the false impression that he isn't acting at all." *Time* opined that Dean "neatly blends tomfoolery and tomcattery." Also in the cast of the film was perennial starlet Joi Lansing who would, in time, catch the eye of Frank, Dean, and others and wind up in many more of their movies.

Dean's second film of 1960 was also based on a Broadway show, the hit musical *Bells Are Ringing*—Vincente Minnelli of *Some Came Running* would again be at the helm—but making the cinematic adaptation was a lot less fun than making *Who Was That Lady?*, mostly because Dean did not get on as well with his costar, Judy Holliday. Dean later said that the whole thing was a waste of his time, but that was primarily because the film didn't do that well at the box office—it was Judy's "first out and out box office bomb," according to writer Gary Carey in his biography of Holliday—and because he had been mightily irritated by her neurotic behavior. Actually *Bells Are Ringing* was one of Dean's best pictures and one that especially provides a brilliant showcase for his particular romantic and light-comedy aptitudes.

Holliday had performed the role of Ella Peterson for 924 performances on Broadway. At the time that shooting on the picture began in October of 1959, she was heavily involved with well-known jazz musician Gerry Mulligan, whom she termed "the love of my life." Judy did not care for the script that had been adapted by Adolph Green and Betty Comden from their play and told producer Arthur Freed that it would have to be redone. This did not endear her to Comden and Green, who were already irritated at her over problems that had cropped up while doing the stage show. Holliday hated the script and the whole approach to the film version—she didn't seem to understand that the story *had* to be opened up for a big-screen movie, nor that a big name like Dean Martin could not do a small supporting part to her star turn—and resisted all attempts by Vincente Minnelli to direct and console her. She was only briefly appeased when Minnelli agreed to hire her lover, Mulligan, for a small part in the picture, but once that was settled she was back to being her usual complaining and difficult self. "Get Shirley MacLaine!" she told Freed one afternoon after only one week of filming when she felt she'd had enough. "She's worked with Dean Martin before. *Get her!*" Freed did whatever was necessary—everything from gentle, flattering persuasion to Dutch uncle talk to, finally, threats of lawsuits—to get her to change her mind about quitting the picture. Anxious over how the film would come off, afraid she was being shunted to one side by Dean (who had no interest in taking over the picture as she feared), and certain that she was too fat to look attractive in Cinemascope, Judy developed a whole host of psychosomatic complaints and more serious afflictions: bursitis, laryngitis, bladder control problems, and finally, a kidney infection. Whatever initial sympathy Dean may have had for her was dissipated as she cried and threw tantrums and ran off to her dressing room to meet with Mulligan or be massaged by an actor named "Big" Ralph Roberts who worked as a masseur when he wasn't working in pictures. Dean finally became so impatient with the woman that when he realized she was going to spend virtually all of her offscreen time in the dressing room and never say a word to him that wasn't part of the script, he breathed a sigh of relief.

As one illness replaced another, Judy also became accident-prone, culminating in a near disaster when an apparatus malfunctioned in the blind date/restaurant scene where her dress catches fire; she was mildly burned but carried on as if she'd been caught in a three-alarmer. Dean didn't appear in this scene but when he heard about the not-so-serious accident, he quipped, "*Now* can we get Shirley?" Although Holliday was a bona fide hypochondriac during this period, she became legitimately ill with throat cancer within a few years and died in 1965. *Bells Are Ringing* was her final film.

Judy's frequent absences for various real and imaginary medical complaints gave Dean lots of time to give on-set interviews. On one occasion he gave the reporter his views on the acting profession. "Acting is a cinch," he said. "The only way to really act is to know what the person you are playing a scene with is saying. This talk of method acting is wacky. You forget your lines and start fumbling and scratching around and you're a 'method' actor—and that's the truth." Of course, Dean, who'd had acting lessons from the likes of Montgomery Clift and (method actor) Marlon Brando, never in his career had to portray roles along the lines of King Lear or Richard the Third, so his lighthearted, rather superficial approach to acting would never have to be challenged; he was smart enough to always play within his comparatively limited range. Not that he didn't have a point in what he said about method acting.

In the film, in which Dean was second billed after Holliday, he plays scribe Jeffrey Morse, who, in a development close to Dean's heart, has broken up with his writing partner and is afraid he's lost the juice as a solo. He's just one of the clients of a phone-answering service cleverly billed as "Susanswerphone" by its owner Susan (Jean Stapleton). Sue's cousin, Ella Peterson (Holliday), works for her at Susanswerphone and is forever being warned not to get involved in the personal lives of her clients. But she's already fallen in love with Jeff Morse's voice and really flips when she finally meets him. In the meantime Sue's beau, who unbeknownst to her is a bookmaker, uses her answering service to take bets by pretending he's running a mail-order record company, with each racetrack represented by a different composer. (For instance, Puccini equals Pimlico. The jig is up when someone orders "one hundred" copies of Beethoven's "*Tenth* Symphony.") To make matters worse, the police are convinced that Susanswerphone is a front not for bookies but for a "lonely-hearts" service (read: prostitution ring). Ella is afraid she's not good enough for the type of sophisticated showbiz crowd Jeffrey hangs around with, but after a few false stops and starts, they fall in love, the bookies are rounded up, and the licentious taint of suspicion surrounding Susanswerphone is finally lifted.

Dean is marvelous in *Bells Are Ringing*, giving a very natural but highly committed performance that shows none of the strain he must have been under while dealing with his costar; in fact, the two play very well together throughout. For obvious reasons he never seems overrehearsed, such as in the scene when he first meets Judy when she drops by his apartment to give him a message because he refuses to answer his phone. He's also quite good in a more emotional (if still on the light side) sequence when he finally tells Ella that he loves her. Holliday, attractive if heavy featured, is also excellent in the picture.

Although Holliday could sing, hers was hardly a great or especially pleasing voice. And while Dean was a crooner and not a Broadway singer as such, he generally does a fine job with the songs composed by Jules Styne. "Just in Time" is probably the most famous song in the picture, a snappy number that quickly became a standard and was recorded by Dean, Sinatra, and just about every other singer of note. "The Party's Over," which Judy sings after she comes to the wrong conclusion that she's not in Dean's league, is also a memorable and well-known ditty. After a false start, Dean comes through on "Do It!" once he adapts the number to his own singing style; ditto for "It's Better than a Dream." Another of the film's highlights is when Dean sings "I Met a Girl" while walking through the mobbed streets of New York City where his joy in love and life and simply being alive is most infectious. Dean knew how to understate a song when it was required. He didn't have to bother asserting himself—he's just there, himself, Dino, always relaxed, always professional.

Bells Are Ringing remains a very charming picture with good dialogue, music, and performances. Jean Stapleton, years before her "dingbat" role on *All in the Family*, scores as Judy's cousin Sue, and Frank Gorshin, in a small role as an actor, does a dead-on spoof of Marlon Brando. The scene when Judy and Dean start saying hello to strangers on the city streets, cutting through the anonymity of the big city, is oddly moving. But the picture also gets a little too silly at times, and it's unbelievable that the determined character Judy plays would be so easily deflated and defeated at the party of "Name-dropping" (as the song goes) showbiz types that Dino brings her to meet. The sequence also presents wealthy, successful people not necessarily as they are but as the snobs other people want to *think* they are.

It was now time for Dean to get back to the relaxed, fun atmosphere of a Sinatra movie, although there was some discussion as to which one it would be. On one of Sinatra's television specials the Voice had Dean, Bing Crosby, and the great comic of the giant schnozz, Jimmy Durante, as guests, and he announced that his next project would be a biopic entitled *The Jimmy Durante Story*. Sinatra, Crosby and Dean—*as Durante!*—would be the stars, (the other two be would Durante's early partners) and the famous Frank Capra of *It's a Wonderful Life* fame would direct. If this project had ever reached fruition it might have been a fascinating feature, but it never got past the planning stages, first because of an actors' strike and then, probably, because the busy schedules of the cast and director couldn't be nailed down to one solid chunk of time. Or it could be that once he'd thought it over, Dean didn't relish the prospect of walking about with an enormous honker again, even if this one were to be made of putty and Max Factor makeup.

The project they filmed instead was *Ocean's 11* (1960). The screenplay had been bought by Peter Lawford, who took it to Sinatra in the hopes he'd film it and give him a part in the picture. By this time Sinatra had formed his Rat Pack, made up of himself, Dean, Lawford, Sammy Davis Jr., and comedian Joey Bishop, and all five would get roles, some more important than others, in *Ocean's 11*. Rat Pack "mascot" Shirley MacLaine would also get a cameo, and Angie Dickinson, who liked Frank as much as she liked Dean, would have a small role as Sinatra's estranged wife, which she made the most of.

The Rat Pack was an outgrowth of a group that had originally been started by Humphrey Bogart and his wife, Lauren Bacall, who saw the others coming home disheveled from a party and christened them "a pack of rats." Sinatra had been a member of the original group, and when Bogie died, it was only natural that he took over. One by one the original members, including David Niven and Judy Garland, fell by the wayside and were replaced by Dino, Sammy, and the rest. They were also known briefly as the clan.

Sinatra had known Sammy since they'd appeared on the same bill very early in Sinatra's career, before he had reached superstardom; later Frank did much to bring Davis into the limelight. Lawford and Sinatra had worked together in MGM musicals and knew each other for years; Peter would soon become "brother-in-Lawford" to John F. Kennedy. Frank met Joey Bishop when the comedian was one of his opening acts at a Jersey club when Frank was in his down-and-out period; when Frank was back on top he did a lot to improve Joey's status. And, of course, Frank and Dean had met in nightclubs, guested on each others TV specials, and become fast friends while making *Some Came Running*.

Ocean's 11 takes place in Las Vegas, where a former paratrooper, Danny Ocean (Sinatra), rounds up eleven of his comrades, all of whom have been disillusioned by civilian life, and gets them to help him in a far-out scheme to rob all five Vegas casinos on the same night. Sam Herman (Dean), who sings at the Sahara, doesn't think much of Danny's plan but eventually agrees to join the others. The robbery itself takes only five on-screen minutes to unfold—not exactly riveting filmmaking after all the build-up!—and does none of the eleven ex-paratroopers, one of whom dies of a heart attack, the least bit of good. The stolen loot is secreted in the coffin of the dead man and Danny Ocean's eleven—now ten—must watch in horrified frustration as the fellow is *cremated*. So much for all their hard work. This last bit was the only really memorable thing about the movie—except perhaps for Dean's rendition of "Ain't That a Kick in the Head" by Van Heusen and Cahn.

Well-respected director Lewis Milestone (*All Quiet on the Western Front, Of Mice and Men*) both produced and directed the film, but everyone knew Sinatra was boss. He and his boys literally took over Las Vegas, as they decided to do a five-man show in the Copa Room at night and film the movie by day. There wasn't a hotel room to be had in the city, and Sinatra had to hire extra bodyguards to keep most—but certainly not all—of the hysterical women away. The boys would report for filming at noon—hours after shooting usually began on a motion picture—because they would stay up until dawn nightclubbing after they completed their shows. With their hip manner, sharp suits, colorful private language ("a little hey hey" was a good time or a sexual experience), they became the epitome of cool—the guys other guys wanted to be and women wanted to be with. They smoked, drank, and caroused in a way that nowadays would be considered not only politically incorrect but downright unhealthy, which is why the Rat Pack has retained its luster, even to young people who weren't even alive during the sixties.

It would have been a miracle if even a gifted director like Milestone could have made much of a movie under these conditions, and *Ocean's 11*, although it does have its entertaining moments, would never make the list of the director's—or anyone in the cast's—classic pictures. Meeting in the steam room after the day's shooting was done, which was never past six P.M., they'd talk about broads and bits of business to do in the act, rarely about the picture. The object was to have fun, get drunk, get laid—not to create any lasting works of art. Everyone had so much fun that Sinatra suggested they make several more of these all Rat Pack extravaganzas, but the way it worked out, they only appeared all together in one more movie. When it was all over, Dean finally got the double hernia that had kept him out of the draft fixed at Cedars of Lebanon.

Unlike the other members of the Rat Pack, Dean was never Sinatra's stooge. Bishop was by no means in the same fame league as the others, and he knew his association with Sinatra was worth its weight in gold; although he wasn't a patsy and occasionally spoke up when he felt it was

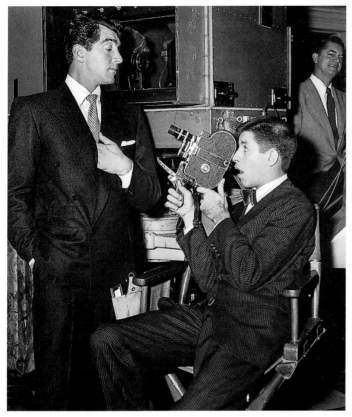

Dean Martin and partner Jerry Lewis clown around on a
Hollywood set, circa late forties.

Dean Martin is exasperated with Jerry Lewis in *Jumping Jacks* (1952).

Dino is surrounded by chorus cuties on the set of *Scared Stiff* (1953).

Janet Leigh wants to marry Jerry, but she's really in love with Dean in *Living It Up* (1954). Janet and Dean were lifelong friends.

Dean in the 1950s: at the top of the world—but still frustrated.

Dean flirts with trapeze star Zsa Zsa Gabor in *Three Ring Circus* (1954). It was around this time that his relationship with Jerry Lewis began to come apart.

Dean with the other members of the Rat Pack (*left to right*): Frank Sinatra, Peter Lawford, Joey Bishop, and Sammy Davis Jr. (*seated*).

(*From left to right*); Dean, Joey Bishop, and Sammy Davis Jr.(*seated*) confer with director Lewis Milestone (*hand outstretched*) on the set of *Ocean's 11*, the first of the all-Rat Pack movies. Things weren't normally so glum when they were making the movie.

Dean and the cast of *Ocean's 11* in a publicity shot. Dean and Frank Sinatra had a friendly but difficult relationship over the years.

Dean and Cyd Charisse getting ready to shoot a scene on the aborted *Something's Got to Give* in 1962. Dean didn't think anyone would believe Lee Remick could steal him away from the gorgeous Charisse—he was right—and he wouldn't complete the film without Marilyn Monroe.

Dean in a pensive moment between shows at the Copa Room at the Sands hotel and casino in Vegas. When he did westerns in a few years, he was just as well rid of the tux, which had been his "working uniform" for decades.

Dean poses in 1964 with his second wife Jeanne, to whom he was married for twenty-two years. They divorced in 1972 when Dean fell for twenty-four-year-old Kathy Mae Hawn. *(AP/Wide World Photos)*

A handsome portrait of Dean for Howard Hawks's production of *Rio Bravo*.

Dean relaxes on the circular moving bed that figures in the action of *The Silencers* and others in the Matt Helm series.

Daliah Lavi (*left*) and scantily clad Stella Stevens argue over which one is telling the truth while Dean seems to be comparing bust sizes in *The Silencers*.

Matt Helm (Dino) ponders his options. Dean's heavy smoking would eventually give him emphysema.

Dean as Matt Helm checks out Stella Stevens's shapely derriere in *The Silencers*. The film made more than enough money to engender three sequels.

Dean flashes a big smile on the set of *The Sons of Katie Elder*, the second film he made with John Wayne.

Dean rides to the rescue in *The Sons of Katie Elder*. Years later he'd walk off the set of *Showdown* after his horse died.

Dean stalks his prey in one of the many westerns he was to make in the sixties and after. His fourth favorite leisure-time activity (after wine, women, and golf) was watching westerns on TV—but never his own.

Dean puts on an eye patch after taking out his "glass eye" and raffling it off in *The Sons of Katie Elder*. He tells the winner: "I have two good eyes!"

Dean Martin's TV show became a tremendous hit in the midsixties and was in the top ten for many years after. Dean was also a top-ten box office attraction for many years.

Dean sings and swings on
his television program in
the early 1970s. A face-lift
kept him looking relatively
youthful.

Dean at the poker game that leads to a series of mysterious murders in *Five Card
Stud*.

When not in front of the camera, Dean would practice his golf swing anywhere he could find room on the set.

Dean in his last starring role, *Mr. Ricco*, as a San Francisco criminal lawyer involved in a bizarre murder trial.

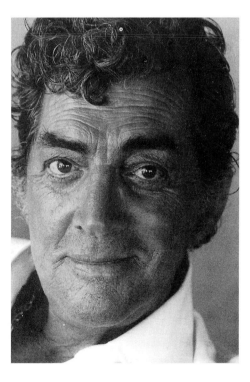

Tanned and rugged, an older Dean relaxes for the camera at the time of the *Cannonball* films in the early 1980s, lame attempts to recreate some Rat Pack magic.

Dean-Paul Martin, or Dino Jr., on the tennis court. "I think his son's tragic death really did him in," says Janet Leigh. "I don't think Dean ever recovered."

Dean laughs as Jerry presents him with a giant cake at Bally's in Las Vegas in honor of his seventy-second birthday on June 8, 1989, one day late. Though the two were friendly with one another, they never had a true reconciliation after the breakup of their partnership. (*AP/Wide World Photos*)

warranted, he was in no position to really stand up to Frank in any serious way. Sammy felt so grateful to Frank that he practically thought the other man walked on water, but inside was a hidden resentment that burst out on a radio show when Sammy was indiscreet with some remarks about Frank, bringing about a rift between the two that lasted for months and forced Sammy out of most of the Rat Pack's future film projects. Peter Lawford would inadvertently offend Frank when he was chosen to deliver the news that his brother-in-law, the new president, would not be staying at Frank's retreat as had been planned but rather at Bing Crosby's; Frank ruthlessly and utterly excised him from his circle.

Although Dean knew that Frank had been instrumental in helping him regain solid footing after the career blow of *Ten Thousand Bedrooms*, he was now a major star in his own right and didn't need Frank. He would follow many of Frank's dictums if he chose to, he would become a member of the "Jack Pack" and stump for Kennedy, but it only went so far. He didn't attend Kennedy's inauguration or entertain at the festivities afterward because he didn't care that much about JFK and also could see that the president was only using Sinatra, who'd never really be accepted by the Kennedys. Dean loved Frank as a friend, but he was always his own man, first and foremost. Over the years he would make it plain to Frank that Dean did what Dean wanted to do, not what Frank wanted.

After Frank, Dean probably liked Sammy the best, although he occasionally would do a double take at Davis's outré outfits and the seedy sex-and-drug stories of his personal life. Dean didn't especially like, or at least have much rapport with, Peter Lawford. And he really didn't get to know Bishop all that well, but they got along. Dean's association with the Rat Pack was an important part of his life, but it wasn't his *whole* life, and it didn't do much for his growth as an artist.

Dean was also busy in the recording studio during this period doing an album called *Dino: Italian Love Songs*, plus many other platters and singles. He did a cover of Nat King Cole's "Non Dimenticar"—the arrangement of swelling violins, insistent organ, and plucky mandolin combined with Dean's casual, effortless style helped put the merely pleasant tune over—and of Leoncavallo's song "Mattinata," which had already been recorded by the likes of Caruso and Nino Martini. While Dean's smooth, nonoperatic version of the tuneful melody isn't awful, it's safe to say it can't compare to the more powerful Caruso's. *Italian Love Songs* was very popular even though those who preferred jazzier arrangements to romantic ones dismissed it as "elevator music." "You're Nobody Till Somebody Loves You," one of Dean's kickier and more memorable recordings, was more on the mark for them; it has rhythm, bounce, and bite, sung by

Dean with a kind of stylish "you might as well face it, buddy" cynicism; Sinatra could not have done better. Dean also recorded everything from Brahms's "Lullaby" to an album of songs from *Bells Are Ringing*. One of the songs that was cut from the film, "My Guiding Star," was issued only as a bootleg.

On the film front, Dean finally cut loose from York Productions, the company he'd started with Jerry, to form his own Claude Productions, which would guarantee him a percentage of the profits of any film he appeared in that came out under Claude's umbrella. Some footage of him performing wound up in the Italian compilation film *Canzoni nel Mondo* (1961), though the picture has never really been part of his legitimate filmography.

Dean, Shirley MacLaine, director Joseph Anthony, and producer Hal Wallis had worked before on *Career*, but now they were in the mood to team up for something that might make a little more money. The answer was obvious: a sex-comedy of the type that was so popular in the sixties, although most consisted of innuendo more than anything else. In *All in a Night's Work* (1961) Katie Robbins (MacLaine), a researcher for a periodical, accidentally winds up in the hotel room of her boss, a publishing magnate, who's dropped dead. When she's seen exiting the room, everyone assumes she was the man's lover. The tycoon's nephew, Tony Ryder (Dean), is sure that Katie intends to blackmail the company, so he schemes to romance to head off her plans. One fly in the ointment is that Katie already has a fiancé, a veterinarian played by Cliff Robertson. It all resolves, expectedly, in a real romance for Tony and his employee.

Dean had three memorable encounters during the filming of *All in a Night's Work*. Because the movie was being made for Paramount, he spent a lot of time on the Paramount lot, where his former partner had the offices for his Jerry Lewis Productions. Dean kept spotting Jerry in the distance, and they almost walked into one another more than once, but the minute Jerry saw Dean he would quickly dart into the nearest doorway or turn on his heels and run away. Dean didn't want to have a professional relationship with Jerry, nor did he especially want to socialize with the man, but he saw no reason why they couldn't be civil, even warm, to each other if they happened to encounter one another during their daily routine. But with Jerry it was all or nothing; he didn't want to speak with Dean if they couldn't be close friends again. At the very least he was embarrassed or didn't know exactly what to say to Dean.

After Jerry had ducked away from him several times, Dean followed him to his office at Jerry Lewis Productions and sat down in front of his desk. Jerry explained that he had only wanted to avoid any awkwardness between them. Dean later said that Jerry admitted his running away from him had been "childish." As the two had a friendly drink, Dean explained that he thought it was ridiculous of them to completely avoid each other and not even speak. Jerry agreed. But the very next time Dean saw Jerry walking toward him on the Paramount lot—*whoosh!*—he was out of sight before you could say Jack Robinson.

Jerry just couldn't get past his sense of abandonment. He also was wise enough to know that just because he and Dean were speaking didn't mean that they would ever really be pals again. And if they weren't friends, why bother? Jerry had thought of Dean as a brother, as family, a loved one, and he was hurt when he realized that such feelings weren't returned on the same emotional level.

Another old friend was acting peculiarly during this period. After a hard day on the set, Dean was home taking a shower when Jeanne told him that he had a visitor waiting for him in the living room. He got dressed, went downstairs, and found his costar Shirley MacLaine sitting on the couch, looking at him expectantly. He sat down beside her, said hello, and asked her if something was wrong. It wasn't like her to drop by uninvited, especially since they were now seeing each other practically every day at the studio. Shirley made chit chat for several minutes, but Dean sensed she had something to say and just couldn't spit it out. Finally she just told Dean how much she was enjoying working with him. Jeanne came in and told them supper was ready—would Shirley like to stay for dinner? Shirley thanked her but declined, kissed Dean good-bye, and said good night.

In fact, Shirley had fallen hard for Dean after three years of seeing him as an older-brother figure. She had been attracted to him since *Some Came Running* but always resisted telling him how she felt because he was married. Now she decided that that didn't make any difference. She had come over to tell Dean she was in love with him—even though his wife was in the other room and his kids were all over the house—but when the opportunity arose, she didn't have the nerve. Undoubtedly Dean would have given her a sympathetic look, a sweet hug and kiss, and sent her, heartbroken but with her dignity intact, on her teary way. At the very least he would have asked, "Couldn't you have picked a better time or place?" In any case, their one-sided love affair never amounted to anything.

The third strange encounter Dean had was with Elvis Presley, who dropped by the studio—he was also under contract to Hal Wallis—to wish Dean a happy forty-third birthday. Elvis sang "Happy Birthday" to Dean, and he and Shirley helped him cut a cake. Inviting Elvis had probably been Shirley's idea because Dean took a long while to warm up to Presley, although he was his usual friendly self on this occasion. After a time he found the rock idol likable enough, but he always detested, and perhaps felt threatened by, the younger man's music. Elvis, on the other hand, was thrilled to meet Dean and even counted him among one of his musical influences.

Dean had happy news that he wanted to share with everyone at the birthday party. He'd become part owner of his own casino, in Lake Tahoe—the Cal-Neva Lodge, which skirted the California and Nevada borders. Dean had only a 7 percent interest in the lodge, however; the biggest shareholder was Frank Sinatra with 25 percent. Dean didn't know that notorious mobster Sam Giancana, one of Frank's closest friends at the time, was the true owner of most of that 25 percent. When he found out, he pulled out of the deal and agreed to sing there for a salary instead. His friendship with Sinatra remained intact, but there was some crumbling around the edges. It made it clear to Frank that Dean did what he wanted to do, not what he was told to do. Shortly before his death, Lucky Luciano, another of Frank's "buddies," let it be known that he wanted his life story to be made into a movie and thought that Dean would be perfect for the part. Since no script was ever written, no producer or director ever hired, it's moot to wonder if Dean would have ever done the picture, but it's fair to assume that his initial reaction would have been, "No dice." He had no great love for the Mafia.

"Martin obviously found small pleasure in his *Night's* work," wrote the *Time* magazine critic when the new picture was released. *Variety* opined that "never for one moment is Martin believable in the role of the youthful publishing tycoon, but his easygoing manner and knack for supplying the comedy reaction gets him by." *Cue* found him "a perfect foil for Shirley MacLaine," while the *New Yorker* found the whole enterprise a "callous farce that blights everything it touches. Martin plays—well, he doesn't exactly play it, it's more a matter of sheepishly allowing himself, for one scene at a time, to be mistaken for—the playboy heir."

Dean would work with love-stricken Shirley MacLaine again in a couple of years as well as with Frank and the clan, but there was someone even more interesting in his future, a certain blond bombshell who'd costar in The Dean Martin Movie that Never Was.

PART THREE

Top of the Heap

THIRTEEN

Marilyn and More

The times they were a changin'. Dean and Frank and Sammy were still the kings of cool; they packed 'em in in Vegas and Chicago; they had millions upon millions of fans; and they were all making lots and lots of money. But since 1956, a new type of music had been sweeping the country—rock and roll—and to some people it was Elvis who was king; Dean (who was now forty-four) and Frank were strictly for their parents. Even so, at this time most of the rock 'n' rollers were one- or two-hit wonders; few became icons like Frank and Dean—or Elvis. There were still enough people who appreciated their sound to make it more than worthwhile for Frank and Dean and Sammy to keep on singing and recording.

Frank had his own record label now, Reprise. When Dean had fulfilled his contract with Capitol Records in late 1961, he jumped ship to Reprise and stayed with the company even after it was bought by Warner Brothers in the late sixties. What made the deal even more lucrative was the fact that Dean retained the rights to these recordings, which were wholly owned by his Claude Productions; Reprise only leased the right to use them. Taking excellent advice from his MCA agents and other advisers, Dean was to find himself a multimillionaire many, many times over.

Dean's three-picture association with director Daniel Mann came about because they both were represented by Herman Citron of MCA. Mann was the director of *Come Back Little Sheba*, *The Rose Tattoo*, *Butterfield 8*, and *I'll Cry Tomorrow* with Susan Hayward as alcoholic singer Lillian Ross. Mann thought Hayward and Dean would be a good teaming and cast them in the film adaptation of a recent best-selling potboiler titled *Ada Dallas*, loosely based on the life of Louisiana governor Jimmie Davis, by the now-forgotten author Wirt Williams. Dean would play the governor—another "southern" role for Dean—and Hayward would be the title character, a former whore who becomes his wife and the true power behind the office. Throughout the film the two battle corruption and each other.

Dean and Susan mixed together as well as oil and water. Susan thought Dean was low-class and vulgar, and hardly sociable or talkative enough to suit her. Dean, sensing her disapproval, did his best to avoid her—he put a net up in one corner of the soundstage and practiced his golf swing—and later remarked that working with Hayward was enough to drive anyone to drink, even though, as he told reporters, "I don't take a drink in the whole picture. Man, I've never acted without a glass in my hand. That was the only method system I knew." Daniel Mann confirmed that Dean was "not much of a mixer" but that he was otherwise a friendly and likable fellow. Mann liked the way that Dean, unlike other movie stars, never tried to direct the picture. Dean always preferred it when he could have a laugh and share a martini with his costars, but Hayward, like Judy Holliday, was just not his cup of java; in fact, he thought she was a total bitch, which accounted for his spending much of his time between scenes addressing his golf balls instead of anybody else.

Ada had some admirers, but it was not a big hit with either the public or the critics. "*Ada* succeeds neither as the story of a woman or the chronicle of a rancid administration. Its characters are sketchy, its political setting routine and synthetic," wrote the *New York Herald-Tribune*. "Dean Martin plays Bo on a note of decreasing emotion," opined *Films and Filming*, and *Variety* found the picture "thoroughly implausible" and added that "Martin is pretty hard to swallow as the governor. His portrayal emerges as an imitation of Dean Martin imitating Bing Crosby imitating a governor. But he's a helluva good singer as he proves when he croons 'May the Lord Bless You Real Good' (by Roberts and Fowler)." *Time* thought that "Mann makes the most of Dean Martin's charm. He directs the show with tact and skill"; they found the film overall "a cute idea—maybe too cute." *Ada* was really just a reasonably entertaining trashy soap opera, no more no less; Dean gave it the performance it deserved. The *Harvard Lampoon* gave Hayward its not-so-coveted Worst Actress of the Year Award for her performances in *Ada* and the remake of *Back Street*, although it was really the pictures that were bad, not Hayward.

Dean next found himself heading out to the wilds of Kanab, Utah, where he and his fellow Rat Packers were going to make *Sergeants 3*, the second remake of *Gunga Din*, with Sammy Davis Jr., in the Gunga Din role, herein known as Jonah Williams, a freed slave. To illustrate the tone of the project one need only note that Frank was cast as "Mike Merry" and Dean was "Chip Deal." Lawford and Bishop also had small roles, making this the second—and last—time that all five Rat Packers would appear together in a motion picture. The main difference between *Sergeants 3* and the original *Gunga Din* was, as one critic put it, "*Gunga* was serious with tongue-in-cheek overtones, whereas the emphasis on *Sergeants* is tongue-in-cheek with serious overtones . . . . Moppet customers will take it seriously while most adult audiences will take one look at the cast and come prepared for the humorous approach." *Sergeants 3* was jointly produced by Frank and Dean's companies, Essex and Claude.

Kanab turned out to be dullsville—the local hot spot wasn't a casino but a Dairy Queen!—so Frank took over the top floor of the only hotel and turned it into one giant suite with freshly carpentered connecting doors. There were the usual card games and drinking as on the set of *Some Came Running*, and Frank even imported some hookers and ran 16mm Laurel and Hardy movies between trysts. The director, John Sturges, who'd helmed such films as *The Magnificent Seven*, *Bad Day at Black Rock*, and Sinatra's *Never So Few*, shot around the antics of The Boys, who pretty much showed up for work whenever they were tired of whatever else they were doing. Frank made sure his Vegas pals got small roles in the film so he'd have them around for company and as a cheering section. When *Variety* noted, "It seems as if half the performing denizens of Vegas went along for the ride," that wasn't far off the mark.

Not only was Dean considered the most fun loving of the bunch, according to fellow cast and certain crew members, but his performance in the film was judged the most noteworthy or at least the most "animated and comfortable"—certainly the most energetic, with Sammy Davis getting the rest of the kudos. Recognizing what kind of movie would result when all the fun, frolic—and occasional filmmaking—was over, Dean got more into the spirit of the picture than Frank and Peter did. Criticized as being much too laid-back in *Ocean's 11*, with some critics wondering if he'd even bothered giving a performance, Sinatra was more businesslike, on camera at least, in *Sergeants 3*, but the approach was all wrong for the movie. The story has the boys battling everyone from buffalo hunters in a saloon to hundreds of angry Indians in the climax.

Reactions to the film from the critical establishment were mixed, with some enjoying the humor and action and others denouncing it as a "$4,000,000 home movie" for Frank Sinatra's "gnat pack." In any case, it did not advance the cause of cinematic art, but it did enrich the coffers of Claude and Essex Productions since it made more than enough money to satisfy Dean and Frank, if not the others, who were strictly on salary, with the exception of Sammy, who got a small piece of the action.

Dean flew over to England for a weekend to do a small, funny bit in Bob Hope and Bing Crosby's ultimate "Road" movie at Shepperton Studios in Middlesex. At the end of *The Road to Hong Kong*, Bob and Bing and Joan Collins have landed on the planet Plutonius. The men immediately get into an argument over who will get Joan—should they share her fifty-fifty? As they sing "Team Work," Joan goes running off to the side and into the arms of . . . Frank Sinatra and Dean Martin. Bob: "The Italians have landed." Bing: "That's the grape and the twig, isn't it?" Bob: "Yeah, and they've got the bar open." Wearing spaceman uniforms and silly beanies with little whirly blades on top, Frank and Dean mix martinis with Joan as Bing and Bob watch with jealousy. Looking a bit snookered—or possibly jet-lagged after flying in Frank's private aircraft—Dean sends his beanie blade twirling at one point and puts on a goofy expression. Bing and Bob ask for "special effects" and have the two rivals for Joan's affections floated away out of sight. Bing then does the same to Bob.

Back in the United States, Dean did his usual club engagements, more recordings, this time for Reprise Records, and reported to the studio for another film with director Daniel Mann, a comedy entitled *Who's Got the Action?* Dean's costar was Lana Turner, and although they got along better than he and Susan Hayward did, they still didn't socialize all that much. A few year's before, Lana had gone to Herman Hover's nightclub, Ciro's, when Dean was performing to try to get close to him after the show, often following him to Hover's house for the informal parties that were held after the club was closed for the evening. Lana had had the hots for Dean and wasn't afraid to let him—and everyone else in the room—know how she felt.

But now it was nearly 1962, and Lana was a lot older—still beautiful and sexy at forty-two, but a bit matronly, comparatively speaking, to appeal to Dean, who liked his women younger and younger the older he got. Dean would invite Lana, along with a dozen others, to his bungalow for lunch, but once she realized that there'd be "more drinking than eating," as she put it, she would simply grab a plateful and head for her own room. Lana was further irritated by Dean because she was anxious to get home to her latest husband, a wealthy real-estate bigwig named Fred May, but Dean's lunches went on so long, she was inevitably late due to the overtime, which did not sit well with hubby. "Dean believed in the value of time a lot less than I did," she remembered. "In his happy-go-lucky way he paid little attention to the shooting schedule. Instead of the ordinary one-hour lunch break, he would stretch his into two or three." Lana complained about it to the film's producer, Jack Rose, who placated her with an "I'll see what I can do." When Dean heard about Lana's grumbling, he shrugged and wrote her off. Mann remembered that Dean put out such a spread that everyone but Lana would go to his dressing room bungalow for lunch—Italian food, lots of Dean's pals, and pitchers of martinis—instead of the studio commissary. Every now and then Dean's bookie would show up to take some bets.

Who's Got the Action? had Dean as Steve Flood, a divorce lawyer who nearly gets separated from his own wife, Melanie (Lana), because of his gambling. Melanie thinks he's preoccupied with another woman, but when she learns it's just the horses, she's at first relieved until she finds out how much money he's lost. She decides to become a phony bookie: Steve will give her the money through a third party, her friend and his co-worker, Clint Morgan (Eddie Albert), and instead of losing anything, she'll present him with a check for the full amount when the year is over. There's just one problem: Steve starts picking winners, and Melanie is going into hock and selling her furniture trying to pay him what he's "won" (remember, she never really places any bets) without him getting wise to her machinations. Before too long she's attracted the attention of a real bookie (Walter Matthau) who uses a computer called a Univac machine to play the horses and thinks Melanie is a rival he'll need to "rub out." This being a movie, eventually everything is straightened out after the amusing but outrageously contrived plan of operations.

Dean is charming and well cast as Flood, and whatever the two thought of each other offscreen, Lana and Dean had the right chemistry when the cameras were rolling. "Nobody bucks the mob," Steve says to Clint when the latter mentions that he's found a "new" bookmaker. He's delightful telling a waiter in a club to "pour Scotch all over us!" and slapping Clint's hand off his knee, which Clint accidentally brushes as he tries to get some cash into Melanie's anxious paws. Melanie also has a funny lunch date with Clint, where she's prepared to tell the romantically inclined fellow that she's divorcing Steve until she learns he's obsessed with horses and not women, to Clint's regret.

Nita Talbot, a latter-day Eve Arden, really scores as Matthau's girl-friend, who tells Melanie, "These days everything's done through a mid-dleman. Well, almost everything." She sparks up every scene that she's in. Oddly, considering that he was the only real comedian of the bunch, Matthau's performance is overdone, a bit self-conscious, and out of sync with the mood, which is frenetic but not quite farcical. Margo makes a good impression as Melanie's maid, Rosa, who was the one who told her that Steve had "something on the side" in the first place. "I'm gonna make coffee good and black," she tells her employer, "then we can start talking about what every red-blooded American woman wants—alimony!" Character actors Paul Ford and John McGiver as a couple of horse-bet-ting judges—as well as George Duning's amusing score—add to the fun. Ford's classic line to an old man who's just married a hot babe a third of his age: "I know how important time is to you."

Who's Got the Action? is a cute picture that eventually gets too silly and involved for its own good, but it is handsomely appointed, smoothly directed by Mann, and has more than enough funny lines and situations to make it work. According to the *New York Morning Telegraph*, "Martin, Albert, and Turner go through their paces with great good will. None of it can be taken seriously, a good deal of it is as ridiculous as it is prepos-terous, but there is no getting away from the magic effect exerted by [Matthau's] Univac machine."

Dean had met sex goddess Marilyn Monroe through Sinatra, and while he was always wary of neurotic women, he basically liked her even if he felt it best to keep his distance. On one occasion, when Marilyn had gone on and on and *on* about her *Misfits* costar, the late Clark Gable, Dean had caused her to throw a drink at him because he half jokingly told her that maybe her behavior on the set of that picture had ultimately given Gable his fatal heart attack. However, when she suggested that the two of them team up in a remake of *My Favorite Wife*, the Cary Grant–Irene Dunne starrer of 1940, he was undeniably intrigued. If nothing else it promised good box office, and Dean thought working with the lady might be fun. At least the two of them got along, which was more than could have been said for him and that other neurotic female Judy Holliday. The picture, retitled *Something's Got to Give*, would be a co-production of Dean's Claude Productions and Marilyn Monroe Productions, everything arranged by the ever helpful MCA.

The notion that Marilyn had to talk 20th Century-Fox into giving Dean the part, that they preferred James Garner—a story which has been bandied about for years—is not very credible. Executives would hardly have preferred Garner, who was to find his greatest success in television, over a superstar like Dean Martin. It's more likely that Garner was an early choice for the role until Dean's availability was ascertained. After that, Marilyn would *not* have had to sell him to the studio.

The story was about a man (Dean) who remarries after his first wife has apparently been lost at sea for years. Shortly after he's set up house-keeping with his second bride (Cyd Charisse), who turns up but the first wife (Marilyn), finally rescued after spending years on a desert island. She does everything in her power to win her husband back from his new wife, but a complication develops when Dean learns that Marilyn was not alone on the island. She was, in fact, shipwrecked with the handsome Tom Tryon, but she tries to fool hubby into thinking her island mate was really the mousy, unthreatening Wally Cox. And so on.

The budget was set at three and a quarter million dollars, of which Marilyn would get one hundred thousand, with Dean and director George Cukor each receiving three hundred thousand (according to some sources Dean received half a million.) Costar Cyd Charisse would get fifty thousand; Tom Tryon, five thousand more. Right from the first *Something's Got to Give* was an unhappy shoot. Fox was greatly concerned with the problems on the set because they were already having enough trouble with the disastrous, money-burning production of *Cleopatra*.

Most of the trouble with *Something's Got to Give* was caused by Marilyn Monroe, who was undergoing, as did Judy Holliday before her, daily panic attacks about her appearance and her performance, developing psychosomatic, and a few legitimate, ailments at the rate of one a day. Afraid that every facial line and crease created by insomnia would show up on camera, Marilyn continually overdosed on sleeping pills. Because of this, she was so groggy that filming in the early-morning hours was generally a total waste of time, which was academic since she rarely showed up on the set before noon. During the early days of filming she reportedly had a temperature of 101 degrees and a bad sinus infection, which turned into acute sinusitis, giving her headaches that were so miserable—or so she said—that they kept her bedridden. Cukor shot around her and filmed scenes with Dean and others, as well as some of Marilyn's subjective point-of-view shots.

Trying to recuperate—or merely get herself together—Marilyn was dismayed by all the script changes and afraid that her "comeback" film would be a disaster. (After a while nothing was left of the original script but four or five pages.) Her psychiatrist gave her more barbiturates and tranquilizers to calm her down but the major effect they had on her was to make her seem alcoholic. Still she was well enough to go and sing "Happy Birthday" for President Kennedy on May 29, 1962, which everyone involved in the production of *Something's Got to Give* certainly took notice of. Marilyn had actually been denied permission to go to the gala because the film was behind schedule; Dean had canceled his own appearance there for the same reason. An expensive dream sequence with Marilyn, Dean, and Tom Tryon on an island was planned for that day, but of course it had to be delayed due to her absence.

Everyone was cool to Marilyn, wondering about her assorted "illnesses" and professional attitude when she returned to work. Then Dean got a cold and couldn't report to the set for several days himself. He may have genuinely caught a bug, but perhaps he also wanted some time off and figured if Marilyn could do it, so could he. Afraid she would catch something from him, Marilyn told Cukor she wouldn't report to the set if Dean did until his cold was gone. Hearing that, Dean was certainly not in the mood to show up for work and spoil that delicate system of hers.

It was while Dean was out sick that Marilyn's famous pool scene was shot. Clad in a skin-toned bikini, she was filmed in the pool virtually all day. At one point when she came out and put on a towel for another shot, her bikini strap was visible, so she obligingly removed the top for the cameraman. Then she decided, Why not have some still photographers take some "nude" shots—she'd actually only be naked under a towel—as a publicity stunt? These poses would never appear in the movie. Cukor loved the idea—if little else about Marilyn—and brought in several freelance photographers to snap her from every conceivable angle.

Dean, now recovered from his cold, finally worked with Marilyn again as well as Cyd Charisse in a scene wherein Marilyn pretends to be a maid in her own home and does a great Garbo imitation. She still had a fever and an ear infection. Dean hated the fact that for one scene, amounting to only five shots in the film, they had to do forty-six takes, and dialogue rehearsals for each scene went on for as long as six or seven hours. Marilyn's last scene—the day of her thirty-sixth birthday—was where she tries to convince Dean that it was Wally Cox who was with her on the island, not Tom Tryon. Footage shows that Dean, Wally, and Marilyn seemed to be enjoying themselves and were pleasant with each other between takes. At one point Dean looks at Marilyn's rear end, points his finger at her as if his hand were a gun, and says, "Haven't I seen that some place before?" Cukor, however, thought these shots were fit only for the scrap heap. "Marilyn was acting as if she were underwater," he said. Yet all but one of the fourteen takes (where Cox flubbed a line) have been deemed by some as "perfect."

After a full day of shooting, there was a small birthday celebration for Marilyn on the set. Besides Dean, it was attended mostly by prop men and crew members and an unenthusiastic Cukor. It quickly relocated inside Dean's dressing room, where Marilyn got a congratulatory call from Marlon Brando. Dean consoled Marilyn on being thirty-six. "Wait'll ya hit forty," he told her, then was teased by her because she knew he was actually forty-five. The party was over—even Dean had left—within half an hour. That night Marilyn took one of Dean's sons to a baseball game at Dodger Stadium, where she threw out the first ball and signed autographs.

The problems with Marilyn were not over, however. More paranoid and hysterical than genuinely ill (for one thing she had already proved that she could work with a sinus infection and fever), Marilyn refused to report to the set. Fed up with her antics, executives at Fox wanted to replace her with Kim Novak, with whom Dean would work in the future. Cukor felt her scenes were completely unusable, and told Peter Harry Brown in the *Los Angeles Times* in 1979: "She should have been in an institution instead of [on] a soundstage."

Was Marilyn's footage "unusable"? Anyone who has seen the footage, including this writer, can't possibly agree. She does seem a little spacey, her eyes a bit unfocused, in some scenes, but not enough to make the footage irredeemable. Her acting is fine throughout, and Dean is wonderful; the two play very well together, in fact. The surviving sequences are also carefully lit and beautifully photographed.

In truth, Cukor had lost patience with Marilyn's neurotic behavior, and he had never particularly wanted to make the movie, with or without her, in the first place. He detested the screenplay, which is the reason it went through so many revisions. Tom Tryon felt that Cukor was making a mistake but also felt that Cukor honestly didn't believe he could get a decent performance out of her. Not unless she had time to fully rest and recuperate and get her act and emotions and assorted neuroses under control—time that the studio simply did not have. Based largely on Cukor's reports, Fox execs decided Marilyn had to be fired, a development that devastated the actress. (There were some who felt that it was Cukor, not Monroe, who should have been fired, since it was Monroe who brought moviegoers into the movie house, not Cukor.) "Cukor was too angry at Marilyn to be objective about her work," Tryon said. "They were oil and vinegar, yin and yang; they just could not find a common human ground to reach each other [on]." Meanwhile Dean, who wanted to get on with his life and career and not be making *Something's Got to Give* for the next ten years, wondered why he had ever agreed to enter into the arrangement with Marilyn in the first place.

Dean didn't hear about Marilyn's firing until late afternoon on Friday, June 8, when Marilyn's makeup artist, Whitney Snyder, told him what he'd heard. Dean immediately had his assistant rush over to the production offices to get confirmation or denial. When he heard that, yes, it was true Monroe had been fired, and Lee Remick had been hired to replace Marilyn, he decided to walk. "I have the greatest respect for Miss Remick as an artist," he said, "but I signed to do this film with Marilyn Monroe." Dean had Herman Citron notify Fox that he was quitting the picture.

Marilyn saw this as payback, a sign of loyalty from Dean, because she had helped circulate the fiction that she'd butted heads with the Fox front office to get him hired over James Garner. Actually Dean had lost patience with Marilyn and was anxious to do *Toys in the Attic*, which he might miss out on if filming on *Something's Got to Give* was delayed any further. It must be remembered that the film was being made under the auspices of his production company as well as Marilyn's, and he stood to lose a lot of profit if the film didn't perform well at the box office. Dean knew that people would come to see him and Marilyn—especially Marilyn—even if the finished film wasn't up to snuff, but Dean and Lee Remick? Remick wasn't box office; her presence in the film as his leading lady would never guarantee a big take as Marilyn's would. Perhaps it was better to pull the plug and cut his losses. *He* was not going to wind up like Gable!

According to Cyd Charisse, Cukor—at least in her presence—seemed sympathetic to Marilyn, but "Dean did not have any patience at all." Charisse recalled being asked to come into the studio days before she was scheduled to do so because of Marilyn's absence. When the studio called, "Dean grabbed the phone to urge me to come in. 'Goddamn it, we haven't been able to shoot an inch of film today.'" When Charisse arrived at the lot, "Dean was pacing up and down, absolutely beside himself. He told me he had another film, a serious dramatic film, waiting for him . . . he was fuming. The next morning I woke up and saw screaming headlines that said MARILYN FIRED! I've long thought that he was, somehow, the one who brought the pressure that resulted in her being fired."

Whether this is true or not, Dean had come to feel, as did Cukor, that Monroe was incapable of finishing the production, either because she was too emotionally disturbed to do so or because she *thought* she was too emotionally disturbed to do so, which more or less amounted to the same thing. Dean may have had sympathy for Marilyn, but he was not there to solve her psychological problems. He certainly would have been capable of applying pressure to get her fired, then refusing to work with any other actress, just so the whole mess could be behind him. But like death and taxes, litigation was a constant factor in Dean's life, as he would shortly discover.

Marilyn's part was offered to Kim Novak, Shirley MacLaine, and Doris Day, all of whom turned it down within hours of receiving the offer. Lee Remick, under contract, was told she had to do the film, and press releases bearing alleged statements made by her about Monroe's "lack of professionalism" were circulated. Remick later denied making these remarks, claiming they were cooked up by the publicity department, and said she was never entirely certain whether or not she would actually have been put into the picture, despite meetings and photo sessions with Cukor and the like.

One newspaper headline, which Marilyn loved, read NO MM, NO MARTIN. Philip Feldman, who was Fox's VP in charge of Studio Operations, importuned Citron to talk sense into his client and have him agree to work with Remick. When this didn't work, Feldman said the studio would file a lawsuit against the actor. Feldman even bypassed Citron at one point and made a special call to his boss at MCA, the powerful Lew Wasserman, but even Wasserman couldn't change Dean's mind.

Not just the studio was furious at Dean. Other actors, crew members, and the unions they belonged to were afraid his heroic actions would shut down the picture for good and deprive gainful employment to an awful lot of people. The studio was already wary of Dean because package deals such as those put together by MCA—standard procedure nowadays—were seen as detrimental and challenging to the old studio system.

At a meeting with Feldman and other execs, Dean was unaware that a $5.6 million "breach of contract" lawsuit was already being drafted by Fox's legal department, this despite Dean's contract that gave him casting approval of his leading lady. Dean explained that no one would believe he would be tempted to leave his beautiful second wife, Cyd Charisse, for Lee Remick. Monroe, yes; Remick, no. Remick was attractive, but not hot and sexy like Monroe. (Dean was right: In the surviving footage Cyd Charisse looks so gorgeous, she would have easily blown Lee Remick right out of the water.) The studio execs argued that the story dealt more with a man caught in an untenable position—between two wives he equally loves—than a married man torn between a wife and a sultry temptress;

the first wife who comes back did not need to be a hot mama. Dean undoubtedly told them his fears about the box office if Remick were Monroe's replacement—money being the major root of the studio's concern—but they were convinced that holding on to Marilyn would just be throwing good money after bad; they wanted some return on their investment, and putting Remick in seemed the only way to get it. Dean felt that shutting down the picture in the long run would not hurt him—careerwise and pocketbookwise—as much as going ahead with Remick and having the movie bomb.

When Dean refused to back down, the studio ultimately sued him for $3 million; he sued them back, charging that they had damaged his reputation and put his career in jeopardy. His suit asserted that Marilyn was capable of completing the film and had been fired for "political motives." Dean's official position was that he and especially Monroe had become scapegoats for studio heads who needed someone to blame at the stockholders' meeting for the implosion of the picture and the monetary losses it would have engendered.

Meanwhile, Marilyn—whose advisers forced her to pull herself together, at least temporarily—invited Fox production head Peter Levathes to her home, where she said she wanted to continue on the film and would behave herself, which led to a renegotiation of her contract. She was not only taken back but offered an additional role; a musical film entitled *What a Way to Go.* For both roles she would receive one million dollars.

Fox wasn't being kind; the studio reasoned that Monroe could still be a big box-office attraction, especially now that all the firings and lawsuits—not to mention Marilyn's sensational "semi-nude" photo spread taken at poolside—would generate millions of dollars' worth of free publicity. With this reinstatement (at least verbally) both Fox and Dean decided to drop their respective lawsuits against each other, as did Fox and Monroe; besides, by this time the power structure at Fox had undergone some changes. It looked as if nothing would stop things from proceeding, with the exception of Monroe's lawyers, who kept stalling because they felt she needed time to recuperate from all the emotional turmoil and the physical toll it had taken before she returned to the soundstage. Filming would be delayed until Martin finished *Toys in the Attic,* which had started production. Now that Dean was certain he would not miss out on that picture, he could tolerate the thought of going back to work on *Something's Got to Give* with Marilyn.

Finally, things began to move. A more sympathetic director, Jean Negulesco, was hired to replace George Cukor, who wanted no part of the movie or Marilyn. The original script by Nunnally Johnson was dusted off, replacing the patchwork quilt created by so many different hands and so many rewrites. But while many of Marilyn's demands were met, she was told to get rid of her disruptive acting coach, Paula Strasberg, whom many people saw as the true reason for all her vicissitudes on the set of *Something's Got to Give*.

Marilyn's death on August 4, 1962, of course made everything academic. Whatever the ultimate reason for her demise—the latest theories seem to indicate that it was accidental—it is clear it could not have been because her career was derailed.

Afterward screenwriter Hal Kanter was brought in to look at the existing footage and see if he could come up with a new screenplay that could incorporate all of Marilyn's scenes without requiring additional footage of her, but Fox decided to pull the plug on this idea (which had been successfully used for the film *Saratoga* when Jean Harlow died in midproduction and a double was brought in to complete the few remaining long shots).

Dean and Jeanne Martin, along with Frank Sinatra, tried to attend Marilyn's funeral and later enter the cemetery where her body would be interred in a mausoleum, but they had been crossed off the list of "suitables" by Joe DiMaggio—who hated Hollywood people and blamed them in part for Marilyn's death—and they were not admitted by the guards.

In the meantime *Something's Got to Give* was completely reshot by director Michael Gordon with Doris Day, James Garner, Polly Bergen, and Chuck Connors in the roles originally played by Monroe, Martin, Charisse, and Tryon. It was released under the title *Move Over, Darling*. Dean didn't make a cent on it and never went to see it.

Had Marilyn and Dean managed to complete The Movie that Never Was, it would undoubtedly have been a much better picture.

FOURTEEN

Hellman

Dean had come a long way from the days when he made a few hundred dollars a week singing in Chinese restaurants. His motion picture salary was at least a quarter of a million dollars per picture and up (not including the money he'd eventually garner if the film were produced by Claude Productions); he got at least fifty thousand a week when he played Las Vegas; and his fee for hosting television specials was also in the fifty-thousand-dollar range. Then there was all the money he got from his recording contracts and residuals.

His chief reaction to all of this moola, besides satisfaction, was, "God! The taxes I'm gonna hafta pay!" Stars on his financial level don't always sit back and relax and enjoy all the loot coming in; they worry about the chunks taken out by managers, agents, and the IRS—and in Dean's case, alimony, child support, the upkeep of his properties, plus all he'd need to maintain his standard of living for his wife and seven children. They worry about what would happen if for some reason all of it were suddenly taken away, which is why celebrities demand top dollar when they can, knowing their glory days may not last forever. This is not to imply that Dean was hurting. He lived like a king.

Like most men in his position, Dean looked for things to invest in, including the aforementioned Dino's and the Cal-Neva Lodge, neither of which turned out to be worth his time or attention. The same was true of the Hancock Raceways in Massachusetts in which he and Frank Sinatra bought stock in 1961. Dean could only roll his eyes and wonder "Now what?" when he found himself co-defendant, with Frank, in yet *another* lawsuit, this one filed by a doctor who claimed that his accountant and the track's president, a man named Rizzo who was alleged to have shady connections, sold his stock illegally and without his permission. Dean's and Frank's lawyers, getting richer and richer all the time, maintained that their clients had no knowledge that the stock was tainted and were no longer co-directors of Hancock Raceways; the suit was dropped. Could Dean have been blamed if he'd turned to Frank and said "This is another fine mess . . ."?

By this time Dean's talent agency MCA, which was already planning to produce pictures by acquiring Universal, also bought Decca Records, which was one step too many as far as the Department of Justice was concerned. They argued that MCA could not continue to control the lion's share of the entertainment industry without becoming a monopoly. Naturally MCA's clients would get the best deals when it came to movie contracts with Universal or recording contracts with Decca. With their back to the wall, MCA had to divest itself of something, and it decided its talent agency, what had once been its backbone, had to go. Then Dean's agent, Herman Citron, got together with a man named Arthur Park, and the two formed the Citron-Park Talent Agency, with a select group of illustrious clients, including Dean. Dean's interests would continue to be protected.

On the home front, Dean and Jeanne seemed to be reasonably happy during this period. Dean didn't like conversation during dinner, so the family would watch TV while they were eating. "You never saw a happier, jollier, gayer house than ours," he told the *Saturday Evening Post*. "My wife, Jeanne, and I make it happy. We tell the others, 'There's going to be happiness in this house, see!' and we do everything we know how to make it happy." He talked about the tennis courts and the pool and the friends that came over on weekends. Of course what this translated into was that Dean wanted everyone happy because he did not want to be bothered with their problems. He also figured that with all the luxuries and conveniences that his wife and children had, there was no reason for anyone *not* to be happy. Dean may have worried from time to time about the IRS and the latest litigation—whatever Sinatra had gotten him into—but he knew he had fallen into the catbird seat.

Dean was also easier to live with during this period because he wasn't under so much tension, as had been the case when he'd been struggling to find his own identity while partnering with Jerry Lewis and during those especially dark days when *Ten Thousand Bedrooms* bombed and everyone thought his days as a superstar were over. Now that he had become a complete success as a solo, most of the tension was gone, he was fulfilled, he was happy. Today Jeanne says, "I have never, ever known a man who was as totally content as Dean was."

Dean heard from Howard Hawks, who asked him what he thought of doing another western with John Wayne, something called *The Yukon Trail*. In the film, to have taken place during the Gold Rush era, he and Wayne would be cattle drivers moving a herd through Alaska, encountering adventure, thrills, and romance every step of the way. Dean told him he'd be delighted to do the film, but Hawks admitted the project was one of several he was mulling over. Hawks never did make the movie; he settled instead on a feeble romantic comedy with Rock Hudson and Paula Prentiss entitled *Man's Favorite Sport?* Five years later Hawks did do another western, *El Dorado*, considered a follow-up of sorts to *Rio Bravo*, in which Duke was a gunfighter helping a drunken sheriff suppress range hostilities, but this time the drunk was played by Robert Mitchum (whom Dean himself would work with in a few years) not Dean, because he was committed to his Matt Helm pictures at the time. When in 1970 Hawks did his *Rio Lobo*, another film in the *Rio Bravo* mold, Dean was busy with *Airport*.

Bud Yorkin, who had once been a stage manager on the *Comedy Hour* program with Martin and Lewis, was directing his first film, an adaptation of Neil Simon's play *Come Blow Your Horn* (1963) starring Frank Sinatra, when Frank suggested it might be fun to have Dean play a small cameo of a street drunk in the picture. Today Yorkin says, "To the best of my recollection, the cameo bit that Dean did in *Come Blow Your Horn* was a last-minute improv done on the set. Dean came over to visit Frank as we were shooting the scene on the street set at Paramount, and everyone thought it would be funny if Frank ran into a drunk and then revealed that it was Dean. As far as I can remember, there was no script for this cameo." Clad in a dusty coat and with five o'clock shadow, Dean approaches Frank and Barbara Rush on the sidewalk sixty-two minutes into the film and says, "Hey, buddy, could you help me out? I ain't et in two days." Frank then hands him a raw steak with which he's been nursing a black eye. As Rush and Sinatra walk away, Dean addresses the camera and says. "Why didn't I tell the truth? Why did I have to lie? Why didn't I tell him what I really wanted?" Presumably, a drink. It's a funny bit.

Doing movies, even bits, with Frank was always fun, but sometimes entertaining with the Chairman of the Board had its dark side. Frank was being pressured by Sam Giancana to appear with the other Rat Packers for the opening engagement of his new club in the suburbs of Chicago, the Villa Venice. Frank also knew that Giancana was furious with Dean since he had pulled out of the Cal-Neva deal on learning of Sam's involvement. Once Sam had wanted Dean to perform there as a quick replacement for an ill entertainer, but Dean, citing other plans, refused; he would entertain there when scheduled, but that was all. Frank figured buddy Giancana would be appeased if Dean went along with him to Chicago and performed at the new club for free. *"For free?"* Dean asked his buddy incredulously. Frank told him they would ultimately make much much more than their usual fees if they recorded the opening-night sessions and released a special album—*Live from the Villa Venice*—to the public. Unfortunately Dean and the others were so footloose, untrammeled, and vulgar in making up risqué substitute lyrics for so many of the songs they sang that the tapes were ultimately deemed unreleasable.

That same year Jerry Lewis came out with one of his most famous movies, *The Nutty Professor*, in which he played a nerdy, buck-toothed, bespectacled chemistry teacher who turns into a smooth, unctuous, and obnoxious lounge singer named Buddy Love after he takes a drink of his special formula. Lewis was terrific in this comic variation on *Dr. Jekyll and Mr. Hyde*, but the real story was the characterization of Buddy Love. Was it *Dean* or wasn't it?

Jerry himself always denied that he'd based the character on Dean— "Buddy Love was a composite of all those rude, distasteful, odious, crass, gross imbeciles whom we can spot instantly at any gathering . . . . He's all those things, but he isn't Dean"—and there are those who maintain that Buddy was actually the real Jerry Lewis, but the real answer isn't hard to figure. Their feuding days may have been over, but as their encounters on the Paramount lot had made clear, the bitterness, irritation, and resentment—at least on Jerry's side—was still there. At the very least, on an unconscious level Jerry used much of what he knew, or wanted to believe, about Dean Martin to create his Buddy. Buddy Love is Dean Martin *filtered* through Jerry Lewis.

Jerry doesn't do a direct imitation of Dean in *The Nutty Professor* but more of a takeoff, portraying him as the uptight, hostile, defensive creature he must have seemed to be to Jerry during the final months of their breakup. The real Dean was probably not as vain (although he *was* vain) or egotistical as Buddy Love, but Lewis exaggerated those traits in his characterization. He holds a cigarette the way Dean does and seems to imitate his singing style but not his voice or vocal "leer," which he may not have been able to do in any case. Sometimes Buddy seems to be a petulant Frank Sinatra practicing wise-guy tactics, which would fit since Jerry now knew Dean was much closer to Frank than he was to Jerry. Jerry also gets in a dig at Dean's lack of intellectual sophistication when the picture's love interest, played by Stella Stevens, says, "If Buddy has any real intelligence, he has a fantastic talent for keeping it hidden."

Buddy Love is self-absorbed, insensitive, miserable to women, none of which may have been true about Dean but all of which Jerry had come to think of his former partner and best pal. It must be remembered that although Jerry himself tomcatted, he somewhat disapproved of Dean dumping Betty for Jeanne. (Jerry never left wife Patti; she divorced him in 1982 after a relationship with one honey became too public.) At that time Dean must have seemed insensitive and unkind to Betty indeed.

If anyone wonders if Jerry had left those early Martin and Lewis days behind him and had no interest in lampooning Dean, they need only refer to the scene where Jerry, as Buddy, listens to the dean of faculty as he lists the entertainers he's invited to the college for a special event. "Who's this Wicker and Watt?" Buddy asks. "Are they the comedy team? I thought they'd split up." It's also true that the idea for *The Nutty Professor* and who Buddy Love would be based on had probably been germinating in Jerry's mind for years.

Is Buddy Love actually Dean? He's Dean Martin as Jerry Lewis had come to see him, as he wanted others to see him and realize him as being, even if only on a subconscious level. But he was not, could not, be the *real* Dean Martin if for no other reason than Buddy Love was completely devoid of charm and a sense of humor, something you could *never* have said about Dean Martin.

Pauline Kael of the *New Yorker* caught on to what Jerry was up to as well as the duality of Buddy Love in her retrospective review of *The Nutty Professor*: "When [Jerry] drinks his formula he turns into a brash, domineering hipster singer named Buddy Love—i.e., a cartoon of Dean Martin. Lewis has reconstituted his former team but now plays both halves, and working within this format he has some scenes that can hold their own with the classic silent comedies . . . . Lewis plays the hapless Julius for childlike pathos, and Buddy for hollow-man Las Vegas loathsomeness; yet in his [Jerry's] TV appearances in the years that followed, he moved even closer to Buddy Love—even down to singing loudly and off key, and being aggressively maudlin as he milked the audience for approval."

Dean had more important things to think about than Jerry Lewis and any vengeance he may have had in mind. He wound up in his next movie, perhaps his most important, at least in his growth as an actor, because his agent Herman Citron went to the theater while on a visit to New York. The play he saw was *Toys in the Attic* by Lillian Hellman, the author of such works as *The Children's Hour*, *The Little Foxes*, and *Another Part of the Forest*.

Hellman got the basic idea for her new play from her lover, Dashiell Hammett, who suggested she write about a man who becomes successful to please his family but, realizing they prefer him as a failure, he deliberately sabotages his success and becomes even more desperate and destitute than before. (In the finished play his success seems sabotaged more by outside forces than by himself). The characters were primarily based on members of Hellman's own family—"Julian" her father, "Lily" her mother, and the two sisters her maiden aunts. As in the play, Hellman's father was helped by his sisters, he married a somewhat vague younger woman, and his wealthy mother-in-law did set him up in a business that failed.

The play was produced on stage by Kermit Bloomgarden and directed by Arthur Penn, better known as the director of such films as *Bonnie and Clyde*, with Maureen Stapleton and Anne Revere as the two sisters, Jason Robards as their brother Julian, and Irene Worth as his mother-in-law, Albertine. *Toys in the Attic* got generally respectful reviews—with reservations—from the New York critics, but it was pilloried in London. It eventually emerged as Hellman's second most successful play, running for 556 performances, and won the Drama Critics Circle Award for best play of 1960—although some felt there wasn't much, if any, serious competition.

Like other playwrights, Hellman was influenced by Tennessee Williams, but as author William Wright put it, "Williams would plumb the depths of his quirky characters and find truths that applied to everyone; Hellman plumbed the depths of her quirky characters and found quirks." Repressed, barely acknowledged psychosexual truths were not Hellman's forte; she was better when she was dealing with such up-front failings as greed and lust for power, as evidenced in the powerful *The Little Foxes* and its devastating prequel *Another Part of the Forest*. Yet *Toys in the Attic* was still a strong, fascinating, well-written play that did not deserve the obscurity it seems to have fallen into. Which is also true of the film adaptation.

Citron immediately thought that Dean would be perfect for the part played by Robards on the stage. (Both Dean and Robards at that time were fond of drink, although it was much more of a problem for the latter.) As soon as he heard that a film version was in the works, Citron told Dean he wanted to go after it for him. "Herman generally gave good advice," Dean said later. "It was really his idea that I do the part. He kept tellin' me how important it would be for me, a Broadway show, all the awards, that stuff. I admit I got all caught up in that. When I found out that Herman got me the part, I was real determined to do right by it. I was workin' with some pretty big, talented actresses, and I wanted to hold up my own end, that's all."

The "pretty big, talented actresses" were Geraldine Page in the part played by Maureen Stapleton on the stage, and Wendy Hiller in the Anne Revere role. Page and Hiller were distinguished serious actors, as was Jason Robards Jr., so tongues wagged along Broadway and out in Hollywood when it was announced that Dean had been signed for the Robards role, regardless of the acclaim he'd received for such films as *Young Lions*, *Rio Bravo*, and *Career*, which had also been adapted from a Broadway play. Those films, despite the literary or theatrical sources they may have been based on, were seen as products of Hollywood, while *Toys in the Attic* (1963), until it was actually released, was seen as a vaunted "theater film." Interestingly, while Jason Robards was given an entire song—"A Great Day, a Bernier's Day"—to sing in the play, Dean only warbles a bar or two of it for a few seconds as he bounces down the stairs.

Kermit Bloomgarden talked a friend, director George Roy Hill, whose first and only directorial assignment to that date had been the adaptation of Tennessee Williams's *Period of Adjustment*, into helming the Hellman play, even though Hill made it clear that he had little interest in heavy dramas; indeed his biggest commercial hits would be such lightweight fare as *Butch Cassidy and the Sundance Kid* and *The Sting*. Dean had already been cast by the time Hill came onto the project, as were Page and Hiller. Actress Gene Tierney met Hill at a party not long after he was signed and mentioned that although she was no longer interested in a full-time career, she did want "to keep a foot in the door." Tactfully, Hill told her the only part in *Toys in the Attic* that had yet to be cast required an "older" woman. Gene was forty-two to Dean's forty-five but she agreed to play his mother-in-law, Albertine, and dyed her hair gray for the role. Yvette Mimieux, who was twenty-three, was cast as Dean's wife, Lily.

In *Toys in the Attic*, Dean is Julian Bernier, who with his young bride, Lily, comes back for a visit to New Orleans where he was raised. He drops by the old house where his spinster sisters, Carrie (Geraldine Page) and Anna (Wendy Hiller), still live. While overjoyed to see him, the women become suspicious when he showers them with expensive presents and tells them he has not only paid off the mortgage but bought them tickets for a cruise to Europe. They have been down this route before with Julian, who has never really succeeded at anything, but Julian insists that this time his ship really has come in. Lily, a fragile, neurotic thing, is afraid that her wealthy mother, Albertine, paid Julian to marry her, a paranoia that Carrie plays on to stop Julian when she learns that he's planning to leave for New York with Lily. Anna confronts Carrie with her own suspicion—that Carrie has incestuous feelings for her own brother. Julian has received a large cash payment from a banker, Cyrus Watkins (Frank Silvera), whose abused wife, Charlotte, told old boyfriend Julian about some valuable property—two acres of swampland that a new railroad will run on—that her husband was planning on acquiring. Tipped off, Julian bought it first, resold it to Watkins, and plans to give half the money to Charlotte so that she can flee her husband and start a new life. Egged on by Carrie, Lily tells Watkins what has happened, and he sends thugs to slash his wife's face, beat up Julian, and take the money. Julian is furious at his wife when Carrie tells him what Lily did, but sister Anna knows that Carrie is really responsible and urges Julian to forgive his wife and leave New Orleans. Since the tickets were already paid for, Anna goes off on the trip to Europe and leaves her sister alone and miserable in the big old empty house.

Screenwriter James Poe, who had adapted some of Tennessee Williams's plays for the big screen, always took a lot of flack for watering down the situations, which was necessitated by the production code. But the screenplay for *Toys in the Attic*, which Hill later claimed he heavily revised, does *not* water down the play nor even de-emphasize the incest subplot in any way. The main difference between play and film is that the movie opens up the locations and has a happier fade-out. At the end of the play Anna does not leave for Europe and leave her sister alone, and Julian is not told by anyone about Lily's betrayal. However, her mother, Albertine, who says some of the lines given to Anna in the movie, is prepared to welcome her daughter back home when Julian finds out the truth; there seems little hope for their marriage. Wisely dropped from the play are all mentions of a revival lady who exchanges Lily's wedding ring for a knife as well as Lily telling Carrie that Julian always said his sister "kept her vagina in the icebox"—excised for obvious reasons. Added scenes include Lily and Julian at their hotel; Julian with the battered wife, Charlotte; Lily visiting her mother at home (Albertine goes to visit Lily at the two sisters' house in both play and film); and Lily looking for Julian in various New Orleans bars.

The new ending for the film version is more Hollywood yet at the same time much more dramatic than the play's finale. There was some criticism that it resembled *The Little Foxes* a bit too much, with Geraldine Page alone in her house, banging her hands on the stairs, instead of Bette Davis, also alone in her house, watching from a window as daughter Theresa Wright runs away in disgust.

Hill wanted to meet with Hellman and discuss the script with her, but for one reason or another the two never did get together, which bothered both of them greatly. Not only was Hill unenthusiastic about the project, but he injured his back during shooting and had to be hospitalized. His stay was temporary, but when he returned to the set he had to direct from a wheelchair, which he later attributed to the stylishness of the film's cinematic technique. Since the material didn't really interest him to begin with, and the back pain was a further distraction, he paid more attention to the visual style of the film than he normally would have. As he set up each shot, he mentally edited the film, something that he had learned to do from working on many television projects in the past.

Toys in the Attic is Hill's most visual and best directed movie, beginning with the shots of New Orleans during the opening credits, with the titles cleverly angled to fit inside striking examples of the city's architecture. The whole movie is beautifully shot by Joseph F. Biroc, and George Duning's warm musical contributions underscore the poignancy of the situations. Throughout the film Hill directs with intensity and sensitivity, making *Toys in the Attic* his best film—even if he himself has undervalued it over the years. Certainly the picture didn't make as much money, nor was it as much the audience pleaser, as his films with Robert Redford and Paul Newman, but those later films, compared to *Toys*, are rather one dimensional, visually uninspired, and mindless. Whatever his reasons for doing such a good job on *Toys*, his work is undeniably superlative.

According to Hill, "Dean Martin was frightened by the demands put on him and so relied on me a great deal." First-billed Dean acts right up to his costars Page and Hiller with great authority and again proves what a *natural* actor he was. While he doesn't *quite* get across all of his character's passion or desperation (perhaps Dean, unlike Julian, was too much of a winner in real life) and adapts Julian to his own persona, his performance is nonetheless extremely effective—with that added force of personality that gets him by and then some. Dean's great likability is also a tremendous asset: Julian is a man of great charm, a good person who's nearly destroyed by his own sister while trying to do someone else, the battered woman, a decent turn. His reactions and facial expressions are always dead-on, and in some scenes he's able to subdue his natural confidence and let the insecurity of the character come through. He's not bad (even if he doesn't quite pull out all the stops) in the café scene after he's been beaten and lost all the money, horrified at what happened to Charlotte, defeated and disillusioned not only by the awful events but the betrayal of his wife. Unlike Robards, he still holds back a bit too much; he could never cry on camera or get *too* emotional in front of others, even other actors and the crew. "Dino came from a school where it was considered unmanly to display emotion," said Ed Simmons, who'd been one of his and Jerry's comedy writers so long ago; and others have made the same observation over the years. No director was really able to get past that self-inflicted barrier.

Although Geraldine Page's performance is generally excellent, to some observers she may seem a bit too dithery as Carrie, more obsessed with language and its delivery than with character and reaction. James Poe had turned Carrie into a more flamboyant villainess than she is in the play, and that's how Page played her. Anna has no sympathy for Carrie's plight—having feelings for her brother that she never asked to have—which begs the question: Is Carrie meant to be that old bugaboo, the evil pervert who ruins everyone's lives through the pursuit of their perversion? To some extent this is true—the film was made in the sixties, after all—though it's also clear to the objective viewer that Carrie's problem isn't her incestuous feelings as such but rather the loathsome things she does to keep her brother near her. As sister Anna, Wendy Hiller has not a false note or an added histrionic reaction; she's quietly superb. Yvette Mimieux is a bit too pretty and sane as Lily to have anyone seriously wonder if she'd have to be sold to a man by her mother, but her performance in the film is one of her finest.

Toys in the Attic is not only one of Dean's best films but also one of his most entertaining, sustaining suspense in the early sections when we wonder where Julian got his money from and if, as before, it will all only come crashing down on him again. The movie continuously twists one's expectations. For instance, the audience and the characters in the film are convinced that Julian is having an affair with the mysterious woman who keeps phoning him, only it turns out he's really helping her to escape from her brutal husband. As a study of lonely, desperate people, *Toys in the Attic* slowly builds up to emotional fireworks. The scene when Anna confronts Carrie with her knowledge of how she hungers for her own brother is very strong—and not at all watered down from the play as many have suggested—and the early scene with Dean handing out the presents as the sisters—so afraid that their brother's latest scheme will come to naught and that everything will have to be returned—react more with sorrow than glee, is very moving. The attack on Dean and Charlotte on the dock is well handled by Hill, who has them cut off by a tractor and trapped inside a rectangle of boxes, seen from high above, as the thugs do their dirty work. There is some amusement amidst the grimness, however, such as a well-acted exchange between Dean and Gene Tierney when Julian and his mother-in-law sit on the porch, and Julian tells her that he's much more comfortable with her now that he has some money of his own. Albertine is forbearing and kind, knowing full well that the money Julian will get, while a fortune to him, is small potatoes to old money like hers.

The film—and Dean—got mixed reactions when it was released. As writer Andrew Horton put it, "Despite a somewhat wooden range at times, [Martin's] performance holds up today much better than one might expect. As Julian, Martin succeeds in conveying a sense of perpetual motion and energy that contrasts sharply with the inertia of those around him." Like *Career*, *Toys in the Attic* is practically a forgotten movie, more's the pity.

That Dean's next film is also fairly forgotten is not as much of a tragedy. *Who's Been Sleeping in My Bed?* (1963), Dean's third and last film with director Daniel Mann, must have seemed a cinch after the serious emoting of *Toys in the Attic*. In this, Dean was an actor who plays a psychotherapist on a television program. Even though Dean could have given them an early variation of "I'm not a doctor—I just play one on TV," discontented wives of his poker buddies keep dropping by to ask for his advice on their dismal marriages as if he were a real therapist. This does not sit well with his fiancée (Elizabeth Montgomery), who wonders why all the women are going in and out of his door. Finally, Dean is so discombobulated by the whole situation, he feels compelled to go see an analyst himself. Carol Burnett, overacting madly, made her film debut in this as the real therapist's nurse-receptionist and Montgomery's friend. Also in the picture is starlet Jill St. John, fresh off her assignment in *Come Blow*

Your Horn with Sinatra. Jill at that time was nicknamed Paramount on ▪ Parade; she was first Dean's girlfriend and then Frank's, among others.

As sex farces go, *Who's Been Sleeping in My Bed?* was fair to middling, with some genuinely amusing moments amid others that were mostly smarmy and foolish. Dean got good notices, however; typical of them was *Variety*'s, noting that "Martin is an amiable performer in light comedy and does fine with the material at hand." But they, and others, felt one bit was particularly tasteless: "Disagreeable is a scene in which Martin graphically demonstrates on his analyst's couch his anxiety about a gal," with Dean's words and movements being a little too licentious. Dean himself had trouble playing this scene and repeatedly and atypically messed up his lines, only because he wasn't certain if he was going over the top or not, and director Mann, willing to let him have his way, wasn't advising one way or the other.

Dean had done Broadway, won acclaim and respect as a serious actor from many critics and peers, and survived working with the likes of Judy Holliday and Marilyn Monroe. But perhaps his greatest challenge was ahead: to essentially play himself in what would turn out to be the most controversial movie of the decade.

FIFTEEN

Wilder and Wilder

Dean was getting older, and—that inevitable by-product—his children were growing up. His oldest son, Craig, was now twenty-one, old enough to have gone into the army—possibly to get away from six siblings and find himself—and get married to a girl named Sandy Pfiffer in June 1963. Craig had no show business ambitions, but that was not true of Dean's oldest daughter, Claudia, now nineteen.

"In the back of my mind I always wanted to be an actress," Claudia said. "A star. But my younger brothers and sisters were so talented. They could sing and dance and mimic people. I couldn't do a thing. I felt way out of it, to tell you the truth." Claudia was getting nowhere when she came to her father and told him that she'd been told by friends that she was lazy. "Daddy got angry." He told her, "You go out and do something about it." But it was "Daddy" who did something about it. He contacted Frank Sinatra, whose company was producing a youth film at Paramount, a moronic musical entitled *For Those Who Think Young*. Frank was only too happy to give Claudia a bit in the picture, although his daughter Nancy, already a recording artist, got a little more to do in the film. Claudia made no attempt to pretend she'd gotten anything on her own merits. "Let's face it, without Daddy I'd still be a little teenage nobody banging on agents' doors and thinking they were out or something."

Ultimately, being Dean's daughter did not do much for Claudia's fledgling career, especially after she angered him by eloping against his wishes to Las Vegas with an actor named Gavin Murrell. As Dean expected, the marriage to an older man who'd already been married before didn't last very long—certainly not as long as the rift between Dean and his daughter, which dragged on for months. On the career front, Claudia let it be known that she had been signed to "star" in something called *Pajama Party in a Haunted House* produced by the prolific combo of Samuel Z. Arkoff and James Nicholson of American-International.

There were other minor changes in Dean's life. Herman Citron had one of his associates, Mort Viner, help him in guiding the contractual ins and outs of Dean's career. Frank Sinatra sold his Reprise Records to Warner Brothers for three million dollars, then gave two thirds of that sum back to Warner Brothers so that he'd retain one-third interest in the firm. The company kept its name, so Dean was still recording on the Reprise label. He recorded some songs from Frank Loesser's *Guys and Dolls* with Sinatra and Bing Crosby (who'd soon be doing a film with them), did a couple of duets with Sammy Davis Jr., as well as covers of "I'm So Lonesome I Could Cry," "Hey, Good Lookin'," and "Second Hand Rose," among many others.

Dean's next movie, *4 for Texas*, had originally been conceived, like *Sergeants 3*, as another Rat Pack film deluxe (the clue is the numeral in the title), but background events had conspired to turn it strictly into a Dino-Sinatra film fest. Frank wasn't speaking to Peter Lawford, and Sammy Davis Jr. and Joey Bishop were busy making a low-budget gangster flick entitled *Johnny Cool* for Lawford's production company, Chrislaw. Considering his feelings for Lawford, Sinatra wasn't thrilled with these developments, but he knew the lesser members of the Rat Pack had to work. Whether he threw Davis and Bishop out of *4 for Texas* because they went to work for Lawford or if they went to work for Lawford because Sinatra gave them no roles in *4 for Texas* is moot: Sinatra's only costars this time around were Dean Martin, two gorgeous actresses named Ursula Andress and Anita Ekberg, and—of all people—the Three Stooges! To make *4 for Texas* Dean and Frank formed yet another production outfit, the Sam Company, with the film's director, Robert Aldrich, who also coscripted the picture.

At that time Aldrich was best known as the director of those aging actress horror hits *What Ever Happened to Baby Jane?* and *Hush . . . Hush, Sweet Charlotte*. After working with difficult, egomaniacal women like Bette Davis and Joan Crawford and having to deal with their feuds and fusses and fights over camera angles and dialogue, all he wanted was to have fun with Frank and Dean and soak up the stunning beauty of Ekberg and Andress—such a contrast to the likes of Bette and Joan. On location, Frank and Dean set up housekeeping again and imported Las Vegas pals, a few idle mafioso, and more than a few nubile hookers. Aldrich employed a few professionals, such as the always-reliable Victor Buono, not to mention Richard Jaeckel and even Charles Bronson, to keep things humming, shooting their scenes while The Boys slept in after their late nights.

"I'm more relaxed with men," Dean said at this time, which was understandable as there was hardly a man alive who could "relax" with the likes of Andress and Ekberg around. Anita and Dean talked a bit about old times—she had appeared in two Martin and Lewis films, with a pretty big role in their last feature, *Hollywood or Bust*—but the one he really bonded with was Ursula. She was a good gal, and the two became friends. Ursula, a sultry, sullen (in movies) beauty who'd made her mark in the first James Bond film, *Dr. No*, the year before, never complained about her role, that of a compliant I-exist-only-for-your-pleasure riverboat gal who falls for Dino. She gave Ekberg a run for her money in the battle of the mammaries, but Ekberg was still the more mountainous of the pair. As for the movie itself, to paraphrase one critic: "Texans may come and Texans may go, but bosoms can always be found."

The film pits Dean as Joe Jarrod against Sinatra as Zack Thomas, both of whom are lovable scoundrels. Zack has just finished lifting some loot from bandits when Joe comes along and does the same thing to him. Joe takes off for Galveston, but most of the town turns out to be in Zack's pocket. After a few minor skirmishes—for instance, Joe wants to open Maxine's (Andress) riverboat as (what else?) a casino, but Zack controls the docks and won't allow it. The two realize that their true enemy is the crooked president of the local bank (Victor Buono) and they join forces to defeat him and his hired gunslinger, played by Charles Bronson.

Following Sinatra's lead, Dean essentially played Dino in the Wild West, and it's clear that, as usual, he's having fun making the picture. Aldrich was to remark that you may have had to give Dean a little push in the right direction, but once he understood what you wanted, he would deliver immediately and without fuss. Like other directors, Aldrich felt that the secret to getting a good performance out of Dean—and indeed most movie star personalities—was to cast them in "something they understood, a character cut from the same cloth as they themselves." Aldrich managed to craft a few good scenes between the boys, such as their opening gunfight over the bandit loot and their final dockside confrontation before they decide to become allies, but other than that—and the surprise appearance of the Three Stooges as ninnies delivering a scandalous nude painting of Maxine to the riverboat—*4 for Texas* is pretty much a mess. Bit by bit the light, often comical, but relatively straightforward western was slowly turned into an out and out farce, with the two distinct approaches never coherently melding. There would be two more pictures before Dean got away from the Sinatra—or Copacabana—School of Filmmaking.

Not that Dean only worked professionally with Frank on pictures; they still did club engagements together, such as a January 1964 gig at the Sands that was billed as "Dean Martin and Friend"—the friend, of course, being Sinatra. Some accounts of Dean's life maintain that he was dispirited at this time, drinking more for real than for show, and that he basically wanted to retire when Sinatra wanted to go on forever. But while this scenario may have eventually come to pass, it was certainly not true as of 1964. He may have been forty-seven and feeling the inevitable strain of encroaching middle-age, but nothing indicates that "he felt like an old man," as one overdramatic biographer put it. It was true that the music scene had undergone a lot of changes, as Dean had noted with some dismay—or perhaps disinterest—but he was hardly over the hill, nor did he look it or feel it. It *was* true that Dean did not enjoy or need the club engagements—or the carousing afterward—as much as Sinatra did. Two months after the joint Sands engagement, Dean received the honor of having his footprints immortalized on the sidewalk outside Grauman's Chinese Theater, taking his place among dozens of other Hollywood luminaries. He had arrived! Although everyone in attendance knew, of course, that he had actually "arrived" years before, Dean was still honored by the tribute, and his family and friends were excited for him.

Had Marilyn Monroe not died a year earlier and *Something's Got to Give* been completed and released, Dean would have found himself in his second film of 1964 with Monroe. After Monroe's death, the movie was retailored for Elizabeth Taylor, with Frank Sinatra set to be her costar. For one reason or another—perhaps because Liz couldn't sing (*What a Way to Go* was originally conceived as a full musical, though only a couple of songs survived)—her part went to Shirley MacLaine, who was just as happy that Frank couldn't do it and her beloved Dino could. She may have gotten over her intense romantic and sexual feelings for Dean, but she still liked him much more than she did Frank, at least during this period. The director, J. Lee Thompson, was a former playwright known for helming such thrillers and action films as *The Guns of Navarone* (1961) and the original *Cape Fear* (1962). Like most directors (unless Dean was under the influence of Frank "No work, please, we're Rat Packers" Sinatra), Thompson found Dean very easy to direct except for a contretemps they had over a red wig that he wanted him to wear. Dean saw no earthly reason why he had to become a redhead for the part he was playing, threw the wig across his dressing room on the very first day of shooting, and refused to discuss the matter further. "Get that thing away from me!" he hollered and would brook no more discussion. The wig was never trotted out again.

As previously noted, far from feeling or looking like an old man, Dean actually looks terrific in *What a Way to Go* and gives his usual charming and effortless performance; he was always at his best in light romantic stuff like this picture and *Bells Are Ringing*, nothing that was *too* demanding or emotional. He plays Leonard Crawley, both the first and final love partner of Shirley's Louisa Foster, who after her first disappointment with money-obsessed Leonard turns to simple, homespun guys. But as they get ambitious, they start turning into carbon copies of Leonard and wind up working themselves to death. Each man is a loser when Louisa first meets him: Dick Van Dyke is the owner of a small neighborhood store; Paul Newman is a starving artist; Gene Kelly is a washed up entertainer. Van Dyke gets fired up to compete with Leonard's department store but drops dead after putting Leonard out of business; Newman makes a name for himself churning out masterpieces created by a special machine, but in his greedy overzealousness he winds up getting caught and crushed in the gears; and Kelly, who manages to become a Hollywood megastar, is stomped on and flattened by overanxious fans. After all this heartache— and inheritances!—Louisa winds up married to now dirt-poor Leonard, whom she probably should have stayed with in the first place.

There was talk in the preproduction phase of putting Dean in the role that ultimately went to Robert Mitchum, playing Rod Anderson Jr., the only other rich guy in the film. He's an airplane tycoon who craves a simpler existence on a farm but makes the mistake of trying to milk a bull: Both kick the bucket. Even more than Leonard Crawley, this part seemed made to order for Dean. At one point Louisa fantasizes about Anderson lying naked on a table surrounded by bathing beauties who are hugging and kissing him, and—the biggest giveaway of all—Anderson's bed is a giant martini glass complete with bubbles! The whole characterization of Anderson is of a rough-hewn guy who's learned to appreciate the finer things in life—Dean in a nutshell. Dean getting the smaller part of Crawley (he's fourth-billed after MacLaine, Newman, and Mitchum) may have had to do with time constraints and scheduling problems. He really had only a supporting part in this picture.

All the vignettes with Shirley and her various husbands are told in different, inventive styles, and the basic ambiance of the film is certainly amiable, although even Thompson felt that the result was a bit overblown.

Some real laughs get lost in all the production values and cleverness, but the film was a tremendous hit. It didn't hurt that in addition to the fine stars, such expert supporting players as Margaret Dumont (of Marx Brothers fame) and Reginald Gardner were along for the ride.

When it came time to make the final Rat Pack movie (although Dean and Frank would team by themselves one more time), the question came up of who would play the role originally conceived for Peter Lawford, who had generally been given more to do in these films than either Sammy or Joey. The Boys needed a star, and they found the perfect one in . . . Bing Crosby. Of course, Frank was not crazy that JFK had stayed at Republican Bing's home instead of at his own (this was the incident that permanently soured Sinatra on Lawford), but he also took perverse pleasure in replacing Peter with Bing just as *he* had been replaced by Bing as JFK's host, as if to say, "Two can play at that game." This was just the sort of childish, petulant revenge that would have appealed to Sinatra.

Bing was also a natural choice because he could sing, which Peter could not, meaning there could be some dynamite song sequences in the picture, and he was already considered a fringe member of the Rat Pack. According to Sammy Davis: "Crosby, though he wasn't at every party, would be there at certain times; he'd leave early if he had to go fishing or somewhere, but he'd have dinner." He had also been an occasional guest at Bogie and Bacall's Holmby Hill gatherings.

The film was entitled *Robin and the 7 Hoods* (1964), and it had fun with Sinatra's well-known association with mobsters; in this he even plays a 1920s-style gangster in Chicago. As usual with Rat Pack movies, the film itself mattered less than the fun they would have while making it, so Sinatra needed a director who was pliable and willing to shoot around them for as long as it took; a martinet need definitely not apply. Frank picked a director he'd worked with ten years previously, Gordon Douglas, who'd given Sinatra some good scenes in *Young at Heart* when he really needed good scenes. (Although *From Here to Eternity* was filmed before *Young at Heart*, Frank hadn't yet won his Oscar when shooting on the latter film began.) Douglas needed work, and Sinatra was happy to comply. The director had had a long but mostly undistinguished career: He'd been a child actor on Broadway, worked on Hal Roach comedies, and directed everything from *The Falcon in Hollywood* to *Sincerely Yours* (with Liberace) to *The Sins of Rachel Cade* with Angie Dickinson. He also directed Elvis Presley in *Follow that Dream* and Bob Hope and Anita Ekberg in *Call Me Bwana*. His best-known movie was the rather well-made thriller *Them* (1954), about ants mutated by atomic testing into thirty-foot, man-eating giants. Monster bugs had nothing on the Rat Pack, but Douglas had already proved with Hope (who liked to goof off as much as Dean and Frank did) that he was flexible and undemanding, essentially a one-take hack instead of an exacting artist, and that he could work around anything from golf games to liaisons with other-than-the-wife broads. Sinatra would work with him again.

Robin and the 7 Hoods is basically the farcical story of the power struggle between Robin (Sinatra) and Guy Gisborne (Peter Falk) who each want to take over Chicago after the latter has rubbed out a racketeer named Big Jim (Edward G. Robinson). Big Jim's daughter, Marian Stevens (Barbara Rush), tries to get Robin to rub out Guy, but Robin gives her proffered murder money to an orphanage run by Allen A. Dale (Bing Crosby), who was left on its doorstep when he was fourteen. Now the charitably inclined Robin is known as "Robin Hood," and Marian tries to enlist someone else in her cause. She'll take over the town herself with the aid of Little John (Dean), but Little John seems more interested in relaxing and, influenced by Robin, no doubt, sending a check to a home for wayward girls. When Little John hitches up with Robin, Marian then joins forces with Guy, but the latter's plan to assassinate The Boys only results in him becoming part of a new foundation—building foundation, that is. Rapidly running out of allies, Marian starts up an anti-crime morality drive with the sheriff (Victor Buono) while starting a romance with the pious orphanage head. After a couple of hours or so, the silliness simply comes to a halt as if nobody had any idea for an ending—or cared to come up with one. Robin and the 7 Hoods certainly has its fun moments, but no one could accuse it of being a memorable picture, more a patchwork of scenes cobbled together as The Boys saw fit—and measured for their talents. As in their last picture together, Sinatra is so laid-back that you can't even call it acting, and Dino does yet another impression of himself, falling back on the usual moves and expressions that had stood him well so many times over.

The best scenes in the film are the musical numbers, not because the songs (by Van Heusen and Cahn) are particularly good but because of the enthusiasm they're delivered in. Dean croons "A Man Who Loves His Mother" as he beats Frank at pool and even joins in for a few bars when Bing and Sammy belt out "Don't Mess with Mr. Booze" at a revival meeting; Sammy kept missing cues because he was so absorbed in watching Crosby work. And Dean, possibly intimidated by doing an on-screen number with his former idol, Der Bingle (as well as Frank), sounds a bit hoarse—perhaps he's singing in too low a register—when the trio performs "Style" while Dean and Frank try to find just the right outfit for Crosby. An album of the songs sung by all the fellows was released when the picture came out.

Crosby was never thrilled with the way the picture turned out. "I just took the part for a lark," he said. "I thought, gee, this will be fun working with these guys like Sammy Davis and Peter Falk—who's a great actor— we'll have a lot of laughs. It was a good part with some good songs, but I don't think they got involved enough. It was right at the time of Jack Kennedy's assassination, and there were a lot of delays. We didn't feel like working for a few days and for some reason the coordination fell apart." Judging from the earlier Rat Pack pictures, that might have happened under any circumstances. In any case, when the picture finished shooting, Dean hung around the set one afternoon so that he could make a short, directed by Douglas, exhorting viewers to contribute money to a special fund to send American athletes to the 1964 Olympics in Tokyo. It was shown in movie theaters along with *Robin and the 7 Hoods*.

If Dean hadn't any reason to feel old or over the hill at forty-seven before, he certainly didn't when his next hit record became so popular that it knocked a recording by the next great thing—which in 1964 was the Beatles—out of the number one spot. Everyone was screaming about the Beatles, including Dean's own children, especially Dino Jr. Dean knew he had a loyal audience for his recordings—they overlapped with the fans of his movies and club engagements—but he never expected to have a record in this time period that was as popular (and with more than one age group) as anything by the superhyped, phenomenally popular megastars from England. Dean couldn't stand the Fab Four's music or the way they looked, and it warmed the very cockles of his heart when his record "Everybody Loves Somebody (Sometime)" became number one on the charts, knocking "A Hard Day's Night" out of the vaunted spot. He almost hadn't recorded the number. It had been written by bandleader Ken Lane several years before, been recorded by Sinatra and others, but had never eased its way into the national consciousness. After two versions—the original recording and a snazzier cover—on two different albums became hits in addition to the hit single (of the second version), everyone in the country knew the tune. It became the song most associated with Dean Martin and helped cement his image as a national icon separate not only from Jerry Lewis but from Frank Sinatra and the other members of the Rat Pack.

Dean must have felt like the king of the mountain, ready to take on any challenge, confident in his skill and ability as well as in his powers of charm and persuasion. He didn't have to be persuaded, however, to do a takeoff on himself in his next film, a comedy directed by Billy Wilder entitled *The Dazzling Hour*. The original choice for the female lead had again been Monroe, who had worked for Wilder in *Some Like it Hot* and *The Seven Year Itch*. It's interesting to speculate on how *What a Way to Go* and *Kiss Me, Stupid* (as *The Dazzling Hour* was eventually released) would have been like had Marilyn lived to make them.

The origins of *The Dazzling Hour/Kiss Me, Stupid* are rather bizarre, and to many it's inexplicable that the project was ever seriously considered by any studio in the first place. For one thing, *The Dazzling Hour* had been a play starring Hollywood actress Olivia de Havilland, only it closed on the road and never made it to Broadway. Not only that, but it was a period piece taking place in France in the latter half of the nineteenth century. Those two factors alone should have precluded any Hollywood studio's being interested in an adaptation; as realized, it could never have been a vehicle for the then-matronly de Havilland.

But *The Dazzling Hour* had even more of a history because it was actually the American adaptation of a French sex farce from the fifties that had taken place in Victorian England. The same basic plot, with a lot of updating and contemporary window dressing, was used in the American version and in the movie that ultimately resulted. In the French play the main character is a church organist who has written an oratorio. His greatest dream is to have his masterpiece performed in London, and when a sheriff from that city arrives in the organist's town on business, the latter contrives to gain his assistance in reaching his goal. At first he plans to curry favor by offering him a night with his own wife, but as she's neither young nor good-looking, she herself offers to let the town's most notorious prostitute take her place. But the results of this scheme are curious. The sheriff becomes close not to the tart but to the organist's wife, and the organist finds himself drawn to the prostitute and vice versa. In any case, the goal is met: The oratorio is played to great acclaim in London.

In Billy Wilder's film version, updated by Wilder and his frequent collaborator, I.A.L. Diamond, the organist has become a hack songwriter and piano teacher, Orville Spooner, who lives within the dusty, dreary confines of the engagingly named Climax, Nevada. The sheriff has become a popular Las Vegas entertainer named Dino (with no last name), very, *very* much like Dean Martin. The prostitute is a likable blond nicknamed Polly the Pistol. Orville substitutes her for his wife, Zelda (without the latter's knowledge in this case) not because Zelda is unattractive but—besides the fact that she *is* his wife—because she's a big fan of Dino's, and he can't bear the thought of the singer being alone with her. He's hoping the lecherous Dino will so enjoy his evening with his "wife"—actually Polly—that he'll record several of his songs. Thinking that her husband is getting it on with the town whore, Zelda gets drunk at the scandalous Belly Button bar and winds up sleeping it off in Polly's trailer. Meanwhile, disgusted by his actions and feeling sorry for Polly, Orville throws Dino out of his house. Still horny, Dino winds up at the Belly Button, asking directions for the Pistol's trailer. Naturally, he finds Zelda instead. Polly spends the night with Orville while Dino spends the night with Zelda in the trailer. Weeks later Dino is singing one of Orville's songs on his television show; Orville wonders why he's doing the song after he threw the guy out on his keister. "Kiss me, stupid," Zelda tells him.

The brilliant comic actor Peter Sellers was originally cast as Orville Spooner. Dean found the actor hilarious and would crack up at virtually his every line and movement—just a glance in that certain way of his could do it—and would always need several minutes to recover before shooting could resume, only to have Sellers crack him up again. If that didn't get on Wilder's nerves, Sellers on-set improvisations did. Wilder wasn't just director and producer but also coscreenwriter, and he felt that his words mattered as much as his camera movements; Peter was throwing too many of them away. For his part Sellers couldn't stand the way Wilder allowed so many damn visitors onto the set. "Who *are* all these people?" he would ask, complaining that he found them too distracting. "How can I concentrate on what I'm doing?" Liking Sellers, Dean would try to prepare him for another invasion. "Blackbirds at twelve o'clock!" he'd say in an attempt to defuse Peter's tension over the many visitors. After numerous clashes between star and director, Sellers finally had a series of heart attacks—one actually "killed" him for several seconds—and he had to withdraw permanently from the picture. (Sellers's costar Kim Novak, cast as Polly the Pistol, remained with the production after she fell during shooting and hurt her back. Most of the time she had to be given shots of Novocain and plenty of pain capsules so that she could keep on working.) Dean was a bit taken aback when Sellers attacked not only all of Hollywood but, implicitly, the production of *Kiss Me, Stupid* from his hospital bed. Dean, Wilder, and others in the cast got together to send Sellers a telegram essentially calling him a stinker who was highly "unprofessional" in his attitude. Whatever problems Sellers had had with Wilder, Dean couldn't understand why he would knock the whole movie and, by association, everyone in it.

It is difficult to say how Sellers's casting in the film might have helped it or hurt it. A strong presence in his own right, he might well have unbalanced the picture and cut too much into Dean's patented charisma. The film works with the character of Dino having much more presence and authority than Orville. At the same time, most agree that the new Orville, Ray Walston, while hardly bad, was miscast. Walston has proved many times over that in the right vehicle he's a superb actor, but it's a question if *Kiss Me, Stupid* was the right vehicle for him. A strong performer, Walston eschews the light touch he evokes in other movies and makes Spooner, who is nearly pathologically jealous of his wife, an almost frightening figure, making some scenes more grim than humorous, such as when he chases a fourteen-year-old student of his out of the house because the kid bought his wife a bunch of flowers. Whether this is over-acting or simply a case of too much intensity or trying too hard is academic. To be fair to Walston, his performance cannot be said to have ruined the movie.

Dean had the same effect on Wilder that Sellers had had on him. "He'd have Billy in stitches, with tears running down his eyes," remembered Felicia Farr, who played Zelda. "He was adorable." Wilder was the exact opposite of the likes of Gordon Douglas and could be both exacting and tyrannical, but Dean knew how to play him and defused his anger with humor. Farr would tease Dean that she knew what his "deep, dark secret" was. "I never saw him drunk or busy with drinking," she said. But this was not exactly a Rat Pack movie, and Billy Wilder, as mentioned, was no Gordon Douglas. Dean behaved himself when he knew it was warranted. Besides, he never got falling down drunk and could easily have a couple of martinis without anyone even knowing he'd imbibed them. Farr later married Jack Lemmon, who would have made the perfect Orville Spooner and been a good foil for Dino—and vice versa.

Dean is wonderful in *Kiss Me, Stupid*, managing the difficult feat of playing a person who is not only a lech but a louse and making him palatable, even likable. He seems to take nothing seriously—certainly not Orville and Zelda's marriage vows—but his saving grace is that he doesn't even take *himself* seriously, something Dean was often accused of in real life. Dino is the personification of the movie's message: It's only sex; let's have fun with it and keep it in perspective. It's not worth getting all excited about—at least not for long.

Billy Wilder biographer Kevin Lally saw Dean's performance as "a devastating portrait of a celebrity's psyche—the star as self-centered, uncontrollable satyr" and also saw the performance as a "broad exaggeration of his Rat Pack image." In a sense, Walston's Orville Spooner is the personification of the reaction—from some disaffected, disenchanted men—to that image. At one point, after throwing Dino out of his house, Orville says: "Him and his Rat Pack. They think they own the earth, riding around in their white chariots, raping and looting and wearing cuffs on their sleeves. To them we're just a bunch of squares, straight men, civilians. Anytime they want to move in we're supposed to run up a white flag, hand over our homes and our wives and our liquor."

Throughout the picture Orville and others refer to Dino as if he's virtually the real deal. When they talk about Dino's records, for instance, they name "That's Amore" and other well-known Dean Martin recordings. At the opening, when Dino is doing his show in Las Vegas, he talks about making a picture with Sinatra, Bishop, etc. Dean even drives his own car in the film, a white Dual Ghia convertible, which breaks down in Climax and forces him to stay until a needed part can be obtained. (Actually Orville's lyricist, who works at the gas station, has made the mechanical difficulty seem worse than it is.) At a roadblock he quips: "Whatsa matter? That Sinatra kid missing again?" Throughout the film he spoofs his image/reality, such as when he makes appointments with half a dozen showgirls and then runs out on all of them.

But Orville's bitter speech would have applied more to Sinatra than to easygoing Dean. Dean may have slept with other men's wives, but he didn't punch out bartenders because they put too much vermouth in his martini. He didn't bully the "little guy" because he'd had one too many. But sometimes the movie Dino is uncannily like the real one, such as when he's told that the small moons on his fingernails means he's "a gentleman and a scholar." "Well you're half right," Dean says. "I'm no scholar." Although Zelda calls Dino "old-fashioned" and says, "I bet the Singing Nun sells more records than you," Dean scores one on the Beatles: "I sing better than all of them put together. And I'm younger than all of them put together." The songs Dean performs in *Kiss Me, Stupid* were Gershwin numbers, most of which had never been published before, including "Sophia," a catchy ditty that Dean recorded, and a pretty ballad about Zelda.

Had Marilyn Monroe lived she probably would have been wonderful as Polly the Pistol, but whereas Monroe had more of a comic gift, Kim Novak was the more vulnerable of the era's two sex goddesses. In pictures as diverse as Hitchcock's *Vertigo* and the oddly named *Phffft!* with Jack Lemmon and Judy Holliday, Novak always played her rather low-class characters with decided dignity. Meant to be a silly sexpot in *Phffft!* she makes the character multidimensional enough for audiences to feel for her when Lemmon simply runs off in the middle of a date and heads for his ex-wife's house for a reconciliation. Similarly, Polly the Pistol could have been played on one note—a dopey slut hardly worth worrying about—but Novak makes us understand why Orville would bust up his whole scheme just because he feels sorry for her. (Although it must be said that Orville's anger at Dino may be more because he realizes how disrespectful he's allowing Dino to be to him by the latter's *letting* him turn over his "wife"; in other words, more male ego than compassion for Polly). In any case, Novak turns Polly into a touching character that the audience can root for. The *New Yorker* noted that Novak "seems exposed, humiliated. Her lostness holds the film together."

Felicia Farr is lovely in the film, playing the thankless role of the wife with grace and humor, and her scene with Polly when the two meet in the trailer in the morning is one of the film's highlights. Dora Morande is hilarious as Zelda's mother, who thinks Orville is a complete loser and doesn't mind telling her daughter so—over and over and over again. Cliff Osmond is gross but good as Orville's writing partner and lyricist, Barney Milsap. His lyrics aren't much worse than a lot of real ones.

At the time of its release *Kiss Me, Stupid* was denounced as smut, not only because of its situations but because of its dialogue. Some of the jokes were lifted right from Dean's act, such as when he says of a showgirl: "Last night she was banging on my door for forty-five minutes—but I wouldn't let her out." One real groaner was even lifted from a previous film, *Who's Got the Action?* Orville says, "Skoal!" to Dino as he's about to take a sip of his drink, and Dino replies, "Sure it's cold. It's got ice in it." But critics objected more to the bit when Orville, referring to his house, says, "It's not very big, but it's clean," and Novak, looking him over, replies *"What is?"* Nowadays there are racier double entendres on television, but in 1964 *Kiss Me, Stupid* was considered unspeakably vulgar. According to Kevin Lally, "The true butts of the jokes . . . are its men, slaves to their sex organs or to their imagined role as dominant partners in marriage."

The film was submitted to the Production Code Administration (PCA) and to everyone's surprise was given the seal of approval by PCA head Geoffrey Shurlock, although most people felt that he was privately appalled by the film. Shurlock told reporters and interested parties that he had approved the film because he knew public taste was changing, and he respected Wilder and knew he often dealt in controversial subject matter; Billy Wilder was not exactly a pornographer, after all. There were those who felt, however, that Shurlock was completely outraged by the picture and actually wanted it released as a kind of wake-up call to the industry, to make everyone see the direction it was heading in. Billy Wilder already knew the answer to that. "Within a few years they'll be making films that we would now call pornographic," he had told Jack Lemmon, and of course he was entirely correct.

Wilder did reshoot some sequences after there were objections from the Catholic Legion of Decency. Originally the trailer scene with Dean and Felicia Farr ended with Zelda singing as Dean tries to kiss her. The camera swings up to the ceiling and the scene is over. In the revised scene, Zelda rubs Dino's back as he falls asleep. "If I weren't so old-fashioned and you weren't asleep . . ." she says. But the very next scene was left intact by Wilder: Dino comes out of the trailer the next morning, smiling, leaving Zelda in bed, undressed, also smiling, with his money in the milk bottle. Regardless of how the previous scene ended, could anyone over the age of twelve *not* know that Zelda and Dino had slept together?

The Legion also pronounced that the word "parsley" in one conversation was too "suggestive," although other vegetables would be OK, and it also dictated that Novak's cleavage be "shadowed" in certain shots. None of this did Wilder any good. Monsignor Thomas F. Little branded the movie C for condemned: "A thoroughly sordid piece of realism which is esthetically as well as morally repulsive." Little was even more incensed when he learned it was planned for a holiday release, calling the action "a commercial decision bereft of respect for the Judeo-Christian sensibilities of the majority of the American people."

Life magazine denounced the film as "a titanic dirty joke." The *New York Times* found it "coarse and vulgar." To the *New Yorker* it was "repellent—the central miscasting is compounded by the chortling tone, the overemphatic double entendres, and the drab look of the film" but admitted that "there's something going on in it." Some critics, such as Judith Crist, used the occasion to attack the morality of *all* of Wilder's films. Bosley Crowther, however, thought that the film *was* moral but that the way it was made, and the casting of Dean Martin, made it seem seamier than it really was. Joan Didion in *Vogue* suggested that it presented a depressing world view as seen through the eyes of a lonely drunk at four in the morning. Dismayed by the notices, Wilder told himself that it must have something to do with the fact that many columnists had been indisposed toward the picture from the day when the press was invited to watch them filming Dino's concert at the Sands (which was actually shot at a theater in Los Angeles). The reporters wanted to be able to get close up shots of Dean, but when this wasn't allowed, many left in a huff.

Because of all the controversy, the film did pretty good business—but only until the shouting died down. Then it was a box-office loser. European critics liked the movie much better, comparing it to the Hollywood sex farces of yore, and indeed many felt that if *Kiss Me, Stupid* had been a foreign film, it would have been better received. Wilder simply fled for the Continent. "The uproar stunned me," he said.

Whatever the intentions of its makers, *Kiss Me, Stupid* remains a fascinating look at the mystique of the Dino persona and more. The picture was ahead of its time with its uncompromising storyline and cynical-realistic ending. It's refreshingly frank and honest about sex and amorality, presenting the world the way it is, not the way moralists want it to be. While still a bit vulgar even by today's standards, the main problem with the film is that it's more silly than genuinely funny, but the interest lies not in its humor but in its subtext. There's something sad and desperate about the movie and its characters: Orville and Barney longing for success and recognition with their songs, willing to resort to virtually any indignity to make it, because they know they're out of the loop and will never have another chance; Polly counting her pennies until she can afford a car to drive her trailer out of the parking lot, away from the dingy town, and on to, hopefully, something better, however unlikely this may be. Even Dino's life seems to have a boozy emptiness to it . . . an emptiness that would perhaps come to haunt the real Dino's existence in the years to come.

PART FIVE

Icon

SIXTEEN

Super-Spy

All the hoopla over *Kiss Me, Stupid* not only didn't hurt Dean's reputation, it may have helped it. People who were mortally offended by the film were not Dean's audience, for one thing. They didn't go to casinos or nightclubs or buy his sexy, romantic records, so they couldn't think less of Dean than they already did. On the other hand, studio and television executives couldn't help but notice that this was a man who was always in the news. *Kiss Me, Stupid* may not have brought in enough box office receipts to please the front office at United Artists—or Dean, for that matter, whose Claude Productions had coproduced it—but it did give Dean a million dollars' worth of free publicity, which was to play a tremendous part in a new career move the following year.

Dean's invasion of television can in part be attributed—although only indirectly—to his old partner, Jerry Lewis. Two years previously, Jerry had guest hosted on NBC's *Tonight Show* when Jack Paar went on vacation. He did the job so well that most Hollywood insiders thought he would be tapped for the job when Paar retired. Instead, Johnny Carson was elected (and probably, at the beginning, got less money than a major star like Jerry Lewis would have expected). ABC had decided to do a two-hour variety-talk show on Saturday nights from nine-thirty to eleven-thirty—part prime time, part late night—and thought Lewis would be perfect as host. They refurbished the old El Capitan Theater in Hollywood and hired a stooge named Del Moore to laugh uproariously at all of Jerry's jokes. ABC had committed to forty episodes, but the plug was pulled after only thirteen weeks. A drop in the ratings caused ABC execs to try to take control from Lewis, who balked at the notion and wanted out of his contract; ABC conceded.

But this left two hours to fill—not to mention a big theater that had been expensive to renovate and was just taking up space and profit. ABC brass rechristened the building the Hollywood Palace and decided to broadcast a show of the same name from the theater. Each week there would be a different guest host and a variety of performers culled from all quarters of show business. Producer Nick Van Off got in touch with Dean's agent and asked if he would do the honors for one installment. The staff writers for *The Hollywood Palace* got to work doing an opening mono-logue for Dean, but they were afraid they might have overdone it and put in too many gags about drinking. "Can't have too many of those," Dean told them when they showed him the material one night at his home. "How do you think I got this big house?" On the show he introduced the acts, flirted with the chorus girls, and told everyone how his doctor had told him it was OK to have a nightcap before bedtime: "I find myself going to bed nine or ten times a night." But he got his biggest laugh when he smiled and said to the audience: "I want to thank Jerry Lewis for build-ing this wonderful theater for me."

His old network, NBC, who'd presented Martin and Lewis on the Colgate *Comedy Hour* broadcasts and also aired Dean's solo specials, thought Dean would make a terrific host of his own weekly television series, and they figured they better snap him up before somebody else did; his well-regarded and highly publicized appearance on *The Hollywood Palace* had reminded them of what a hot property he was. Although tele-vision had become more respectable to Hollywood stars by the sixties, it was still more the rule than the exception that most movie people, such as Lucille Ball, only defected to TV when their film careers were washed up, which was hardly the case with Dean. NBC found him attractive *because* he was still a major player; Dean thought mostly about the money. If each weekly segment could go off as *The Hollywood Palace* did—he just sang a number or two, introduced the guests, told a couple of jokes, had nothing, really, to rehearse—maybe a weekly gig wouldn't be out of the question if the money was right. NBC kept making offers; Dean kept turning them down. The money wasn't right.

Finally Dean's agents got an offer that they felt he couldn't refuse, and *The Dean Martin Show* became a reality in 1965. The producers were Hal Kemp and Bill Colleran, and the director was Greg Garrison, who'd become very influential on the program in years to come. *The Dean Martin Show* was not an immediate success, and Dean never got along with the first producers. He saw no reason to spend a lot of time on rehearsing and had little interest in appearing in sketches with the guests. Not only would he have to learn a lot of lines (he eventually just read off cue cards), but doing skits smacked too much of what he had done with Jerry Lewis, particularly if the guest he was acting with was some kind of screwy comedian.

When he did deign to perform in a sketch, he refused to rehearse with the other performers. The producers begged him to see it their way—his hands-off approach wasn't exactly adding up to blockbuster ratings—but Dean was adamant. Kemp and Colleran eventually quit, and the powers that be debated whether or not it would be prudent to simply drop the show. They were reluctant to do this because the ratings, while not spectacular, were not that bad and Dean was still seen as a television performer of great promise.

Greg Garrison, who'd previously worked on *Your Show of Shows* and *The Milton Berle Show*, thought he knew how to handle Dean and could make the show even more successful simply by cooperating with his star—that is, by letting Dean participate in the rehearsal process to the barest minimum allowable. Garrison gave Dean the time off to work on films or play golf, structuring the schedule so that he could stay away from the studio for days at a time and just come in for taping on one afternoon and maybe a *teensy* bit of rehearsal. It wasn't so much that Dean was lazy, although many considered him so, but that he wanted the time to *enjoy* all the money he made, and he honestly felt a lot of rehearsal simply wasn't required.

His record producers had also learned that this was the way to get around the demands on Dean's time. He no longer rehearsed in the recording studio with the musicians. The band would go through its paces until they got it right, then Dean would come in at his leisure and dub in his voice over the music tracks. This kind of thing would eventually become very commonplace in the recording industry, especially with vocalists whose natural voices would need to be electronically and otherwise enhanced. But while the musicians may not have necessarily minded Dean's absence, the guest stars and regulars on his show weren't as thrilled when it occurred to them that rehearsing with a stand-in instead of the real Dean Martin might hurt their own performances in the long run.

To accommodate Dean and somewhat appease the guests' fears, the sketches would generally be built around the guest; Dean could just stand there, react if he wanted to, and read the occasional line off the cue card.

He never bothered trying to disguise the fact that he was reading his lines; it was part of the fun. A typical sketch had Dean coming over to guest Phyllis Diller's house for a visit. Dean sat down and let Phyllis carry the ball as the comedienne first shoved everything on the table onto the floor to make room for teacups, then went on a panicky search for a used teabag that she had forgotten she was drying. Phyllis then launched into what was basically a monologue about her trip to a "crummy Italian restaurant." The food was so bad, she got drunk on wine. "I don't remember much about it, Dean," she told the crooner. "All I remember was that as I was leaving, some *slob* stepped on my tongue." Dean, his timing as impeccable as ever, waited just a beat before saying, "Was that you?" It got the biggest laugh of the evening.

The new Garrison-Martin combo was an immediate hit, and *The Dean Martin Show* became a television staple with more or less the same format for many years to come. As *TV Guide* put it: "[Dean] missed his cues, stumbled around the set, tossed off risqué innuendoes, and mispronounced his guests' names. After all, he rehearsed for only one day. But his quips were witty, and his charm overwhelming, and the audience loved it." For years to come the show was generally rated in the top fifteen of the country. Fans were so anxious to attend a taping of the program that they would wait over a year to receive tickets.

However, Dean had his critics from the first. There were, of course, those who found him too vulgar, his jokes too redolent of Las Vegas and the barroom. He once made a reference in Italian to anal sex that had the NBC switchboard more flooded with outraged phone calls than it had ever received in the network's history. And there were those who thought that his casual demeanor and unrehearsed attitude suggested he had nothing but contempt for the medium, the process, and the audience.

But this very unserious approach is what endeared him to millions who thought he was cool, unflappable, a completely refreshing character, like someone you'd like to meet in a bar and have a few beers, trade a few jokes, with. He didn't seem like a superstar; he seemed like a funny, regular fella. And the booziness of his delivery, the way he talked to the wrong camera and screwed up the names of his guests, made him seem vulnerable, fooled the audience into thinking that Dean probably wasn't a much better host than they would be, made them feel he was almost one of them. And since most of his largely middle-aged fans were obsessed by sex, booze, or both, they could relate to him. Guys in their forties, dismayed by long-haired rock stars and jealous of pimply studs in their twenties, were glad Dean portrayed a man their own age as a lothario, some-one who not only could still cut the mustard but attract women by the cartload. And middle-aged women looked at Dean, still attractive even if he was pushing fifty, and imagined him a more accessible, realistic lover for them than, say, Troy Donahue or Paul McCartney.

A number of comedians reached national prominence as regulars on the show, including Paul Lynde and Dom DeLuise, who'd help get Dean involved in his final film projects many years later. As mentioned, Phyllis Diller made many appearances on the program, as did Kay Medford, eventually playing the neurotic mother of musical director Ken Lane, who had about as much personality as a blond cadaver. Other regulars over the years didn't quite catch on with the public, however, and had lit-tle professional life beyond the show. Dean had a whole host of people both on-stage and off carrying the ball. "There's one thing I'll say about me," he explained after a couple of years of doing the program. "I'm always on time. I don't argue with the director or producer. I just ask, Where is the chalk mark, where do I stand, and what do I say? and I do it. That's why I never get in trouble." He claimed that he and Garrison never had a fight, but that was because Garrison, now the guardian of an extremely popular series, never asked Dean to do anything his star didn't care to do.

Eventually Jerry Lewis was given his own program on NBC in the hopes that it would do better than his two-hour ABC version, which it did for a while. For several weeks, Dean urged his viewers to tune in to Jerry's series, although in a sort of half-joking manner that made one wonder if he really meant it or was just doing a goofy plug to please the NBC brass. For his part, Jerry was not offended by Dean's hawking his show—Dean was doing it in character so it was OK—but he himself could not do Dean Martin jokes, even affectionate ones, on his own show because it was still so painful. They never appeared on each other's programs. "I don't see any reason for exchanging guest spots," Jerry said at the time. When Jerry's show ultimately failed, Dean said during an interview, in which his tongue had been loosened by a couple of cocktails: "Too bad about Jerry. The guy just didn't grow with the times. You can't do that. You gotta change." He didn't help relations between the two when he added, "I always knew in my guts that I was funnier than he was."

Though a star of the small screen, Dean still kept up his profile for the big screen as well. He found himself in a second picture with John Wayne—this one produced by Hal Wallis (Dean was still working off that old contract with Wallis)—entitled *The Sons of Katie Elder* (1965). The picture had to be postponed for some months after Wayne came to see Wallis and told him he had "the Big C." Eventually half of his left lung and one of his ribs were removed during surgery, and he reported for work four months later. The picture was directed by another cancer survivor, Henry Hathaway, whose colon had been operated on some years before. Hathaway, who was sixty-seven, had directed Marilyn Monroe in *Niagara* (1953) and also helmed parts of *How the West Was Won* (1962), among many others.

The Sons of Katie Elder concerned four brothers who gather in their hometown of Clearwater for their mother's funeral. Tom (Dean) is wanted for murder; John (Wayne) is a notorious gunslinger; Matt (Earl Holliman) and Bud, the youngest (Michael Anderson Jr.) are more socially acceptable. The older boys want Bud to stay in school and become the one among them who amounts to something, as their mother would have wanted, and John is also obsessed with finding out who shot their father in the back many years earlier. Said villain, Morgan Hastings (James Gregory), and his hired gun, Curly (George Kennedy), cook up a scheme to get the Elder boys out of their hair, arrest them for the shooting of the sheriff, and ambush them as they're being taken by crooked deputies to see the marshall in Laredo. After a major gun battle outside town, the bad guys are routed and mother Katie's rocking chair swings back and forth to indicate, presumably, that her tired soul is finally satisfied and at rest.

Much of the picture was shot in the town of Durango, Mexico, which Dean—and other western stars—would return to several times in the next few years. Durango was if anything more spartan than Kanab, Utah, where *Sergeants 3* had been filmed. There was one hotel, which the cast and crew took over, and a greasy diner served as the local hot spot. The Mexican nights at this time of year were so frigid that scenes would often have to be postponed for a warmer evening. After two months the company left Durango and headed for the much livelier Mexico City, where interior scenes were shot at the Churubusco Studios. Still pinching a penny, Wallis knew it would be cheaper to make the flick in Mexico than in Hollywood, and the Mexican extras, technicians, and laborers could be employed for a comparative song. With Old West-style locations at convenient distances, Mexico made a great place to shoot a western.

John Wayne was determined to show that he was as macho as ever after his surgery, and Hathaway was just as determined to help him prove it, driving Wayne even more than he did the rest of the cast. "[Henry] was charming socially but miserable to work with," said costar Martha Hyer, who had also appeared in *Some Came Running*, "reducing strong men to tears on every picture." By this time Hyer was married to Wallis and had been given a part in the movie. Wallis told her not to look *too* glamorous or it might upset Wayne, who had put on weight and aged after his operation and was sensitive about it. Because Durango was at an elevation of 6,200 feet, Wayne often had to use an oxygen inhalator to breathe. In spite of this, Hathaway insisted that Wayne do all of his own stunts, including the lengthy shoot-out in the river wherein Wayne and the others had to lie in freezing water for hours several days in a row. Wayne took out his displeasure on most of the cast, but Dean did his best to perk up his costar's sense of humor and save the day.

Dean and Wayne remained good friends and were often joined on binges by Dennis Hopper, who had a small but pivotal role in the film as the villain's neurotic son. Although they would try to limit their drinking to the weekends, playing cards and swapping jokes on week nights, occasionally they'd turn up rather red-eyed and weary on the morning of a shoot, which only made Hathaway drive them harder. One night Dean and Wayne woke up everyone in the hotel, including reporters, by marching down the street outside arm in arm, singing at the top of their lungs. Hathaway was not amused and kept them in the river the next day even longer than required.

In spite of this rough treatment, Dean had fun making movies. During one interview given during this period, he said, "I don't understand all these actors who say they've had a tough time at the studio all day. They have aches and pains. They can't go out to dinner at night because they worked hard. Who are they kidding? All you do is say a few lines. If you make a mistake, a director tells you to do it over again. What's so tough about that? Show business is a ball. I've been in it thirty years, and I felt the same way about it when I was broke as I do now."

Dean betrays his obvious camaraderie with Wayne and the other actors in every scene of *The Sons of Katie Elder*. A highlight has the boys punching each other out in sheer joy, joining up to throw Bud into the river with his clothes on. Dean's in full command of his charm in one scene when he good-naturedly scams some barflies by pretending he has a glass eye, which he raffles off after putting a black eyepatch over the supposedly empty eye socket. He collects his money only to tell the, fortunately, amused crowd that he actually has two good eyes. When shot at the end of the movie (he survives) he does a dramatic face-front fall into the sawdust. Playing the sleaziest and least likable of the Elder brothers, his performance paved the way for somewhat darker characterizations in later films. Other than that, Dean doesn't really put himself out that much; he's OK in the film but not that energetic (although not as laid-back as Sinatra ever was). *The Sons of Katie Elder* was hardly a stretch for him.

Martha Hyer has a fine underplayed scene when she tells off the brothers for neglecting their mother for so many years, and Dennis Hopper gives a nice, nervous performance in the showiest role of David Hastings, who's shot by his own father before he can betray him to the Elders. The others in the cast are all solid, and the movie is creditable but nothing special. Under Hathaway's workmanlike but uninspired direction, there are no great scenes, and Elmer Bernstein's music is too derivative, but Dino would make worse movies in the years to come.

Marriage on the Rocks, his next to last film with Frank Sinatra, was, happily, not one of the most awful ones, although at least one chronicler has inexplicably labeled it "one of the worst movies ever made." *Marriage on the Rocks* is actually a pretty funny movie about a wife who winds up divorcing her boring husband and marrying his swingin' business partner. Dean was typecast as the swinger, and Frank Sinatra was amusingly cast against type as the boring, unromantic husband who'd rather stay home on his anniversary than go out to a club. Jack Donahue, who'd already directed Dean and Frank on some of their TV specials, was at the helm and knew how to get the best out of them. Instead of phoning in their performances as they were wont to do on Rat Pack movies, the two worked hard (in a way that made it seem as if they were hardly working) to put over the script, which had its lapses into silliness. Some critics noted that it also seemed a bit old-fashioned, like a screwball comedy of the thirties.

Sinatra importuned the distinguished Deborah Kerr to play his wife, who accidentally winds up married to Dean after getting a cheap Mexican divorce from Sinatra; she refuses to have it annulled so as to make the man she really loves jealous while her husband pretends that he just loves playing the field. Meanwhile swingin' Dean tries to explain his marriage to his numerous babes. Initially wary about working with the duo, Kerr wound up having an absolute blast and was impressed by Dean's healthy attitude toward his profession. As he had said earlier that year: "Show business is a ball," and he set about proving it to Kerr, who had the time of her life laughing at his jokes and behavior. Dean could have walked through the film and gotten away with it, but instead he displays his expert timing and generous sense of humor in scene after scene, such as when he exchanges drinks and one-liners with Frank and Hermione Baddeley in an encounter at the wet bar in Sinatra and Kerr's living room. Perennial starlet Joi Lansing also had a small role in the film, but whether Frank or Dean got it for her is beside the point, as she had been girlfriend to both.

An interesting aspect of *Marriage on the Rocks* is that Dean and Frank, unlike other movie stars, made no attempt to hide the fact that they had ascended into middle-age in their choice of on-screen roles. Their characters were as old as they were, with grown children, and like most men of their age they hated the music and fashions that had come into prominence in the sixties, which was made clear in several sequences. They did not try to come off as hip, as other members of the Rat Pack, particularly Davis and Lawford, did in their later years. Of course, to their fans they were hardly hip, but cool—which was hipper than hip. Frank even had his daughter Nancy play his daughter in the film.

While Nancy had a pretty good part in *Marriage on the Rocks*, Claudia Martin was nowhere to be seen, which was almost the case in the haunted house–beach party hybrid she'd signed to do some months before. It was finally released as *Ghost in the Invisible Bikini*. Along with such "teen" luminaries as Deborah Walley, Tommy Kirk, and Aron Kincaid, the film had also improbably snared such genuine talents as Patsy Kelly, Boris Karloff, and even the inimitable Basil Rathbone of Sherlock Holmes fame. Claudia Martin was eighth billed after Nancy Sinatra. Although as Kincaid's girlfriend, Vicki, Ms. Sinatra had lines and a characterization, Claudia (as Lulu) only stood around in the background and had not a single line of dialogue. Dean's daughter at this time was a tall, attractive twenty-one-year-old girl with long black hair, big teeth—and not a lot of that all-important presence. Even Piccola Pupa, a tiny Italian girl singer who had a short run in the sixties, had more to do in *Ghost*. All the girls paled beside buxom, saucy Quinn O'Hara, however. The movie has only one laugh, when Karloff, who'd been told that certain dark forces could make him "younger," is turned into a child. Claudia could only cross her fingers and hope she'd have a bigger part in the upcoming *Ski Fever*, which she did. She also got engaged again, to a British disc jockey named Lord Timothy Hutton, who was twenty-four. Dean didn't like him any more than he did Claudia's first husband; Claudia and Hutton never made it to the altar.

Her sisters Gail and Deana had decided that they, too, would like a career in show business. Deana signed a recording contract at Columbia at the ripe old age of sixteen, while Gail was the first of the daughters to appear on Dean's television show (the other two soon followed suit). The *New York Daily News* was kind, noting that Gail "is a good-looker with a fair voice, and her modest delivery shows signs of careful preparation. Somewhat hesitant in her manner—understandable under the circumstances—she is yet, of course, far from being in her father's league, but the girl does have definite promise." Deana also got some club dates, thanks to her father's intervention.

As for Dean's sons, although Craig had never had any interest in performing, now that Daddy had a TV show, he was interested in working behind the scenes; Dean made him an assistant producer. Fourteen-year-old Dean-Paul, or Dino Jr., had his own ideas and formed a band with another Hollywood Junior, Desi Arnaz Jr., and their mutual friend Billy Hinsche. Christened the not-exactly-euphonious "Dino, Desi, and Billy," the band released a record on Reprise called "I'm a Fool." It didn't do badly, but Dean's son had another love. Some years later Dino Jr. remembered: "I really enjoyed the music. It was the time of the Beatles. Kids were really turned on. But the music kind of interrupted my tennis. Those years—fourteen, fifteen, sixteen—are really important years for tennis development. The music was a distraction, but I always considered myself an athlete first."

While the kids pursued their varied careers, Dean went in front of the cameras again in a new movie—this time as a super-spy. Donald Hamilton had written a series of novels about a secret agent named Matt Helm that some considered the American answer to Ian Fleming's James Bond, although the books—and character—were never as popular as the adventures of 007. Columbia Pictures, via producer Irving Allen (not to be confused with *Irwin* Allen) had bought the rights to the novels and let it be known that they were instituting a nationwide search to find the right actor for the part. The search didn't last very long since it had occurred to Allen that Dean would be perfect for the part—or at least the Hollywoodized version of Matt Helm that resulted. Dean agreed to play Helm in the first of several projected films, *The Silencers*, but he wanted a piece of the action; his Claude Productions would have to be involved or it was no go. Allen agreed.

In *The Silencers*, which screenwriter Oscar Saul based on the book of that title and another one called *Death of a Citizen*, Dean is an agent of ICE (Intelligence Counter Espionage) who does photospreads for *Slaymate* magazine on the side. Assigned to "Fall Out," an operation to block an attempt to start World War Three, he first teams up with agent Tina (Daliah Lavi) and then must pretend to be married to another woman, Gail Hendricks (Stella Stevens), whom he suspects of being an enemy agent. Actually it is Tina who is the worm in the apple, as she is secretly in the employ of Tung-Tze (Victor Buono) who works for an organization called—believe it or not—the Big O, which Helm and Hendricks defeat in the end. Clearly *The Silencers* was not meant to be taken even as seriously as your average James Bond feature.

Director Phil Karlson had made mostly undistinguished films, including *Kid Galahad* with Elvis Presley, before being assigned to *The Silencers*, and his direction of the film overall is second-rate. According to Karlson, "Dean Martin was a good sport and did just about everything that was asked of him except the more outrageous stunts for which we used stunt men. I'm not certain, but I think Dean worked his way through the Slaygirls one by one. He did drink a bit, though never excessively, though I must say he did get a little wobbly if we had to shoot in the evening hours. He just took a little nip now and then throughout the day, in between scenes, but by the time it was night he had consumed quite a bit. He wanted to go have some fun; he'd put his day in, his time in, and now he wanted to go home or something. I'd say he got pleasantly high as the day proceeded as opposed to drunk. Most people didn't even notice it, though I think it's apparent in some scenes in the finished film."

Indeed, Dean looks rather loaded in a couple of scenes, and his drinking may be the reason why he's a bit *too* relaxed in his portrayal of Matt Helm, though he's certainly not bad in the part. He never overplays the comedy or camps it up too much, which a more intense actor might easily have done. "What am I doin' here? A guy can get killed like this!" he says during a well-executed chase scene when two cars on either side of him try to crush his vehicle in the middle. When a make-out session with Stella Stevens is interrupted by gunplay, he seems both appalled and disappointed instead of constantly smug like Sean Connery in his James Bond portrayal. Dean doesn't do any actual song numbers but he can be heard singing several songs in the background—"Red Sails in the Sunset," "Sunny Side of the Street"—with even more than his usual sleazy insouciance.

Second-billed Stella Stevens was at the height of her good looks when she made *The Silencers* and critics wisely took note of her excellent comic performance. Often dismissed as a *Playboy* beauty and glamour queen, Stevens was one of the most underrated actresses of the sixties. A cute bit has her turning on the radio and hearing Frank Sinatra. Dean says, "Oh, turn him off—he's terrible!" Stella switches channels, and Dean is heard singing "Everybody Loves Somebody." "Now, this fellow can sing," Dean tells her. Stevens is genuinely amusing sinking into the mud outside Helms's car as she tries to get away from him (a sequence which the *New Yorker* noted was lifted from 1948's *Julia Misbehaves*) and also has a terrific drunk scene.

Asked about her costar some years later, Stevens said: "Dean appeals to most women simply because he is Dean Martin—a wonderfully pleasant, easygoing guy. He is a great-looking man with a wonderful sense of humor. On top of everything else he's charming and polite. There's no doubt he's a real ladies' man." She did note that he got a little grumpy when filming went overtime and also noticed that he generally *didn't* have "soda" in his drinking glass. She claimed that their sexual camaraderie in the film never protruded into the real world, though she might not have minded if it had.

Also good in the picture was the super-busty Daliah Lavi of the chic mushroom cloud hairstyle, who plays her role of an enemy assassin and counterspy just right: sexy and serious but with a wink. At one point when Lavi's character is hurled over someone's shoulder and tossed across a stage, a stunt man in drag was substituted for the actress. Dean had a field day mercilessly—but good-naturedly—kidding the guy, who could probably have bent him into a pretzel. Lavi's estimation of Martin: "He's one hundred percent male, and there aren't too many of them around today." Victor Buono, whose evil character tries to kill Matt with red laser beams, had worked with Dean on two previous occasions; these two very different actors became good on-set friends. Dean's affectionate nickname for the portly Buono was "Chubbins," which always amused the latter as he knew it was all in fun. Cyd Charisse, as attractive as she had been in the aborted *Something's Got to Give*, appeared as a "special guest star" in *The Silencers* as the exotic dancer Sarita. Her dance number in a skintight leotard to "Santiago" and her sexy delivery of the title song under the credits (actually vocalized by Vicki Carr) are two of the picture's highlights.

One of the movie's "Slaygirls"—the equivalent of *Playboy* bunnies only with guns—was played by a hopeful starlet named Marybeth Jaymes. Today she remembers, "What I liked about Dean is that he was accessible. I mean, I didn't even have any lines, I was really just an extra, but he would kid around and joke with anyone in the vicinity, make you feel at ease. On the first picture—I did another of the Matt Helm movies—I found him almost paternal. He told me he had daughters my age who were also trying to make it in showbiz. 'It's a great way to make a living but a tough profession to get started in,' he said, and I had to bite my tongue to keep from saying, 'Not if you're Dean Martin's daughter.' But I think that's what he was trying to communicate with me—that even with the best connections it was hard to get some place. He was very sympathetic, fatherly, very gentle and kind. He didn't make any passes—at that time. I knew he drank a little during the day, in his dressing room, because I could sometimes smell it on his breath."

The Silencers has an expensive look and beautiful art direction—lush bedrooms, hotel lobbies, and the Slaygirl Club are all exquisitely furnished and color coordinated by Joseph Wright (*Gentlemen Prefer Blondes*) and beautifully photographed by the talented Burnett Guffey—but the gadgetry is a little feeble, to say the least. When not clad in Sy Devore turtlenecks, Helm wears buttons on his jacket that are in reality miniature grenades, and gets a lot of help in defeating the villains from a gun that fires backward. But his greatest technological marvel is the big round bed in his apartment that at the press of a button sails across the room and dumps him into a huge poollike bathtub complete with redhead. In the amusing postscript, Stella Stevens accidentally presses the same button and dumps both her and Dean in the drink.

While *The Silencers* doesn't compare to the best of the Bonds, it does have its moments and isn't a total waste of time. The story, as taken from Hamilton's books, is quite reasonable, and everything is played fairly straight (if tongue in cheek) for the most part, although certain absurd elements and characters add to the feeling that you're seeing a parody and not a serious picture. In this blatant male fantasy, every woman is ready and eager for action at a moment's notice, and the Slaygirls that Dean photographs are all quite luscious, even sexier than the gals in the Bond flicks. Helm's secretary, played winningly by Beverly Adams, is named Lovey Kravezit (pronounced "craves it").

Apparently the public craved it—this was the era of the super-spy sensation as personified not only by Bond in the bijou but *The Man from U.N.C.L.E.* on television—and *The Silencers* was one of Dean's biggest hits. The critics were not as enthusiastic as the public, however. "Most of Dean's throwaway lines should have been thrown away before the film ever went into production," said *Films and Filming*, "and Martin's lethargic delivery helps not at all." The *New York Herald-Tribune* reported that "it's the *Kiss Me, Stupid* Dino, the Las Vegas Dino—eyes at half mast, suntan at full blast, the image projected of the lecherous buffoon burbling songs, guzzling whiskeys, and nuzzling wenches with the suggestion that either cirrhosis or satyriasis will finish him off any minute." Brendan Gill declared that "Dean is the worst and most self-confident actor in the world." However the critic from *Saturday Review*, who got the point, opined that "he risks his neck, embraces his girls, and drinks his Scotch with the same easygoing good nature," while Pauline Kael found it "Crude but good-natured." Some reviewers likened *The Silencers* to the *Batman* TV show of the period and were surprised at the casting of Dean as an action hero.

"I had laughs," Dean said. "The audience had fun. There were pretty girls. We had laughs."

Did anything else matter?

SEVENTEEN

Rough Nights

Dean had not only become a national icon, but he was well on his way to becoming one of the wealthiest men in show business. His income in 1967 was well over five million dollars—from his TV and movie salaries, club engagements, and profits from recordings and Claude Productions—but it would triple within a couple of years when NBC, anxious to retain their most valuable property and the star of one of the country's most popular programs, raised his salary from forty thousand dollars a week (for the one day's actual work he put into the program) to two hundred and eighty-five thousand—for just *one day* each week. No wonder he thought showbiz was "a ball."

Like other movie stars, however, Dean would make his real fortune in investments and real estate. Following Bob Hope's lead (and to a certain extent Sinatra's), Dean bought many valuable properties via his Claude Productions. One of the first things he did was join a consortium to buy up land adjacent to an airport in Carlsbad, California. He made plans to build his own youth-oriented country club and golf course in Beverly Hills and planned to charge members—the younger the better; this was not to be a stuffy old men's club—twenty-five thousand dollars a year. He bought real estate in San Francisco, Tarzana, and Los Angeles as well as Ventura and Riverside Counties. He bought a ranch from Jimmy Stewart and also owned ranches in Ventura and Camarillo. He owned two apartment houses and several hundred acres of park land. He was still a part owner of the Sands along with Sinatra, and he had over a quarter of a million shares of stock in RCA, which owned the National Broadcasting

Company. By selling many of these properties at the right time, Dean increased his investment a thousandfold.

And the records kept coming: "Welcome to My World," which became another signature tune; a cover of "I've Grown Accustomed to Your Face" from *My Fair Lady*; the amusingly titled "I'm Not the Marrying Kind," which expressed sentiments his wives might have agreed with; and a duet with Frank's daughter Nancy called "Things." He never recorded a duet with his own daughters, even though he put them on his television show. Perhaps it was because Nancy, despite the undeniable help from her father, seemed to have proven herself and worked hard at her career. She'd had a big hit with "These Boots are Made for Walking" and demonstrated real charisma and personality in her movie assign-ments, such as *Marriage on the Rocks*. Dino saw Nancy as a fellow profes-sional, which was not how he felt about his children, no matter how much he may have loved them. At this time, for instance, Claudia seemed more interested in marrying one unsuitable fellow after another than she did in pursuing her career.

Dean also did covers of a variety of records that had been hits for other people: Roger Miller's "King of the Road," Glen Campbell's "By the Time I Get to Phoenix," Bobby Goldsboro's treacly "Honey" (in which a dead wife is compared to a tree), plus "Gentle on My Mind" and "The Green, Green Grass of Home." Most of these songs were not really appropriate to Dean's style, but it didn't seem to matter. Some fans would accept him singing anything, and his version of these records became the only ones that they were familiar with.

When he wasn't working, Dean played golf with such buddies as Nick Hilton, son of the hotel king Conrad Hilton; Fletcher Jones, who ran an L.A. auto dealership; Bill Bastion, a meatpacker who was known as the "Corned Beef King" of Los Angeles; and Bill Ransom, a Beverly Hills realtor. Presumably Dean would have made allowances and let these com-parative old fogies play with him at that youth-focused country club he was building—although the matter became academic when he decided that he and his family would be better served if he funneled the money elsewhere, and he canceled the project.

The part of Sam Hollis in Dean's next movie, *Texas Across the River* (1966), was perfectly suited for him, and he gives an excellent perform-ance in yet another western-comedy, his light touch much in evidence. The director, Michael Gordon, was a former stage actor who had helmed such films as *Another Part of the Forest* (1948), based on the Lillian Hellman play, *The Lady Gambles* (1949) with Barbara Stanwyck, and even

Doris Day's *Move Over, Darling* (1963), the picture that had started life as *Something's Got to Give*. Gordon felt that Dean was "great to direct"—but only after things had been arranged so that he wouldn't have to do to much rehearsing or sitting around between scenes. Gordon told reporters that Dean "didn't like acting," but it was really that he didn't like the minutiae that came with it: sitting for hours while shots and sets were adjusted; sound and light checks that could be done with stand-ins, all those sort of things that took up unnecessary time for the *actor*. He also wanted to be able to have plenty of time off to enjoy his extracurricular pursuits while he was making a picture.

In *Texas Across the River*, Dean is a cowboy who encounters Don Andrea (French sex symbol Alain Delon) out West, where the latter is fleeing from a trumped-up murder charge. The two ride together through Comanche territory to meet up with Don's fiancée, Phoebe (Rosemary Forsyth), in Texas, where the two had agreed to rendezvous. Unfortunately, Phoebe finds herself falling for Sam while his lady pal, a pretty squaw, is attracted to Don. After a battle with Indians, Sam and Don decide to have their own well-directed, comical showdown over the gals, but ultimately agree that it would make much better sense to remain friends and just switch girlfriends.

Although they came from very different backgrounds, Dean and Alain were both romantic men who loved the ladies as much as the ladies loved them, so they bonded on the film and enjoyed working together. Their interplay is one of the movie's strong points. Joey Bishop turned up now and then as a stereotypical—and rather wooden—Indian named Kronk. Years later he said, "I remember Dean most of all for his honesty. He hated anything that was phony and would not partake of it. He was one in a trillion."

Director Gordon was able to fashion some fine sequences for the film, including a lyrical bit with Don and the native gal frolicking with tame bulls in a river and a nifty sword fight between Don and Phoebe's ex-boyfriend in her bedroom. The story had enough interesting twists that it would have worked just as well had it been told with a totally straight face, although it trivialized the horror of the Indian attacks on settlers and the reverse. In any case, it was not a film that Dean need have been embarrassed by. The picture did fairly well with the critics and made money to boot.

By this time the huge grosses for *The Silencers* were in, and there was no question but that a sequel was in order. This time the director would be Henry Levin, best known as the director of *Journey to the Center of the*

Earth (1959) as well as *Jolson Sings Again* (1949) and Pat Boone's *April Love* (1957). (During filming Levin also shot Dean hawking U.S. Treasury Bonds in three direct-to-theater shorts.) Columbia Pictures was so sure the sequel would bring in lots of moola that they wanted to do a lot of expensive location shooting, but Dean, thinking of what that might mean to his share of the profits via Claude Productions and not especially wanting to spend weeks and weeks overseas, suggested it would be more prudent—and cheaper—to stay at the studio. For this reason *Murderers' Row* (1966) has little of the production sheen and elaborate settings of the previous picture. Very few sets were built for the film. Instead, the studio used existing sets or exotic California locations that could double as Big O headquarters: a spooky castle, a factory with high-tech derricks and so on. The only real glamour was provided by the sexy Slaygirls, and there was even less gadgetry than in the first film: The villain's hovercraft was really just a land/sea hydrofoil, exotic at the time, perhaps, but hardly an outlandish invention of the screenwriters. Aside from a gun that actually fires nine seconds after the trigger is pulled, the only other technological bit has to do with a lame "death device," actually one of a series of pistonlike tubes that Dean is placed inside at one point. Dean wanted to do the movie—he liked the idea of being in something hip and trendy, of being cool and popular like the Beatles—but not at his own financial expense.

The story of *Murderers' Row*, taken from Donald Hamilton's book of the same name, begins with a series of international intelligence agents being murdered one by one around the world. Matt Helm is also on the death list and is almost dispatched by one of his models, who's posing for a *Slaymate* centerfold as Miss January. ICE decides to fake Matt's death and have him sent to Monte Carlo as James Peters to investigate the disappearance of a heliobeam inventor named Dr. Solaris. He's instructed to either get Dr. Solaris out of enemy hands or kill him. He's even told he must kill himself if the situation warrants so that he can't be brainwashed and turned into an enemy spy. Since James Peters is supposed to be a Mafia hit man, it's under that guise that he's recruited by Big O agent Julian Wall (Karl Malden), who plans to use Solaris's heliobeam to destroy Washington, D.C. Naturally our hero makes sure that his plans don't come to fruition, and all is soon right with the free world once again.

Even more than the first film, *Murderers' Row* is essentially a parody of the Bond films, down to the villains and situations and clever, suggestive dialogue. As Helm, Dean is again smooth, casual, enjoying himself; he's fine as a flip, laid-back caricature of an agent, but one senses he could never have really played the honest-to-goodness 007 as well as those who did tackle that role. Essentially playing himself, he's, ironically, more real than Connery and the others, but his unique persona would not have worked against the stylized tone of a serious spy piece.

Dean was forty-nine years old when he made *Murderers' Row*. All the women are hot for him and openly admire his looks, but he seems a dated, middle-aged sex symbol by the standards of today's hard-bodied, healthy, muscular hunks with their poetic drop-dead good looks. Still, what matters are his priceless reactions, such as his double take when his boss at ICE, McDonald (James Gregory), tells him he might have to kill himself. "I don't get you," Dean says. Fleeing from police officers who think he's a mafioso with costar Ann-Margret, he puts an electronic message on the back of his car: ATTENTION: FRENCH POLICE. DON'T SHOOT—THERE'S AN INNOCENT GIRL IN THE CAR. When the cops continue shooting, he says, "That's the French. They don't believe any girl is innocent."

While Ann-Margret, in her typical sex-kitten mode, is OK in the second-billed babe role of Solaris's daughter, neither she nor her character are as much fun as Stella Stevens's in the previous film. She and Dean seemed to enjoy their smooching scenes together. There was an unfortunate side effect of dancer Ann-Margret's casting, which was that the picture was jazzed up with all the latest awful dance crazes and music. At one point Ann-Margret frugs in front of a poster of Frank Sinatra, who detested this kind of pop-rock music. More attention is paid to her dancing than to Dean's escape in a hydrofoil occurring at the same moment. Eventually the intercutting between both scenes just turns into an Ann-Margret dance exhibition while Dean is all but forgotten! The other babe in the picture, pretty Carmilla Sparv, is competent as a femme fatale named Coco.

Employing a multitude of dialects—an "international mishmash of an accent," as he put it—for his role as Julian Wall, Karl Malden did not care for himself in the picture—"Instead of coming across like an international con man, I made an international ass of myself," he said—but he actually plays it well without going over the top, a style that would fit both a serious and not-so-serious picture. He greatly enjoyed working with Dean. "I thought it would be a kick to work with Dean, and it was," Malden said. "His whole style was built around making fun of himself and the situation with that easygoing charm of his. He knew what he could do and he did it well. And he always did it the first time. Dean was definitely a one-take actor: One day after we had done a scene together, he asked me, 'Do you like doing just one take?' I said, 'It doesn't bother me. Two, three, that's OK, too. I don't care.' Dean jumped in, 'Don't say that to anyone.' He wanted to keep it his way—one take and print it."

James Gregory had already appeared with Dean in *The Sons of Katie Elder* and in the previous Helm flick. "Dean was always great to work with," he remembered, "because he never took himself too seriously. Some actors get all messed up if you or they blow a line, or they want to do the same scene a hundred times over, over, and over again, never satisfied, but Dean was relaxed, always relaxed—if it doesn't work do it over, but for heaven's sake you oughta not need more than that one or two times to get it right. Nobody screwed up that often—not because they knew he didn't want to have to do it again, but because *they* were relaxed because *he* was relaxed, and when everybody's relaxed the work goes better, there's fewer mistakes, everyone is satisfied, and that was that."

Dino Jr.'s rock group, Dino, Desi, and Billy, were "introduced" in this film and appear in a nightclub sequence as themselves. As his father dances—or what passes for dancing—with Ann-Margret, Dino Jr. says from the bandstand: "Hey, now you're swingin', Dad!" To which Dean says, "Dad?" "It's a wise son knows his own father," intones Ann-Margret. The Royce and Hart number they perform, "If You're Thinking What I'm Thinking," was typical sixties schlock. As in *The Silencers*, Dean has no actual song numbers but can be heard on the radio in his hotel suite doing "I'm Not the Marrying Kind." The Schifrin-Greenfield melody emerged as a blatant rip-off/variation of "King of the Road," which, as noted, Dean had also recorded.

Herbert Baker's screenplay has a couple of good laughs amid a lot of groaners and is top heavy with breast jokes. Matt Helm tells one of his calendar models that they're going to do a layout on the Spirit of '76. "But I'm only a forty-four," she moans. To a model who's posing in front of a map of Minnesota, Matt says, "Lower your arms; we don't want to hide the Twin Cities." One bit of dialogue that Dean would certainly have appreciated is spoken by a club kid to his girlfriend: "After I graduated my dad wanted me to join his firm, but I wanted to make it on my own. So he gave me $250,000 in traveler's checks, and here I am!" Ladling out money to his children and doing the occasional bit to help their careers hadn't done much to ease Dean's cynicism, although he didn't exactly see his children as the "parasites" who had plagued him earlier in his life.

Told straight, *Murderers' Row* might have made a great, interesting movie, but as was the case with *Silencers*, taken on its own terms it's not a total loss. There's a lively opening showing the mock destruction of Washington, D.C., in Wall's secret base, and a well-executed climactic chase between Wall in his hovercraft and Matt and Suzie Solaris in a smaller hydrofoil. There's a bald hired gun with a black metal head plate who seems to be the forerunner of Jaws, the weird assassin who turned up in the Bond films eleven years later. "You mind turnin' off your head?" Matt screams at him as light reflects off the guy's skull cap and bounces into his eyes. Like Jaws in *The Spy Who Loved Me*, the metalhead is defeated when Matt lifts him off the floor with a big dangling magnet. And any movie that has a Judy Garland impersonator singing "Roll Out the Barrel" at Matt Helm's funeral can't be all bad. The public ate it all up, although it didn't go down quite so well as its predecessor and didn't make quite as much money. The critics could only shrug.

It was before filming that Dean got upsetting news about his mother's health. He had bought his parents their own home, and the two had lived quietly and happily for several years, proud of how incredibly successful their son had become. Angela Crocetti had developed cancer of the bone marrow, and it spread throughout her system, making her so fatigued that she could hardly leave the house. Her condition worsened as the months went by, but there was nothing anyone could do. Angela passed away on Christmas Day 1967 at seventy years of age. Dean got the call from his father. In her memory, Dean sent money to St. John's Hospital back in Steubenville so that they could build a Cobalt Treatment Center.

Dean had inherited much of his outward emotional stoicism from his father, Guy, but inside both men were hurting and did their best to console one another. It was worse for Guy; Dean had lost a mother, but Guy had lost his life's mate. Dean could never understand exactly how devastating that was for his father because Dean had never had that kind of all-consuming, long-term relationship with any woman. After his wife's death, Guy deteriorated rapidly and soon had to be placed in a nursing home, where he died on August 29, 1968, at the age of seventy-four. Both of Dean's parents were buried in the Crocetti mausoleum in Westwood Memorial Park. Dean took it all in stride. He couldn't know there was worse to come.

It was through a scriptwriter for a couple of old Martin and Lewis movies, Martin Rackin, that Dean acquired his next project, a western entitled *Rough Night in Jericho* (1967), in which Dean played a very nasty character named Alex Flood. The director, Arnold Laven, like Gordon Douglas before him, had helmed a nifty creature feature, *The Monster that Challenged the World*, about ten years previously as well as the second film version of *Anna Lucasta* starring Sammy Davis Jr. Dean got top billing, as usual, with the names of George Peppard and Jean Simmons also above the title.

Alex Flood is a former lawman who originally came to Jericho to clean up the town but has stayed to take control of it because he can't live on "fifty dollars a month." Worse than any of the bad guys he routed, he rules over Jericho with an iron fist, destroying anyone who challenges his rule. The only one who has the guts to stand up to him is Molly Lang (Jean Simmons), who wants to run a stagecoach line with the help of a retired marshall named Ben Hickman (John McIntire), who shows up in Jericho at her invitation with an ex-deputy named Dolan (George Peppard) in tow. The two men have no idea how bad things really are in Jericho and at first want to move on posthaste, but in the end they agree to team up with Molly and the disgraced Sheriff Jace (Don Galloway) to take care of Flood, who's stabbed to death by Dolan during a fight.

Probably because of the seamier side of his character in *The Sons of Katie Elder*, Rackin and Laven thought Dean would be perfect as Alex Flood, but he was not at all a great casting choice for an unrepentant villain. His natural charm works against his coming off as really nasty as he needs to be. "How long will it take you to round up a jury?" he asks one of his men after they decide to lynch a storekeeper who dared kill a Flood crony who had roughed him up. He does have his moments—repeatedly knocking the head of a punk gunslinger against the bar; grabbing Molly by the hair after slapping her and throwing her on the floor of her kitchen—but his performance, while not bad, lacks the dynamism required to make Flood really come alive. He seems to appropriate that certain John Wayne half-serious/half-breezy approach in this film but is, if anything, even less intense than the Duke. He has a good, horrified, somewhat panicky and disbelieving expression on his face as he's hit by Dolan's thrown knife, but even here he's simply Dino biting the dust: "Don't take less than fifty-one percent," he says to Peppard as he dies with a smile on his lips.

While more visceral and energetic than *Rio Bravo*, the whole production of *Rough Night in Jericho* is second-rate. It holds the attention but is nothing special despite a pretty solid screenplay. The best scene has Slim Pickens, cast against type as a sadistic whip-wielding associate of

Dean's, using his bullwhip to discipline Peppard, which leads into a drawn-out confrontation between the two in which chains, bars, rods, and all manner of implements are brutally employed. Don Costa's music does absolutely nothing for the picture, which might have seemed much more effective with a better score.

Christy Dodd played one of the saloon girls in the picture. "I don't think Dean enjoyed making this movie," she recalls today. "He seemed pretty grumpy and irritable at times, although he was always polite with everybody. I think he had a lot of charm; he just didn't seem inclined to use it that often." Arnold Laven remembered that Dean told him more than once that he only made movies to "get away from the wife." Laven assumed Dean was joking, but like his buddy Sinatra, Dean generally preferred working to the not entirely convivial domesticity at that point in his life. "He always looked forward to making a film," Jeanne Martin says today, "he just wasn't obsessed with it."

Although *Murderers' Row* may not have done as well at the box office as *The Silencers* did, it still did well enough to convince Columbia that they should come out with a third entry in the series—only with a substantially reduced budget, which unfortunately was mirrored on the screen. *The Ambushers* was also directed by Henry Levin and written by Herbert Baker from the novel of the same name by Donald Hamilton. In this entry, ICE launches a tacky *Plan Nine from Outer Space*-type flying saucer, which is brought down by an even tackier electromagnetic jamming device employed by agents of Big O (now revealed to stand for Bureau for International Government and Order). The saucer's pilot, Sheila Summers (Janice Rule), is sent back in a daze to ICE, white-haired and incommunicative. Seeing Matt revives her memory, but she thinks he's her husband because she went undercover as his wife in a previous assignment. Together they go to Acapulco to locate the saucer; Sheila must fly it because the electromagnetic field in the saucer is somehow deadly to males and therefore only a trained female can act as pilot. In Acapulco they come afoul of Big O operator Leopold Caselius (Albert Salmi), his assistant (Kurt Kasznar), who runs a beer factory, and his lover Francesca Madeira (Senta Berger), who uses a sleep drug in her lipstick to subdue Matt. But with Sheila's help and the assistance of a bevy of Slaygirls, Matt is able to put the kibosh on Salmi and the others.

By now Dean could have acted Matt Helm in his sleep, but he does it smoothly and professionally, if half awake. At fifty, he looks good if a little long in the tooth next to all the young girls in the picture. Perhaps that's why he was given a more sensible leading lady, Janice Rule, who seemed an odd choice to many not because she wasn't attractive—she was a very good-looking woman—but because she was an intelligent dramatic actress with serious credits and not just a sexpot. She and Dean play extremely well together and have just the right sexual chemistry. Although Rule looks a bit uncomfortable in the Kewpie-doll outfits— miniskirts and knee boots—that the story line called for, taking her cue from Dean she plays with a light touch and never loses her dignity. "It certainly was nothing to be embarrassed about," she said of being in *The Ambushers*.

As usual, Dean never sings outright in the film, but this time he plays "Everybody Loves Somebody" over the radio to put a gal in the romantic frame of mind. When she tells him "I'm not in the mood," he switches stations only to hear Sinatra singing *his* big hit, "Strangers in the Night," to which the girl is finally receptive. "You like Perry Como that much?" Dean asks her. In addition to the Sinatra gags, he also gets to sneak in references to his hometown, such as when he tells the leader of a firing squad who gives him a last cigarette: "I'll remember you from the Great Beyond. Hopefully around Steubenville." The title song, a dreadful pop-junk tune by Baker and Montenegro, is sung by a boy group and not by Dean, who was probably grateful not to have the assignment.

By this time the Matt Helm series had begun to resemble the *Batman* TV show even more than *The Man from U.N.C.L.E.*, and the gadgets were pathetically low-tech. In addition to the cheesy spaceship jamming device, there is an infrared heat camera that looks like a common if outsized Polaroid, Caselius's unimpressive telekinetic antigravity device, and a totally timid metal melting ray that an ICE operative demonstrates on the belt buckle of a male dummy whose pants fall down. "That's when the danger usually starts," says one of the Slaygirls. Later Janice Rule enters the fray during a battle in a beer factory wearing a metal exoskeleton that adds bulk and heft to her arms and legs. Along with the breast jokes, there are brassiere devices, such as a message bra with a built-in transmitter worn by Lovey Kravezit, and a bullet-pumping bra gun worn by Janice Rule, (the idea for which had come from *The Tenth Victim*, in which such a device was wielded by Ursula Andress). The only technical bit that's even remotely impressive is a tiny compressed bit of material that rolls out of the trunk of Helm's car and expands—via what appears to be stop-motion trick photography—into a full-size tent big enough to set up housekeeping in. As with the previous film, there was little if any location work, and the expensive sets had been replaced by "exotic" southern California locales.

Badly paced, directed, and written, *The Ambushers* starts OK but goes nowhere from there, representing a step backward, if possible, for the series. It's hard to tell which is the film's lowest point: Dean sliding down a train rail on his backside and a branch or the entire climax, when Dean rescues Rule from a runaway rail car that the saucer has been placed on. We never realize the woman is in any danger until the car reaches the end of the track and goes over a hitherto unseen cliff—talk about minimizing suspense! It makes no sense at all that Rule wouldn't save herself by simply flying off in the saucer or that Matt wouldn't use Salmi's antigrav device to lift the saucer off the train car along with Rule. Both of these "top operatives" allow a highly expensive piece of equipment (as far as ICE is concerned, at least) to go crashing off the cliff along with the train!

Nevertheless, even *The Ambushers* has a couple of memorable scenes. Dean rides through a river on a motorcycle and emerges with an alligator as a passenger. Later he winds up in a giant vat of swirling beer with Kurt Kasznar, to whom he says, "Drink your way to the bottom!" A genuinely hilarious and clever bit has Dean participating in a training exercise on a bogus train with three other agents: a pretty girl with a compact, an old lady eating a snack, and an older man with a briefcase. Every time the lights go out, these three switch positions and accouterments as Helm stays in the same place. When the lights come up for the final time, the older man is holding the compact and the girl is in her undies. "Well," Helm tells his superiors, "you *told* me to uncover the secret agent." Basically the film, like Dean's TV program, is too good-natured and silly to be offensively sexist, presenting almost a parody of machismo.

According to Marybeth Jaymes, who was back as one of the bodies beautiful in *The Ambushers*, Dean had changed, too. "He was still sweet, but not so fatherly anymore," she remembers today. "I knew he had flirted with a lot of the other girls, but I thought he would cut that out once he got to know you, once you became a person in his eyes. He didn't really seem to remember me that well, even though we'd worked on *The Silencers* only a short time before and had lots of talks. He definitely came on to me, asking for dinner dates and inviting me back to his dressing room for a 'drink.' I think he was crazy about Janice Rule, who he thought was real sexy and on top of that classy. I know he wanted her, but

I don't know if he got to first base with her or not. They did seem to enjoy working together, but everyone liked working with Dean—he was *fun*. I do know that he fooled around with at least two of the other Slaygirls. One tried to keep it a big secret, but you could tell from the way they looked at one another and all the time she spent with him. The other one blabbed it all over the lot. I think she thought it meant great things were in store for her. Talk about naive women. I knew that once you put out they lost interest, and that's just what happened. Besides, I didn't fool around with married men, even if Dean didn't act like he was married. A lot of the girls thought he was divorced or separated at the time, but he wasn't. Not divorced, at least. He just *acted* like he was."

It wouldn't be too long before Dean would be divorced—again—for real.

EIGHTEEN

The Unold

In late 1967, Dean signed to make a film entitled *Band of Gold* with his leading lady from *The Silencers*, Stella Stevens, as his costar. The film was directed by Fielder Cook, who had previously helmed *Patterns* and *A Big Hand for the Little Lady*. By the time the new film was released the title had been changed to *How to Save a Marriage (and Ruin Your Life)*. Today all Cook will say about the film is that "my experience with Dean was very satisfactory in the end, and I keep all my relationships with actors very private." Reportedly, Cook complained to higher-ups about Dean's refusing to rehearse or do more than one take, but it did him no good—Dean had much more clout. The writer-producer was Stanley Shapiro, who'd worked on a number of "eternal virgin" Doris Day's sex farces. The *New York Times* would charge that he was "obsessed with virginity."

Dean plays a bachelor who discovers that his best friend, played by Eli Wallach, has taken a mistress (played by Wallach's real-life wife Anne Jackson), and makes up his mind to steal the woman away from Wallach so that his buddy's marriage can be preserved. Unfortunately, he comes under the mistaken impression that Stella Stevens is the mistress and targets the wrong woman with his romantic campaign. When she learns the truth, Stevens is so morally outraged that she retaliates by giving him the impression she's been "had" many times over. Eventually everything is worked out, but Dean's life is "ruined"—by marriage to Stella. Meanwhile Jackson joins a league of discarded mistresses.

Stevens was twenty-six at the time and had just done her third layout in *Playboy*. She was thrilled that *How to Save a Marriage* was the first of her films to play Radio City Music Hall and felt she could identify with her part, saying at the time, "It's the closest thing to *me* I've played. This girl wears clothes like I wear, and she's a hard worker, too. For me, it was just like a piece of cake. I didn't have to build a character."

Today Eli Wallach remembers: "We were filming this comedy two weeks after our closest friend died—so our mood was sober and glum. We enjoyed doing the film with Dean Martin, but a lot of the time his mood paralleled ours. He was a pro, but below the surface he seemed *sad*—we often wondered if it was trouble at his home or career blues or just that he'd had enough of light comedies. We were invited to his home and spent a number of evenings together—we were 'New Yawk' actors, but he identified with us and our work. When Dean sang we were impressed with his ease of delivery, his humor and his warmth.

"Problems?" Wallach continues. "Some. He would get impatient with the time the director took in setting up the scenes—lighting took an eternity—after all [he was] brought up on the nightclub and vaudeville stage. His movie work with Lewis is very interesting—watch the films carefully and you'll see a masterful foil for Lewis's joviality. He was a wonderfully skillful straight man—although the term 'straight' is distasteful to an actor. Martin was a gifted man—and Anne and I miss him."

Dean is as adept as ever in this lightweight role, with good support from Stevens and especially from the ultratalented duo of Wallach and Jackson. *How to Save a Marriage* is yet another Dean Martin comedy that might have been more effective if it had been played straight. The picture begins well, with some very funny dialogue, but after a while it becomes more silly and predictable than amusing, although it must be said that it holds the attention, no doubt because of that cast.

"Does anyone who is even moderately interested in movies need to be warned off *How to*?" asked the *New Yorker*. "A Doris Day reject . . . The dialogue has the desperately strained sound of burned-out gag writer's dialogue—the wisecracks come out sourcracks—nastiness pretending to be low-down wisdom . . . . Fielder Cook's direction manages to eliminate the last vestiges of behavioral charm from Dean Martin and Stella Stevens." *Newsday* opined that the picture was "witless, predictable, obnoxious." On the other hand, *Motion Picture Exhibitor* called it "A slick funfest . . . The message seems to be that the male of the species can reap all the bliss and benefits of wedded life without the need for license, ring, and all that jazz."

Even Dean got mixed notices, with *Variety* noting that he "delivers a more restrained, mature performance" than in the Matt Helm features and the *Observer* deciding, somewhat obtusely, that "Mr. Martin's emotional range is bounded on both ends by a calf look."

Dean had good reason to be sad while making *How to Save a Marriage*. His mother was dying at the time, and his own marriage was not in the best of shape, although it would be a while before things reached the breaking point. Mostly it was that he was never there, taking on so many projects that all the free days he had (because he only took one day to do his TV show) were being eaten up by movies and club engagements. His mother's and then his father's deaths put him at a crossroads. He had tried to have the kind of happy, long-lasting marriage they had, the good Catholic boy in him wanting not only to please them but to do the right thing, but he had never really been the same kind of man as his father. That whole way of life just didn't mean as much to him. His parents had strongly disapproved of his first divorce, so there hadn't been a second— not while they were alive. As if there was no one to watch over him any longer, this orphan boy would soon become much less discreet about his indiscretions.

He certainly wasn't unhappy with his earnings. In 1968 *TV Guide* reported that he earned "more money in a year than anyone in the history of show business. His record singles now outsell Sinatra's, his movies outgross Sinatra's, and his total income surpasses Sinatra's. Surpasses the Beatles as individuals." He was being paid $750,000 per picture (not counting percentages); $825,000 for records; and $150,000 for three weeks at the Sands. He was now considered "the largest individual landowner" in Ventura Country, adding restaurants, music companies, blue-chip stocks, more ranches, a house in Palm Springs, and so on to his portfolio. Dean was number four in a box office poll of most popular movie stars; in fact, throughout the sixties he was never out of the top ten.

Perhaps Dean had realized that all that money didn't necessarily add up to a perfect life—or could keep one's mother from wasting away from an awful, terminal illness. Never mind that Sophie Tucker had once said: "I've been rich and I've been poor, and rich is better." Perhaps what Dean needed to hear was someone telling him: "It's better to be rich and unhappy than poor and miserable. If you're rich you can always fly away." Dean had enough money to fly away, more than enough money for any form of escapism. But even with all his money Dean's favorite form of escapism—besides sex and booze—was to sit in front of the TV set (there was one in each room of his Beverly Hills mansion) and watch a western.

When he wasn't watching a western, he was off making one. The latest was called *Bandolero!*—his first and only film with Jimmy Stewart, whose ranch he had bought some time before. Dean also had Jimmy as a guest on his TV show singing "Ragtime Cowboy Joe." The sex symbol of the moment, Raquel Welch, was also in the cast, along with George Kennedy, who'd had a supporting role in *The Sons of Katie Elder*. The film had begun life as *Mace* and was a project initiated by studio head Darryl Zanuck, who pretty much dictated that it would be written and directed by James Lee Barrett and Andrew McLaglen and star Jimmy Stewart, the same trio that had combined on the acclaimed *Shenandoah* three years previously. The son of actor Victor McLaglen, Andrew had also directed *McLintock!* (1963) with John Wayne and *The Rare Breed* (1966) with Stewart, among many others. Zanuck also wanted Dean and Raquel in the cast, so Barrett tailored the script for their talents.

Aside from a few scenes shot in the studio, most of the picture was made on location in Brackettville, Texas, where there were old sets originally built for *The Alamo*, and in Page, Arizona, where the adjacent Glen Canyon National Recreation Area could be used for some striking background scenery. According to Welch, there was also a detour to Utah, where a "torturing"—as she put it—sandstorm flew up to bedevil the players; Welch had it the worst because unlike the men she didn't even have a bandanna to protect her. "That night," she said, "I must have washed a ton of red sand out of my hair, and all day my eyes were watery." On top of that she was thrown off her horse at a Rio Grande crossing called the Devil's River, where she hit the rocky bottom and bruised her ankle.

Bandolero! begins in Val Verde, Texas, in 1867. Dean plays Dee Bishop, a member of a gang that's caught and imprisoned during a bank robbery. Sheriff Johnson (George Kennedy) sends for the hangman, but Dee's brother Mace (James Stewart) manages to take the man's place and surreptitiously helps free his brother and the others before they can be executed. As they make their escape with a hostage named Maria (Raquel Welch), whose husband was killed during the robbery, Mace holds up the bank himself and takes off after the others with the loot concealed in his saddlebag. Sheriff Johnson, who has a thing for Maria, grabs Deputy Roscoe (Andrew Prine) and pursues the robbers into "bandolero"—bandit country—where the banditos "kill every gringo they can find." It all ends with everyone biting the dust except for the sheriff and Maria.

Dean, close to fifty-one, was aging well and looks good in the movie. As with *Rough Night in Jericho*, however, he was really not the best choice to play a bad guy, even if this character had some slight redeeming features, unlike Alex Flood in the earlier picture. Many felt he and Stewart never seemed remotely related, let alone like brothers, but the real problem was that Dean played the less sympathetic of the Bishop boys with too much charm—although he "tried awfully hard," according to the director—and isn't crude or rough enough to be terribly convincing. He does, however, *react* very well to Stewart's better delivered lines and speeches. Stewart emits the intensity that Dean should have projected—even though one senses that Mace has the weaker personality of the two brothers—yet Stewart is also too cute at times (as is the character). Dean can't quite work up the right emotion or conviction for his death scene, probably because the thought of him and Raquel Welch settling down on a farm in Montana—Dee's aborted dream—was hilarious to him. The romance that develops between him and Raquel never seems remotely believable; offscreen the two didn't exactly bond.

Although fan mags and some entertainment columnists tried to suggest that there was a love triangle on the film between Dean, Jimmy, and Raquel, today Andrew McLaglen confirms that nothing of that nature ever happened between Raquel and Dean—"their relationship was nice and professional," he says—let alone Raquel and Jimmy, although Dean certainly noticed the charms of his shapely costar. Raquel was married at the time and said later that she didn't have a very enjoyable experience making the picture. She kept wanting to question her motivation, which Dean found a touch exasperating. "It was an inoffensive, nine-to-five project," she said, "with a lot of very senior people, the old John Ford gang. Very cliquish. Except for Jimmy, who'd always kind of throw out little things, I felt pretty lonely the whole shoot." Shooting a western on location in somewhat rugged conditions was not the kind of glamour Welch had envisioned when she became a movie star. She didn't understand that she was working with solid professionals with strong, *proven* talents and couldn't expect to be instantly respected. Sensing her unease, McLaglen and the others did their best to loosen her up. "We took her out for dinner," McLaglen remembers, "when her husband wasn't around so she could have a glass of wine and smoke a cigarette, which her husband wouldn't allow." Stewart recalled that they got her "good and drunk, and she was OK after that." With the exception of one or two sequences, including, oddly enough, Dean's death scene, Welch's performance is only adequate. "She comes across more as a tartish camp-follower than as an outraged widow," wrote film historian Lawrence J. Quirk.

Dean was a bit in awe of the great Jimmy Stewart and was on his best behavior, cooperating in every way and hardly drinking during the day, if at all. McLaglen remembers that he was nothing at all like the image he conveyed on his television show. "He told me, 'When I'm drinking with Frank, every third one goes in the pot.'" He was convivial and "eager to please," remembers McLaglen. "I was impressed by his exuberance." As for retakes? "I'll do it one hundred times if you want to," McLaglen recalls him saying. This change in attitude from his usual One-Take Charlie approach could only have been induced by his great respect for Stewart and McLaglen. McLaglen remembers that there was one shot left at the end of filming, a close-up of Dean in a jail cell when he's supposed to be talking to his brother. Even though Stewart wouldn't appear on camera and no one had asked him to show up on the set, "Jimmy put on all his wardrobe just so he could do the scene with Dean," says McLaglen. He recalled Dean telling him afterward, "Boy, I never had any of them do *that* for me before." McLaglen says, "It was a really great experience for me, working with a guy who really loved making movies, who was so much different than the TV persona that he played perfectly for the TV audience." Jimmy and Dean liked and respected one another, although Stewart wouldn't exactly carouse with Dino the way John Wayne had. When Jimmy wasn't talking to Dean or others in the cast, he was taking care of Pie, his equine companion in many movies whose last film appearance this would be; the horse was simply too weak and too old.

Although critics agreed that McLaglen had done his usual solid job of moviemaking and kept things moving, *Bandolero!* was nearly undone by the superficial characterizations in the screenplay. An entertaining picture, the most "fun" scenes in *Bandolero!* have to do with the attacks of the banditos: They strike silently, without warning, stabbing and hacking with machetes, then remove the clothing and all valuables from the corpses of their victims in seconds flat. Considering how relatively negative the "heroes" of the picture are, the film achieves a kind of moral closure with their deaths at the end. Jerry Goldsmith contributed a nice whistling overture for the picture, and the stunt coordinator was Hal Needham, who'd work with Dean in another capacity a few years hence.

Barely had the dust settled on the streets of Brackettville, Texas, when Dean was on his way to Mexico to work on yet another western. For a man who had been called lazy by some, it was ironic that he should push himself to take on virtually every filmic assignment that he was offered (and that paid the right price) in addition to hosting his show, appearing on other people's shows, and doing club and casino engagements. Of course this was why he only had one day a week to spare for *The Dean Martin Show* and why he preferred to do a scene in one take. He not only wanted time to do other work but to enjoy his leisure activities. The popular theory among friends and associates was that Dean had never forgotten his early days of struggle and debt and wanted to make sure he and his loved ones would be set and secure for the rest of his life, no matter what happened. "It's all coming my way, and I want to take advantage of every opportunity," he said. On another occasion he added, "There'll be a time when I'm not so much in demand. That happens to every entertainer. I can do plenty of relaxin' when that day comes, right?"

When he was home, he slept in his own separate bedroom, watched TV incessantly, spoke little to Jeanne and even less to the children. He was not trying to be cruel; in the words of the sixties, he "needed his own space." He was not an intellectual, well read, well versed in the arts (aside from his hit movies) or politics; he had little to say. In addition to his wife there were seven children, not all of whom were married and out of the house, and one mother-in-law. Jeanne's mother, Peggy, whom Dean was very fond of, lived with them throughout most of their married life.

Like other active movie-star husbands—Bob Hope, for example, or Paul Newman, who had a separate everyone-else-keep-out retreat built on his property—he left the child raising and disciplining, almost all domestic issues, to the wife. Jeanne may have wanted to travel with him when he went on location—a few times she did—but someone had to be there for the children, someone they had a more emotional attachment to than a nanny, someone who could applaud them at the school plays and root for them at Little League. Dean did picture after picture so that he could make enough money to see to their every need as well as his own; that was his contribution. But while the kids had their own friends and even spouses—their own lives—Jeanne wanted to live life with her *husband*, and he was hardly ever there. Some movie-star wives, like Joanne Woodward, had their own careers and coped; others, like Delores Hope, accepted that their marriages were somewhat shallow and false but somehow managed to weather it. Ultimately Jeanne would not be able to do either.

It was as Jacqueline Susann described it in 1966 in her blockbuster novel *Valley of the Dolls*. In Hollywood "a wife held the same social status as a screenwriter—necessary but anonymous . . . . Starlets could garner plenty of attention at parties, but a wife lived in limbo. Too respected to be approached, too unimportant to rate respect." Whatever her original ambitions, which she might have suppressed for Dean's sake, Jeanne had never had a career of her own. Perhaps her only real taste of show business, besides appearing on Dean's show for Christmas, was an *I Love Lucy* episode back in the fifties when, playing herself, she was one of the movie-star wives (along with Lucy Ricardo) who were trotted out sans dialogue and with upswept hair to show off Don Loper's latest designs. "The very, very pretty Mrs. Dean Martin is wearing a dancing costume in re-embroidered lace with a coat of Italian satin," says Loper. Elegant and chic, Jeanne not only looks every inch the movie-star's wife, but every inch the movie *star*.

Jeanne did a very frank interview with *Ladies Home Journal* in 1968 where she put it all on the line. Friends suspected that this was her way of reaching out to Dean, making him understand exactly how she felt—and how much she hurt. "Dean was not and is not, nor will he ever be, the ideal husband," she told the interviewer. "I could be with the man I love a tremendous number of hours a day. Obviously, he's not about to give them. As a matter of fact, Dean gives minimum amount." She admitted that she put up with his affairs because "I receive a fantastic amount of love from Dean. So it balances out." Jeanne figured that what she didn't know wouldn't hurt her and didn't want to hear about his carryings-on from friends, although she would occasionally throw a tabloid detailing his latest indiscretion into his room.

Far from being a swinger or night owl, Dean in his fifties, while not exactly a homebody, wanted to be in bed by eleven when he was in Beverly Hills. When parties at his house went on too long, including his own anniversary party, he would anonymously call the police from his bedroom and complain about the noise! When the police showed up, Jeanne says today, laughing, "We'd go out and give them some Scotch."

Perhaps because he sensed the marriage was on its last legs at this point and wondered how it would impact on his public life, Dean had a new woman in his life in 1968 but only in a professional capacity—although Mrs. Temme Brenner claimed she had been in love with Dean since the fifties when she worked for Paramount. "He's a man's man, and men love him just as much as women," she said. She worked for the public relations firm of Rogers and Cowan; snaring Dean as a client earned her a partnership. Dean would now be advised and protected by the powerful firm of Rogers, Cowan, and Brenner.

It was while Dean was making his latest western in Mexico that daughter Gail debuted her act at the tony Persian Room of the Plaza Hotel in New York. Dean didn't attend, ostensibly because he was in the middle of shooting; he sent flowers instead. One columnist lambasted him for being a no-show: "It would have taken less time for Dino to have jetted to New York than it did for the posies to come across town from the florist." But Dean knew that Gail and his other children knew that wherever he was, he was with them in spirit. Dean had seen Gail perform before. To a multimillionaire megastar like Dean, her little act was hardly different from an appearance in the high-school dramatics society; he just didn't want to bother flying all the way to New York to see it. That didn't make Dean a bad father, just not the overly devoted, slavishly paternal, "I wouldn't miss it for the world" kind of old man. Was he selfish? Self-absorbed? In some ways yes, but never malevolently. "It's not that he doesn't care," Claudia once said. "He cares very much, but he just doesn't want to hear anybody else's problems. It's almost as if not hearing them means they really don't exist."

The latest western, *Five Card Stud* (1968), Dean's last picture for producer Hal Wallis and his second with director Henry Hathaway, began life as an untitled project that, during filming, was simply called *Durango* after the location where it was being shot. As he had been in *The Sons of Katie Elder*, also helmed by Hathaway, Dean was back in the high-altitude Mexican Sierras, only this time his buddy John Wayne wasn't with him. In *Five Card Stud*, a mystery-western, Dean portrays Van Morgan, a Colorado gambler who tries to stop what he feels is the excessive punishment of a card cheat: lynching without benefit of trial. Even though he fails, it seems as though someone else who either participated in or witnessed the execution is gunning for the murderers. One is found smothered in a barrel of flour; another is strangled with barbed wire; and so on. Who is picking off the lynch mob one by one? Morgan? One of the men who wants to eliminate witnesses? Nope—it's the new gun-totin' preacher in town, Jonathan Rudd (Robert Mitchum), getting justice for his dead brother. After romancing the new owner of the barbershop (Inger Stevens) and tangling with the desperado (Roddy McDowall) who gave Preacher Rudd the names of the other murderers, Morgan and Rudd have it out, with only one—guess who?—emerging the winner.

Dean should have been better in this movie than he was in *Rough Night in Jericho* and *Bandolero!*—although he was playing a somewhat shady character, Van Morgan is essentially decent—but he hardly bothers to give a performance. He's in the picture but never really *occupies* it. This may have been because he wasn't too fond of producer Hal Wallis, plus the fact that director Hathaway was up to his same bullying tricks, and Dean would have none of it. In any case, he seems to be preoccupied through most of the movie. (Perhaps with wondering why Morgan is moral enough to try to stop the hanging but not enough to rat out the killers to the marshal?)

Dean and Robert Mitchum both appeared in *What a Way to Go!* but had no scenes together, thus they really worked together for the first time in *Five Card Stud*. Cut from the same cloth, they got along well, if not as well as Dean and John Wayne. Mitchum had been a major star even before Dean did his first picture, so he wasn't too crazy about being second-billed below him. Almost every critic noticed that his part in *Five Card Stud* was too reminiscent of his role in the far superior *Night of the Hunter*. Roddy McDowall was ludicrously miscast as a cowboy, and his accent is hardly western let alone American. At one point the audience is asked to believe that Roddy could knock Dean out with his gun with one blow, and while the fight they have is rather rousing, the fisticuffs never look quite real. "I didn't know what to expect when I found out I'd be working with Dean," Roddy said. "But he was likable if a little crude. I must say I expected a barrel of laughs, but I found him a little morose. Don't know why." Intellectual Roddy was not really the kind of guy Dean liked to hang out with. Dean didn't really know what to say to highly intelligent, cultured people like McDowall, and while both men were witty, their wit cut in different directions entirely.

Inger Stevens and Dean have an interesting love scene with some compelling, provocative dialogue that in today's movies would be delivered in a sexier style. Inger was a little too bony for Dean's tastes. After being dumped by the likes of Bing Crosby and Henry Fonda, among others, not to mention additional personal vicissitudes, Stevens would, sadly, commit suicide about a year after finishing this picture. Yaphet Kotto, who would later appear in *Alien* and on TV's *Homicide*, plays the bartender George with dignity and intelligence. His death struggle at the hands of Mitchum's Rudd is one of the movie's better scenes, but it might have been nice if Dean had Morgan evoking more of a sense of moral outrage over his murder; George, after all, did not partake in the lynching.

Marguerite Roberts's screenplay for *Five Card Stud* isn't bad, but the film would have needed practically an entirely different cast to be effective. Hathaway was able to build up some suspense over the murderer's identity, but the picture has almost no atmosphere. Maurice Jarre's musical score is all wrong for this kind of movie. An interesting aspect of the picture is that at the end Morgan goes off with the bad girl played by Inger Stevens instead of the good girl portrayed by Katherine Justice (who is excellent). Dean recorded the fairly standard title tune, which he warbles over the opening credits.

By this time Dean's father had passed away in his nursing home. Then Dean's brother, Bill, who'd been diagnosed with cancer of the brain shortly before his father's death—another reason for the depression that some of Dean's friends and co-workers noticed in this period—succumbed to the disease on October 20, 1968, not even two months after his father's death. He was only fifty-two. The only saving grace is that his parents died without knowing how soon their first-born would follow them.

It is strange to contemplate the fates of these two brothers, Dino and Guglielmo, Dean and William, one of whom had become a multimillion-aire and famous entertainer who lived to a ripe old age while the other toiled in relative obscurity and died in misery at fifty-two. Dean, who, as Jeanne today puts it, "got down on his knees every night to thank God for his success," could not have explained it. "I have never missed a night without praying," he said. He believed in God but not necessarily in all the ritualistic trappings of religion, just as he liked to act but could do without everything else that came with it. He was continuously grateful for all that he had been given and knew that things could have been so much worse, that his loss, as awful as it was, could have been even more devastating. In time it would be.

While it could never make up for his personal losses, Dean seemed to have the Midas touch when it came to the professional front. Earlier in 1968 he learned from the Record Industry Association of America that two of his Reprise albums had gone gold, each bringing in over one million dollars in sales. Most of the performers who had sales similar to or greater than Dean's sang hard or acid rock and had an entirely different audience from his. His television show remained the greatest place to hype his latest recordings to millions of viewers. It was all synergistic, all feeding off everything else, dividing and multiplying—endless money. He had the occasional rock group as guests on his show, and it did him a world of good to know that his records were outselling most of these long-haired freaks who might have considered him—him! one of the most popular and wealthiest men in show business—an old fart and a has-been. By now Dean, the American icon, had become too big to ever become a has-been. He would retire, he would leave show business; it could never leave him. Even the rock stars, the kids, knew that Dean could get away with things that their parents or other entertainers couldn't.

For instance, when he opened at the Versailles Room of the Riviera casino in Las Vegas, the tab per person was a record-breaking $15.50, which the Riviera had no problem getting or charging. They had wooed Dean away from the Sands after his contract there expired and offered him one hundred thousand dollars a week, another twenty thousand per month, and part ownership of the hotel. Execs at the Sands, which had recently been taken over by Howard Hughes, tore their hair. Some believed Dean had left the Sands to show loyalty to Frank Sinatra, who had parted company with the place in some silly huff and was now a headliner at Caesars Palace, but Dean could not be bound by Sinatra's drunken rages and mood swings. The Riviera had simply made him a better offer. Sinatra was aware of this—in spite of Sinatra's actions Dean had been in no hurry to get away from the Sands until he heard from the folks at the Riviera—and for a while the two were incommunicado. Sinatra was angry at Dean, and Dean knew there was no point calling Frank when he had a chip on his shoulder. He had put up with such behavior from moody Jerry Lewis, and he was not about to put up with it again from anybody else. Sinatra had to learn that Dean did things his *own* way or not at all. As for the Riviera, Dean eventually had his own problems with them when he told them in no uncertain terms that he would perform only one show per night, which not even the great Dino could get away with. He sold his interest back to the casino, and they sold his contract (which still had some months to run) to the MGM Grand only on the condition that he do *two* shows per night for them, not wanting any precedents to be set.

In the meantime, daughter Claudia had come out in a new movie, *Ski Fever* (1969), costarring Martin Milner (of *Adam 12* fame), as a guest at a ski lodge in a mediocre comedy directed by Curt Siodmak. She had also found another husband in Keil Martin née Mueller, who took his wife's—or actually his father-in-law's—last name after the wedding, most likely because it would look better on his resume; he, too, was an actor. Deana found the man of her dreams with another artistic type, an aspiring screenwriter named Terry Guerin. Also an actress, Deana had a tiny role in *Young Billy Young* with Robert Mitchum. Craig divorced his first wife and married one of the dancers on his father's TV show, then divorced *her* to marry—ironically—Lou Costello's daughter, Carole. Watching their father divorce their mother, Betty, and marry Jeanne, had not exactly impressed upon either Craig or Claudia the sanctity of wedding vows or the permanence of the marital state. It's no wonder that Dean's next flick was called *The Wrecking Crew*.

The Wrecking Crew was the fourth and final entry in the Matt Helm series. Phil Karlson, the director of the first installment, was back as director, with a new scripter, William McGivern, adapting Hamilton's novel. In Denmark, during "Operation Rainbow," a billion dollars' worth of gold is hijacked from a train by sinister Count Massimo Contini (Nigel Green). A team can't be sent in to get it back—it must be a one man/Matt Helm operation—because news of the theft might leak out and cause a panic on the world market. Helm is told he must bust the case within forty-eight hours by order of the president, LBJ. Flying to Copenhagen, he goes to talk to mysterious Lola Madina (Tina Louise), an associate of Contini's, but she's blown to bits by a doctored bottle of Scotch before she can talk to him. Helm and Freya Carlson (Sharon Tate), a klutzy Danish agent with the tourist bureau who turns out actually to be an agent of ICE, go to Contini's house undercover as photographers of fashionable interiors. They wind up in a big battle in the House of Seven Joys, which is run by another Contini associate, Yu Rang (Nancy Kwan). After more misadventures, Dean finds the gold bars cleverly disguised as a wall, and the rest is history.

Dean looks tired, a bit bored, and boozy in *The Wrecking Crew*. Lying on a bed with sexy Elke Sommer, smooching, he looks like he'd rather be sleeping; he just hasn't the energy for sex. He shows more energy making karate moves (trained by Bruce Lee, no less!) with an Oriental opponent later in the picture. Dean saw how tired he looked next to all the young girls, and part of him wondered if it might be time to call it quits, at least with the Matt Helm movies. Throughout much of the movie he wears a kind of white jumpsuit that doesn't suit him at all. Dean is heard singing voice-over songs several times during the movie, but he changes the lyrics as he did on his TV show. "If your sweetheart puts a pistol on your bed, you'd do better sleeping with your Uncle Fred" is sung to "Cry," while "Grab your hat and grab your pail, let me take you in the barn, just sit back and watch, 'cause I found a cow that gives Scotch" is sung to "Sunny Side of the Street." Dean is shown dreaming of voluptuous women that he doesn't seem to have the energy to satisfy as his racy new version of "Red Sails in the Sunset" plays on the soundtrack.

Pretty Sharon Tate—later senselessly murdered by Charles Manson's followers—proves to be a fairly deft actress/comedienne, though not on the level of Stella Stevens. When she switches from outsized glasses and a severe hairdo into sexpot mode halfway through the film she loses her appealing vulnerability. She seems very uncomfortable kissing fifty-two-year-old Dean in the pop-out bed on the train at the end of the picture. James Gregory was no longer playing Matt's boss; the part went to John Larch instead. As the other resident babes, Tina Louise and Elke Sommer are no better than they should be.

The budget for *The Wrecking Crew* wasn't much by big movie standards. The phony grass outside the villain's chateau actually wiggles when Dean lands on it. The high-tech weapons include a camera that emits incapacitating green gas and a two-seater open-air whirlybird that Dean doesn't even get into. One effect Dean hated was a table in a Chinese restaurant that goes around and around as one wall comes down to cut them off from the rest of the room and another goes up to reveal Count Contini. The spinning motion almost made Dean sick, particularly if he'd indulged the night before. The film briefly introduces a Q type (but American and very unlike Desmond Llewelyn, who plays the part in the Bond movies), who explains the gizmos before he gives them to Helm.

The pace is too languid for a thriller, and Hugo Montenegro's awful, boppy score does nothing to add tension or suspense to the proceedings; it even spoils halfway decent scenes such as a car crash on a country road. Another train climax (after the one in *The Ambushers*) lacks excitement and features some very crude process work. A karate catfight between Sharon Tate and Nancy Kwan isn't badly staged (again courtesy of Bruce Lee), but it's much too brief and civilized—a catfight in a politically incorrect Matt Helm movie should have hair pulling, face scratching, and heaving bosoms. Also Matt's meeting with Tina Louise at her apartment turns into a fashion show when surely the mostly male audience for these movies would have preferred to see her *un*dressed, not modeling clothing that would be of interest only to the wives back home.

Once again, this Matt Helm flick has a perfectly good story with interesting situations almost completely undone by bad execution and a silly script that never lapses into out-and-out hilarity. The Helm films may have been parodies in a sense, but aside from a few vulgar chuckles, they aren't especially funny. By now—if they hadn't always been—the Matt Helm movies were sex fantasies for pot-bellied, middle-aged men: Helm, a super-spy for couch potatoes. By now Dean was not *too* much different from the men watching in the theater.

Although a fifth movie, *The Ravagers*, was announced at the end, it never materialized. In that installment Matt was to attempt to bring to justice the murderer of a congressman, with the added complication that the assassin is his own perfect double. In a switch from previous films, Matt would indulge in various disguises to catch his prey, no doubt to keep the cops, who might mistake him for the assassin, off his trail: an elderly "Mother Helm," a bewigged lawyer, a hippie-dippie ice cream vendor. Dean refused to do the picture and was soon back in court, making the lawyers happy. Columbia held back $300,000 of his *Wrecking Crew* profits because they claimed that was only a portion of what they would lose if there weren't a fifth Matt Helm.

Dean had several reasons for refusing to do *The Ravagers*. Even before the withholding, he hadn't been *that* impressed with the profits from *The Wrecking Crew*, for one thing; the Helm films were co-produced by his own company, and he felt that there were better ways to invest his money. He was fairly sick of the whole formula. The westerns he did—and which he loved—may have been formulaic, but not so much as the Helm series; each picture had a nagging sameness to it. He had never been that crazy about spy movies to begin with and only did the films to make a great deal of money and reinforce his popularity. He had accomplished his goal; now it was time to move on. Besides, it was one thing to flirt with the young girls on his television program and another to be shown in bed with them, to run around like a loon with pistols and karate moves in a big-screen color movie that showed every wrinkle. Perversely, Dean had no problem seeing—and putting—himself in an actual offscreen bed with women just as young as the girls in the pictures. Perhaps he needed a reaffirmation of his appeal, his sexuality, needed to feel he could still cut the mustard. To hedge his bets, he got a face lift. He considered it no different from a nose job: a good career move.

Let everyone else get *ravaged*. Dean Martin would remain unold.

PART SIX

The Two Deaths of Dino

NINETEEN

How to Ruin a Marriage

Women. There were lots of women.

One of the more significant was Miss World, USA, Gail Renshaw, who was crowned in 1969 when she first met Dean. Five years earlier at seventeen she had married the son of an Arlington, Virginia, realtor named Edward Shoup Jr., but within three years they were divorced, and Gail was once again single and therefore eligible to compete in the Miss World contest. As the winner, she had to honor all personal-appearance contracts—she did television ads for Frostie root beer, one of the pageant's sponsors—and at *all times* be chaperoned; otherwise she could lose her title.

Gail had a manager, and when he and his pretty client were in Las Vegas for one meeting or ribbon cutting or another, the manager, Al Patricelli, decided to get in touch with Dean, who was appearing at the Riviera at the time, via the club's press agent. Dean agreed to meet with the gal and pose for some pictures with her; it was the American way, after all. Besides, everyone knew that Dean had always been partial to beauty queens.

Gail Renshaw and Al Patricelli invaded Dean's dressing room after his show, and Dean liked what he saw. For her part, Gail was thrilled to be in the presence of this magnetic superstar. They did the picture bit, and then Dean asked her if she'd have dinner with him, but of course she needed a chaperone. Dean didn't want Patricelli along; instead, he asked the other Gail in his life, his *daughter*, to come with them!

One can only imagine how bizarre that dinner must have been, Miss World Gail bonding with Dean's daughter Gail (who was only a couple of years older than her namesake), Dean making boozy chitchat while holding the beauty queen's hand under the table and hoping his daughter wouldn't notice. Eventually, as Jeanne reported to columnists, Renshaw would meet all of Dean's children in one way or another. On this occasion Dean managed to whisper sweet nothings to Renshaw while Gail Martin was in the ladies room: Could they meet privately? He thought she was so lovely. It wasn't long before their very private meetings were definitely *un*chaperoned. Registered under the name of his agent, Mort Viner (Gail also used a pseudonym), Dean had repeated trysts with Miss World in bungalow nine of the Beverly Hills Hotel. After a while he refused to come out of the bungalow and told his wife that he wanted a divorce.

What made it all the more infuriating to Jeanne was that Dean had refused so many times to go out on the town with his own wife, yet he often objected when she went by herself or with a chaperone, usually Dino Jr. One night Dean even went out to the popular disco the Daisy Club and almost literally dragged Jeanne off the dance floor and back home. Apparently what was good for the gander wasn't good for the goose—the usual philosophy with philandering husbands. Instead of helping to raise his family, Dean was shacking up with one woman after another. For instance, Dean boycotted his son Craig's second and short-lived wedding (to the dancer on his TV show) in Las Vegas while Jeanne took care of all the arrangements. Dean found all the demands on his time by his family to be too smothering. And he could only stand to be smothered—barely—by someone if there were a sexual component in it. Jeanne, while still attractive, was more than twenty years older than when Dean had first met her.

Jeanne was stunned by Dean's announcement that he wanted to divorce her and marry his new beauty queen, but her emotions were otherwise mixed: a desire to hang on to her man through thick and thin, to wait for him to come to his senses and an equally fervid desire to be done with the sham marriage and his intoxicated, exasperating ways once and for all. "I wouldn't want to live with a man who's not happy with me," she told reporters. "Now he can hide—which is what he does best." Dean's first wife, Betty, wouldn't have been human had she not thought of Jeanne: *Now you know what it feels like.*

As for Dean, he could hardly keep his mouth shut—comparatively speaking—about Gail and the boundless joy she brought him. "I'm not a good bachelor," he said. "I like being married, although I know it means giving up a lot of freedom. But I can't help it—*I like being married.*" He confirmed that part of the problem with Jeanne, as he saw it, was that she was always nagging him to go out, but he never answered the question: Wouldn't his new beauty queen want to go out on the town just as much? Dean maintained that, as he saw it, the problem with Jeanne wanting to go out every night when he was tired was that it contradicted her claims to want to spend more time with him. "She's mad because I'm never home—working, always working. But then when I come home—she wantsta go out! Who can figure?" He told friends he was tired of the struggle and while the married state per se didn't appeal to him, he did not want to be a bachelor. He still needed that one special woman looking up to him; he still needed to be somebody's hero, which after all these honest years and disappointments he could no longer be for Jeanne.

Or Gail Renshaw, either, apparently. Almost as quickly as they'd announced their engagement, the marriage was off. Sensing that Dean was still attached to his wife—if for no other reason than all of the children she gave him and their reaction to this crisis—Gail was afraid the wedding would never take place. "I'm not cut out to be mistress to a superstar," she said to him. She went back home to Virginia and told him not to call her. Another bone of contention was that Gail knew Dean was seeing other women besides her, and that was too much to bear.

One of these women was an aspiring twenty-five-year-old actress named Linda Chesley, although she was using a stage name at the time. She claims to have had a five-year-long on-and-off affair with Dean Martin that began when she met him one night at a Las Vegas casino, where she had come with three girlfriends. She has pictures of herself and Dean, some more intimate than others. "Although I had acting ambitions," she says today, "I was also a divorcée with a young son and an ex-husband and ex-in-laws who kept threatening to take back custody of him. I was not a high-profile beauty queen like Gail Renshaw. I told Dean we had to be *absolutely* discreet or I simply could not see him.

"I had a small apartment in Los Angeles, and Dean would call up, ask if he could come over, and visit. Mostly it was sex, good sex. He was a very pleasant man to be with. I admit at first I just thought of him as a 'connection'; what girl wouldn't have? But over the years I really came to love him, to realize what a sweet and in some ways really lonely man he was. He wanted to be married, and he wanted to be a bachelor. He knew I was having a tough time, so he gave me money and brought me presents. I was not a whore, he didn't treat me like a whore. But he was kind and generous. My son was seven years old, and he adored Dean. Dean was very good with children and very warm, buying him presents and giving him change. But there was always a cutoff point. It wasn't like, 'Get the kid outa here, I want to have sex," but Dean could only take kids in small doses. It was the same way with conversation. We'd be talking politely, having a few laughs and a drink; then he'd just sort of freeze up, if that's the word. Chill on you. He'd had enough. He'd play with my son for a while, but then the same thing would happen. He was never mean; he'd just say, 'Off you go,' and you'd go. Or he'd go. It was as if he portioned out his time with everyone. You only got so much."

Linda says there was never any serious talk of marriage. "I didn't go there. I knew about Jeanne, but I didn't talk about her. He would talk about her now and then, not unkindly, but joking a bit. One night he asked me what I thought about marriage, and I wondered what it was he wanted me to say. I would not have minded marrying him and would have done it in a minute if he'd asked. I knew about Gail and a couple of others."

Dean continued to call on her "out of the blue" the whole time he was seeing Gail Renshaw as well as during the period when he divorced Jeanne, married his next wife, and afterward. "I would say five years or so. Sometimes weeks would go by and I wouldn't hear from him. I never called him. Then finally he just stopped calling. Until one time when he rang up at two in the morning, pretty drunk, and wanted to come over. By that time I had a new man in my life—not the one I'm married to now— and it was just impossible. I was not 'Miss Quick 'n' Ready' for Dino or anybody else. But all in all my memories of him are very positive. He was not an angel—he did a lot of wrong things and he hurt people—but he was not a bad man when you balance the scales."

Apparently Dean had never considered a long-term relationship with Chesley, but now that he had broken off with Renshaw, and Jeanne seemed more or less amenable to going on without him, he still needed to find a "wife." He was in the Candy Store nightclub in Hollywood one night when an actor named Frank Calcagnini introduced him to a pretty twenty-four-year old from Ohio, also a divorcée with a young child, named Catherine (Kathy) Mae Hawn. As Dean became closer and closer to Kathy, who was a receptionist in a beauty shop, Jeanne got closer to Calcagnini, enjoying a short-lived romantic relationship with him. It would be a while, however, before Dean and Kathy decided to get married. Or before they *could* get married. Wondering if the relationship with Hawn would last any longer than the one with Renshaw, Jeanne wasn't in a rush to divorce Dean, and it would take months to work out property settlements considering *all* of the property that there was to divide. In the meantime, Dean did his TV show and made *Airport* (1970).

The story goes that Dean first turned down the role of the pilot in the adaptation of Arthur Hailey's best-selling novel because he thought his boozy TV persona would be at odds with the image of a nerves-of-steel airline pilot. While this thought may well have occurred to him, he was more concerned with the money than with anything else. If he could play a cowboy and a spy, he could play an airline pilot. Producer Ross Hunter met his asking price, and the deal was set. The director, George Seaton, had won an Oscar for adapting Clifford Odets's moving drama *The Country Girl*, which he also directed; he had also helmed the Christmas classic *Miracle on 34th Street*. An uncredited Henry Hathaway, one of Dean's least favorite directors, replaced Seaton temporarily when Seaton caught pneumonia on the day before shooting. The studio wanted to completely replace Seaton but Hunter preferred to have Hathaway fill in by doing second-unit stuff and the like for approximately two weeks until Seaton felt well enough to report back to work.

According to Ross Hunter, "Both Burt Lancaster and Dean Martin accepted their roles even before a script was written, banking on the success of the book and my promises to develop their roles implicitly within the framework of a superior production." Most of the movie was filmed on soundstages, but some exteriors were done at the Minneapolis Airport. Seaton said, "Minneapolis gave us exactly what we wanted. Between nine at night and four in the morning, there were only two flights coming in and going out, so it gave us time to work in the field and also in the terminal." For both the jet that gets stuck in the snow at the beginning of the film and the one that's endangered in the air above, Hunter contacted Flying Tiger Airlines and asked if he could rent a Boeing 747 as well as a flight crew. With a minimum of fuss, things were arranged to everyone's satisfaction.

Burt Lancaster plays Mel Bakersfeld, the general manager of Lincoln Airport in a large, unnamed metropolitan city and a man with a lot of problems. First he has a plane stuck in the snow on an important runaway during a blizzard, and protesters are picketing because of flights from another runway that rattle their houses. His marriage has become stale and unpleasant—his neglected wife (Dana Wynter) wants him to go to work for her father—and his heart burns for Tonya Livingstone (Jean Seberg), the beautiful widow who works for Trans-Global airlines. Then there's his brother-in-law, Vern Demarest (Dean Martin), a pilot and "overaged juvenile delinquent" who is cheating on Mel's sister (Barbara Hale) with now-pregnant stewardess Gwen (Jacqueline Bisset). A former war hero, Bakersfeld has an adversarial relationship with Vern, who has to fly 747s and is sick of hearing Mel's old war stories—"A bomber can't compare to an airliner," he says. But the biggest problem both men have is that a passenger on Vern's flight is carrying a bomb and plans to kill himself—and everyone else on board—so his wife can get the insurance money. With the help of Gwen and an elderly stowaway (Helen Hayes), Vern doesn't quite outwit the bomber but manages to bring the plane down safely even after a hole has been blown in its side. Vern goes off with a badly injured Gwen as his wife watches sadly from the sidelines, and the bomber's despondent widow desperately apologizes to the passengers.

Dean is good in the film. As was often the case, he turns Vern into a variation of Dean Martin. With attractively styled salt and pepper hair (his natural state without dye), he also *looks* good as Vern but sort of old. The scene in the cockpit with Dean and co-pilot Barry Nelson discussing women is so natural and spontaneous that it seems almost improvisational. While Dean enjoyed making the movie, he didn't enjoy being dragged along the floor in the scene where he's nearly sucked out of the plane after the bomb goes off. Dean demonstrates his trademark jauntiness after stewardess Gwen tells him that she "doesn't have a thing to wear." "Great!" he says. Dean also has a very nice scene with Jackie Bisset, who gives one of her loveliest performances as Gwen, when she tells him that she's pregnant with his child. He reacts with compassion and concern, telling her he'll take care of her.

Offscreen, Dean had had lots of practice being compassionate to women who were in love with him, although some might not have agreed. Linda Chesley, however, claims that she got pregnant by Dean, and he *did* show solicitation and concern, though there was absolutely no question about her keeping the child or him marrying her. "He was never nasty about it, just determined that I would have an abortion, which he arranged through a friend and paid for. There was no question that he was the father. I don't know what he would have said or done if I'd told him I wanted to keep the child. It never came up because I wanted an abortion as much as Dean did. Some women might have seen it as a way of getting their hooks into Dean, but that wasn't the type of person I was. Who needed another mouth to feed? Although Dean struck me as the kind of man who would stick by me and the child, financially at least, I didn't want to test him on that score—or any man for that matter. We both agreed an abortion was best, it was taken care of, and that was all there was to it."

Asked if she ever considered the publicity value of having Dean's child, she responds curtly. "I would never use a child for that purpose. I know a lot of other actresses would have used their association with Dean to get everything out of it that they could—maybe I should have; my career never did amount to anything—but I just couldn't use people that way once I got to know them. I've admitted that at first I just saw Dean as someone to use, but he was just too *sweet*. He did try to do me favors, make a few calls for me, but nothing much ever came of it. I once broached the idea about being on his show, but he never pursued it. I think the whole idea made him nervous. The two of us weren't *public* like he was with those other women. Remember, I didn't want to lose custody of my son." No wonder Dean is so good in that scene with Gwen: In some ways he was reenacting his real-life scenes with Linda Chesley. Unlike in the film, however, Dean was more practical. He did not need or want to be a father again at fifty-three; he didn't need the complications and he undoubtedly figured that neither did the unborn child nor the mother.

As for *Airport*, today costar Jacqueline Bisset remembers that "working with Dean Martin was certainly one of the most amusing of my Hollywood working experiences. He joked and made light of everything. He played with a golf club around the set, drank apple juice (as if it were whiskey)—on stage also, so I'm told—and generally kept the spirits up of all around. *Airport* was like two different films—one intense, with Burt Lancaster (no one dared whisper while he worked) and the other hilarious and relaxed. We talked about golf, Vegas, Italian food, and Jerry Lewis mostly; his sons, his wife, Jeanne, and a dozen explanations of why he didn't rehearse anything. In spite of all his joking, one could feel a sad side, but he was a great guy."

Jacqueline Bisset was not the first or last co-worker to notice Dean's "sad side." He was still bothered, of course, by losing his entire family—mother, father, brother—all in the space of a few months, but many friends also theorized that he had not yet accepted the fact that he was ultimately going to lose Jeanne and perhaps even the love of his children by her. There are sources who insist that Dean called off his wedding to Gail Renshaw because he didn't really want to leave Jeanne, but that when she in her understandable outrage—he had *flaunted* the affair with Renshaw so!—indicated that she didn't want him back, he had run to Kathy Hawn more out of his "need to be married" to someone than anything else. The truth was, Dean didn't really know *what* he wanted, and it was eating him up inside. He kept up the happy-go-lucky front—which the more sensitive of his companions could easily see through—because that was his nature. He had been raised to believe that worrying did not do a bit of good. You put your faith in God and prayed. But what would

God think of the hedonistic, extramarital activities of this not-so-good Catholic boy? There were those who felt that Dean had brought all of his problems on himself due to his profligate philandering. And he might well have agreed with them.

There were also those who were certain that all this internal tension was *literally* eating Dean up, giving him ulcers and ultimately necessitating stomach surgery, although not for a couple of years. Whatever was going on in his psyche, Dean enjoyed making *Airport*, and it shows in the finished film. Helen Hayes, who won an Oscar with her expert comic performance as the stowaway, said, "I don't know if he took anything at all seriously, but he was fun to work with and be around." Another good performance came from Jean Seberg, one of the screen's great beauties, as the widow who secretly loves Lancaster as he does her. Perhaps the film's greatest performance, however, was from Maureen Stapleton as the bomber's wife. The final scene in which she goes tearfully from one shell-shocked passenger to another and says, "I'm sorry, he didn't mean it; I'm sorry, he didn't mean it" is heartbreaking. The scene when Vern, Gwen, and the others corner the nervous bomber (Van Heflin) is nail-bitingly tense—although none of the principals seem nearly nervous enough about the bomb—and quite a bit of suspense is generated from a scene when the empty snowbound plane is pushed to full power on the ground in an effort to move it, with everyone afraid that it will instead topple over and cause another, if lesser, disaster.

With fast-paced direction and editing from George Seaton and Stuart Gilmore, respectively, and striking aerial shots courtesy of cinematographer Ernest Laszlo, *Airport* is an extremely entertaining motion picture; it's not art, but it works. Like most disaster flicks—and this one engendered the rash of such films in the seventies—it's a bit exploitative but not as much as subsequent productions. Although the movie was and is held in contempt by many critics, they seem to be reacting more to the inferior sequels than to the original movie, which no one need apologize for. *Variety* ultimately reported that *Airport* was the last big hit of Dean Martin's career; he worked for 10 percent of the receipts and earned over five million dollars from this one assignment! Burt Lancaster didn't do too badly, either, although he opined about the picture: "It's the biggest piece of junk ever made." *Airport*, which cost ten million dollars to make, raked in over fifty million when the dust cleared. No wonder there were so many sequels.

About Dean's five million: He may have earned it, but it was not that easy to get it. Once again his lawyers wound up in court, suing Universal for his share of the take. It was years before he saw most, but probably not all, of what was due him—a familiar story in the motion picture business, the industry that, as one wag put it, "invented double-booking."

Still, with all that loot on his plate or about to be put there, Dean figured he could safely take a year or two off from moviemaking, which he did after one more quick picture in 1971. He concentrated on his show—for one day a week, at least—playing golf, and squiring Kathy Hawn around town. His wife and children went out to the ranch in Hidden Valley and Dean's lawyer and Jeanne's lawyer—both of whom worked for the same law firm—continued to argue over settlements.

Dean was also kept busy attending political events. He only got involved in politics because his friends, usually Frank Sinatra, importuned him, but usually he would only go so far as to sing a song or two, not make a speech extolling the virtues of the candidate. In the seventies he joined the Democratic group Californians for Reagan, which helped re-elect the then-governor to a second term of office. Dean, Sinatra, Sammy Davis Jr., and even old buddy John Wayne went out to Sacramento to celebrate the occasion by performing at an inaugural gala at the Memorial Auditorium. In all likelihood Dean saw it more as a chance to hang out with old friends than anything lofty. As the evening progressed, three hundred antiwar protesters gathered outside in the hopes of confronting Reagan and his celebrity courtiers when they came out the front exit. Instead, police hustled Reagan, Dean, and the rest of the Rat Pack out the side door and into the night while Wayne, refusing to be intimidated by the protesters, simply marched right through them. Whatever Dean thought about it all, he kept to himself. Like most men of his age during this time period, he probably thought the protesters were long-haired hippies and worse, but he didn't feel the almost maniacal outrage against them that Wayne did; he couldn't be bothered.

He was back with a director he liked and worked well with, Andrew McLaglen—as well as back in Durango, Mexico—for the lowercase *something big* (1971), his penultimate western in which he was perfectly cast and gives a lively, engaging performance. Today McLaglen says that Dean was an absolute joy to work with, as with the earlier *Bandolero!*. He knew his lines perfectly, never pulled any stunts, got along with everyone, and made shooting the picture a pleasure. "There was a little dog in the film," McLaglen remembers, "and Dean used to say, 'Look. I get in front of the camera even before the dog does!'" Honor Blackman, who'd played the Pussy Galore character unthawed by James Bond in *Goldfinger*, was also unthawed, figuratively speaking, by Dean's charm, finding him "lovely, affable, delightful. I never imagined that working with him could be so much fun." McLaglen thought that Dean was "a very underrated actor." The first choice for star had been Peter O'Toole, but, especially after *Airport*, Dean was considered more box office.

In *something big* Dean plays Joe Baker, who was, as one critic put it, "a bandit who covets all the gold in a bandit hideout." Baker needs a Gatling gun to succeed in his mission, but Cobb (Albert Salmi from *The Ambushers*) will only trade him one if he finds him a woman. After rejecting several prospects, Baker finally targets Mrs. Morgan (Blackman), the wife of fort commander Colonel Morgan (Brian Keith). Morgan gets his wife back, however, and Cobb winds up with two lascivious sisters while Baker uses the Gatling gun to get the loot and ride off into the sunset.

A lighthearted look at comic outlaws, *something big* was probably made because of the tremendous success of *Butch Cassidy and the Sundance Kid* two years previously. Burt Bacharach, who'd been hired to do the rather awful score for *Butch*, was also called in to write a number for *something big* (although the score itself was composed by Marvin Hamlisch). But whereas critics were willing to overlook the glamorizing and glorification of desperadoes in *Butch*, they would not do so for *something big*. The same critics who ignored the fact that Butch and Sundance steal payrolls from hard-working men trying to feed their families and shoot down dozens of Mexican soldiers trying to arrest them as they take a final stand were apoplectic over the fact that Joe Baker and his cronies "unleash the Gatling and kill at least a thousand men." Perhaps Dean wasn't considered as pretty as Newman and Redford and therefore not entitled to get away with it. Sam Peckinpah's graphic (for the time) *The Wild Bunch* had been released the same year as *Butch Cassidy*, and critics who had hated *that* movie now complained about the "bloodless slaughter" of *something big*, even though a lot of bloodletting would have gone against the light tone of the piece as did, many critics charged, the slaughter of the Mexicans at the end, which some found similar to the mindless slaughter of Native Americans in so many earlier westerns (political correctness had also hit the motion picture industry). Some would argue that *Butch Cassidy* was less offensive than *something big* simply because it was a better movie, but the fact is that *Butch Cassidy* has not held up at all well over the years. Perhaps the problem is that Butch and Sundance bite the dust and pay for their misdeeds at the end of *Butch Cassidy*, but Joe Baker gets away with robbery and murder at the end of *something big*. Unlike *Bandolero!* wherein the bad guys get their just deserts, *something big* simply has no moral closure.

The Hollywood Reporter opined, "Dear old Dino is a way-out robber, kind of cute in his own way " and that the film was "clever but suggestive, violent without blood . . . precisely the same sort of mindless goo that corrodes TV airwaves." Another critic found Dean "as convincing as called for." Dean, who was fifty-four, was pretty mellow with the reporters who came to the set—and more talkative than usual. "I like the feel of old boots, cowboy shirts, and this western garb," he said. "All my life I've been stuck in a stiff tuxedo—in the old days when I was a croupier and now in Vegas nightclubs. I dig these threads; they're simple and uncomplicated, like me." He also claimed, "I'm going to quit [show business] when my TV contract runs out in two and a half years. I'm just longing to go to my ranch [the one in Thousand Oaks, California], bum around unshaven, let my hair go gray, and get pleasantly stewed every night until I finally die."

He also gave his opinion of movie love scenes. "Screen love is the bunk. You got so many technical things to concern yourself with that kissin' the girl, regardless of how beautiful she is, becomes real work. The hairdresser stands by looking daggers at you, just in case you muss her hair. So you loop your arms around her neck, makin' sure you don't tilt her collar, and you look to your own appearance. There's too much on your mind to enjoy what you're doin'. When you finally get to kiss the girl, you can't kiss her square on the lips because if you did, your nose hides her eyes. You kiss her just off center and she smacks the air in response."

His comments on movie kissing may have been innocuous, but it seemed Dean was attracting moral outrage from all quarters nevertheless. In early 1972 *Life* magazine ran a column by their anonymous columnist and social critic "Cyclops" entitled "The Witless Reign of King Leer." It read, in part: "[*The Dean Martin Show*] is the equivalent of solitary confinement with nothing to read but *Playboy* Advisor. A kind of plastic smut, a Las Vegas of heart is locked upon the screen. It isn't necessary to be solemn about sex—but what keeps that wit from being dehumanized—from being, in fact, a mask to cover up aggression—is that everyone partakes of it. The women are just as witty as the men; *people* are involved, they relate to each other as personalities, as individuals with individual styles and individual dignity." Cyclops felt the program was as antimale as it was antifemale, "a calculated degradation" and "entertainment only to monsters or to people wholly incapable of love (which is probably the same thing)."

Cyclops may have had a point, but his rather pretentious overreaction to Dean's show read more like the vanguard of what would come to be known as political correctness than any astute or justifiable social commentary. Priggishness masquerading as social concern. Nevertheless, a great many people, few of whom were fans of Dean's show, took it seriously. By the early seventies all the assorted movements in the country were in full swing—Women's Lib, Gay Rights—and Dean's bust-size gags and generally mean-spirited "fag" jokes (a variation of the "nance" or "swish" humor he had done with Jerry) *were* beginning to seem awfully dated, at least to the hip and aware. The mostly straight white male execs at NBC could probably not have cared less about being aware, except about dollars and cents, but once the calls and letters of protest came in, they began to get nervous. There had always been negative comments from viewers who found Dean's show too raunchy, but now a political storm was brewing that might turn off the demographically desirable younger viewers, baby boomers with money to spend, who, attracted by the naughty, risqué nature of the program, had watched the show with their parents when it premiered eight years before and were now watching it on their own. It might also frighten advertisers—who steered clear of controversy the way Howard Hughes avoided contaminants—into pulling their expensive ads from the show. NBC execs, of course, masked their money and ratings worries under a cloak of social concern. Memos were filed, and phone calls were made.

Producer Greg Garrison had already acceded to the network's requests to tone down the sleazy nature of the show, but annoyed by their hypocritical pressure, his reaction this time was to push the show to the limit and to hell with the network brass. In 1968 he'd been importuned to hire some squeaky clean, fresh, wholesome, straight-out-of-Iowa farm girls to play "the Golddiggers," a dance troupe of long-legged daises with more freckles than lipstick. "Boy, were we dull that year!" he remembered. "They were like ten virgins surrounding Dean!" He replaced them with the four Ding-a-Ling Sisters—who were a lot sexier, like old-time burlesque queens—and, if possible, even stupider (as portrayed). His one concession to political correctness? He hired the black Jayne Kennedy and the Japanese-American Helen Funai as two of the Ding-a-Lings. There—now let someone say *The Dean Martin Show* wasn't culturally aware.

"We had been in a monastery for a year," Garrison complained to the press. The show was "going back to the booze jokes, the girl jokes, the double entendres. As I pointed out in a memo to my staff, now that we're in our eighth year, it would be easy to continue with the old format, the weekends in Palm Springs, and let things slowly slide downhill until we closed up shop. But that's not the way I do business." He assured everyone that the complete overhaul of the show was *not* due to complaints from the censors or anybody else. Other innovations for the new season were a set called Club Ding-a-Ling, a series of barbershop skits with Dom DeLuise and Nipsey Russell as barbers, and another series presenting Lou Jacobi and Kay Medford as, respectively, the owner and waitress of a crummy diner. Another bit would have a "voluptuous gal in a tiger's outfit" be Dean's personal pet as his guests paraded by with normal animals on leashes. Dean's "pet" would also be on a leash. This last bit particularly outraged the feminists.

What Garrison never told the reporters was that the real reason for jacking up the sensationalism on the show was because of the dip it had taken in the ratings, not all of which could be blamed on squeaky-clean Golddiggers. Dean's opening monologue had always contained affectionate jokes about and references to "Jeannie"—she was always Jeann*ie*, not Jeanne—and everyone in the country knew about his pretty wife and had even seen her on his Christmas broadcasts. But now everyone in the country knew the couple was about to split. It was one thing for Dean to *play* a lewd, skirt-chasing playboy on his show and quite another for him to be one in real life. Dean had forgotten that his older audience was generally conservative. They may have disapproved of women's libbers and Viet Nam protesters, but they didn't think a man should cheat on his wife and brag about it in the papers. Dean had gone too far. The ratings for the new season weren't bad by any objective standards, but Dean was no longer in the top ten.

There were changes in the wind for *The Dean Martin Show* . . . and for Dean Martin.

TWENTY

Showdown

Dean went down to Chama, New Mexico (popula-
tion: 1,000), near the Cumbre Pass Wilderness (and the Cumbres and
Toltec Scenic Railroad, which was used in the picture) in early 1973 to
film one of his better latter-day movies, *Showdown*, with Susan Clark and
Rock Hudson. The director was George Seaton of *Airport*. Cast and crew
took over a hunting lodge on the outskirts of Chama, while Dean stayed
by himself in a log cabin on the Brazos River, where he did his usual practice swings with a golf club. Sunning himself on the porch, he would
attract the interest of patrons of a nearby restaurant. By all accounts, Dean
did not have a particularly good time making this movie. He was not as
well prepared as he had been for McLaglen, blew many of his lines or forgot them (assuming he had bothered to memorize them in the first place),
and seemed to many to be totally strung out. By now he was getting bored
of going to out-of-the-way locations for weeks, working all day for a few
seconds' screen time. And while his current amour, Kathy Hawn, had
stayed with him for a long time in Durango where they'd shot *something
big*, for one reason or another she could not come down for extended visits in New Mexico. When she did come, she and Dean spent time at a
place called Ghost Ranch. When Kathy left, Dean was utterly bored.

"It's so dull up here," he told a reporter, "that last Sunday when they
took my car to wash it, I went along for the excitement. I ask myself, 'Why
are you doing this, Dino?' I guess one reason is I'm a ham. The refriger-
ator light came on last night when I opened the door, and I did four
songs." Another problem was that Dean didn't bond with anyone on the

film. He and George Seaton respected each other, but that was as far as it went. Susan Clark was a bit of an intellectual and a real actress, not Dean's type, although he was too much of a gentleman not to be his usual charming self with her. Dean and Rock Hudson did not get along well at all. It's likely that even then Dean had heard the rumors of Hudson's homosexuality, but what probably bothered him the most was that Rock, even taller and manlier than Dino, was not the stereotypical "faggot" he was used to. Being in show business and living in L.A., Dean had known and worked with lots of "nelly queens"—he'd even had Paul Lynde as a regular on his show—and he could tolerate and even kid around with them, but he didn't quite know what to make of a macho guy like Rock who was secretly gay. Perhaps he was afraid Rock was attracted to him, but Dean was not Rock's type.

Dean was polite to his co-workers—most of them, anyway—but some later described him as distant, cool, off in his own little world. That little world was not so much one of emotional distraction and exhaustion—although that was certainly part of it—as one of pure physical pain. For the past few years he'd been having back trouble (the last thing a man with a fresh young squeeze wanted to have), and as he rode around on horses for hours, the agony only intensified. His back didn't always bother him, but when it did it was excruciating. Since he was still relatively fit and slender, the lower back distress had probably been caused by something pulling the wrong way as he did a scene in too over-active a manner in one of his previous movies. Years earlier an associate had introduced him to Percodan, a morphinelike painkiller, which Dean had previously used for headaches and hangovers. Now it was just about the only thing that knocked out the back pain so that he could work. He had a tendency to take more of the pills than he should have, wanting the pain to *go away* —and fast—so he could work, relax, or make love. That would come to cause problems for him in the future.

But for now he was the one causing problems. As uncooperative with Seaton as he had been cooperative with McLaglen, he told the director he was through with the film and went back to Beverly Hills and Kathy. He claimed the reason for this action was his distress over the death of his eighteen-year-old horse, Tops, who literally collapsed under him as they were filming a scene. But Dean was not as attached to Tops as Jimmy Stewart had been to his horse, Pie; it was just that everything was getting to him, primarily the boredom, and he wanted to go home. Universal Pictures would have none of it. Before he knew it, Dean was being sued again, this time for six million dollars. Hardly a week had gone by when he was back in Chama, not exactly in the best of moods, the lawsuit withdrawn.

Rock Hudson had his own problems. To begin with he was depressed because of the death of his friend Marilyn Maxwell and the news that another friend, actor George Nader, had glaucoma and could no longer act because the strong lights used for television and films would adversely affect his vision; Rock hired George's companion as his secretary. Then while driving an antique car for a scene in the picture (later cut from the film), Rock hit a wall and suffered a concussion as well as several fractures and a few cracked ribs. He had to be hospitalized, and production was shut down for several weeks. Dean was just as glad to be out of it for a while—and it wouldn't cost him six million, either. But soon his natural good humor reasserted itself, and he was a good sport about everything. He actually threw a wrap party at the only hotel in Chama; even Rock was invited.

In *Showdown* Dean and Rock play childhood friends Billy Massey and Chuck Jarvis. In the back story, much of which is shown in flashbacks, the two bought a ranch together with winnings from a shooting competition, but Billy figures it's time to leave when their mutual girlfriend, Kate (Susan Clark), decides to marry Chuck. Unfortunately, his life goes on the downswing after leaving town, and he winds up joining a bunch of robbers in holding up the local train. When Billy left town, the sheriff was a slow old codger; he doesn't realize he has since been replaced by Chuck, who now has to track him down. When Billy's partners try to cheat him out of his share, he holds them up and winds up killing one of the men in self-defense. Billy pays a call on Kate, where Chuck finds him and urges him to give himself up and return the money, which he does. But when he mistakenly fears that he's going to be hung, he escapes and is soon being tracked by Chuck once more. The two join forces against the other robbers who have come for the loot Billy took from them, and Billy is killed in the gunfight that follows.

Considering the difficulties in making the film, it's surprising how successful *Showdown* turned out and how delightful Dean is in the picture. None of his emotional or physical distress is evident on camera, and he plays very well with both Clark and Hudson. Sure, sometimes he seems like a Las Vegas lounge singer out West, but mostly he's lovable and even a bit poignant as the rascally if well-meaning outlaw. The first scene makes it clear that while this is a western drama, it's not above having a sense of humor: During the train holdup that opens the picture, Billy, a passenger, pretends to be a sheriff, complete with prisoner in handcuffs, so he can get the valuables from everyone—for safekeeping from the robbers outside—without any alarm or struggle. Dean impresses his own personality on top of Billy's, and there are scenes in the script that seem to be made to order for the actor. "Do I get a kiss or a handshake?" he says to Kate before grabbing her in his arms and planting a wet one on her. In a flashback we see him lying in her arms, supposedly unconscious, in the back of a wagon, only to start wrestling with the woman the minute she relaxes. Another funny flashback has Billy and Chuck looking morosely at their unromantic cow and bull. "They better start humping soon," Billy says, "or we ain't gonna have much of a herd." To which Chuck replies, "If that bull was only half as horny as you are, we'd be in business!" Dean has a very nice, quieter scene wherein Billy tells Kate why he left the ranch and of his feelings for her in which he trades on all the natural charm and appeal he had for women. He's also good in a chillingly prophetic scene when he looks down at the tombstone of Kate and Chuck's one-year-old boy and notices that they named the baby after him. Hudson gives one of his best performances in the film, and Susan Clark, a fine actress, is simply excellent and consistently genuine as Kate. "If they took half of you and half of Chuck," she says to Billy, "and kind of latched it up into one human being, it'd really be something."

Showdown is by no means another schlocky Rat Pack-type western but a fine, well-paced picture (with superior editing from John W. Holmes) that pulls the viewer along from the very beginning and makes the audience care about its well-written characters (courtesy of Theodore Taylor) and what happens to them. There are many fine scenes, such as a lively, realistic fight scene when Billy and Chuck protect an Indian from a couple of guys who want to beat him to death. When Chuck punches out one fellow, he nearly breaks his hand and hollers in pain, which is what *does* happen when someone smashes a fist into someone's face, although movies usually ignore this fact. The flashbacks are heralded by frozen sepia daguerreotypes that suddenly come to life. Ernest Laszlo's widescreen cinematography is stunning, and while David Shire's score is not a great one, it is often poignant, perhaps evoking more sorrow for Billy than is warranted, although as Dean portrays him he's rather pathetic and affecting.

The movie is essentially a fascinating variation on the old story of two buddies who grow up to be on opposite sides of the law and is also old-fashioned in that it expects one to have faith that "bad'uns" are really good guys at heart. The only scenes that don't quite ring true concern a self-righteous prosecutor who collapses into cowardly, overplayed fear

when Dean confronts him—a bleeding heart's portrait of a prosecutor—
and Billy and Chuck swapping quips when cornered by the other robbers.
When Chuck is shot in the backside, Billy says, "Better you than me; that's
where my brains are!" Cute, but it smacks too much of the Rat Pack era.
The script harkens even further back than that, however, when, referring
to his friendship with her husband, Kate tells Billy that she "stepped in
between Damon and Pythias." When Billy asks, "Who are they?" Kate
says, "A juggling act—they played all the better saloons." Of course,
Damon and Pythias was to have been the title of the next Martin and Lewis
movie had the pair stayed together.

Dean would make only one more movie in the 1970s, and his recording output was also relatively limited. He made his last record for Reprise
in 1974 and wouldn't do another for nearly ten years. There were covers
of "Little Green Apples," "Raindrops Keep Fallin' on My Head," "Tie a
Yellow Ribbon," and even that immortal standard "You Made Me Love
You," which Judy Garland had first sung of Clark Gable many, many years
before. One of the records that was most suitable for him was Smokey
Robinson's "Tracks of My Tears," and one of the most ironic was "My
Woman, My Woman, My Wife," almost as if he were referring to Gail
Renshaw, Kathy Hawn, and Jeanne Martin. Who *was* his wife, by the way?
the public might have wondered.

Before shooting *Showdown* he had determined it would be Catherine
Mae Hawn. Part of his emotional distress for the past few months had
been due to the way the lawyers—and Jeanne—were dragging everything
out when he just wanted her to divorce him as quickly and as cleanly as
possible. He chose a romantic opportunity to speed up the process by fil-
ing for divorce himself on Valentine's Day 1972. Learning that Dean had
bought an expensive new half-million-dollar home for Kathy and her six-
year-old daughter, Sasha, in Bel Air, Jeanne was afraid he was determined
to *spend* as much of his money as he reasonably could so there'd be a lot
less to share with her. She quickly fired her lawyer at Arthur Manella's
firm—as noted, the same firm used by Dean—and hired herself a top
divorce attorney named Eugene Wyman.

Meanwhile, Dean had announced his marriage to Kathy for October
1st, but as the lawyers picked and probed into his financial affairs and
dickered with each other, the wedding kept being postponed again and
again and again. Kathy wondered if all the delaying was a tactic on *Dean's*
part—did he want to marry her or not? By this time, Dean was convinced
he was in love with Hawn and she with him—she was the princess, he the
white knight—and at Hawn's urging told Jeanne that he'd do whatever it

took to end their union. Jeanne's lawyer told him exactly how much it would take, and while Dean balked, he was determined to go through with it or risk losing Hawn forever—or at least that's how he imagined it. "Hawn was not about to give up a good thing when she had one," a columnist observed. By the time his divorce was granted, ten months had gone by. It was good that he had gone back to work on *Showdown*; the settlement he finally paid Jeanne was six and a half million dollars. On March 20, Judge Jack Ryburn declared their divorce final, their marriage of twenty-three years over. Dean and Kathy set another date for their wedding, which was almost postponed because Dean finally got his ulcers operated on in L.A.'s Midway Hospital, the same place he'd gone for some nip and tuck work. Finally the two were wed on April 25, 1973. Dean was fifty-five years old.

The wedding was held at their new Bel Air mansion, with the living room converted into a makeshift chapel. Frank Sinatra was the best man and little Sasha, the flower girl. About a hundred guests and members of the press ate and drank heartily at a reception at the Crystal Room in the Beverly Hills Hotel. The newlyweds' names were carved out of an ice sculpture, and the buffet featured beluga caviar, beef Wellington, and trout stuffed with lobster mousse, while bottles of Dom Perignon kept popping and flowing all night. A story that made the rounds at the time, possibly true, was that whenever Dean and Kathy lost sight of one another in the throng, Dean would turn to whomever he was talking to and say, "Pardon me, but I have to go burp my baby." He was referring to wife Kathy, although shortly after the wedding he did legally adopt her daughter, Sasha.

The Bel Air mansion—"a redbrick Tudor fortress" according to one visitor—had a big curved stairway in the main hall, down which bride Hawn had made her entrance. Dean's main headquarters in his new home was a den—"long, narrow, multileveled and vaulted" as one writer described it—with comfortable sofas, game tables, TV sets, a sunken bar, natch, and a "Cinemascope-sized" motion picture screen at the end. The driveway was cluttered with a variety of automobiles, most conspicuous among them a Stutz Blackhawk with plates that read DRUNKY. All visitors had to speak into a slot in the thick oak front door and were turned away even if they had an appointment unless one of the staff recognized them personally. Hawn-Martin, who was described as being "Ophelia-like" and who vaguely resembled Jeanne, was a perky blond with an upturned nose and wide mouth. Visitors noted that she would often use a stethoscope on Dean, as if she were afraid he might get a heart attack, and doctors would come periodically to inject B12 into his lower back in an attempt to control the pain.

Dean claimed that the only reason he had bought such a tremendous house was that there would be room for his children when they came for a visit, except they rarely did. They all were busy with their own lives, careers, lovers, spouses. Claudia, determined to make her latest marriage work, had left show business for good; even being Dean Martin's daughter couldn't help her overcome the fact that she didn't stand out in a crowd the way a star was supposed to. Craig, now thirty-one, would leave his job as production manager on Dean's show and try for a career making government documentaries. Gail also forfeited her showbiz aspirations and moved to Palm Springs with husband Paul Polena, a lawyer. Shortly after they would file for joint bankruptcy. Deana went out on the road with a show, while Gina stayed in school. Young Ricci had cut a record for Capitol, and Dino Junior had married Olivia Hussey, who'd made a big splash in Franco Zeffirelli's 1968 film version of *Romeo and Juliet*. While Dean bemoaned the fact that he rarely saw his kids—just as they'd rarely seen him when they were younger—Kathy went out and looked for a smaller house.

It wasn't long after the marriage that Arthur Marx, the son of Groucho, came out with a dual biography of Dean and Jerry Lewis which was amusingly titled *Everybody Loves Somebody Sometime (Especially Himself)*. Although the book was pretty frank about Dean, it was especially merciless with Jerry. Apparently Marx, who was a comedy writer himself, felt that Jerry had not always been fair with his writers, and neither on some occasions, he suggested, had Dean. It's unlikely Dean ever read the book, as he hadn't read an actual book (as opposed to a comic book) since he was in school.

Although Dean was still a big draw at casinos, he didn't do so well at other venues, such as the Boston Garden, in which half the seats were empty. He opened at the MGM Grand in Las Vegas in 1974 at an astonishing two hundred thousand dollars a week. He was also given a three-picture deal with MGM, one picture a year, for a fee of five hundred thousand dollars per picture. His TV show, however, was on its last legs. Divorce and remarriage didn't help it any, although it was also probable that audiences were simply getting tired of it—the same old gags, the same guest stars: Kay Medford, Ken Lane, Nipsey Russell. For the ninth season, its last, the name was changed to *The Dean Martin Comedy Hour*—a nod to the old Colgate *Comedy Hour* with Dean and Jerry, perhaps, ashes to ashes—and the skits were given even more weight than before. Ronald

Reagan was the first person to be guest for a running sketch called "Roast of the Week," which took its cue from the Friars Club "roasts" in which the guest of honor was affectionately skewered and honored at one and the same time. When the *Comedy Hour* was canceled due to low ratings, Dean did a couple of *Dean Martin Celebrity Roast* specials with Lucille Ball and then Jackie Gleason, "the Great One," as the guest-victims. The ratings shot up dramatically, and NBC execs insisted that Dean do only celebrity roasts if he wanted to stay on TV. He was allowed a couple more variety specials but these tanked in the ratings. The old formula was no longer attracting enough viewers. The old formula was offensive and controversial. The old Dean Martin show was gone forever.

So were the silly chicks, the bust jokes, most if not all of the other sleazy stuff replaced by put-down humor as practiced by the genius of insult comic Don Rickles. The gags the celebrities told about the guests of honor had more to do with their age than their longevity, with suitable aspersions placed on their talent or lack of same. At first the honorees were distinguished or at least big in name—after Ball and Gleason there were Bob Hope, Jack Benny, and Johnny Carson, then Dean himself—but then there were so many roasts that the comparative dregs had to be scoured: Muhammad Ali, Michael Landon. Anyone and everyone might turn up on the dais, sometimes people who actually knew the honoree (Vivian Vance for Lucille Ball, for instance), other times anyone from Barry Goldwater and Henry Fonda to Freddie Prinz and Billy Crystal, and sometimes a crew of regulars that included Rickles, Phyllis Diller, Foster Brooks, Milton Berle, and others. Then there were all of Dean's movie costars: Angie Dickinson, Jimmy Stewart, John Wayne, Zsa Zsa Gabor, Joey Bishop, even Cliff Robertson in a wig almost as bad as Howard Cosell's, which Muhammad Ali tried to snatch off.

Occasionally deep truths were uttered beneath the laughter, such as when Ali said to Cosell: "You are living proof that you don't need *nothin'* to make it!" and now and then the remarks were politically incorrect, such as when Johnny Carson told Redd Foxx, "It's apropos that Redd is here tonight because his ancestors originated the idea of roasting people," which got raised eyebrows from Dionne Warwick. With one eye on the TelePrompTer that almost everyone read their lines from, Ed McMahon would sometimes laugh at the jokes before the performer had a chance to say them. Of course there were the booze jokes, mostly from and about Dean. Introducing Bob Hope, Dean said, "He's the fifth son of a stonemason, and I'm the stoned son of a white mason with a fifth." And jokes about Jerry Lewis. Rickles: "It takes many years to become a great comedian." Dean: "And you ain't reached that year yet." Rickles: "Thank you, Jerry." When Dean was roasted, Rickles took over as guest host. Getting up to honor Dean, Paul Lynde said with a straight face: "Dean and I have very different tastes. I prefer museums, gourmet cuisine, and the legitimate stage. Dean likes bocci ball, pizza, and the Pussycat Theater." And not so above it all, there on the dais was the fallen genius Orson Welles, a three-hundred-pound Buddha who'd descended from the heights of art and culture and shattered career dreams to the burp-and-giggle humor of the hoi polloi.

It would be all too easy to condescend to the *Dean Martin Celebrity Roasts* were it not for the fact that they were often very funny. Although one chronicler has suggested, somewhat pretentiously, that the roasts were amusing only to those who "lived canned lives, who found release through canned laughter"—and no one would exactly accuse the roasts of intellectual or unpredictable wit—they featured some great performers who made good material sing and bad material seem better. Draped across his chair next to the podium, sometimes staring off into space, Dean seems half shot through most of these roasts, but when it's his turn to stand and speak, his timing is still good, his delivery perfectly professional.

At first the roasts were taped at the Ziegfeld Room of the MGM Grand, with all the participants in assemblage. As the roasts were broadcast with more frequency, getting everyone together was a little more difficult. Since almost every single line was scripted beforehand, it was possible to have a guest come into the studio and tape his little bit at the podium, then take a few close-up shots of him sitting behind a duplicate dais and laughing hysterically at somebody else's joke. Sometimes the guest of honor wasn't even there at the Grand; Dean and Rickles would come in and sit on either side of the studio podium as he took potshots at those who'd insulted him or her one by one. A shot of Milton Berle getting out of his chair with arm raised in a mock fist at some slight from the podium was used over and over again. After a while the patchwork roasts were mostly put together in this fashion, with long shots taken from previous programs.

While television career was perpetuated by the roasts, the 1970s saw his final turn as a film headliner, *Mr. Ricco* (1975), which was filmed on location in San Francisco. The director, Paul Bogart, who'd done a lot of TV work, was a former puppeteer who'd helmed such films as *Cancel My Reservation*, Bob Hope's final fling—which should have served as a warning to Dean—and *Marlowe* with James Garner. Others in the cast were Cindy Williams of *Laverne and Shirley*, Eugene Roche, and Geraldine

Brooks. In this film Dean plays criminal lawyer Joe Ricco who represents black militant Frankie Steele (Thalmus Rasulala) who's been accused of murder. Ricco drinks nothing but milk for his ulcer and is terrible at golf. After Ricco gets the man acquitted, the "grateful" client tries to kill him with a rifle. A wild chase ensues, during which several innocent bystanders are slaughtered. It turns out that the activist is actually a white man disguised as a black. As in his last film, *Showdown*, the cast and crew of *Mr. Ricco* found Dean remote and dispassionate but thoroughly professional—except for the fact that he had trouble learning some of his lines. He behaved for director Paul Bogart as he had for Andrew McLaglen; he just wasn't interested in what he was doing although he did want to come through for everyone else. The Percodan, which he took too much of, affected both his personality and his memory. And he was not very happy with his new bride. Again he superimposed his own personality over that of the character he was playing, but this time to less felicitous results.

MGM refused to let its distributor, United Artists, run trade previews for reviewers, a sure sign they thought the movie was a dog and didn't want the word to get out until after the day it opened. Predictably, when they finally got to see the film, the critics were merciless. The *New York Times* found *Mr. Ricco* to be "a very bad melodrama . . . Dean Martin plays a brilliant San Francisco criminal lawyer as if brilliant San Francisco criminal lawyers modeled their behavior on successful TV personalities such as Mr. Martin. Everything about the character Mr. Martin plays looks like displaced southern California: the tan, the hair set, and even the boredom, which suggests the fellow wants to get back to that old gang of his in the Polo Lounge as quickly as possible." Another critic noted, "It's such a clumsy movie it makes all the actors look dreadful, which may or may not be the fact."

The movie was a bomb.

So, it seemed, was the marriage to Kathy Hawn Martin, which lasted barely three years.

TWENTY-ONE

Bumming Around

Kathy Hawn Martin had finally found another house
that pleased her, a smaller place out in Malibu, but just as she divested herself of the large estate in Bel Air, Dean divested himself of Kathy.
Approximately two weeks after moving to Malibu, Dean walked out on his
new wife and adopted daughter and filed for divorce. He withdrew the
petition a few days later, then filed for divorce again within a couple of
months. He was still a man who didn't know what he wanted.

Linda Chesley says, "Dean had told me—and he may have been
talking about Kathy or me or any number of women—that he didn't want
to be a 'golden goose' for anyone. I think he meant the goose with the
golden eggs. He didn't want to feel trapped, and he didn't just want to
represent security or a 'step up' to anyone. He said he had been through
all that before. I could be pretty frank with him at times, and I said to
him, 'Then why run to women who are so much younger, struggling,
women on the fringes of show business all the time? If you don't want to
get used, stay away from the users.' He looked at me in that way of his, a
sort of puppy-dog way, and said, 'Who else would want me? I'm an old
man.' I just smirked and tickled him. He knew he [would] still [be] attractive to younger women even if he hadn't been rich and famous, not that
that hurt. To tell you the truth, I was real surprised that he ever married
Kathy or left Jeanne. I think after a while he realized he'd been a fool. He
never seemed to doubt that Jeanne loved him. She just got disgusted,
that's all."

Dean had the same problem with Kathy that he'd had with Jeanne.
Dean lived in a big beautiful home with a private den equipped with

anything a man could want. But his back hurt, and the booze and pills made him tired, and he didn't want to go out; he wanted to watch TV with his honey at his side, rubbing his back. When he did go out he preferred to be with his cronies or by himself, so he could cruise for women. But Kathy was young and attractive and wanted to do the town. She wanted to show off her movie-star husband and wanted him to want to show her off, too. Before too long there were the inevitable disagreements, then arguments, finally shouting matches. Kathy was intruding into his personal space. Now that he had become Sasha's father, Kathy expected him to act like a dad, but he hadn't been able to do that for his own children let alone an adopted child. He was panicking, he was suffocating—it was Jerry, it was Jeanne, all over again. He had to get out. Once he was out, staying in hotels or at his agent Mort Viner's, he would reconsider—Kathy was sweet, Kathy was young—but every time they reconciled, the pattern would begin all over again. Dean and Kathy's lawyers argued over the settlement while Dean hung out with a new squeeze, a thirty-eight-year-old club hostess named Peggy who had briefly been married to Bing Crosby's son Phillip. The tabloids had a field day: one crooner squiring around the former daughter-in-law of another; but the affair didn't last much longer than Peggy's marriage. In addition to paying child support for Sasha until she turned eighteen—another eight years at that point—Dean agreed to give Kathy five thousand dollars a month for three years (the length of their marriage). The divorce was final on February 24, 1977. Dean never looked back. As far as he was concerned he'd been the biggest goose—and jackass—in the world, and he never again entertained the thought of marriage, no matter how much he had once claimed he loved the state of matrimony. A reconciliation with Jeanne seemed out of the question.

Frank Sinatra was responsible for another reconciliation—of sorts. It had never been Dean's idea to cut off all ties to Jerry Lewis, and it wasn't Dean's idea to surprise Jerry by going on his muscular dystrophy telethon with Frank in 1976. But Dean bore no particular grudges—it wasn't as if he had ever *hated* Jerry—and after a couple of martinis with Frank, Ole Blue Eyes had no trouble in getting Dean to go along with his plan. Standing on stage with Jerry, Frank said, "There's somebody here who'd like to say hello." And Dean strode out with a big smile on his face. Dean and Jerry hugged, and Dean kissed Jerry on the cheek. "I think it's about time, don't you?" Frank said. Dean said, "Thank you" and then kissed Frank on the cheek. As Dean and Jerry affectionately patted each other on the face—Dean more misty eyed than Jerry—Frank quipped, "Break it up! What is this? Break it up!" Then, rather obtusely, he said, "We could whip the world without the guns of Navarone!"

Years later Jerry explained why the two men had never run into each other at Hollywood parties. "They were all very respectful of the fact that the breach had scarred us. When Frank felt it was time, we saw one another, knowing full well we never stopped loving one another—I guess it was one of the greatest two-man love stories . . . . When he brought Dean on that stage and I saw him, what came into my mind first was, 'I can't believe it.' And second: 'That's the most courageous thing I've ever seen in my life' because he was coming onto my turf, and he didn't know how I'd react. But he came because he knew in his heart I loved him, I'd never hurt him. And when we embraced, we said it all in that embrace."

But the reunion—although it made the telethon's take that year go through the roof—did not lead to a true resumption of their friendship. As Jerry remembered in his memoirs, to him the occasion meant that "[we'd] maybe look forward to better times ahead, to a friendship we never had before. And now that we were older, perhaps a little wiser, there would be so much more to learn about each other. . . . As tired as I was, before going to bed I wrote Dean a letter and had it hand-delivered to his hotel. No reply. A few weeks passed and I sent off another letter, enclosing a twenty-dollar gold piece with the telethon symbol embossed on one side, a love inscription composed specially for him and Frank on the other. Frank responded immediately. As for Dean, not a word."

Privately Jerry was hurt that Dean had obviously imbibed a few cocktails before going on the telethon, wondering if the warm sentiments he'd expressed in front of millions of people were honest emotion or just a feel-good, love-everybody sensation caused by alcohol. Jerry wanted to have Dean on the telethon a year later, but when arrangements were made for a meeting, Dean failed to show. Dean never returned Jerry's phone calls, either.

There was a simple reason why Dean kept Jerry at bay. He thought of Jerry the way many think of certain friends or relatives that they love but cannot live with or spend too much time with. They love these relatives, enjoy them, and even feel close to them when they meet—but once a year, or even once every two or three years, is more than enough. Dean knew that if he started returning Jerry's phone calls, if he met with him or agreed to go on the telethon as a guest, Jerry would see it as a sign that they could resume the friendship, the closeness, they'd once enjoyed, but Dean was done with all that. He cared about Jerry, but he did not want to work with him, hang out with him, or be with him all that often—not as he had so many years before. He would be perfectly pleasant, even loving, when he saw Jerry, but such times had to be strictly controlled and kept to a minimum—whenever *he* felt like seeing Jerry. He knew Jerry would be *at* him all the time otherwise, wanting to work on projects together, to hang out, and Dean couldn't handle that. Plus there was the fact that Dean never felt comfortable showing or feeling such strong emotions with another man, platonic as that emotion might have been.

Esquire wanted Dean to pose with Jerry on the cover. Dean nixed the idea. The resulting article by Jean Vallely is perhaps most memorable for its title: "Dean Martin's Closest Friend is Frank Sinatra (He Sees Him Twice a Year)." Sinatra was another person who had to be kept at bay, or he could swallow you whole. Film director Peter Bogdanovich, who'd once made great movies like *The Last Picture Show* before churning out tripe like *At Long Last Love* and *Nickelodeon*, wanted Frank and Dean and Jerry to star in another of his hapless productions of that period. They would be down-on-their-luck gamblers who wouldn't actually speak to one another until the end of the movie. Again, Sinatra urged Dean to agree to work with Jerry, but it never came off, probably because Bogdanovich couldn't get financing. One senses that the world didn't exactly lose a cinematic masterpiece when this project bit the dust.

It's not that Dean wanted to shut himself off from everyone. He just wanted to be *left alone* when he felt like it. When he wanted company, he would ask for it. It seemed like everyone in his life—Jerry, Sinatra, his women, his children—were larger than life personalities who had such *needs*. Dean was a simple, uncomplicated person—relatively speaking— and he didn't understand what everyone wanted from him, nor did he analyze why he required privacy. Jerry Lewis's take on the matter was, "Dean was never really that [introspective]." Dean was always seen as a bad guy by some because of his need to be apart from others—at least certain others—at times, but people forgot that this was a man who was recognized and pursued by fans wherever he went. He had no problem with being a public personality. But when he simply wanted to be alone, he was worse than Greta Garbo.

Despite his reclusive tendencies, Dean still desired romantic relationships. His next inamorata was a nineteen-year-old college co-ed named Andre Boyer, who was introduced to Dean by her golf pro at the Riviera Country Club in the Pacific Palisades in March 1977. Dean was nearly sixty at this time. Boyer attended Dean's opening at Lake Tahoe and shared quarters with him; they were seen billing and cooing like a couple of kids. Andre lived with her mother in a house in Rolling Hills but after meeting Dean, as her mother reported, went out with the singer virtually every night. Meanwhile, Jeanne and Kathy wondered what had happened to his perpetual need to stay home and take care of his back. Dean was looking for another hero worshiper but definitely not a wife. Mrs. Boyer didn't think the age difference would be a problem. "It really doesn't seem to make a difference with them because they enjoy so many of the same things." Andre, a fairly attractive light brunet had big eyes and a wide mouth just like Kathy Hawn's. There were people who thought that between Mrs. Boyer, her daughter, and Dean, the crooner's life was more and more beginning to seem like something out of *Kiss Me, Stupid*.

Dean was due to perform at a concert with Sinatra at the Westchester Premiere Theater in Tarrytown, New York, and took Andre with him where they holed up at the hotel in between shows. Dean's name wound up in secret FBI files—the theater was run by mob boys who planned to hide the profits of the Sinatra-Martin concerts—which asserted that the concerts were attended by, among many mobsters, one Alfredo "Skippy" Felice, a Philadelphia crime family member. Dino was godfather of Felice's son—also named Dino—and gave one hundred thousand dollars to his wife, or so claimed the FBI, when Felice was incarcerated in a Florida prison earlier in the decade. After one of the concerts, Felice was supposed to have a drink with Dean in the dressing room, but since Governor Hugh Carey and his security people were there, Dean sent word that Felice should probably not drop by. Dean had probably figured what was the harm in being a godfather to his namesake when Felice had cornered him and asked if he would do him the honor. The one hundred thousand he sent to Felice's wife was not some kind of mob payoff but a sincere effort to help a husbandless woman and her child. Years before Dean and Jeanne had made a likable oil millionaire named Ray Ryan godfather to their son Ricci, but it was hardly Dean's fault that the man later got involved with and came afoul of the mob, being blown to bits by a car bomb. But all that this and the Felice business did was make Dean seem more of a "mob singer" in the eyes of some government officials and writers. Felice and some of the mob boys involved in the Westchester Premiere Theater wanted to hang out and play golf with Dean, but he pretended that he was the lousiest golfer in the world so they'd stop bothering him—if he wouldn't put up with Jerry, what did he need these bums for?—but this was later seen as evidence of his deterioration due to pills and liquor. The drugs would eventually catch up with Dean, but he was not quite *that* bad yet.

The second Dino—Dean-Paul Martin Jr.—was embarking on his own film career in 1979. First he had quit showbiz—Dino, Desi, and Billy didn't have much staying power—and entered medical school. His predilection for collecting guns—they were for show, not for use, and were kept in display cases—got him arrested in 1974 when he inadvertently sold two combat rifles to agents from the Bureau of Alcohol, Tobacco and Firearms. The problem was not that he collected guns— Civil War pistols, machine guns, antitank guns—but that he had failed to register them and transported them illegally. He was fined two hundred dollars and sentenced to a year's probation. A chip off the old block, he had squired around the likes of Jill Haworth, Julie Christie, Christine Kaufmann, and French actress Dany Saval before dropping out of school to marry Olivia Hussey. His four-year marriage to her ended later in 1974.

Dino Jr. was introduced to his next wife, ice skater Dorothy Hamill, by his old buddy Desi Arnaz Jr. after her 1976 Olympic victory. "I thought Dean was so handsome and funny and sweet," she told reporters of their first meeting. She was sheltered; he was a Hollywood sophisticate. After their marriage, her career in the Ice Capades and on television far outstripped her husband's. He moved out after less than two years. "Whatever problems we've had in this relationship have come from not being together," he said. Dorothy said, "We are still the best of friends, we still love each other, and the divorce will be amicable."

Dean-Paul had a pretty good idea of what made his father tick. "There is no way he is going to sit down and open up. He doesn't do that to his closest friends. He never really tells you what he feels, what he's really thinking. I don't know him very well. We never had a tremendous heart-to-heart conversation. To the public he is very simple, but the truth is he is very complex. What he always liked to do best was get into his car, drive to the golf course, drive home, play some cards, watch the football game on TV, and then go to bed. Early. Then he'd get up early and do it all over again. He is very, very easygoing, because he knows exactly what he is doing. What he does he has done for so long, it has become a part of him. He wants to maintain the thing." Dean-Paul and his siblings never saw their father as "the big swinger," not only because he behaved differently at home and had slowed down a bit in his later years but because he was, after all, their *dad*. They probably saw his romances with much younger women more as aberrations to be indulged than "swinging" per se. Dean gave the kids little attention but in exchange for this emotional neglect Dino Jr. had his own helicopter—he got his license at sixteen— Ricci his own extensively equipped yacht, and so on.

"It's tough being a kid anywhere," Dean-Paul also said, "and if your dad's famous, that is an added pressure because you have to find your own identity. I never felt the need to compete with my father. I got into sports instead." Dean-Paul got a two-year contract to play on the World Team Tennis League, though his global ranking did not rise above 250th. Movie producer Robert Evans got in touch with twenty-eight-year-old Dean-Paul through a mutual friend named Gene Taft and offered him the lead in a film about tennis entitled *Players* (1979). Dean-Paul would play a tennis pro torn between the game and a fallen woman played by Evans's ex-wife, Ali MacGraw of *Love Story* fame. Evans offered him a five-picture deal and told reporters, "Dean would rather be Björn Borg than Robert Redford, but I think he will be Redford." Much of the six-million-dollar production of *Players* was shot at Wimbledon, while the rest was filmed in Cuernavaca, Mexico.

Although Dean-Paul had no trouble letting loose with his emotions in real life, like his father he had trouble doing it in front of cameras. He eschewed the use of an acting coach and instead called upon his father's *Career* costar Anthony Franciosa to give him some pointers before he tested for the film. Then he went to a psychiatrist for tips on how to express anger in public. "If the acting doesn't work out," he said, "it's not the end of the world. There are other things I can do. If I don't become the next whatever—well, that's OK with me." This was a fortunate attitude on his part because *Players* was denounced by most critics as one of the worst movies of the decade, and Dean-Paul's acting received few accolades—although he did receive a Golden Globe nomination for Male Newcomer of the Year. He appeared in smaller roles in a few more films, such as *Heart Like a Wheel* in 1983, then costarred with Courtney Cox (of *Friends* fame) in the short-lived sci fi/superhero show *Misfits of Science* in the '85–'86 season, playing a doctor who organized some superpowered freaks into the Human Investigation Team (HIT). But he'd already made up his mind on his true avocation when he attended an air show at Edwards Air Force Base and wished he could fly a jet fighter. In a few years, his dream would become both a reality and a tragic nightmare for his parents.

Unlike his son, Dino the elder wanted to stay before the public in some capacity. "I vowed I would never make a commercial," Dean had said, but in 1980, at sixty-three years of age, he changed his mind when he got a solid, high-paying offer from the people at AT&T. Consumer research pointed to Dean as the perfect spokesman for the company because he was "generally well-liked, enjoyed above-average awareness as a celebrity, and appealed to all age groups." Dean was primarily interested in the several million dollars that the company paid him. Aside from some guest spots on TV shows like *Vegas*—and that was only because he was dating one of the show's stars, Phyllis Davis (Andre Boyer having been dumped)—Dean's profile was rather low during this period. He would make only two more movies, and he had to sue Warner Brothers, which owned Reprise Records, for money he'd lost due to their failure to release any more of his albums—though the company claimed Dean was less interested in recording the albums than they were in releasing them. Although he had done his final recordings for Reprise in 1974, the label released a final platter of hitherto unreleased material, *Once in a While*, in 1978. As previously noted, it would be several years before he was back in the recording studio. Again stories circulated that the combination of Percodan and liquor was leaving him besotted; it was said that he was too drunk to perform as scheduled at the Reagan Presidential inaugural-eve gala in January 1981.

As for Dean's drinking, his family and press agents said one thing; his co-workers—some of them at least—another. Claudia once said, "My father enjoys taking a drink and will take one or two while doing his TV show or making a movie. But no one has ever seen my father drunk—not even his oldest friends. Dad uses liquor. It doesn't use him." Dean had often said, "Why would NBC offer me a multimillion contract if they thought I was a drunk?" Today Jeanne Martin says, "When he worked, he had fun with it—when the show was over, he was out of there, he did not want to play, he stayed out of bars . . . he did not drink much." A lot of how much Dean drank depended on the particular periods of his life. When he was younger, Jeanne says, he caroused a lot more, but as he got older he liked to stay home.

There is no question that Dean liked his liquor, but he could hold it well and refuse it if he wasn't in the mood for it. He would rarely if ever get out-and-out drunk to the point where he couldn't perform, and often that had as much to do with fatigue and painkillers as liquor. But there were periods in his life—when he was having particular fun or undergoing special stress—that he drank fairly heavily and consistently, nipping throughout the day to keep up the high without ever getting absolutely drunk. Teetotalers were fooled—they thought it was apple juice (as it sometimes was), but other drinkers could tell, which is why there has been so much inconsistency in comments regarding his drinking from co-workers and friends. Another problem Dean had with his wives—and another reason why he didn't want to hang out with Jerry Lewis, who did not drink—was that he didn't want these people pestering him about his alcohol consumption, nagging him about his health or anything else. What his family and friends feared was that Dean would be unfairly labeled an alcoholic, which would have had a negative impact on his career. One thing cannot be denied: Dean *was* a drinking man.

Dean's drinking didn't slow down his movie career, though he no longer landed plum roles. He made two films in the 1980s that were among his worst, *The Cannonball Run* (1981) and *Cannonball Run II* (1984). The director, Hal Needham, had formerly been a stuntman and stunt coordinator as well as a second-unit action director on many pictures, including Dean's *Bandolero!* Dom DeLuise, a good buddy of the films' star, Burt Reynolds, had known Dean for years—appearing on Dean's television program had been his first major break—and brought him into Needham's fold. The film was going to be a barrel of laughs, DeLuise and Needham told Dean. Why, it would be like the Rat Pack all over again. Hal, Burt, and Dom fancied themselves a new version of the Rat Pack, only the public never took to them the way they did the originals, despite the surprising success of the first of the *Cannonball* films. The film's producer, Albert Ruddy, got in touch with Dean's agent, Mort Viner, and over time the two came to terms. Dean certainly didn't need the money, but he happily took the one hundred or so thousand that Ruddy offered. Sammy Davis Jr. also got a part in the film, which costarred everyone from the ex–James Bond Roger Moore to Mick's ex-wife Bianca Jagger. For boobs—gotta have those boob jokes—there was saucy Adrienne Barbeau. Needham gathered together pals like Jimmy the Greek and Terry Bradshaw, anyone and everyone who could make it seem like Las Vegas in the sixties.

The cast had a lot more fun than the audience viewing the picture, although there was no problem getting an audience and the movie made enough money—quite a bit, in fact—to engender a sequel. Both films were about car races with very odd vehicles—souped up ambulances, a computerized car—with even odder drivers, including Jackie Chan and an orangutan. These people (or apes) pull just about anything to get to the finish line ahead of everyone else. Dean and Sammy dress up in priests' robes so they can pretend they're rushing to give someone the last rites. The sequel brought in mobsters and an Arabian sheik to add some flavor to the stew, but by that time the meat had already spoiled. The second film also had a cameo by Frank Sinatra playing himself, the "king" of Las Vegas, with Shirley MacLaine thrown in for good measure as a bogus nun. Sinatra was on the set for only a couple of hours one afternoon. Dean and Sammy were again phony priests but turned into phony cops before the race was over.

All of this might have amounted to some good-natured fun (and admittedly there are a few very amusing sequences) if Needham had paid as much attention to the direction and the pacing of the films as he did to the superior stunt work. *Cannonball II* gets somewhat higher marks than the first picture because it has a little more of a plot and slightly more enthusiastic performances. Dean's billing went up from seventh to third.

Dean was in his early sixties when he made the films, but he looks very healthy, tanned and fit, if a little soused, as usual, though not everyone agreed. "Certainly he looked weird enough to indicate that some strenuous denial of the aging process was going on," *Film Dope* speculated years later. Dean did the films because he wanted to enjoy the camaraderie of the old Rat Pack days, and while they could never be entirely recaptured—the level of talent and commitment wasn't exactly the same, for one thing—he did have a lot of laughs, and that's all that counted. In the afternoons, he had martini parties with the other cast and many of the crew members and poured sugar all over MacLaine's trailer when Shirley, giving Dean some of her "health crap," chided him sanctimoniously for putting too much of the refined sweet in his coffee. As to be expected, the pictures exploited the usual Dino personality, having him flirt shamelessly with two much-younger female drivers, trying to talk them into having a threesome—wearing his priest's garments, no less! He also fixes a pitcher of martinis for a blond waiting in his bed as Sammy climbs in the window and spoils the moment.

Terrance Glynn was one of a team that worked on and patched up many of the strange automobiles that coasted through the *Cannonball* pictures. "Out of all the actors, some of whom were or had once been pretty big names, Dean was by far the most approachable. He never seemed drunk, just merry, friendly. And I saw him drinking a beer on one occasion and pouring martinis on another. He was certainly not dissolute. The first time I spoke to him, I went over to him and said something stupid along the lines of, 'I want to thank you for giving me so many years of pleasure.' Then I quickly said, 'Boy, I wished I had phrased it another way.' He pulled back his head and really laughed. '*You* know what I mean,' I said, embarrassed. He clapped me on the arm. 'I'm glad I've given you so much *pleasure*, sweetie,' and laughed again. He was really good-natured about it, though. Throughout the movie he would make jokes and keep everyone's spirits up. I think everyone knew the movie was going to be a dog, and nobody could believe how much money it made. I think Dino's presence made the whole experience fun for everyone. I think Burt Reynolds got a little jealous because everyone clustered around Dean, even Burt's pal Dom DeLuise. Dean was the king of the road, that was for sure." *The Cannonball Run* took in over thirty-seven million dollars; the sequel barely broke even. As far as the audience was concerned, once bitten, twice shy. *Cannonball II*, sadly, was Dean's last appearance on the big screen.

Between the two *Cannonball* films Dean went back into the recording studio for the first time since 1974. What emerged was a new album, *The Nashville Sessions*, on Warner Brothers's own label. Dean did some duets with the likes of Merle Haggard and Conway Twitty as well as solo covers of "Don't Give Up on Me" and "Hangin' Around." Another song, "Since I Met You Baby," which was also released as a single, became Dean's first music video.

By this time Dean's son Ricci was a graduate of the film department of the California Institute of Arts; Ricci wrote, produced, and directed the video for "Since I Met You Baby," using twenty thousand dollars of his father's money. The video was shot in L.A., partly at the Beverly Hills mansion Ricci's mother, Jeanne, had gotten from Dean in the settlement package. The video featured Dean cavorting with a bevy of models all dressed exactly alike. *On Location* magazine described it thusly: "A parody of current rock videos, with a retinue of new-wave actresses in spiked heels, dark dresses, and sunglasses put through a variety of unusual situations while Dean Martin casually strolls along, performing his version of the classic '56 Ivory Joe Hunter hit." *Rolling Stone*, which apparently did not see the humor of it, gave it a special DINO Award for "1983's Worst Rock Video."

Dino almost made another movie in this period, *King of Comedy*, for director Martin Scorsese, who was miles beyond Hal Needham, certainly in terms of prestige. Scorsese originally thought of Johnny Carson for the role of the kidnapped talk show host in his movie, but when Carson turned it down, he next considered Frank Sinatra, who would not have been right for the part. Next on his list was Dino, who would have been perfect, but Scorsese instead came up with Jerry Lewis by a process of association. Lewis is excellent in the movie, so there was no harm done, but it's interesting to speculate on what *King of Comedy* would have been like with Dean Martin in the lead. It would have had Dino taken captive by and interacting with a crazed Robert De Niro.

There were some good experiences during this period, and there were some bad. Among the good ones were a trip to London and Paris in

1983; all ten performances at the Apollo Victoria, a theater that had 2,800 seats, were sold out weeks in advance, and the engagement would have to be characterized as a triumph. As for Paris, Dean hadn't been there since the late fifties when he'd filmed *The Young Lions*, but he was warmly received at a charity function at the Moulin Rouge to aid the mentally challenged.

After that, Dean got a reported million and a half a year to work in the newly opened Golden Nugget casino of Atlantic City, which had finally legalized gambling. No wonder he said, "I love working. I don't care what anybody says. I love working. I can't wait until tomorrow to open. That's the truth." In 1984 Dean was hailed as the "Man of the Year" by the Friars Club (in a private, not televised, ceremony) at a $250 to $1,000 a plate dinner at the Grand Ballroom of the Waldorf-Astoria in New York. It was not much different from the *Dean Martin Celebrity Roasts*. Thirteen hundred people were in attendance as Dean sang, ate, and drank. When Shirley MacLaine took to the podium she said, "Even in the middle of the night I can pour out my heart to Dino, confident that in the morning he won't remember a thing I said." Frank Sinatra was toastmaster.

The bad experiences included an incident on May 8, 1982 when Dean was arrested one night after a California Highway Patrol officer saw his car weaving suspiciously in traffic. A bigger problem arose when the officer found a loaded .38 caliber pistol in the vehicle. Dean had to submit to a blood-alcohol test and wait two hours in the drunk tank for the results of the analysis, which revealed plenty of oxycodone, the main ingredient of Percodan, in his bloodstream, but not enough alcohol to make him legally intoxicated. But there was still the question of the unlicensed gun, which Dean had kept in the glove compartment in case of emergency. Considering what had happened to son Dino a few years before, he should have registered the gun, but he figured police in California would recognize the peculiar dangers faced by wealthy, recognizable celebrities and cut him some slack. No dice. Dean was arrested and arraigned on June 18 on one count of carrying a concealed weapon and one count of carrying a loaded weapon. The latter charge was the more serious of the two, but it was dismissed in a plea bargain. Dean pleaded no contest, and on August 5 he was fined $192 in Beverly Hills Municipal Court and given one year's probation. There were those who felt the whole business smacked of "let's dump on the big shot" and others who felt even Dean Martin was not above the law. The whole thing was enough to drive him to drink.

There was more TV of a limited kind—NBC permitted a few *Celebrity Roast* specials to air, though the caliber of the men of the hour had descended to the likes of such celebrities of the minute as Mr. T—and guest appearances on an NBC-TV show entitled *Half-Nelson*, whose star, Joe Pesci, would make a bigger splash in Martin Scorsese's *Goodfellas* five years later. Dean played himself on the series, which debuted with a two hour TV movie special in March of 1985. He made his last recordings—this time for MCA Records—in 1985, as well: a single of "L.A. is My Home" with "Drinking Champagne" on the flip side. Any albums that followed were compilations of previously recorded material.

Dean was not as busy professionally as he had once been, but his life was more or less full. He had more time to relax and enjoy himself. He saw women. A frequent companion in his later years was the actress Edy Williams. He went out and saw buddies when he felt like it. There were health problems relating to his steady drinking over the years, the Percodan consumption, and just plain aging, but nothing too severe just yet. He couldn't complain. He was in some ways as happy and contented as a clam.

All that was about to be shattered.

TWENTY-TWO

Final Years

Back when he'd first enrolled in the Air National
Guard in the late seventies, Dean-Paul Martin had nearly been too old to
join. He went to Washington and personally pleaded his case to Major
General John C. Conaway, the ANG's director. "If you give me a shot and
I make it through," he said to the major general, "I'd be willing to help
out with recruiting, promoting the guard." Conaway agreed to give him
his shot, and the young man was sent to Officer Candidate School in
Knoxville, pledging to turn over at least one weekend a month for drilling
as a guard pilot. He eventually made captain.

On March 21, 1987, three jets left March Air Force Base east of Los
Angeles for a practice bombing run. One jet was piloted by Dino Jr. with
Captain Ramon Ortiz as weapons officer. Dean-Paul's twelve-year-old son
by Olivia Hussey, Alex, watched the jets take off. Dino and Ortiz were flying near Mount San Gorgonio at a radar altitude of 9,300 feet when their
plane plunged almost 4,000 feet and hit the side of a mountain going 400
miles an hour. Apparently Dino Jr. had requested a change of course, but
weather conditions prevented the affirmative response from getting
through over his radio. An ANG spokesperson, Sgt. Carolyn Hamilton,
later said that "Captain Dean-Paul Martin and Captain Ramon Ortiz per-
ished instantly at the time of impact." Dino Jr. was thirty-six, and Ortiz
was thirty-nine.

Before the wreckage was found, all that was known was that the F-4
Phantom Jet had disappeared during a training flight. Dean was notified
and was told by a Major Steve Resnick that the two men may well have
bailed out before the crash. He did not tell Dean what he told reporters:

"We are looking for a needle in a haystack." A blizzard in the area had created eight-foot-high snowdrifts. Dean-Paul's friends tried to look on the
bright side. Doris Day's son, Terry Melcher (whom Charles Manson had
actually been looking for when he butchered Sharon Tate) said: "He's the
sort of guy who you would not have been surprised if he'd bailed out and
survived up there for five or six days. He was that tough."

But it was not to be. Dean called Jeanne, and the two huddled together for days, desperately hoping for good news, while the rescue operation continued. Finally, the wreckage of the jet was found in Wood
Canyon in Riverside County. The remains of the two men were airlifted
off the mountain along with what remained of the F-4 Phantom. Dean
and Jeanne may have been more well-off than the Ortiz family, they may
have lived in more glamorous surroundings and had more possessions, but
none of that mattered one iota in the face of the death of their child.
Jeanne was disconsolate and says that she and Dean never spoke of what
happened to Dino Jr.; it was just too painful.

Jerry Lewis immediately called Dean to offer his condolences and
also attended Dean-Paul's funeral. "I'm absolutely devastated," said Ali
MacGraw, Dean-Paul's costar in *Players*. Many more of Dean and Jeanne's
friends and co-workers sent their condolences and asked, futilely, if there
were something they could do. There was nothing.

"I think his son's tragic death really did him in," says Janet Leigh
today. "I don't think he ever recovered." Alan King noted that Dean "went
downhill. Everyone who knows him agrees with that. That took whatever spirit he had out of him." Bob Newhart concurred: "He lost a lot of his
drive after Dino was killed." Milton Berle said, "I don't think [Dean] had
the desire to go on after the accident." Yet today some family members
insist that this was not true. Dean was of course horrified and deeply sad-
dened by what had happened, but they claim it did not "do him in" as
much as people later claimed. In one sense this is true. Dean did not stop
living after his son's death; he did not entirely stop working, either,
although he had to be talked into it in most cases. Dean went on, he persevered, but something had been cut out of his heart, and this is what so
many of his friends were referring to. He had been rather proud of Dean-
Paul, who after a few false starts had his life in apple-pie order. Dino Jr.
had followed in his father's footsteps as an actor but also had his own
interests and enthusiasms.

Still, Dean-Paul hadn't always been a very big part of his father's
life. Did Dean feel guilt or regret that he had never had that heart-to-
heart with his son and namesake? Jeanne and little Alex felt the loss more

keenly, which perhaps subconsciously made Dean feel even more guilt. Only a short time after Dean-Paul died, Dean's first son, Craig, lost his wife, Lou Costello's daughter, to a stroke; she was forty-eight. Dean Martin was now seventy years of age and undoubtedly wondered why these much younger people had to die when an "old fart" like him went on and on and on. Gradually the pain eased, and he did go on. Sources say that Dean began drinking more heavily than ever—usually Scotch and soda—after his son's death.

Frank Sinatra got an idea for taking Dean's mind off his grief, although the idea was equally self-serving. He and Dean and Sammy would go out on a tour, the ultimate tour, together; they'd call it the "Together Again Tour;" and it would be a smash. They'd eschew clubs, the smaller venues they were used to, and book themselves into stadiums. Why should people who couldn't afford to fly to Vegas be deprived of seeing them, the greatest entertainers of their generation, in person? They'd entertain the *masses*. Dean had never done anything just to please Frank, but though he was now tired and weakened, after a while he agreed to do the tour, although at the first press conference at Chasen's he mused, "Is it too late to call the whole thing off?"

Frank should have listened to Dean. The first show was held at the Oakland Coliseum where the boys managed to fill a hall that was usually reserved for big-time rock acts. Subsequent shows were sold out weeks in advance. But Dean was not having as much fun as Sammy and Sinatra. His back bothered him; the Percodan affected his memory; he didn't have the all-consuming need to perform and be in front of an audience that Frank did. Frank was the *artiste*; Dean was just an entertainer. Dean had used his talent to make a good life for himself, to get out of debt and enjoy all the endless bounty that life had to offer. Now that he had everything, the energy and the desire were relatively absent. He had genuinely loved show business, loved doing his act and making his movies, but now he was elderly, and he wanted—needed—to relax; he just didn't have the drive anymore. He missed his cues, he forgot his lines, he didn't take it seriously enough for Frank. Frank told Dean off, and the emotions of the two men began to simmer. Things didn't boil over until the act reached Chicago, however.

Another bone of contention that Frank had with Dean was that Dean didn't feel like cruising the bars all night as they had done during the height of the Rat Pack era. It was one thing to go out with some sweetie pie, have a drink or two, then go home to watch TV; it was another to hang out until all hours with crazy Frankie getting drunker and drunker and more and more demanding of everyone around him—slow waitresses, recalcitrant bartenders, even Dean. He had already thrown a fit at their hotel because of one thing or another, and Dean wasn't in the mood for putting up with Sinatra's nonsense when they weren't doing the show. Like Jerry Lewis, a little of Frank Sinatra went a long, long way.

Frank was annoyed because he told himself—and Dean—that this tour was about getting Dean out of his shell and not his own ego. The two had the famous "spaghetti" confrontation one night at the hotel when Frank was trying to persuade Dean to go out and have a few drinks with him. Dean was quietly eating a spaghetti dinner he'd ordered from room service and waiting for a western to come on TV when Frank, half jokingly/half seriously, picked up the plate and dumped its contents on Dean's head. Dean said nothing. He sat there a spell, avoided looking at a grinning Sinatra, then got up and went into the bathroom. He slammed and locked the door and cleaned himself off, waiting until he was certain Frank had finally left for his night on the town before emerging. The next day he checked out of the hotel and left the tour for good. Frank had mixed emotions. Not only was Dean no fun, but he felt his disinterest was undermining his performance as well as the show itself; Dean was so bored and petulant, he was even flicking cigarettes into the audience. There were still a dozen cities and dozens of concerts remaining. Jerry Lewis wanted to replace Dean, but Frank chose Liza Minnelli instead. The tour continued in Europe sans Dino.

Dean and Frank had always had problems when they worked together. Shirley MacLaine recalled the time Frank complained that Dean was getting all the laughs. They agreed to switch lines so that Dean "played straight, and Frank had the punch lines," as she recalled. "Nobody laughed at Frank. In fact, they laughed at Dean's straight lines. Frank began to understand on a visceral level the depth of Dean's timing. No one could compare, and it was all because Dean had hit on the identity of Dean the Drunkie."

Dean's agent, Mort Viner, was afraid that Dean would as usual get sued for leaving the tour, so he suggested he check himself into Cedars-Sinai Medical Center citing numerous health complaints so that he could claim he left the tour because he was ill. The official story was that he had kidney trouble; he'd had kidney flare-ups in the past, so perhaps there was some truth to the story. A little over a month later Dean was doing his solo act at Bally's Grand. He told the crowd: "Frank sent me a kidney, but I don't know whose it was." Reviewers argued over whether or not Dean was actually inebriated or just doing what they felt was a tasteless parody of a pathetic alcoholic. Women's libbers had protested the bust jokes on Dean's show; now AA got into the act.

It was also on the stage at Bally's Grand that Jerry Lewis wheeled out a cake for Dean's seventy-second birthday the following year. Dean and Jerry had developed more of a phone relationship since Dino Jr.'s death. Jerry always did the phoning; Dean still kept his distance. "He's not having a ball," Jerry would say, "but he wants me to think he is." Dean wound up back in Cedars-Sinai for a variety of complaints at the same time Sammy Davis Jr. was being treated for throat cancer. Tests showed that his prostate would have to be operated on. His doctors told him that his chain smoking had given him emphysema, but he still loved to smoke when he wasn't in the hospital. Later, he attended a tribute for Sammy Davis, who was dead within a few weeks' time.

Dean did his last concerts in Las Vegas in September of 1991. Mike Paskevich, a columnist for the *Las Vegas Review-Journal*, remembered that "his last shows were very sad. In one of them he set up a couple of jokes, then started talking about his [deceased] son. He looked upward and said, 'Why, God, didn't you take me instead?' I've never seen a showroom so uncomfortable. Some were crying, some walked out. He was cheered at the end of the act, but it was probably out of sympathy."

The following year a new biography of Dean called *Dino* by Nick Tosches was published. Along with the dates of every single one of his club engagements, the book supplied the names and minibiographies of virtually every mafioso Dean had ever encountered, no matter how fleetingly. Tosches painted Dean as a drug-addicted recluse who rarely left his home and also hinted he had Alzheimer's. Tosches cites Sammy Cahn regarding Dean's Percodan addiction. Cahn claimed that a man named Mack Gray, who had been George Raft's personal assistant before taking on the same duties for Dean, had gotten Dean started and eventually hooked on the stuff. Dean undoubtedly took Percodan for his back pain, but whether or not he was genuinely addicted to it is perhaps open to question.

Although Tosches claimed Jeanne Martin wanted to arrange a meeting with Dean after the book was published, it's unlikely that Dean ever read the book or would have enjoyed it if he had. Despite the liberal sprinkling of cuss words in the passages that were meant to seem like Dean's internal thoughts, *Dino* emerged as a kind of literary biography, a style that's odd for a star of Dean's breezy nature. Aside from a brief prologue, Dean himself doesn't even show up until chapter four. Mort Viner felt compelled to respond to the book. "How can Dean be called a recluse," he asked, "when he dines out every night of the week? He's done that for several years. He loves to go out to restaurants. What he doesn't like is to be with a lot of people or attend parties. Does he drink? Of course. Unfortunately, when he quit working he lost interest in golf. When you don't exercise, you're bound to deteriorate. But I'm sure he'll return to performing." The last did not come true.

According to girlfriend Edy Williams, "Every night when he would arrive back at his house, the first thing he'd do is take off his St. Christopher medal, kiss it, and give thanks for safely making it home. He was still very young at heart and still loved a romantic evening." Bob Newhart said, "He's still very sharp and with it." Others, such as Milton Berle, felt differently. Berle said, "I just saw him two weeks ago. He was sitting there by himself, and he looked very bad, very sick. I feel that he didn't care anymore." Mort Viner had another explanation: "People see him in a restaurant and say, 'What's the matter with Dean?' He just likes to eat alone. He keeps his head down to prevent people from bothering him."

Dean and Jeanne had started to become close again after his divorce from Kathy Hawn, and today she says that she and Dean were good friends "for the last eighteen years of his life." The two would dine every Saturday night at Dean's favorite restaurant La Famiglia in Beverly Hills. Owner Joe Patti had a seventy-seventh birthday party for Dean at his place in 1994. "He doesn't ever want anyone to sing to him," he said at the time, "but tonight let's gather 'round." Everyone in the restaurant sang "Happy Birthday" to Dean. He saluted the crowd. "I love you," he said. "I love you all," then told a woman who asked his age that he was "forty-seven."

There were a lot of concerns about his health at this time. His old producer Greg Garrison told a reporter, "I'm not telling you Dean doesn't drink. Dean is a drinker. But Dean doesn't drink when he drives, and Dean doesn't drink when he's onstage. Smoking, that's another thing, and that's caused him more than a few problems." On Sundays Dean would go to his favorite hamburger joint. "The word got around," said Viner, "and people were standing three deep waiting for his arrival."

When La Famiglia closed, Dean would go to Da Vinci's every night at seven-thirty. He would always order the same thing: a Scotch on the rocks, spaghetti with fresh tomato and basil, tiramisú for dessert. Often Jeanne would join him, but only for drinks. She couldn't eat with Dean because "he didn't want me to see him eat without his teeth"—another reason why he kept his head down and avoided others in restaurants. (Presumably, his dentures bothered him, and he could slurp spaghetti without them.) A few weeks before Dean's death he and Sinatra reconciled and had dinner, at which occasion they laughed and threw bread sticks at one another, still twelve-year-olds at heart.

Jeanne recalls today how Dean loved to watch westerns but never his own movies. She has no idea what he thought of them or of his performances. "He never talked about it. He did not take anything seriously." He didn't dislike being famous as some stars, such as Paul Newman, seemed to. "He loved the money it brought him, the time off to play golf. I never heard him complain. I never knew a man as totally content as Dean was." While she admits Dean didn't get along with everybody, "I never heard him speak untoward of anyone. He didn't have a mean bone in his body."

Dean had six surviving children and eleven grandchildren. Craig had retired and played golf with his wife. Claudia worked on a magazine and lived in Reno with her husband. Gail had three daughters and was "extremely happy." Deana, also married, was a personal trainer. Ricci ran a recording studio in Park City, Utah. Gina moved to the mountains of Colorado and married Carl Wilson of the Beach Boys (she would be widowed in early 1999). It still hurt to think about Dean-Paul and probably always would.

In late 1995 Dean was two years short of eighty. There is no great mystery to his death. He was an old man who'd been smoking and drinking steadily (even if not excessively) all his life and in addition had the fairly typical health complaints of someone his age, conditions that were exacerbated by the smoking and drinking. Dean figured there was no point in staying alive if he couldn't do the things he enjoyed. "Don't start me with the machines to give me another five months or five years," he said. "I've had a good run." Still, at the importuning of his family he did try to change his act. His son Ricci said, "He decided to quit smoking and cut down on drinking" a year or so before his death, but by then it was too late.

Two weeks before his death, Dean stopped eating. "We sort of knew he wanted to go," said Jeanne. "He was perfectly lucid." Jeanne was at his bedside when he died of respiratory failure. He passed away on Christmas Day just as his mother had.

Jerry was performing in *Damn Yankees* in Denver when he heard the news. He was "devastated." He planned to hold a press conference to talk about Dean but had to cancel because he was too emotional. After Jeanne, Jerry was the one who had loved Dean the most. His manager said that he was "completely shattered and grief stricken." Sinatra told reporters: "Dean has been like the air I breathe. He was my brother. Not through blood but by choice." He was too overcome with grief to attend the funeral, which was by invitation only at Westwood Village Memorial Park. Lewis skipped a performance of *Damn Yankees* to attend, along with Shirley MacLaine, Don Rickles, Bob Newhart, Robert Stack, all of Dean's surviving children, and many others. Instead of flowers, it was suggested that donations be given to Dean's favorite charity, the Barbara Marx Children's Center at the Eisenhower Medical Center in Rancho Mirage, California. In Las Vegas all the casinos dimmed their lights in honor of Dino.

Dean wouldn't have wanted the occasion to be *too* somber. He had left instructions that there be no tears at his funeral, so everyone made affectionate jokes to keep each other's spirits up. "First of all," MacLaine said, "I talked to Dean about an hour ago . . . ." (The supermarket tabloids picked up on this, and before long it was speculated that "Shirley and Dean are having a love affair beyond the grave.") Then Jerry got up and said, "Rest well and don't forget to short-sheet my bed when I get there." He added that Dean had "exquisite tranquillity despite a great inner turbulence" along with "steel balls." If Dean had seen him leave the stage in tears, he probably would have thought: "Same old Jerry; never does what I tell him." But he would have been touched in spite of himself.

Despite whatever disillusionments or disappointments Jeanne Martin may have weathered with Dean, today she speaks of him with great warmth and affection. "He was just a very, very content, quiet, happy-go-lucky guy. A sweet and very gentle man." She never married again and says she has "never been in love with anyone else. Dean was my soul mate."

Dean's own words will be his epitaph: "I've done it all. I've lived a full life, and I've been blessed with more opportunities than a lot of people. "I have no regrets."

SOURCES AND OTHER NOTES

Parts One and Two
Information on Dean's early years in Steubenville came from Mary Braxton and Joseph Pirone as well as from published and unpublished interviews with Dean Martin (DM) and members of his family. They also offered a wealth of information on Dean's Manhattan nightclub days and his association with Ernie McKay and Sammy Watkins—not to mention his assorted debts, Bryant Hotel days, and nose job—as did press reports and reviews. Sunny Daye—she would not allow her real or married names to be used in this book; "I'm living a new life now, honey, and I never look back"—provided much information on Dean's early years in New York. Press reports and court documents were also consulted. DM and Jerry Lewis were always frank in interviews about each other, Lou Perry, Abby Greshler, their years together, and their breakup. Virginia Wyscott viewed Dean's anger at snide "homosexual" remarks. Janet Leigh recalled making *Living It Up* with Martin and Lewis as well as the latter's home movies. Dean's involvement with Lori Nelson was an open secret in Hollywood. The business with Mitchell and Petrillo was covered by the press. Court documents and press reports were consulted for various lawsuits DM was embroiled in as well as his marriage, separation, and divorce from his first wife, Betty, and marriage and separation(s) from second wife, Jeanne, who was interviewed by the author. Kinescope tapes of old Colgate *Comedy Hour* shows were consulted as was rare footage of Martin and Lewis's nightclub act, not to mention numerous press reports of their shows, movies, and activities. Larry Quirk passed along certain information on Hal Wallis, who was also never shy in expressing his feelings about Martin and Lewis, among others.

Dean Martin and MCA (chapter three): It was largely because of the irresponsible fiscal behavior of talent like Dean Martin that led agencies like MCA and William Morris to change their policies in regard to how their clients got paid. Instead of allowing them to be paid by the employer directly and expecting them to responsibly deduct and forward 10 percent to the agency, employers must now send all payments directly to the agency, which deducts its 10 to 20 percent and forwards the remainder to the client. When it began producing pictures as well as representing actors, MCA was accused of being a monopoly and eventually had to get out of the talent agency business. Sticking to the production end of things, it bought Universal in the sixties.
Dean Martin's screen test for Joe Pasternak (chapter three): Although George Sidney directed Dean's screen test for *Till The Clouds Roll By*, the picture itself was helmed by Richard Whorf.

Jerry Lewis's lip-syncing (chapter four): Jerry Lewis was a highly influential comedian, not only affecting the styles of Jim Carrey (who practically borrowed his whole shtick from Jerry) and the minimally talented Adam Sandler, but his lip-syncing bit—an entire act built around mouthing the words to old records—was revived decades later by, of all people, numerous New York and Los Angeles drag queens, the most publicity-grabbing of whom is billed as Lypsinka. Lewis was gifted enough to get beyond this type of act into something that would require genuine talent; most of the drag queens, alas, are not.

The Stooge (chapter six): It's also possible that Capitol Records had a hand in the release delay of *The Stooge*. As Dean recorded *all* the numbers from the movie, they may have wanted time to plan a major publicity push for the album to coincide with the release of the movie. Due to Dean and Jerry's hectic schedules, there may have been a problem setting aside time for rehearsing and recording the numbers.

Living It Up (chapter seven): Between the time of *Nothing Sacred* and *Living It Up*, the same story was the subject of a Broadway musical entitled *Hazel Flagg*.

You're Never Too Young (chapter eight): Arthur Schwartz, who composed the songs for the film, was the talented Broadway composer of *A Tree Grows in Brooklyn*, among others.

Parts Three and Four
The creation of Reprise Records, the involvement of Frank Sinatra and DM, and its subsequent sale to Warner Brothers were covered in numerous press reports and official releases, as was the final breakup of Martin and Lewis and their last show at the Copa. Ditto for DM's involvement with the Cal-Neva Lodge and Dino's. The controversies over *Something's Got to Give* and *Kiss Me, Stupid* were covered exhaustively, as were the problems MCA had with the Department of Justice, in press reports of the period. Studio memos were also consulted, as was surviving footage from *Something's Got to Give*.

The personal dissolution of Dean's first wife, Betty, was another open secret in Hollywood. Janet Leigh recalled working on *Who Was That Lady?* with Dean. Shirley MacLaine wrote of her love for Dean and other impressions of him in one volume of her memoirs. Bud Yorkin recalled Dean's cameo in *Come Blow Your Horn*. Details on *Toys in the Attic*, *Rio Bravo*, *Career* and other films were gleaned from press reports, reviews, and contemporary interviews, some provided by Lawrence Quirk. Claudia Martin's career and marriage were covered extensively by the press. Private and published interviews with Dean Martin and Jerry Lewis were consulted as were tapes of Dean's early TV specials. Other sources include Jeanne Martin, Lawrence Quirk, Virgina Wyscott, and confidential sources.

Hal Wallis (chapter nine): The four films Wallis produced starring Dean Martin are described in the text. The four he produced starring Jerry Lewis are *The Sad Sack* (1957), *Don't Give Up the Ship* (1959), *Visit to a Small Planet* (1960), *Boeing Boeing* (1965).

Damon and Pythias (chapter nine): The film was finally made as *The Delicate Delinquent*, Lewis's first solo film, with McGuire at the helm and Jerry producing under the auspices of York. In the poor film that resulted, Jerry is still playing the lonely kid who needs an older buddy, this time played by Darren McGavin, who acts more perplexed by Jerry's antics than anything else. The strange thing about the movie is that this time it's the older guy who seems to have the crush on his younger buddy. When the cop McGavin portrays calls on troubled youth Jerry and asks him how he likes his steaks, it's as if he's asking him for a date. Later McGavin is shown frantically cleaning up his apartment, we assume, for his girl, Martha Hyer. Hyer shows up, but the person he's actually expecting—and cleaning for—is Jerry!

Rio Bravo (chapter eleven): Auteur theory has it that the filmmaker is the author of his films and impresses his personal vision on each work. This theory works well for such directors as Alfred Hitchcock, who tend to tread somewhat similar territory and generally stay within one genre, but many felt, rightly or wrongly, that applying it to Hawks, whose films go all over the lot (although this would not necessarily preclude a similarity of theme and structure), was stretching it a bit. Hawks's fans certainly did their best to interconnect all of his pictures by linking supposed common themes and elements. Todd McCarthy, Hawks's biographer, maintains that *Rio Bravo* "fully justifies serious appreciation of Hawks, since it represents the most detailed and elegant expression of his typical concerns—self-respect, self-control, the interdependence of select chosen friends, being good at what you do, the blossoming of sexual-romantic attraction—as demonstrated by characters utterly removed from the norms of routine existence. The Hemingway imperative of grace under pressure could not be rendered more perfectly, and the stoicism is shot through with fun . . . ." All well and good, except that Hawks's "typical concerns" seem to be fairly typical of most artists, and none of this means that the film is genuinely *deep*, or meant to be, by Hawks or anyone else working on the production.

Kiss Me, Stupid (chapter fifteen): Although made under the United Artists imprint, the film was released under the Lopert banner because UA was afraid of all the fallout due to its controversial nature. Decades later *Film Dope* magazine noted that "it was rather courageous of (Dean) to have made the picture." Billy Wilder was right that the country was on the verge of a new dawn of frankness and that one day stuff like *Kiss Me, Stupid* would be more typical than not. For instance, a February 1999 episode of ABC-TV-sitcom *Dharma and Greg* had Greg trying to convince Dharma to let him park a Ferrari. When she asks him why, he says, "I guess the 'I'm a guy' thing won't work." To which Dharma replies: "Not unless you park it with your penis." The rest of the half hour featured innumerable (and admittedly humorous) jokes and gesticulating about premature ejaculation. And to think that back in the 1950s the cast of *I Love Lucy* wasn't even allowed to say the word "pregnant" on TV!

Parts Five and Six
Dean's TV show, his appearance on *Hollywood Palace*, and Jerry Lewis's TV shows were covered in contemporary press reports; tapes of some of DM's shows were also consulted. His children's private and professional struggles, their marriages and divorces, were also well detailed by the press at the time and revealed in court documents. DM's real estate holdings were uncovered via press reports and documents as were his earnings, also revealed in *TV Guide*. Details on his various films were gleaned from new interviews with participants as well as from some contemporary published and unpublished interviews. Marybeth Jaymes provided information on *The Silencers* and *The Ambushers*, as did Karl Malden for *Murderers Row*. Christy Dodd was a source for *Rough Night in Jericho*. Jacqueline Bisset and others provided details of *Airport*. The author also spoke with Andrew V. McLaglen, who provided information on *Bandolero!* and *something big*, the two pictures he directed with DM.

Information on the *Cannonball* films came from Terrance Glynn and others. Lawrence Quirk recalled Roddy McDowall's comments on Dean and *Five Card Stud*, among other tidbits.

Dean's marital problems were discussed frankly by both Dean and Jeanne and other participants and were covered extensively in the press. Information on the Westchester Premiere Theater and the relationship of DM and Alfredo Felice came from FBI files. Dean's relationships with Gail Renshaw, Kathy Hawn, and other women were covered by the press and in frank contemporary interviews with Dean and the other participants. Terms of DM's divorce from Kathy Hawn were detailed in court papers; other aspects of his relationship with his third wife came from confidential sources. Linda Chesley spoke frankly with the author on her five-year on-and-off affair with Dean. Tapes of the 1976 telethon that reunited DM with Jerry Lewis were viewed. Both DM's and Dean-Paul's arrest for illegal weapons were covered in police reports as well as press accounts. DM's Man of the Year Award and his recordings were chronicled by the press, as was his relationship with Andre Boyer. Information on Dean-Paul Martin's marriages and career highlights were gleaned from press reports and from his private and published interviews; his tragic death was covered extensively by the press. The controversy over Dean's TV show in the seventies was described in *Life* and elsewhere. Tapes of DM's *Celebrity Roasts* were also consulted. Court records were reviewed for details over the lawsuit concerning *The Ravagers*. DM's involvement with Californians for Reagan and his appearance at the Memorial Auditorium were covered by the press. Jeanne Martin provided information on Dean's home life and his religiousness, (which Dean also referred to in interviews) as well as the current professional activities and marital states of his children. She also spoke with the author about Dean's life in his final years and his enduring relationship with her.

The Matt Helm series (chapters sixteen through eighteen): In the capsule review of *The Ambushers* in Leonard Maltin's *Movie and Video Guide*, it says: "Third entry in the series may be the weakest, but few film scholars will want to take time making certain." This author has had the dubious distinction of determining that *The Ambushers* actually runs neck in neck with *The Wrecking Crew* as the worst of the series so that future generations won't have to.

Ghost in the Invisible Bikini (chapter seventeen): Noteworthy for no other reason than that it had such bizarre acting pairings as second-string, slack-jawed beachboy Aron Kincaid doing a scene with the distinguished artist Basil Rathbone!

Valley of the Dolls (chapter eighteen): When Susann's novel was published, there was much speculation as to which real-life stars corresponded to the characters in the book. It was generally agreed that "Neely O'Hara" was meant to be Judy Garland. There was also some comment that the singer "Tony," who was so simple (and sex obsessed) that his sister rarely allowed him to speak in meetings (and actually turned out to have a serious, debilitating mental condition), was modeled—although *very* loosely—on Dean Martin.

Cannonball Run and *Cannonball Run II* (chapter 21): The films were based on a real-life road race that had already inspired two previous movies, *The Gumball Rally* and *Cannonball*.

FILMOGRAPHY

Songs that Dean sang in movies that he also recorded are denoted by + following the title. The number of stars that follow the title denotes the (subjective) quality of film. (Note: Important films are set in bold.)

1. *My Friend Irma* ★★ (1949) Director: George Marshall. Dean sings: "Donkey Serenade."
2. *My Friend Irma Goes West* ★★ (1950) Director: Hal Walker. Dean sings: "I'll Always Love You (Day After Day)"+.
3. *At War with the Army* ★★ (1950) Director: Hal Walker. Dean sings: "Tonda Wanda Hoy (It's Easier to Say 'I Love You')"+, "You and Your Beautiful Eyes,"+ "Tarra Ta-larra Ta-Lar"+ (as Bing Crosby).
4. *That's My Boy* ★★ (1951) Director: Hal Walker. Dean sings: "I'm in the Mood for Love;" "Ballin' the Jack."
5. *Sailor Beware* ★★ (1952) Director: Hal Walker.
6. **Jumping Jacks** ★★ ½ (1952) Director: Norman Taurog. Dean sings: "Parachute Jump," "Big Blue Sky is the Place for Me," "I Know a Dream When I See One,"+ "Keep that Dream Handy."
7. **The Stooge** ★★ ½ (1953) Director: Norman Taurog. Dean sings: "A Girl Named Mary and a Boy Named Bill,"+ "Just One More Chance,"+ "I'm Yours,"+ "With My Eyes Wide Open,"+ "I Feel a Song Comin' On,"+ "Who's Your Little Who-Zis!"+.
8. *The Road to Bali* ★★ ½ (1953) Director: Hal Walker. (A cameo with Jerry Lewis in a Crosby and Hope movie.)
9. *Scared Stiff* ★★ (1953) Director: George Marshall. Dean sings: "When I Meet My Baby," "San Domingo," "When Someone Wonderful Thinks You're Wonderful," "The Enchilada Man."
10. *The Caddy* ★ ½ (1953) Director: Norman Taurog. Dean sings: "That's Amore"+ "You're the Right One,"+ "What Would You Do Without Me," "A Wonderful Kind of Whistling Moment."
11. *Money from Home* ★ (1954) Director: George Marshall. Dean sings: "Love is the Same All Over the World," "I Only Have Eyes for You," "Moments Like This"+.
12. *Living It Up* ★ ½ (1954) Director: Norman Taurog. Dean sings: "Money Burns a Hole in My Pocket,"+ "How Do You Speak to an Angel?"+ "Kiss Me Baby," "I Love New York"+.
13. *Three Ring Circus* ★★ (1954) Director: Joseph Pevney. Dean sings: "It's a Big, Wide, Wonderful World."
14. *You're Never Too Young* ★★ ½ (1955) Director: Norman Taurog. Dean sings: "Simpatico,"+ "Every Day is a Happy Day," "Love is All that Matters,"+ "I Know Your Mother Loves You"+.

15. *Artists and Models* ★★ 1/2 (1955) Director: Frank Tashlin. Dean sings: "Artists and Models," "When You Pretend,"+ "You Look So Familiar,"+ "My Lucky Song,"+ "Innamorata (Sweetheart)"+.

16. *Pardners* ★ 1/2 (1956) Director: Norman Taurog. Dean sings: "Pardners,"+ "Me and You and the Moon,"+ "Whistling Wind"+.

17. *Hollywood or Bust* ★★ 1/2 (1956) Director: Frank Tashlin. Dean sings: "Let's Be Friendly,"+ "Wild and Woolly West," "Hollywood or Bust,"+ "It Looks Like Love,"+ "A Day in the Country"+.

18. *Ten Thousand Bedrooms* ★★ (1957) Director: Richard Thorpe. Dean sings: Title song,+ among others.

19. *The Young Lions* ★★ 1/2 (1958) Director: Edward Dymtryk.

20. *Some Came Running* ★★ 1/2 (1959) Director: Vincente Minnelli.

21. *Rio Bravo* ★★ 1/2 (1959) Director: Howard Hawks. Dean sings: "My Rifle, My Pony and Me"+ (Note: Dean recorded both a solo of this record as well as a duet with Ricky Nelson), "Get Along Home, Cindy, Cindy."

22. *Career* ★★★ 1/2 (1959) Director: Joseph Anthony.

23. *Who Was that Lady?* ★★ 1/2 (1960) Director: George Sidney. Dean sings: Title song+.

24. *Bells Are Ringing* ★★★ (1960) Director: Vincente Minnelli. Dean sings: "Do It!"+ "It's Better than a Dream,"+ "I Met a Girl,"+ "Just in Time"+.

25. *Ocean's 11* ★★ 1/2 (1960) Director: Lewis Milestone. Dean sings: "Ain't That a Kick in the Head"+.

26. *Pepe* ★★ (1960) Director: George Sidney. (Dean did only a cameo in this picture.)

27. *All in a Night's Work* ★★ 1/2 (1961) Director: Joseph Anthony. Dean sings: Title song+.

28. *Ada* ★★ 1/2 (1961) Director: Daniel Mann. Dean sings: "May the Lord Bless You Real Good."

29. *Sergeants 3* ★★ 1/2 (1962) Director: John Sturges.

30. *The Road to Hong Kong* ★★ 1/2 (1962) Director: Norman Panama. (Dean does a cameo in this film with Frank Sinatra.)

31. *Who's Got the Action?* ★★ 1/2 (1962) Director: Daniel Mann. Dean sings: Title song+ (very briefly over closing credits).

32. *Come Blow Your Horn* ★★★ (1963) Director: Bud Yorkin. (Dean has an unscripted cameo as a street drunk in this film.)

33. *Toys In The Attic* ★★★ 1/2 (1963) Director: George Roy Hill.

34. *Who's Been Sleeping in My Bed?* ★★ (1963) Director: Daniel Mann.

35. *4 for Texas* ★★ (1963) Director: Robert Aldrich.

36. *What a Way to Go* ★★★ (1964) Director: J. Lee Thompson.

37. *Robin and the 7 Hoods* ★★ (1964) Director: Gordon Douglas. Dean sings: "A Man Who Loves His Mother,"+ "Don't Mess with Mister Booze,"+ "Style"+.

38. *Kiss Me, Stupid* ★★★ (1964) Director: Billy Wilder. Dean sings: "Sophia,"+ among other (often reconstituted) Gershwin tunes. (Note: The original title of "Sophia" was "Wake Up, Brother, and Dance," composed in 1937.)

39. *The Sons of Katie Elder* ★★ 1/2 (1965) Director: Henry Hathaway.

40. *Marriage On The Rocks* ★★★ (1965) Director: Jack Donahue.

41. *The Silencers* ★★ ¹/₂ (1966) Director: Phil Karlson. Dean sings: "Sunny Side of the Street,"+ "South of the Border,"+ "Red Sails in the Sunset"+. (Note: Dean had no actual song numbers. A few bars from these and other songs from his latest album could be heard in the background.)
42. *Texas Across the River* ★★ ¹/₂ (1966) Director: Michael Gordon.
43. *Murderers' Row* ★★ ¹/₂ (1966) Director: Henry Levin. Dean sings: "I'm Not the Marrying Kind"+.
44. *Rough Night in Jericho* ★★ ¹/₂ (1967) Director: Arnold Laven.
45. *The Ambushers* ★ ¹/₂ (1967) Director: Henry Levin. Dean sings: "Everybody Loves Somebody (Sometime)"+. (Note: Dean is heard singing this song over the radio; he does not perform it.)
46. *How to Save a Marriage (and Ruin Your Life)* ★★ ¹/₂ (1968) Director: Fielder Cook.
47. *Bandolero!* ★★ ¹/₂ (1968) Director: Andrew McLaglen.
48. *Five Card Stud* ★★ (1968) Director: Henry Hathaway. Dean sings: Title song+ (over credits).
49. *The Wrecking Crew* ★ ¹/₂ (1969) Director: Phil Karlson. Dean sings risqué, voice-over versions of "Sunny Side of the Street," "Cry," "Red Sails in the Sunset," others.
50. *Airport* ★★★ (1970) Director: George Seaton.
51. *something big* ★★ ¹/₂ (1971) Director: Andrew McLaglen.
52. *Showdown* ★★★ (1973) Director: George Seaton.
53. *Mr. Ricco* ★★ (1975) Director: Paul Bogart.
54. *The Cannonball Run* ★ 1/2 (1981) Director; Hal Needham.
55. *Cannonball Run II* ★★ (1984) Director: Hal Needham.

DISCOGRAPHY

Dean Martin made literally hundreds of recordings and dozens of albums. The following is a selective, alphabetical list of most of the standards and important or popular songs that he recorded, followed by the year they were released. (Some of these tunes were recorded more than once; the date is for the first recording.) Albums are in italics. An asterisk denotes a particularly important song, and Dean's three greatest songs are highlighted in bold print.

Absence Makes the Heart Grow Fonder (1948)
All of Me (1946)
April in Paris (1962)
Artists and Models (1955)
Baby, It's Cold Outside (1959)
Bells Are Ringing (1960)
Bésame Mucho (1962)
Brahms's Lullaby (1958)
Buona Sera (1958)
By the Time I Get to Phoenix (1968)
Bye Bye Blackbird (1950)
Carolina in the Morning (1954)
Come Back to Sorrento * (1951)
Crying Time (1969)
Cuddle Up a Little Closer (1958)
Darktown Strutters' Ball (1950)
Dean Martin Sings 'The Silencers' (1966)
Dean Martin; Capitol Collector's Series (1989)
Dinah (1955)
Dino: Italian Love Songs (1962)
Dream a Little Dream of Me (1958)
Everybody Loves Somebody (Sometime) * (1964)
Everybody Loves Somebody (1964)
Fools Rush In (1964)
Gentle on My Mind (1968)
Georgia on My Mind (1954)

Gigi (1962)
Green Green Grass of Home (1967)
Guys and Dolls (1963)
Guys And Dolls: Reprise Repertory (1963)
Hey, Good Lookin' (1962)
Hollywood Or Bust (1956)
Honey (1968)
I Can't Give You Anything But Love (1957)
I Don't Know Why (1964)
I Got the Sun in the Morning (1946)
I Love Paris (1962)
I Take A Lot Of Pride In What I Am (1969)
I Walk the Line (1962)
I Wish You Love (1961)
I Wonder Who's Kissing Her Now (1972)
I'll Be Home for Christmas (1966)
I'll Be Seeing You (1964)
I'm Gonna Sit Right Down and Write . . . (1970)
I'm Not the Marrying Kind (1966)
I'm Sitting on Top of the World (1972)
I'm So Lonesome I Could Cry (1962)
I've Grown Accustomed to Her Face (1960)
If You Knew Suzie (1966)
If You Were the Only Girl (1964)

In a Little Spanish Town (1962)
In the Cool, Cool, Cool of the Evening
(1951)
Innamorata (Sweetheart) * (1955)
It's Easy to Remember (1957)
Jingle Bells (1966)
Just in Time * (1960)
King of the Road (1965)
Let It Snow! (1959)
Let Me Go, Lover (1954)
The Last Time I Saw Paris (1962)
Little Green Apples (1968)
Living It Up (1954)
Louise (1947)
Make the World Go Away (1970)
Mambo Italiano (1954)
Manhattan At Midnight (1946)
Mattinata (1961)
Memories Are Made Of This (1955)
Memories are Made of This * (1955)
Mimi (1962)
Moments Like This (1953)
My Melancholy Baby (1963)
My Rifle, My Pony, and Me * (1958)
My Woman, My Woman, My Wife (1970)
My Woman, My Woman, My Wife (1970)
Nashville Sessions (1983)
Naughty Lady of Shady Lane (1954)
The Night is So Young and You're So
Beautiful (1947)
Non Dimenticar * (1961)
O Sole Mio (There's No Tomorrow)
(1961)
Oh, Marie * (1947)
On an Evening in Roma * (1958)
On the Street Where You Live
(1960)
On the Sunny Side of the Street (1966)
Once in Love with Amy (1948)
Pardners (1956)
Pennies from Heaven (1951)
Please Don't Talk About Me When I'm
Gone (1960)
Pretty Baby (1957)
Raindrops Keep Fallin' on My Head
(1970)
Ramblin' Rose (1972)

Red Roses for a Blue Lady (1965)
Red Sails in the Sunset (1966)
Release Me (1967)
Return To Me (1958)
Return to Me (Ritorna a Me) * (1958)
Robin And The 7 Hoods (1964)
Rock-a-Bye Your Baby with a Dixie
Melody (1950)
Rudolph the Red-Nosed Reindeer (1959)
Second Hand Rose (1963)
Send Me the Pillow You Dream On
(1964)
Side by Side (1966)
Silent Night (1963)
Silver Bells (1966)
Since I Met You Baby (1983)
Smile (1972)
Standing on the Corner (1956)
Sway * (1954)
Sweetheart of Sigma Chi (1946)
Swingin' Down Yonder (1991)
Ten Thousand Bedrooms (1956)
That's Amore * (1953)
Tie a Yellow Ribbon (1973)
Tracks of My Tears (1970)
Until the Real Thing Comes Along (1960)
Volare (1958)
Volare * (1958)
Waiting for the Robert E. Lee
(1954)
Walkin' My Baby Back Home
(1947)
Way Down Yonder in New Orleans (1954)
Welcome to My World (1965)
Welcome To My World (1967)
When the Red Red Robin . . . (1972)
When You're Smiling (1952)
White Christmas (1959)
Winter Wonderland (1959)
You Belong to Me * (1952)
You Made Me Love You (1972)
**You're Nobody 'til Somebody Loves
You * (1960)**
You're the Best Thing that Ever
Happened (1973)

BIBLIOGRAPHY

Author's note: The following books were consulted primarily to double-check and compare certain anecdotes or to provide direction for further research. A great many articles and court and studio documents and the like were also consulted for similar reasons, but a lengthy list of these has been omitted for space considerations.

Bosworth, Patricia. *Montgomery Clift: A Biography*. New York: Harcourt Brace Jovanovich, 1978.

Braun, Eric. *Deborah Kerr*. London: W. H. Allen, 1977.

Brown, Peter H. *Such Devoted Sisters: Those Fabulous Gabors*. New York: St. Martin's, 1985.

Brown, Peter Harry, and Patte B. Barham. *Marilyn: The Last Take*. New York: Dutton, 1992.

Carey, Gary. *Judy Holliday: An Intimate Life Story*. New York: Seaview, 1982.

Costello, Chris, with Raymond Strait. *Lou's On First: A Biography*. New York: St. Martin's, 1981.

Davis, Ronald L. *Duke: The Life and Image of John Wayne*. Norman: University of Oklahoma Press, 1998.

Dewey, Donald. *James Stewart: A Biography*. Atlanta: Turner, 1996.

Fishgall, Gary. *Against Type: A Biography of Burt Lancaster*. New York: Scribner, 1995.

———. *Pieces of Time: The Life of Jimmy Stewart*. New York: Scribner, 1997.

Gil-Montero, Martha. *Brazilian Bombshell. The Biography of Carmen Miranda*. New York: Donald I. Fine, 1989.

Haining, Peter. *Raquel Welch: Sex Symbol to Superstar*. New York: St. Martin's, 1984.

Henreid, Paul, with Julius Fast. *Ladies Man: An Autobiography*. New York: St. Martin's, 1984.

Horton, Andrew. *The Films of George Roy Hill*. New York: Columbia University Press, 1984.

Hudson, Rock, with Sara Davidson. *Rock Hudson: His Story*. New York: Morrow, 1986.

Kael, Pauline. *5001 Nights at the Movies*. New York: Holt, Rinehart, and Winston, 1982.

Katz, Ephraim. *The Film Encyclopedia*. New York: HarperPerennial, 1994.

Laguardia, Robert, and Gene Arceri. *Red: The Tempestuous Life of Susan Hayward*. New York: Macmillan, 1985.

Lally, Kevin. *Wilder Times: The Life of Billy Wilder*. New York: Henry Holt, 1996.

Levy, Shawn. *King of Comedy: The Life and Art of Jerry Lewis*. New York: St. Martin's, 1996.

Lewis, Jerry, with Herb Gluck. *Jerry Lewis In Person*. New York: Atheneum, 1982.

Linet, Beverly. *Susan Hayward: Portrait of a Survivor*. New York: Atheneum, 1980.

MacLaine, Shirley. *My Lucky Stars: A Hollywood Memoir*. New York: Bantam, 1995.

Malden, Karl, with Carla Malden. *Where Do I Stand? A Memoir*. New York: Simon and Schuster, 1997.

Maltin, Leonard. *Movie and Video Guide*. New York: Signet, 1998.

Martin, Tony, and Cyd Charisse, as told to Dick Kleiner. *The Two of Us*. New York: Mason/Charter, 1976.

Marx, Arthur. *Everybody Loves Somebody Sometime (Especially Himself)*. New York: Hawthorne, 1973.

McCarthy, Todd. *Howard Hawks: The Grey Fox of Hollywood*. New York: Grove Press, 1997.

Murphy, Mary. "The Days and Nights of Dean Martin." *TV Guide*, July 16, 1994.

Neibaur, James L., and Ted Okuda. *The Jerry Lewis Films: An Analytical Filmography of the Innovative Comic*. Jefferson, NC: Mcfarland, 1995.

Quirk, Lawrence J. *The Kennedys in Hollywood*. Dallas: Taylor, 1996.

———. *Jimmy Stewart: Behind the Scenes of a Wonderful Life*. New York: Applause, 1997.

Roberts, Randy, and James Olsen. *John Wayne, American*. New York: Free Press, 1995.

Rodriguez, Elena. *Dennis Hopper: A Madness to his Method*. New York: St. Martin's, 1988.

Schickel, Richard. *Brando: A Life in Our Times*. New York: Atheneum, 1991.

Schoell, William, and Lawrence J. Quirk. *The Rat Pack: The Hey Hey Days of Frank and The Boys*. Dallas: Taylor, 1998.

Spoto, Donald. *Marilyn Monroe: The Biography*. New York: HarperCollins, 1993.

Summers, Anthony. *Goddess: The Secret Lives of Marilyn Monroe*. New York: Macmillan, 1985.

Tierney, Gene, and Mickey Herskowitz. *Self-Portrait*. New York: Simon and Schuster, 1979.

Thompson, Charles. *Bing: The Authorized Biography*. London: W. H. Allen, 1975.

Tosches, Nick. *Dino: Living High in the Dirty Business of Dreams*. New York: Doubleday, 1992.

Turner, Lana. *Lana: The Lady, the Legend, the Truth*. New York: E. P. Dutton, 1982.

Wallis, Hal, and Charles Higham. *Starmaker: The Autobiography of Hal Wallis*. New York: Macmillan, 1980.

Wallis, Martha Hyer. *Finding My Way*. San Francisco: HarperCollins, 1990.

Wayne, Jane Ellen. *Lana*. New York: St. Martin's, 1995.

Wright, William. *Lillian Hellman: The Image, the Woman*. New York: Simon and Schuster, 1986.

Periodicals consulted include the *New York Times*, the *New York Post*, the *New York Daily News*, *Variety*, *TV Guide*, *Filmfax*, *Outré*, *Film Dope*, *On Location*, *New York Herald-Tribune*, *Motion Picture Herald*, the *Hollywood Reporter*, and many others.

INDEX

Numbers in *italics* indicate photographs.